Founding theory of American sociology 1881–1915

International Library of Sociology

Founded by Karl Mannheim

Editor: John Rex, Research Unit for Ethnic
Relations, University of Aston in Birmingham

Arbor Scientiae
Arbor Vitae

A catalogue of the books available in the **International Library of Sociology** and other series of Social Science books published by Routledge & Kegan Paul will be found at the end of this volume.

Founding theory of American sociology 1881–1915

Roscoe C. Hinkle

Professor of Sociology
The Ohio State University

Routledge & Kegan Paul

Boston, London and Henley

First published in 1980
by Routledge & Kegan Paul Ltd
39 Store Street, London WC1E 7DD,
Broadway House, Newtown Road,
Henley-on-Thames, Oxon RG9 1EN and
9 Park Street, Boston, Mass. 02108, USA
Photoset in 10 on 11 Times by
Kelly Typesetting Ltd, Bradford-on-Avon, Wiltshire
and printed in the United States of America by
Vail-Ballou Press Inc.

ISBN 0 7100 0401 X

Contents

CONTENTS

Tables

Preface

Two objectives have been paramount in this undertaking of analysis and synthesis in sociological theory. One has been the development of a scheme for comparing and contrasting, generalizing and characterizing the (comprehensive or macro-) theories of individual sociologists. A second has been the exemplification of the scheme by its application to the classification and periodicization of the works of a particular aggregate of theorists in the history of American sociological theory, i.e., the period of 1881–1915. Admittedly, a third, accepting the ultimate desirability, if not necessity, of the explanation of the character of any prevailing sociological theory, has also been acknowledged and preliminarily formulated. Chapter 3 sets forth the analytic scheme. Chapters 4 through 11 offer an illustration of its application. And chapters 1 and 12 suggest a possible strategy for explaining the character of early theory in relation to later developments of general theory in American sociology.

Undeniably, selection of a title for the present study has been a peculiarly perplexing task. Adequate typification of the complex interrelationships between problems and the several theoretical stances, which are signified by the prevailing assumptions, could not be represented by the minimum of words ordinarily demanded in a title. 'Evolutionary naturalism' perhaps comes closest to meeting the requirements. But it also has certain disadvantages: it does not possess a broadly identifiable meaning among sociologists; it ignores entirely the predominant epistemological-methodological views of the period; and it fails to recognize the diversity of subpositions even within the substantive-ontological realm of early American sociological theory. Consequently, an

entirely different approach – one emphasizing a temporal dimension and significance – was adopted. 'Founding theory' is, of
course, the (general) theory of the founders of American sociology.
Furthermore, 'founding' also suggests the initial formulation and
establishment of a distinctive and persisting set of assumptions in
and about theory and in and about the interrelationship among
theory, the discipline of sociology and its societal context(s in the
US). By no means is inquiry into (even earlier) precursors and
antecedents (e.g., in Europe) precluded.

Because prosecution and completion of *Founding Theory of
American Sociology* has extended substantially over a decade (and
more), it has tended to acquire a history that has become significant
for an understanding of the study itself. Actual research began in
1958 (i.e., four years after publication of *The Development of
Modern Sociology*), but the character of the motivating interest
was generated during graduate training in sociology at the
Universities of Wisconsin and Minnesota. In part, the interest had
its origins in a course in American Sociology offered by Professor
John H. Useem at the University of Wisconsin in 1949 (before he
joined the Department of Sociology at Michigan State University).
In part also, the interest stems from an (even earlier) introduction
to the approach of Frederick J. Teggart to the history of the major
methodological ideas of the social sciences which Professor Joseph
F. Schneider had provided in his theory courses at the University of
Minnesota in 1944–5 and at Indiana University in 1947–8. (He had
been one of Teggart's graduate students at Berkeley along with
Gladys Bryson (Smith College), John M. Foskett (University of
Oregon), Henry H. Frost (University of Utah), Edward Rose
(University of Colorado), and Robert A. Nisbet (University of
California – Berkeley and Riverside, University of Arizona, and
Columbia University).) Understandably, then, the conviction that
the study of early American sociological theory must ultimately be
justified by its contribution to an understanding of the nature of
current sociological theory stems from Teggart's own insistence
that historical inquiry must necessarily be concerned with the study
of how the present has come to be as it is (Teggart, 1977, pp. 165,
168, 237–9).

Actual research began with detailed individual studies of major
figures of early American sociology (e.g., Ward, Small, Ross,
Sumner, Giddings, and Cooley). Systematic summary accounts of
the specific theoretical orientations of the first four (though not the
last two) figures were completed during the late 1950s and early
1960s. The analyses were reported at the annual meetings of several

professional associations over a decade and a half. Papers on the antecedents of the action orientation in American sociology before 1935, the conceptions of theory in earlier American sociology, and the older and newer social evolutionisms in American sociology were presented at the American Sociological Association conventions in 1963, 1966, and 1967. Two papers on Cooley were part of the American Sociological Association and Eastern Sociological Society programs in 1965 and 1966. (Some of these papers subsequently appeared as articles, e.g., Hinkle, 1963, 1966, 1967.) Substantial portions of an analysis of Ross were published in 1969. The programs of Cheiron (The International Society for the History of the Behavioral and Social Sciences) afforded an opportunity for presenting analyses of the social forces notion, evolutionary naturalism, and a variety of aspects of Sumner's orientation in 1969, 1972, 1973, 1975, and 1977.

But from the very beginning of the inquiry the most significant problem seemed to involve just how a methodological device could be developed for eliciting generalizations about similarities and dissimilarities in the basic assumptions among the early theorists themselves and between them and still earlier and later figures in the history of the discipline. Versions of the analytic scheme were offered at the American Sociological Association meeting of 1969, the Cheiron convention of 1974, and the North Central Sociological Association meeting of 1977. Modifications were published in 1975 and 1978.

Throughout the twenty years of study, academic and personal circumstances have sometimes been favorable and sometimes unfavorable for energetic pursuit of the project. Initially, the enterprise was envisaged as a joint venture which was to culminate in a textbook in sociological theory, but this plan had to be abandoned. A sabbatical research leave in the Spring (semester) of 1970 (just before departure from Temple University and return to Ohio State University) provided a major opportunity for a provisional formulation of the social evolutionary theory of social change in American sociology. But the final impetus to and inspiration for completion of this study was generated out of a seminar in early American sociological theory in the spring of 1976. Members of this group – many of whom have continued to engage in related research – included Patrick J. Gurney, Inese K. Neiders, Norman E. Smith, and Drs Danny L. Jorgensen, David M. Orenstein, and Stephen J. Pfohl. Judith A. Cook, Keith Ewald, Judith A. Golec, Linda W. Romero, and Drs Edward E. Armstrong, Israel L. Barak, Gideon Fishman, Rodney M.

Kueneman, and Aldo Piperno have also given significant stimulation and encouragement.

The roles of three persons especially deserve comment. I am particularly indebted to Professor J. David Lewis (University of Notre Dame) for his careful, considerate, and constructive criticisms of various versions of the manuscript. And although Professor Gisela J. Hinkle has not been directly involved in the preparation of this work and is not responsible for any of its content, she has contributed incalculably. Theoretical reflection and analysis have always been a part of life. To her late father (and my father-in-law), Professor Fritz Karl Mann (Emeritus Professor of Economics at the University of Cologne and American University and one of the founders of the first Deutsche Gesellschaft für Soziologie), I am grateful for his vivid personal accounts, interpretations, and re-creations of the social science world of Dilthey, Windelband, Rickert, Tönnies, Simmel, and Alfred and Max Weber – a world with which the first generation of American sociology has been recurrently compared and contrasted.

Roscoe C. Hinkle
Columbus, Ohio

Acknowledgments

The author wishes to express his gratitude to the Yale University Library for the right to cite and to quote from unpublished documents in the collections of the William Graham Sumner Papers and the Albert G. Keller Papers in the Yale University Library.

He is also grateful for invaluable information on the doctorates in sociology conferred by the University of Wisconsin and Yale University before 1915 which has been provided by Professor Michael T. Aiken, Department of Sociology, University of Wisconsin, Madison, Wisconsin; and Professor Jerome K. Myers, Department of Sociology, Yale University, New Haven, Connecticut.

And he is appreciative of permission to use a 1973 unpublished paper on 'The Pioneers of American Sociology: An Empirical Study' by Professor Paul J. Baker (and his associates Martha P. Long and Susan L. Quensel), Department of Sociology, Illinois State University, Normal, Illinois.

The author gratefully acknowledges his indebtedness for quotations:

Reprinted by permission of Charles Scribner's Sons from *Social Organization* by Charles Horton Cooley. Copyright © 1909 Charles Scribner's Sons; renewal copyright © 1937 Elsie Jones Cooley.

Reprinted by permission of Joan Kennedy Slocum and William W. Slocum, Jr, executor of the Estate of Mary E. Cooley, deceased, from *Social Process* by Charles Horton Cooley. Copyright © 1918 Charles Scribner's Sons.

ACKNOWLEDGMENTS

From *Folkways* by William Graham Sumner, © Copyright, 1906, by William Graham Sumner. Used by permission of the publisher, Ginn and Company (Xerox Corporation).

Reprinted by permission of Yale University Press from *The Science of Society* by William Graham Sumner and Albert Galloway Keller. Copyright © 1927 Yale University Press.

Reprinted by permission of Augustus M. Kelley from *Pure Sociology* by Lester Frank Ward. Copyright © 1970 Augustus M. Kelley.

1 Toward a sociology of the history of sociological theory

Although the field of the sociology of sociology has a venerable intellectual ancestry, its actual birth dates from the socio-academic turbulence of the 1960s. It originated with proclamations of crisis, which betokened an acute sensitivity to the character of the theory of the discipline and its changing socio-historical context. Both Gouldner (1970) and Friedrichs (1970) have pronounced the discipline in a state of crisis akin to the paradigm revolution ascertained by the sociological adaptors of Kuhn's conception of the history of the physical sciences. For Gouldner (1970), 'crisis' is signified by the demise of functionalism and the ascendance of a social dramatology, ethnomethodology, exchangism, and radicalism (especially neo-marxism). More particularly, he has asserted (1970, p. 410) that the dominant functionalist and Parsonian models have been drifting towards a convergence with marxism; younger sociologists alienated from functionalism, their dissatisfaction crystallized in collective and organized forms; alternative theories (e.g., Goffman, Garfinkel, Homans) have emerged; and a middle-range social problems research and theory – 'often oriented to the values of "freedom" and "equality" rather than of "order"' – have developed. Other sociologists who seem to have drawn their formulations from Kuhn (e.g., Friedrichs, 1970, pp. 12–13; Effrat, 1972, pp. 11, 31; Lehman and Young, 1974, pp. 16–17, 25) have also envisaged sociology as beset by a crisis which is reflected in the declining acceptance of functionalism. Yet, just what the larger temporal or historical significance of crisis within the sociology of sociology is is not immediately apparent here, but when it has been divulged it may well require a more searching

1

methodological concern with historically-oriented inquiry than has so far been contemplated.

The implications of crisis for the history and sociology of sociology

Perhaps Gouldner (1970, pp. 341–2) comes closest to specifying the general implications of crisis. He discerns change, especially basic and permanent change, the possibility of a fundamental metamorphosis or transformation of a system (i.e., sociology). A crisis implies that changes are taxing, relatively rapid, involve great tensions and conflict, spiraling costs, along with the possibility of a fundamentally different system-state. A time perspective is manifestly entailed. Something differs from something else in temporal sequence. What seems to be emerging is different from what has been. Crisis suggests an awareness of (some degree of) discontinuity between the future emerging out of the present and past. There is a sense of 'fin de siècle' in the literal sense, the end of an era or a period, on the one hand. And on the other, such crisis implies (at least potentially) the beginning of another period or era.

In the present instance, therefore, 'crisis' signifies the end of a period of relative intellectual consensus, homogeneity, or orthodoxy centering around structural functionalism (generally intertwined also with the social action orientation). Intellectual dissensus, heterogeneity, and heterodoxy have become increasingly evident, as witness the rise of social exchangist, conflictual-neo-marxist-critical, ethnomethodological-phenomenological, and even structuralist orientations. Whether the present intellectual conflict will soon be superseded by another period of consensus or orthodoxy or will itself persist indefinitely to become a (full) period of dissensus and heterodoxy cannot now (or here) be determined.

Periodicization as a problem in the history of sociology and sociological theory in the US

However, the basic and fundamental problem is not merely to account for the ending of one period and the beginning of another. The apparent recent transition from one period to another is only a particular symptom or manifestation of a more abstract, general phenomenon of intellectual change and historical succession, i.e., periodicization. What is significant, therefore, is not merely the characterization and demarcation of one (recent) particular period but the problem of how periodicization in general (in the discipline) is accomplished. The particular and concrete sense of crisis must be recognized for what it is: a symptom, manifestation, or instance of a more general problem phenomenon. Thus, the inquiry which is the focus of this monograph involves the general problem of developing a tenable methodology for periodicization in the history of sociology.

But even this problem statement is insufficiently precise and circumscribed. Those who have referred to the crisis of the present (e.g., Gouldner and Friedrichs) have in effect spoken as though that which was beset by crisis was indeed the entire field, discipline, or science of sociology. Significantly, these chief spokesmen of 'crisis' are identified professionally with the domain of (general) sociological theory. And the 'crisis' whose dimensions they have sought to describe has been basically or essentially characterized as theoretical in nature. Whether or not it is appropriate and accurate to approach the entire discipline in terms of the controversies of (general) theory might at least be open to question. Consequently, a first restriction or qualification of the history of that which is to be periodicized is that the object of inquiry is (the periodicization of) the history of (general) sociological theory. No especially compelling a priori reason can be offered for necessarily identifying (or subordinating) the histories of the sociology of the family, bureaucracy, stratification, or the polity – for instance – with what is essentially the history of (general) sociological theory. Professional candor and detachment thus seem to commend initially the recognition that the field whose history is to be subject to periodicization is (general) sociological theory (rather than sociology in general).

A second circumscription is as necessary as the first and will, perhaps, invite even more controversy. It is imperative to recognize that the periodicizing methodology to be developed is to apply not merely to the history of sociological theory but more narrowly and precisely to the history of American sociological theory or, stated more accurately, to the history of sociological theory in the United States. Again, it appears to be the case that professionals in sociological theory in the United States have in effect spoken and acted as though the developments in American theory have dominated and in essence constituted sociological theory generally. Manifestly, the character of German sociological theory before World War I and between World Wars I and II was distinguishably and distinctively different from American theory. (Admittedly, developments in American theory have been influential abroad since World War II, but this fact does not warrant a general unreflective Americano-centrization of sociological theory.) Indiscriminate intermingling of the histories of sociological theory in the US and elsewhere (especially France, Germany, Great Britain) can only obfuscate and complicate the task of accurate historical analysis. (Cross-national intellectual similarities must be consciously and intentionally demonstrated rather than unconsciously and unreflectively assumed.) Thus, a second restriction to be imposed on the present study is that the periodicizing methodology is to apply to the history of sociological theory in the United States.

Approaches to the study of the history of sociological theory in the US

Unfortunately, a scrutiny of the past works in the history of the discipline in general and in sociological theory in particular – which have tended to be designed prevailingly as textbooks rather than as research monographs – does not yield any major helpful clues for dealing with the problem of periodicization. Many seemingly relevant books have been published since World War II, including, for instance: Harry Elmer Barnes (ed.), *An Introduction to the History of Sociology* (1948); Nicholas S. Timasheff's *Sociological Theory* (1955); Howard Becker and Alvin Boskoff (eds), *Sociological Theory in Continuity and Change* (1957); Joseph S. Roucek (ed.), *Contemporary Sociology* (1958); Don Martindale's *The Nature and Types of Sociological Theory* (1960); Robert A. Nisbet's *The Sociological Tradition* (1966); Pitirim A. Sorokin's *Sociological Theories of Today* (1966); Alvin Boskoff's *Theory in American Sociology* (1969); Robert E. L. Faris's *Chicago Sociology 1920–1932* (1970); Robert W. Friedrichs's *A Sociology of Sociology* (1970); Alvin W. Gouldner's *The Coming Crisis of Western Sociology* (1970); Larry T. and Janice M. Reynolds's *The Sociology of Sociology* (1970); Lewis A. Coser's *Masters of Sociological Thought* (1971); Nicholas C. and Carolyn J. Mullin's *Theories and Theory Groups in Contemporary American Sociology* (1973); Herman and Julia R. Schwendinger's *The Sociologists of the Chair* (1974); Jonathan H. Turner's *The Structure of Sociological Theory* (1974); James T. Carey's *Sociology and Public Affairs: The Chicago School* (1975); George Ritzer's *Sociology: A Multiple Paradigm Science* (1975); S. N. Eisenstadt's (and M. Curelaru's) *The Form of Sociology: Paradigms and Crises* (1976); Graham C. Kinloch's *Sociological Theory* (1977).

Certainly, these works do provide some basic indications of just how sociologists tend to write the histories of their discipline and its theories. At least two dominant modes of historiography can be identified. The first envisages history as a succession of creative personalities who constitute a kind of sociological pantheon and who are presented with their chief contributions in accordance with their order in chronological sequence (e.g., Coser). The second mode endeavors to classify sociologists into leading schools or theoretical orientations and to arrange them by sequence of appearance and then by dates of the careers of their leading exponents (e.g., Martindale, Timasheff). Less common, however, is the effort to write a history of the discipline in terms of its societal contexts (e.g., Barnes, Roucek), or its major subfields (Becker and Boskoff), or its current dominant problematics (Boskoff). Nisbet is the only sociologist who analyzes the sociological tradition through basic unit-ideas or major notions. Faris and Carey provide major monographic studies of the Chicago School which they both identify with the years from the end of World War I (or 1920) to 1932. Both are inclined to ascribe the pre-eminence of the Chicago Department to the research eminence of its members (1970, pp. xiii, 123) or to the 'remarkable flowering of empirical inquiry on urban problems during this period' (1975, p. 3), though Faris claims that the 'period of interest has no precise beginning or end' (1970, p. xiii). But Carey notes that Chicago sociology arose under a 'specific set of social conditions,' had representatives who 'came from an identifiable social stratum, and directed its studies toward a particular audience who used . . . [the] research' (p. 3). Carey's concern for the distinctiveness of the era (pp. 4–7) suggests an interest in the phenomena of periods or the problem of periodicization in the history of sociology or sociological theory.

Three of the above volumes do concern themselves in effect with one or perhaps two periods in the history of the discipline. Friedrichs's book is preoccupied with the intellectual changes in the discipline since World War II. Though placed in a historical context, Gouldner's work is *predominantly* concerned with an analysis and critique of structural functionalism and the years of its intellectual dominance in sociology. The Schwendingers have offered a radical analysis of the formative years of (North) American sociology, 1883–1922. Again, none of them directly confronts the problem of temporal delimitation.

However, at least four of the historically-oriented volumes on theory utilize the notion of 'paradigm,' which in its original usage by Thomas Kuhn in *The Structure of Scientific Revolutions* carried an explicitly temporal or durational meaning and whose employment in sociology thus warrants consideration. Friedrichs's *A Sociology of Sociology* makes Kuhn's work in general and his notion of paradigm the basic point of departure for his own inquiry. He is unmistakably aware of the varied meanings of Kuhn's ideas of paradigm (p. 5). However, the more recent works by Eisenstadt (and Curelaru) on *The Form of Sociology: Paradigms and Crises* and by Kinloch on *Sociological Theory: Its Development and Major Paradigms* either ignore Kuhn completely or virtually so. Eisenstadt never explicitly defines what a paradigm is and tends to use the term modified by adjectives, e.g., 'explicative paradigms or sociological theories,' 'explicative paradigms or paradigmatic models.' Although he doesn't refer to Kuhn, he does declare that such models tend to derive from the basic analytical problems (or *Problemstellungen*) of the discipline, which are 'seen as essential for the working of societies and patterns of social behavior' (p. 82). Such a notion is at least consistent with, if it does not actually stem from, Kuhn. Kinloch, who makes only two abbreviated allusions to Kuhn, is also remarkably brief in his delineation of the notion of paradigm. He remarks that the 'foundation of any theory is its paradigm or model of reality,' which consists of a 'conceptualization of [the] phenomena being explained' (e.g., society) and 'an assumed underlying causal relationship' about the phenomena (p. 5). He identifies only three basic paradigms in sociology: the organic, conflict, and social behavioristic (but each with its own variants). Eisenstadt designates individualistic, sociologistic, cultural, and environmental paradigms in sociology (p. 85). Neither Kinloch nor Eisenstadt follows Kuhn to indicate how their alleged sociological paradigms acquire intellectual acceptance and dominance, undergo development and elaboration, encounter anomalies and contradictions, and finally experience refutation and rejection – all of which are durational and temporal in nature.

However, it is Ritzer in his *Sociology: A Multiple Paradigm Science* who invokes the notion of paradigm most directly and extensively. Kuhn is his alleged point of departure, though in reality it is Masterman's re-analysis and typology which are Ritzer's base. Curiously, Ritzer nowhere explicitly and systematically defines the main components of his own conception of paradigm (as applied to sociology): exemplar, image of the subject matter, theories and methods. He treats the meanings of these components as though they were self-evident, clear, and exclusive of one another – rather than as elusive, ambiguous, and overlapping in their actual use. He doesn't provide a direct justification of his conception of paradigm in relation to Kuhn's own multiple meanings (as opposed to Masterman's simplified typology). He fails, for instance, to indicate why it is legitimate to regard 'theories' as a component of paradigms in the face of Kuhn's own declaration that a paradigm is 'prior to . . . theories' (Kuhn, 1962, p. 11). Ritzer's 'methods' seem to refer to techniques and procedures of data collection and analysis, but without direct association with epistemological-methodological assumptions so significant for Kuhn. Importantly, too, his analyses of 'the social facts paradigm,' 'social definition paradigm,' and the 'social behavioral paradigm' are all devoid of any demonstration that they are in fact accepted by and expounded by an integrated group (or 'community') of practitioners across a particular interval of time. Ritzer is, indeed, indictable for the same omission just observed above in the case of Kinloch and Eisenstadt. In company with the other exponents of 'paradigm' in sociology, he has failed to recognize that in effect the duration of the dominance (or orthodoxy) of the paradigm does define a 'period' in the history of the discipline. Actual usage of the notion of paradigm in sociology does not commend it for its temporal, historical signification.

A proposed scheme for periodicization

Clearly, the histories of the discipline and its general theories have offered no precise prescriptions or substantial intimations for dealing with the problem of periodicization and the explanation of the characteristics of any such demarkable time-intervals (as a sociological history of sociological theory). Yet, past analyses of sociological theory did more or less imply the existence of periods associated with the ascendance or dominance of particular orientations, such as the 'Chicago School' or 'Structural Functionalism.' But these designations (and such other possibilities as 'organicism,' 'conflict,' 'formalism,' or 'social behaviorism') appeared to be incomparably concrete or particularistic or vacuously vague and ambiguous. Some way is required to secure access to more fundamental generalized similarities and dissimilarities in the nature of sociological theory.

The present procedure in which a classificatory-periodicizing scheme has become a central and crucial device evolved out of the pursuit of the clues, implications, and possibilities contained in the writings of such sociologists as Timasheff, Martindale, and (Walter) Wallace. In his introductory *Sociological Theory*, Timasheff (1955, p. 11) suggested that 'sociological theories of the

7

past and present' have revolved 'around a few problems . . . the various answers to' which might be made the basis of a formulation of (a sequence of) fundamental theoretical orientations in the history of sociological theory. (Unfortunately, Timasheff never implemented his idea systematically.) A decade later (but only five years after *The Nature and Types of Sociological Theory* had been published), Don Martindale concluded in his chapter in *Functionalism in the Social Sciences* (1965) that two central and fundamental problems can be identified: what is the nature of social phenomena (or social ontology) and what is the nature of social knowledge and how is it acquired (or social epistemology-methodology). His chapter also suggested the main alternative answers which Sorokin's last book (in 1966) corroborated in somewhat different terms and which reflected Sorokin's more elaborate analysis in volume 2 of the earlier *Social and Cultural Dynamics* (1937). Patently, too, in his introduction to his *Sociological Theory* (1969) Walter Wallace advocated taking a similar stance, though he did not implement his approach in the way Martindale intimates and this book proposes.

But the more immediate point of departure for the development of the periodicizing scheme (below) was the analysis of the (explicit or implicit) notions of 'sociological theory' espoused by major sociologists who have been self-identified and/or other- (or publicly-) identified as sociological theorists and whose professional careers in the aggregate extended from the 1880s and 1890s up to the 1960s. Their views implied that two fundamental questions are involved: What makes 'sociological theory' genuinely 'theory'? And, in turn, what renders such theory distinctively 'sociological'? The concern with theory as a technical notion (as an array of concepts or categories, as a set of empirical generalizations, or as a logico-deductive (i.e., hypothetico-deductive) system) ultimately led back to the question of the nature of explanation or interpretation and, even more basically, to the nature of social knowledge and the method of study (or social epistemology-methodology). The main referent or objective of 'sociological' concern involved a preoccupation with the nature of the social (or social reality), i.e., with a social ontology. Thus, two problem-domains are evident. The former encompasses (the theory of) how the social is to be known and studied, whereas the latter comprehends (the theory of) what the (nature of the) social is. Together, the two sets of problems become the foundation for the classificatory-periodicizing scheme as indicated in chapter 3.

In turn, each of these two problem-spheres or domains is further specifiable into a series of basic questions or issues and possible answers (or positions) in terms of which the scheme can be further differentiated and elaborated. For instance, the epistemological-methodological domain involves such questions as what the bases of social knowledge are (e.g., empiricism, rationalism, intuitionism); implementing investigative methods, procedures, techniques (with the subsidiary questions of whether these methods are like or unlike those used in the natural sciences (positivism versus humanism), focus on the whole or parts (methodological holism versus atomism)); whether and how explanation is to occur (with subsidiary issues and positions concerning reduction versus emergence, deductive versus pattern form, causation versus interaction, etc.), and the issue of 'truth' in knowledge (e.g., correspondence versus consistency).

The other domain, that of social ontological theory, also entails its typical issues or questions and responses (or positions). First is the basic issue of the conception of the 'social' itself: as (inter- and/or multi-personal) relation or relationship; as (inter- and/or multi-personal) activity; and as (persisting, structured) group. A second concerns the relations of the social to other phenomena and realities, such as whether the social is a domain, realm, or system itself (in nature versus outside), what the relation of the nonsocial to social phenomena is (e.g., the non-human biophysical, human organic, human psychic, human quasi-social, human cultural), analogies or models between the non-social and the social, the social in relation to basic forms of reality ('materialism' versus 'idealism'), part-whole or whole-part in the constitution of the social ('social nominalism' versus 'social realism'). Finally, the third sector of social ontological theory comprises the basic problems around which the study of the social focuses (e.g., *genesis* (origins, emergence), *stasis* (statics, stability, persistence, structure), and *dynamis* (dynamics, instability, change, variation, including transformation and possible dissolution of structures)).

The actual procedure of periodicization (with the scheme) involves the demarcation of time-intervals (or 'periods') during which particular generalized sets of (theoretical) notions among theorists are ascendant or dominant. A 'period' is established by comparing – and thus generalizing from – a series of statements extracted from publications of a number of theorists whose professional careers intersect or coincide and thus form a relatively unbroken continuum through time. The categories of questions and answers-positions from the scheme serve as a guide to the extraction of statements, which are subsequently compared to

9

develop more general categories or types. Some one or two of these types will, presumably, be ascertained eventually to represent the dominant, orthodox, or 'mainline' position(s). (In most instances, numerical predominance of cases in the categories should be sufficient to determine dominance. But perhaps in a few circumstances more subtle 'prestige' manifestations may have to be analyzed.) Other (remaining) types will constitute subordinate, heterodox, 'marginal,' or peripheral positions. As the inquiry is extended to include the analysis of statements of figures who are both earlier and later than those used as the original point of departure, differences of shifts in what is the dominant position(s) in relation to minor positions will be encountered. These differences signal the (temporal) boundaries of time-intervals or periods.

Either partial or full periodicization of the history of sociological theory might be undertaken. The former entails delineation of only one or a few periods. A particular period is constituted of one or more major and minor orientations which involve both social epistemological-methodological and social ontological premises persisting through a determined interval of time. Total or full periodicization of the history of (macro-) sociological theory (in the US, for instance) entails the delineation of a succession of generalized intellectual orientations (or 'periods') – as defined through and determined by changing more or less dominant or prevalent answers to the questions in the scheme – across the full range of history in the discipline.

Delineation of periods in the history of theory does provide a signal opportunity for creating a history of theory that is genuinely sociological, i.e., a sociological history of sociological theory. It means, among other things, that the history of theory can be approached in terms of and as a potential contribution to the sociology of sociology. Each period and the transition to the next can be subjected to sociological explanation. As a period, the major and minor field domain concepts, ideas, postulates, assumptions and their interrelationships can be related to such considerations as professional origins, educational characteristics, patterns of productivity, political preferences, communication networks, etc., of theorists. The characteristics of periods can be related to the impact of ideas from (sociological or non-sociological) movements or personalities from abroad, developments in other fields of (American) sociology, the changing professional organization of (American) sociology, influences from other disciplines or sciences (e.g., anthropology, linguistics, biology), modifications in the social structure of academia (i.e., colleges and universities), alterations in the broader environing social structure (e.g., research funds from the federal government) and culture (such as priorities in major values).

Furthermore, each such period so interpreted sociologically can be linked temporally with others (preceding and succeeding) to form a unified sequence extending backward (or forward) so that eventually a complete historical chain between the present state of affairs in sociological theory and the earliest can be established. Each period will thus be both a problem to be explained (an explanandum) and a contribution to an explanation (an explanans) of what follows. Each period is thus in part explained by its current social and intellectual situation or context and in part by the prior past or historical background setting. Presumably, both continuities and discontinuities will be discerned and become explicable. And it should become possible eventually to ascertain whether or not some deeper structural unity persists between the apparent discontinuities between periods.

An illustrative application of the scheme to the early history of sociological theory in the US

Unfortunately, any analysis of the content of general sociological theory which is conducted with the aid of the scheme (noted above), which is pursued rigorously, intensively, precisely, and systematically across a particular interval of time, and which is buttressed by an inquiry into the related socio-intellectual context (as just proposed), can scarcely aspire to encompass the total developmental span of sociological theory in the United States. What this means is simply that the endeavor at periodicization must be attempted within a limited or partial interval of years rather than across the total historical horizon of the field (in the US). Consequently, the question must be addressed as to which segment of the history of theory can be most advantageously subjected to study with the aid of the periodicizing scheme.

Undoubtedly, considerable interest exists in the recently preceding decades in which structural functionalism was apparently the prevailing theoretical orientation and which has more recently experienced a noticeable decline. Nevertheless, several major works have attempted to study the rise and decline of structural functionalism and thus the justification for another would seem to be somewhat less than compelling. In addition, much of the interest in theory of recent years is also associated with evident partisan

11

commitment. Detachment is likely to be won with considerable difficulty. Even more reason for rejecting the study of this recent 'period' is the persistence of 'crisis' and thus the likelihood of substantial difficulty in demarking more or less temporal 'beginning' and 'ending' boundaries of the recent period. Transition has begun but the 'outlines' of the new theoretical stances are still blurred and indistinct.

By contrast, some persuasive arguments can be offered for investigating the theory of earliest American sociology and for attempting to apply the scheme to demark the beginning and ending of this period. Although interest in the theory of these years may not be as intense as in the more recent years, partisanship and commitment should be minimal and, therefore, detachment easier to achieve than in the more contemporary period. Second, our knowledge of the general or composite nature of theory from the early decades of the discipline is scandalously inadequate. We have no major investigations centering on the generalized similarities and dissimilarities among the early theorists. (The Schwendingers' *The Sociologists of the Chair* is actually oriented to other objectives.) What we possess are isolated (and but rarely published) dissertations, articles or monographs on single theorists (which were usually made long before the present interest in the sociology of sociology and the new histories of science) or textbook summaries which at best draw individual theorists together under vague conceptual umbrellas. Third, the ostensibly divergent character of American sociological theory after about the mid 1930s seems to recommend a study of the earlier (and largely ignored) years if the possibility of ascertaining fundamental theoretical continuities through the use of the scheme is to be contemplated seriously. Modern theorists such as Parsons and Gouldner at least imply that earliest theory in the US is relatively irrelevant to, and perhaps basically different from, the allegedly European-inspired social action and structural functional theories generated after about 1935. In order to test the possibility of long-range theoretical continuity, it becomes absolutely indispensable to command an in-depth knowledge of the characteristics of general sociological theory from the earliest decades of the history of the discipline. Certainly, the appropriate point of departure for the eventual development of a comprehensive sociology of the history of sociological theory in the US is a study of early American theory.

To facilitate the demarcation of the period (with the use of the scheme below), it seems advisable to begin the search with the earliest published works of sociologists in the 1880s and to pursue the inquiry into the literature of the 1920s. The analysis which is to be reported in the subsequent chapters reveals that the contributions of such early sociologists as Lester Frank Ward (1841–1913), William Graham Sumner (1840–1910), Franklin Henry Giddings (1855–1931), Edward Alsworth Ross (1866–1951), Albion Woodbury Small (1854–1926), and Charles Horton Cooley (1864–1929 were consciously and pre-eminently theoretical. These men were the founders of the discipline and its major theoreticians. They wrote what was and is regarded as the general theory of sociology during its first several decades. Accordingly, the period of earliest American sociological theory begins with their first publications: Sumner's articles on sociology and the science of society in 1881 and 1882 (see his 1918 work), his *What Social Classes Owe to Each Other* and Ward's *Dynamic Sociology*, both in 1883, Giddings's *The Principles of Sociology* in 1896, Cooley's *Personal Competition* in 1899 and Ross's *Social Control* in 1901. Extension of comparative inquiry through the years of World War I offers maximum opportunity for discerning signs of intellectual discontinuity and the boundedness of the first period, for World War I had a substantial impact on American life generally. Ward's, Sumner's, and Small's academic careers and/or major publication activity had come to an end before 1920. Cooley's last major publication, his *Social Process*, the third of his trilogy, appeared in 1918. (But his *Sociological Theory and Social Research* was published posthumously in 1930.) The fact that Giddings and Ross continued to publish important works throughout the 1920s does suggest possible problems in the determination of the terminal boundary of the first period.

Other reasons can be cited for ascribing significance to the works of Ward, Sumner, Keller, Giddings, Ross, Small, and Cooley. These individuals were the major contributors to the literature in sociology generally. Admittedly, only one periodical existed in the field before World War I, the *American Journal of Sociology*, which was published by the University of Chicago with Albion W. Small as its first editor. The most prolific contributor to this journal during its first two decades of existence (1895–1915) was Small himself (with some thirty-eight articles). Author of twenty-two articles, Ward is second in the list of contributors. (Next are faculty members and former graduate students in the Chicago Department of Sociology, e.g., Charles R. Henderson, W. I. Thomas, and Charles A. Ellwood, all of whom were authors of from fourteen to seventeen articles in those years.) A fourth category of productivity includes first the (ex-) Chicagoans E. C. Hayes and George A. Vincent (with eight and seven articles) but also includes Ross, Giddings, Keller, and Cooley (who range from seven down to four contributions). Sumner, who died in 1910, was the author of two articles which appeared in the *American Journal of Sociology* during its first two decades.

Ward, Sumner, Keller, Giddings, Ross, Small, and Cooley were also conspicuously active in the meetings of the American Sociological Association (then Society) during its first decade of existence (1906–15). Of the ninety-seven papers presented during its first ten years, the seven pioneers delivered nineteen (or about 20 per cent). Giddings, Ross, and Small each offered four papers, Ward three, Sumner two, and Keller and Cooley each presented one.

Presumably the respect which these men commanded also contributed to their election to the presidency of the American Sociological Society (as it was then called). Ward was the first executive officer (1906, 1907). Sumner followed (1908, 1909). Giddings was the third president (1910, 1911), Small the fourth (1912, 1913), and Ross the fifth (1914, 1915). Cooley was the eighth person to hold the chief office of the organization (1918).

It is of major consequence that these pioneers and founders were associated with departments of sociology which were (or eventually became) the chief graduate training centers in the discipline. During the period 1895–1915 perhaps as many as ninety-eight doctorates in sociology were conferred.[1] The largest number (thirty-five) were awarded by the University of Chicago, with which Small was associated. Twenty-four doctorates were granted at Columbia University, where Giddings was the dominant figure. Ten Ph.D.s were conferred by Yale, under the direction of either (first) Sumner or (later) Keller. (Interestingly, thirteen doctorates in sociology were awarded by the University of Pennsylvania and eight by New York University!) The Departments at the Universities of Wisconsin and Michigan, with which Ross and Cooley were prominently associated both before and after World War I, apparently did not produce substantial numbers of advanced degrees until the 1920s. Wisconsin conferred six doctorates in sociology (the first in 1909), Michigan one (1907), and Ohio State one (1914) before 1915.

Finally, evidence exists that within the decade after World War I the sociologists in question had already achieved a pre-eminent position in their generation. One of the questions of L. L. Bernard's unpublished 1927 questionnaire-investigation of the professional backgrounds of sociologists asked for specification of which earlier sociologists had been most influential as teachers-professors or authors-writers or both.[2] The 184 respondents to this question (out of the total of 276 whose answers to all of the questions could be located) listed the names of Cooley, Giddings, Ward, Ross, and Small as the five most influential figures. Sumner was listed in the ninth position (after Park, Thomas, and Ellwood).

Manifestly, the publications of Ward, Sumner (and Keller), Giddings, Ross, Small, and Cooley do warrant consideration for a variety of reasons. But the primary reason is that their works do constitute the theory of the first several decades of the discipline in the United States. Thus, their publications will provide the chief data for analysis, i.e., characterization and periodicization, with the aid of the schema.

An overview of the inquiry

Although the actual organization of the analysis of early American sociological theory is in part dictated by the nature of the structure of that theory and in part by the use of the analytical scheme, the organization of the inquiry cannot be meaningful if it entirely ignores the conventions of how phenomena of the past are to be treated. Early theory existed in a much broader socio-historico-intellectual context or contexts which must be delineated and understood prior to the analysis of the theory itself. Theory becomes meaningful or makes sense only in relation to the context or contexts. Indeed, these contexts provide an indispensable orientation for the application of the scheme to the data of early theory.

Accordingly, chapter 2 on the 'Contexts of Early Sociological Theory' indicates the existence of five different (though inter-related) contexts, the characteristics of which provide clues for adapting the scheme to use in the period of American sociology within the later decades of the nineteenth and the earlier decades of the twentieth centuries. Of broadest significance is the changing character of post-Civil War (i.e., post-1865) American society and its culture. In turn, these changes make meaningful the profound modifications in the structure of American higher education which also occurred and which constitute the second context. Together, the alterations in American society and higher education provide a basis for the emergence of the social sciences as academic disciplines in the late nineteenth century as the third context. Sociology as a discipline is the obvious immediate and fourth context for early American theory. The last of the five contexts is constituted by then contemporary (and earlier) European sociological theory.

In the following chapter 3, the basic outlines of the analytic scheme are presented as a preliminary overview of the total inquiry. This chapter indicates what the major data are (i.e., published works in 'general' sociology), and why on the basis of their explicit objectives these works constitute treatises in general sociological theory in accordance with the scheme. But before any major analysis in terms of the scheme is undertaken, the actual embodiment of the theories in concrete expositional presentations is first described. Subsequently, it is evident that early general theory in American sociology does endeavor to provide comprehensive definitions of the phenomena studied by the field (e.g., 'society,' 'social phenomena,' 'social process'). Like more modern theory, the earlier period bespeaks the fundamental division of sociological theory into two fundamental branches, the first identifiable as epistemological-methodological theory and the second designatable as substantive-ontological theory. Each of the branches is preliminarily characterized. For instance, acceptable sociological knowledge of that era tends to be based dualistically on both sensory experience and the logic of reason. Prevailingly positivistic and humanistic methodological orientations have already emerged in this first era of American sociology. Manifestly, knowledge aimed not merely at description but also at explanation which tended to be emergentist (rather than reductivist), deductive, teleological, genetic, and emphatically causal in character. (Chapter 4 elaborates the features of early epistemological-methodological theory.)

But this overview chapter also notes that sociological theory of the first era is predominantly associated with substantive-ontological theory. As the second branch of theory, it is concerned with the nature of the 'social' and with the basic problems of (1) social origins or genesis, (2) persistence-stability-structure, and (3) instability-change (both modification and transformation). However, ontological theory of the first period is distinctive because it was especially preoccupied with the problems of origins and change. These concerns are especially reflected in the common overarching sociological orientation of 'evolutionary naturalism.' This latter term designates three appropriate tenets: (1) it is possible and desirable to offer a naturalistic, rather than a supernaturalistic, explanation of social or societal phenomena (which are thus a domain in and of nature and which involve social forces); (2) the

16

appearance of social phenomena can be accounted for (causally) in terms of other more basic, elementary or generic phenomena, states, or conditions, out of which social phenomena arose gradually; and (3) Darwinian (and Spencerian) views of organic evolution are held to afford an acceptable model for interpreting the stability-instability of modes of human association as effective adaptations or adjustments to the conditions of human existence.

All of the subsequent chapters (on ontological theory) are dependent on and interrelated with the implications of this pervasive evolutionary naturalism of early American sociological theory. Chapter 5 presents an account of the (two modes of) evolutionary origins of social phenomena – one arguing for the post-(human) organic and the other for the pre-(human) organic genesis of the social. It also reveals the relevancy of the general ontological distinction between materialism and idealism in the scheme for characterizing the nature of the social: as inter- and/or multi-personal relations or relationships; as inter- and/or multi-personal forms of activity or process; and as relatively permanently structured and persistent group. Chapter 6 extends genetic analysis into the basic structural features of the early human group-society and supports the basically dualistic view of social reality. (Structural notions such as 'place,' 'status,' and 'institution' appeared in early theory.)

Early sociologists did endeavor to develop structural classifications of groups and societies within their theoretical formulations. Chapter 7 reveals that their efforts included (Sumner's) 'in-group' and 'out-group,' (Giddings's) 'social composition' and 'social constitution,' (Cooley's) 'primary group' and 'nucleated group' (but no 'secondary group'), and (Ross's) 'community–society' dichotomy. However, society itself was the most significant structural notion, with perhaps 'primitive' and 'modern society' being the most common designations. Early theorists provided impressive profiles of the characteristics of these two types of societies.

Nevertheless, early ontological theories were considerably more interested in instability-dynamics-change than in stability-statics-structure. Two types of change theories appeared and the characteristics of both are more or less specifiable in terms of the analytic scheme: unit undergoing change; model; investigative method; magnitude and rate; directionality; and the explanation or modus operandi of change. Chapter 8 contains an analysis of the theory of social evolution, which emphasizes human society, humanity, mankind, or the race as a whole as the unit of study;

17

organismic growth, especially adaptive growth as the model; the resort to the comparative method for studying dynamics; the naturally small, imperceptible, infinitesimal amount, with a slow, gradual, continuous rate of change; its linear or rectilinear directionality (as exhibited in passage through certain stages); and finally, a tendency to explain change internally or intrinsically by the acceptance and dissemination of inter-individual adaptations or adjustments in relation to the changing conditions of existence. Ward, Keller, and Giddings appear to be social evolutionists.

Chapter 9 indicates the opposition and criticism of such early theorists as Sumner, (W. I.) Thomas, Ross, Small, and Cooley to one or more features of social evolution and the character of a separate social process conception or theory of social change. They rejected the monistic and, indeed, monolithic view of the unity of all human societies as one whole undergoing change. They controverted the conventional organismic growth analogy. They repudiated the use of the comparative method. They allowed for considerable variation in the rate and magnitude of change, even though slow, gradual, small-scale change might be most common. Directionality might be denied altogether, or the notion of a straight and uniform line of development might be rejected or some general direction might be accepted in conjunction with progress (as opposed to the necessity of adaptive social differentiation). Finally, Sumner, Ross, Small, and Cooley did attempt to invalidate both (Social) Darwinian and Lamarckian notions of the mechanisms of social change.

Instead, they explained change in a much more dialectical, Hegelian fashion through a cycle of processes invoking both internal and external sources. In contrast to the Social Darwinist view, conflict does not necessarily involve the elimination of the vanquished. Indeed, conflict is only one form of opposition, which is conceived as a stage or phase of interaction concluding in structural modification and creativity. For the processualists, some degree of compromise, accommodation, adaptation or adjustment tends to succeed conflict (between the opponents or thesis-antithesis) and eventually to be followed by innovation (accompanying synthesis). Social processualists tend to be predominantly idealistic-subjectivists or more balanced materialist-idealists rather than prevailingly materialist-objectivists.

The analysis of the problem of social change is concluded in chapter 10. Evolutionists do use specific social processes in their theories of change and both evolutionists and processualists accepted the idea of progress as a significant (and recognizably normative) component of their conceptions of change. This chapter summarizes the major points of agreement and disagreement about social change in early theory.

Chapter 11 provides a summary characterization of the founding theory of American sociology in terms of the basic features of the analytic scheme. Initially, it recalls the place of theory within the total perspective of the early discipline. In turn, the nature of early theory was further specified in terms of the relative interest in the epistemological-methodological versus the substantive-ontological divisions. Although early theory was preponderantly ontological, its epistemology can be identified as substantially dualistic (empiricist-rationalist (or rationalistic-idealist)). Cooley was uniquely idealist (or more precisely, an affective or romantic idealist). Methodologically, both more positivistic and humanistic stances can be distinguished.

By virtue of the dominant questions asked about the social (as inter- and/or multi-personal relations, activities, and persistent organized group or society) and the modes of their resolution, the basis is provided for characterizing the overarching ontological orientation as evolutionary naturalism. Although this orientation encompasses three somewhat distinct sub-positions, early American ontological theory is not merely dualistic (i.e., a combination of a social materialism-idealism) but is significantly idealist. Analysis of the distinctive formulation of that idealism reveals, further, that this founding theory is both nominalistically and voluntaristically inclined (i.e., is committed to a voluntaristic nominalism).

Chapter 12 seeks to complete the analysis required by the basic problem-objective of this monograph: a case-study illustration of a possible technique for periodicization in the history of American sociological theory. To periodicize is, of course, to demarcate periods of time and, in the present case, to do so by use of the analytic scheme. A period has a temporal duration, with a 'datable' beginning and ending between which certain features are predominant. Because the founding period is literally the initial period of American theory, its beginning boundary is more or less arbitrarily given by the onset of continuous publications, i.e., the early 1880s (c. 1881–3). However, determination of the ending temporal boundary of the first period involves the difficulties more characteristic of periodicization generally. It means isolating within an interval of a few years the decline-recession of one set of features and the ascendance-predominance of another. In this instance, the publication of Thomas's and Znaniecki's *The Polish*

Peasant in Europe and America during World War I is perhaps the most apt indicator-barometer of basic intellectual change.

Using the analytic scheme, it is evident that some very basic changes in theory (and the discipline generally) seem to be occurring by the middle of the second decade of the twentieth century (*c.* 1915–18), but become prominent only some years later. The very rationale for the acquisition of knowledge (i.e., progress) altered (Scheme II, D, 1, c). The relationship of theory to the discipline was modified. The position of epistemological-methodological theory was reversed so that the former acquired a predominance after World War I that it did not have previously. (Science became the hallmark of the discipline and empiricism-positivism-quantification acquired an unprecedented prominence.) The bases of the older social ontological theory in general (the social forces) and of dynamics theory in particular (social evolution) were severely challenged and controverted. Not only did interest in large-scale theory decline but it actually became intellectually suspect in the eyes of many members of the oncoming post-World War I generation of American sociologists. On the basis both of the characteristics of theory which had become predominant during the first decade of the century and those which had become ascendant during the 1920s, the interval of years around World War I (i.e., 1915–18) seem to represent a crucial temporal boundary setting off the first period from the second and the second from the first in the history of American theory.

Certainly, periodicization involves establishment of more than merely one period in a history. But it would appear to be impossible to develop an adequate argument for demarking the more recent periods in theory within the limits of less than one chapter – given the more than seven required to present the characterization and delineation of only the one first period. Nevertheless, the dating(s) and character(s) of the successive periods are proposed. In effect, then, this suggested delineation of periods constitutes a declaration of certain intellectual *dis*continuities in the history of American theory.

Yet the consequences of this endeavor must not be misconstrued. To assert discontinuities (i.e., periods) at a certain level of analysis does not necessarily preclude determination of continuity (or continuities) at another level (or levels). So, it becomes important to assess the capacity of the scheme to reveal continuities between and among the basic social ontological assumptions of major representatives of the different theoretical orientations ascendant in different periods (e.g., Park with his community-society theory;

20

the social action theory of Parsons, MacIver, Znaniecki, H. P. Becker; the symbolic interactionism of Blumer, the structural functionalism of Parsons, and the social phenomenology based on A. Schutz's works). Tentative conclusions are offered and a possible theoretical formulation of a sociology of the history of sociological theory is proposed.

2 Contexts of early sociological theory

Characterization of sociological theory by application of the scheme to particular, relevant statements of theorists from a given period of time does presuppose a context or contexts which must be delineated and elaborated if the endeavor is to be meaningful. What theorists say becomes interpretable only in relation to coexisting and preceding orthodoxy and heterodoxy in sociology and outside. Indeed, even the scheme itself acknowledges the interrelationship between the nature of theory itself and other sub-fields between sociology and other disciplines, and between the state of knowledge in general and the surrounding society. For instance, the scheme recognizes (II, D) that one of the functions of theory is to formulate the relationship between the discipline and the larger society and to analyze the rationales for that relationship. The earliest (general) theorists in American sociology did expound a justification for the development of the discipline which argued for a utilitarian or instrumentalist – more specifically, an ameliorative – relationship between the field and the larger society.

Admittedly, it is difficult initially to define the nature of (relevant) context (or contexts) without in advance assuming a potential causal relationship. 'Contexts' signify domains, settings, or situations to which theory (and/or the discipline) are more or less consciously oriented. They may be more or less concrete or abstract, immediate or remote, stable or variable. Manifestly, they possess both a spatial and a temporal character.

For sociology and its general theory which emerged in the 1880s and 1890s, five major contexts can be delineated.[1] Perhaps first and foremost is American society itself as a socio-cultural setting after the Civil War. Second is academia, the organizational context of higher education, the social structure of colleges and universities. The emerging social sciences comprise the third context. A fourth context is provided by the special (or more particularized) sociology to which theory (as the core of general sociology) is related and oriented. The fifth (and last) context of American sociological theory is the related and then current European sociological theory which was so often the point of departure for American theory.

Changes in the structure of American society

Significantly, the very justification which early sociologists offered for their discipline required its conscious orientation generally to the conditions of modern society and particularly to those in the context of their own society. Their rationale was predicated on the premise that human societies had experienced (evolutionary and) progressive change which was being threatened in their own era and thus could be no longer taken for granted. Construed as a natural object reflecting its own distinctive realm of forces, society could and would reveal to sociologists – upon appropriate investigation – regular, uniform, and predictable laws. This knowledge would permit social progress to become a conscious objective and would facilitate amelioration of those social conditions construed to be 'social problems.'

What Ward had termed natural progress would no longer occur automatically. It was threatened by the squandering of natural resources, under- or mal-adjusted production of the means of subsistence, depression, monopoly, financial mismanagement, the periodic outbursts of social reaction, the disproportionate rewarding of occupations concerned with the status quo, the sanctity of established institutions, the masses' ignorance of their own interests, the unorganized pursuit of knowledge, and the necessity to accelerate the dissemination of knowledge to overcome the developing lag between the appearance and mechanical application of scientific discoveries and the masses' understanding of them (1968, I, pp. 16, 73–81, 704–5; II, p. 15).

Giddings, Ross, and Small were all convinced that the growth of sociological knowledge would permit the effective formulation and rational criticism of public policies. According to Giddings, it should be possible to decide, therefore, 'what policies under given conditions further human progress, and what retard' (1922, p. 124). Ross contended similarly that scientific knowledge should permit public 'focus upon an ever small[er] number of measures [in] the discussions relating to family, property, association,

education, crime, pauperism, colonization, migration, class relations, race relations, war, and government' (1919, p. ix). Although
Small declared that sociology 'is not reformation of criminals, nor
administration of charities, nor solution of the poverty problem,
nor prevention of labor conflicts, nor reform of government, nor
improvement of education, nor the making of religion practical,' it
'would be an abortion if it did not eventually promote each and all
of these things' (1905, p. 34). But this ameliorative outcome could
obtain only if sociologists devoted themselves to 'constructing a
general science of society' and to formulating a 'general theory'
rather than becoming directly and primarily involved in 'the
solution of practical problems' (1905, p. 654). Like most of his
colleagues, Giddings asserted that sociological knowledge could
and should be used to redress the undue hardships and misery of
those who suffer from change by the enactment of legislation
(1922, pp. 244–5). Cooley also adhered to this prevalent melioristic
interventionism in arguing that sociology should facilitate the
formulation of 'measures having a good chance of success . . .'
(1966, p. 403). Understood as the development of knowledge useful
in ameliorating the social conditions associated with social
problems, the 'greatest practical concern' of virtually all early
sociologists was the 'promotion of progress' – as Ross had declared
(1919, p. 185). Necessarily, they were oriented to the context of
their larger society.

Processes of structural change

Early sociologists were aware that American society as the context
of social problems was undergoing basic, rapid change after the
Civil War. It was a society experiencing industrialization and
urbanization, differentiation, integration-centralization, stratification and concentration of power, and secularization.[2] In some
respects, industrialization and urbanization were perhaps the
primary processes. Certainly, these two contributed to the
economic and occupational differentiation of the population and,
in turn, the new media of communication permitted a new rational
integration and centralization. The unprecedented creation of
wealth through corporate capitalism became the basis for a new
system of stratification and the concentration of power, which
became evident in expressions of unrest by farmers and industrial
workers. Eventually, too, the belief and value-systems of American
society experienced secularization.

24

But among all these processes, industrialization was central and basic. Ellwood noted (1910, pp. 230–1), for example, that the factors which have made possible 'a great growth of manufacturing industries . . . have [also] tended to centralize manufacturing industries in the cities.' Indeed, (industrialism-) 'manufacturing has been a prime cause of the modern city . . .' (1910, p. 231). In spite of their close association with economics, early sociologists generally failed to recognize the complex nature of industrialization and its ramifications.

Not only did industrialization involve the application of the mechanized factory system to the manufacture of increasing numbers and types of products but also an expansion of major markets to include the entire country. Such national markets could emerge only if national systems of rapid and efficient transportation and communication developed and only if agricultural production became specialized, commercialized, and vastly enlarged. (See Nash, 1971, pp. 12–14, 7–8.) Between 1877 and 1890 railway mileage expanded from about 37,000 to 200,000 miles and mergers of railways had resulted in four major systems. Highway mileage more than doubled between 1860 and 1890 as new towns and cities were connected by main roads with improved surfacing and paving. The telegraph, telephone, and typewriter were important instruments in improving communications in the period. Most importantly, the specialization of productive activity implied by industrialization would not have been possible without major technological improvements in agriculture (e.g., the chilled iron plow, improved reaper, and mechanical twine-binders) which reduced the number of persons required for the production of food and released thousands from the farms to take industrial jobs in the cities.

Although the modern factory system with its (inanimate) power-driven machinery and its permanent working force, whose tasks were subdivided and specialized, had appeared in the US as early as 1814, it had remained relatively limited to textiles and related industries until an all-weather transportation network appeared. Factory production expanded into new fields in the late 1840s and 1850s, but it was the Civil War which provided a major impetus. Following the War, mechanized mass production enlarged further. By 1880, the Census reported that of the 3,000,000 people employed in industries using machines, some four-fifths (or 80 per cent) worked under the factory system. And at the turn of the new century, three of four major industries making the US the world's leading industrial power involved factory production (i.e., food processing, textile and clothing manufacture, and iron and steel fabrication; Nash, 1971, pp. 10–11).

Although the importance of technological innovation is not to be depreciated in the rise of large-scale industry in the post-Civil War US, it was not sufficient unto itself. Financing and the legal structure of the enterprise were other important considerations. Either initially or subsequently, the funding of the operations often could and did become a major problem and thus rapid industrialization could occur only because 'big finance' – investment banking houses (e.g., Morgan), securities markets, stock exchanges, and new banks (e.g., First National of New York, National City Bank of New York, National Bank of Commerce) – developed.

In addition, the legal form which industrial enterprises might assume was also important in the ease with which increasing size of operations might occur. The single entrepreneurship and partnership were not conducive to the easy amassing of capital. But this and other advantages were afforded by incorporation, the requirements and procedures for which were generalized and standardized by states only after the Civil War. The evident attractiveness of incorporation is indicated by the fact that by 1900 two-thirds of all manufacturing was done by corporations.

Simultaneously, enterprise was transformed from a single-purpose to a multi-functional, vertically-integrated organization (in the same era) (Chandler, 1967, pp. 71–102). In 1880 nearly all manufacturing firms simply manufactured. Their owners (or managers) purchased the raw materials and sold the finished goods through wholesalers, who were sometimes commission agents and at other times jobbers who took title to the goods. A concomitant of expanding size, which culminated in the first great merger movement in American history between 1897 and 1902, was the differentiation of function within the same organization. By the first years of the twentieth century many American industries were dominated by enterprises which had created their own distributing organizations, sometimes including even retail outlets, had formed their own purchasing systems and in some cases controlled their supplies of semi-finished and even raw materials.

As Ellwood suggested in his popular *Sociology and Modern Social Problems* (1910), industrialization and urbanization proceeded concomitantly in the decades after the Civil War. The urban proportion of the American population expanded from just under 20 per cent in 1860 to almost 40 per cent in 1900. (And it rose to 45.7 per cent in 1910.) The smallest increase was 2.5 per cent between 1870 and 1880 and the largest increase of 6.9 per cent occurred between 1880 and 1890, with changes between other decades varying between percentages of 4.7, 5.9, and 6.0. Manifestly, the rates of urban growth were extremely variable, accelerating in times of prosperity and diminishing in years of depression. The decade of the 1880s reveals the highest rate of urbanization, with many smaller cities – especially those in the Midwest – demonstrating striking increases (Glaab, 1963, p. 174). Significantly, the 16 per cent of the population in cities of 8,000 or more in 1860 had increased to 33 per cent in 1900 (and to 38 per cent in 1910). The number of such cities increased from 141 in 1860 to 546 in 1900 (and to 778 in 1910). By 1910, New York was approaching 5,000,000 inhabitants, Chicago (which had 1,000,000 only twenty years earlier) had moved beyond 2,000,000, and Philadelphia increased to about 1,500,000.

Significantly, the decades of urban expansion also coincided with substantial immigration (with which so much of the social problems of the urban poor tend to be associated). In the decade 1871–80, some 2,812,191 immigrants arrived. Their numbers increased considerably to 5,246,613 in the years 1881–90, but decreased to 3,687,564 in the 1891–1900 decade. The 1901–10 period involved the peak of immigration: 8,795,386 persons. In the succeeding decade of 1911–20 a decline to 5,736,811 immigrants occurred.

Not only were these years those of the greatest volume of immigration but also a time during which the sources changed from Northern and Western to Southern and Eastern Europe. (Ellwood expressed concern (1910, p. 175) because these newer immigrants do not have 'the same social and political standards and ideals' as we do and tend to aggregate 'in large communities of their own.') Of the total of 744,788 immigrants in 1882, Northern and Western European countries contributed 71.3 per cent in contrast to the 10.5 per cent from Southern and Eastern European countries. In 1907, the situation had become exactly opposite. Of the total of 1,285,000 immigrants, Northern and Western Europe provided 17.7 per cent, whereas Southern and Eastern Europe was the source of 75.5 per cent. More specifically, Austria-Hungary provided 26.3 per cent, Italy 22.2 per cent, Russia 20.1 per cent, and Greece, Serbia, Romania, etc., 6.9 per cent.[3]

Furthermore, these new immigrants were inclined to settle in the more urban North Atlantic and North Central States, where the possibility for industrial employment was at a maximum (Ellwood, 1910, p. 175). The 294,000 Italians who arrived in 1907 settled in

New York, Pennsylvania, Massachusetts, and New Jersey. Of the 138,000 Polish immigrants, the majority settled in Pennsylvania and New York, with lesser numbers in New Jersey and Illinois. The 149,000 Russian and Polish Jews (who also arrived in 1907) distributed themselves in New York, Pennsylvania, and Massachusetts.

Figures from the Commissioner of Immigration indicate that the immigrants had had prior occupational backgrounds which would fit them only for the least demanding of urban industrial or personal service jobs (Commons, 1967, p. 108 opposite). Only one of the fourteen ethnic entities contained in the Austro-Hungarian empire and one of the three ethnic divisions of Russia had less than 90 per cent of its previously employed persons in the 'unskilled' category. (Only the 'Bohemian and Moravian,' 'Italian (North),' 'Italian (South),' and 'Russian' had substantially lower percentages of 53.9, 76.9, 82.3, and 83.6.) All of the other major ethnic categories ranged from 90.4 to 97.2 per cent 'unskilled.'

E. P. Hutchinson's findings on the relative concentration of certain Southern and Eastern immigrant males in (American) occupations in 1900 are consistent with the data on pre-migration backgrounds (Hutchinson, 1956, pp. 173–4, 178, 179). Generally, foreign-born males were most frequently employed in domestic and personal service and in manufacturing in 1900 (as well as in 1890), though they shifted somewhat more strongly to manufacturing, professional service, and trade and transportation during the decade 1890–1900. Hutchinson's analysis of Bohemian, Hungarian, Polish, Russian, and Italian males in 1900 do suggest relatively low socio-economic status, which might well be associated with residential concentration in slum or tenement (or near slum-tenement) conditions. (Ellwood was curiously silent about this circumstance. He merely noted (1910, p. 177) that the industries such as manufacturing, mining, and transportation in which substantial concentrations of foreign-born were found evidenced 'the greatest demand for cheap labor.'

Manifestly, the members of the recently arrived ethnic groups from Southern and Eastern Europe were subjected most acutely to the disabilities of tenement-slum existence in such large urban centers as New York, Chicago, Philadelphia, Boston, Cleveland, Buffalo, and Milwaukee in the first decade of this century. Slum existence was characterized by inadequate ventilation, sanitary and cooking facilities, light, water supply, healthfulness of surroundings and play room for children (Fairchild, 1920, p. 251). Slum residents tended to require relief, to contribute to the high rate of illiteracy of the period, and to have children who exhibited an exaggerated tendency to crime. (But this high rate seeming to stem – Ellwood remarks (1910, p. 181) – especially from the slum, is 'perhaps largely a product of urban life, and possibly a lack of adequate parental control in their new American environment.') Foreign-born were generally alleged to contribute a disproportionate number of persons (in relation to their representation in the population as a whole) to poorhouses, orphanages, and insane asylums.

Although Ellwood recognized (1910, p. 224) that the city is a problem in itself and is 'even more an intensification of all of our other social problems, such as crime, vice, poverty, and degeneracy,' he was not explicit about why and how this intensification obtained under urban conditions. Apparently, cities do produce 'mental and moral degeneracy, such as increases in the rates of insanity, suicide, poverty and pauperism, crime, desertion and divorce, and illegitimacy' (1910, pp. 118, 234–5, 255; cf. pp. 126, 127, 147). Ellwood was representative of the prevailing view of early sociology that industrialization, urbanization, and immigration were fundamental to an understanding (and eventually an explanation) of the major social problems phenomena. (The intellectual problem definition was thus established for the sociology of the second period which had its emergence with Thomas's and Znaniecki's *The Polish Peasant in Europe and America*, the Americanization-assimilation studies, and the Park and Burgess urban sociology-ecology inquiries.)

Patently, the social phenomena represented by social problems did direct early sociologists' attention to the changing character of the larger American society. But to observe that social problems phenomena are associated with societal change after the Civil War is not a fully adequate characterization of their genesis. Social problems became intellectually problematic because they were construed in relation to certain basic and dominant moral values in American society and culture. An understanding of the responses to change requires a comprehension of the orienting moral framework.

Basic values

In one sense, it is true that a comprehensive grasp of the problematicity of social problems phenomena in the context of American society requires an understanding of all of the major American values, such as the ultimate relevancy of a divine will, the sanctity of individual life, self, ego, or personality, equality, freedom, democracy, external conformity, a categorical moralism, activism and work, efficiency and practicality, the exploitability of physical nature, optimism and progress, material comfort, occupational achievement and financial success, science and technology, education, and humanitarianism and reform.[4] But in another sense, it is evident that some of these values are more immediately and directly consequential than others. Of most immediate relevance are 'optimism and progress' as linked to 'science,' on the one hand, and to 'humanitarianism and reform,' on the other.

Optimism and progress   Certainly, the idea of progress tends to imply an optimistic assessment of the future, though optimism would apparently not have to be formulated in the characteristic terms of modern progress. In the period after the Civil War, the idea of progress acquired a broad popular support previously lacking, though the more urban literate and educated, commercial and professional sectors of American society (the more prosperous ascendant middle class) had always substantially endorsed and supported progress even before the Revolution.

The increasing secularism of urban industrial life after the Civil War afforded a congenial context for the idea of progress which won broad popular acceptance. The (religiously) orthodox or fundamentalist notion of the sinfulness or depravity of man and the eventual degradation or cataclysmic termination of terrestrial human experience became less and less threatening and meaningful to urban Americans as the nineteenth century drew to a close. Progress meant then (and continues to mean now) that human experience can be properly envisaged as a comprehensive unity through time and does evidence an ascertainable (linear) directionality – just as Christianity had earlier contended. But unlike the earlier religious view, progress adopted an optimistic rather than a pessimistic notion of the directionality of human history on this globe. It was anthropocentric and this-worldly rather than theocentric and other-worldly in outlook. True, it was a faith, but a faith born of confidence of what man and his acquisition of secular knowledge about the external, observable world of nature had done and could do to achieve a constantly improving and happier condition of life. Americans were encouraged by comparisons of the present with the past and they assumed that the future would bring continued improvement.

Progress became an intrinsic part of Americans' image of

themselves, their country, and its manifest destiny. America was in the vanguard of the progress of Western European civilization and their conception of themselves and their country in this progressive movement became a crucial ingredient in the developing American nationalism. It became a part of the rationalization for Westward territorial expansion and even for American military undertakings later in the nineteenth century. In its more idealistic aspects the notion of a unique American destiny entailed the conviction that American democracy could become, through the power of its peaceful example, the form of government for all nations. This same faith had its religious counterpart in the spread of Christianity under American auspices. In conjunction with the prosperity of American society, the belief in the unique efficaciousness of American values and institutions 'fostered a sentiment of nationalism which was only temporarily interrupted by the Civil War' (Ekirsch, 1944, p. 36). Most importantly, it also contributed 'the proper material and intellectual setting for the mass reception of the idea of progress' (Ekirsch, 1944, p. 36).

Advancement or improvement in the course of time (i.e., progress) involved at least two separable dimensions, the material-technological on the one hand, and the intellectual-moral on the other, though the former was generally considered to be compatible with and conducive to the latter, and the different domains of progress lead to and interlace with the other basic values of the American ethos. For perhaps the great mass of Americans, the fundamental criterion of progress was a generally rising standard of living as evidenced especially in enhanced material comforts. Each individual was held to have a right to compete occupationally for the good things of life. Thus, occupational achievement and financial success became important values. Science (i.e., expanding scientific knowledge) and technology (as the application of scientific knowledge to the control of the world of nature) were the chief means to progress. Education, generally formal education, came to be regarded as the major agency by which science and its results were to be disseminated and popularized (and thus become available to individuals to use in their competition with one another). Science was conceived to have basically good and desirable results – once it was made broadly accessible. In a word, the values of progress and science were linked with a broadly humanitarian commitment, i.e., scientific, technological, and material progress were believed to be compatible with and conducive to moral progress. And obstacles to moral progress were removable through programs of reform. Accordingly,

31

humanitarian values are associated with gradual reform (through education, legislation, etc.) rather than by abrupt revolution. Progress is thus conceived to transpire within the framework of the existing (middle class) social order as more and more individuals come to share the desired ends. As Rush Welter remarks (1955, p. 408), 'the most that needed to be done in order to progress . . . was to find a way to extend the benefits of existing perfection to as large a part of the population as possible . . .' The belief in progress in conjunction with humanitarianism-reform thus clearly demanded the amelioration of the social problem conditions of the urban poor.

Humanitarianism and reform   As a concern with and sensitivity to the conditions of the mass of persons in a society or broadly within mankind itself who are disadvantaged or suffer through no fault of their own, humanitarianism tends to evoke efforts at reform either from a more religious or more secular basis. If they issue from a more secular foundation, they tend to presuppose or at least to be associated with the doctrine of progress. Interestingly, progress can rarely be limited only to the material-technological domain. And if progress is linked with the intellectual-moral realm, as it ordinarily seems to be, it tends to involve the welfare of increasingly broader aggregates of persons up to mankind as a whole. It becomes cosmopolitan and humanitarian. In turn, humanitarianism also involves a concern for the welfare of broader wholes, assumes human perfectability as in the philosophy of the French Enlightenment, and holds that in an equalitarian democracy the political state should function as the servant of the common well-being (i.e., for purposes of reform). In its older religious form, humanitarianism conceives of the Christian brotherhood of all mankind under one universal God, the Father, with the unavoidable implication that each person is indeed his brother's keeper.

Humanitarianism may assume a variety of expressions. It may be manifested in sympathy for people who are in distress by no fault of their own; in anger at the bully, the overbearing individual, group, or nation; in pride in America as a haven for the downtrodden and oppressed; and in expressions of generosity toward other societies whose members have faced mass disasters in the form of earthquakes, floods, fires, famines, etc. It may involve personal kindliness, aid, and comfort, spontaneous contributions in mass disasters, and more formally organized forms of relief or philanthropy.

A more directly and ultimately religious basis of humanitarianism, which occasioned more or less directly religiously inspired social reform activities in the last several decades of the nineteenth century, had its precedents in the era before the Civil War. The social backgrounds of the ante-bellum reformers reveal the significance of Christianity, especially the doctrine of human brotherhood (through Puritan, Quaker, and Evangelical traditions) and the sense of community responsibility for sin (particularly in Puritanism and Quakerism). Arguments against the privileges and practices of business enterprise and in support of the working class, for temperance reform, peace, women's suffrage, and against capital punishment and slavery were profoundly religious in nature.

Similarly, too, the more secularly oriented social reform activities had pre-Civil War antecedents. Among them were a more secular humanitarianism (which was based on the earlier doctrine of natural law from the Enlightenment era) and a revival of the idea of progress (which stemmed substantially from the amazing growth of the West and the achievements of science and technology before the Civil War). Both the influence of American Transcendentalism and the impact of European Romanticism contributed to the reinvigoration of the doctrine of American individualism as did Jeremy Bentham's utilitarianism with its famous formula of the 'greatest good of the greatest number.' Just how important the many (pre-Civil War) efforts to establish more perfect secular social orders through collectivistic communities along the lines proposed by Robert Owen and Charles Fourier were for later social reform is a matter of some controversy.

Admittedly, the four principal forms of the (humanitarian) social reform movement after the Civil War were interconnected and interrelated. The more religiously-inspired and ministerially-organized segment did involve cooperation and some overlap of membership with the three more secularly oriented and organized segments, such as those which had a basis in political organization, in literature and journalism, and in organized relief, charities, philanthropy, and academic social science.

The religious segment of the reform movement began in the 1870s and 1880s as the actualities of industrial capitalism contradicted Christian ethics (especially the notion of the law of love as applied to everyday relationships) on a broad scale sufficient to awaken a strong protest among the clergy. Protestantism's responses were guided largely by two English influences: one from the settlement house movement and the other from the

CONTEXTS OF EARLY THEORY

social gospel and Christian socialism. Washington Gladden and Charles Sheldon were among the conspicuous leaders of the social gospel movement in the US. (Books of a number of early social scientists were obviously aligned with the social gospel movement, e.g., T. H. W. Stuckeberg's *Christian Sociology* (1880), John Common's *Social Reform and the Church* (1894), and Richard T. Ely's *Social Aspects of Christianity* (1889).) W. D. P. Bliss, George D. Herron, and Walter Rauschenbusch were among the major advocates of Christian socialism. (A number of social scientists contributed selections to Bliss's *Encyclopedia of Social Reform*, e.g., Franklin H. Giddings, William Dunning, Arthur Hadley, Frank Persons, John R. Commons, and E. W. Bemis.) Nor can the relevance of the Chautauqua movement – which provided a meeting place for interchanges between clergy, college presidents, notables, and radical social scientists – be ignored.

In turning to the more secularly-oriented segments of the social reform movement, it is appropriate to begin analysis with the farmers and (skilled and semi-skilled) workers, who were among the first to experience social disadvantages as the enlargement of the market and centralization of the economy occurred with industrialization. Indeed, the actual organization of farmers and workers as the Grangers (or Patrons of Husbandry), the Knights of Labor, and later the American Federation of Labor (now AFL-CIO) can be and have been regarded as part of the post-Civil War reform movement. Farmers endeavored to use political action to win more favorable rates of interest in borrowing money, to increase the volume of currency in circulation, to secure reduced freight rates and grain storage (or elevator) prices, and to protect themselves against fraudulent bond issues. Although labor endeavored to avoid direct political endorsement and affiliation with a political party before and after the turn of the century, it did try to secure enactment of legislation which would be beneficial. Trade unions did fight for factory inspection by governmental authority, for regulation of working conditions in factories, for workmen's compensation, and for the eight-hour day.

However, efforts to 'right' the 'wrongs' or remove the disabilities associated with farming and factory work could not be and were not narrowly confined within economic-occupational limits but moved inevitably to issues of political power and political organization-reorganization. New political parties developed or older ones became substantially reformist-oriented (e.g., the Greenback, Single-Tax, Populist, Democratic, and Progressive Parties). Reform candidates were successful (e.g., Mayors Tom

Johnson, Hazen Pingree, and Sam Jones, William Jennings Bryan, Governor and then President Theodore Roosevelt, Governor and then Senator Robert LaFollette, Governor and then President Woodrow Wilson). More efficient methods of government and administration (e.g., the initiative, referendum, recall, direct primary, direct election of US Senators) were adopted. And the franchise was extended (women's suffrage).

Another important segment of the secularly-oriented post-Civil War reform movement centered in the efforts of literary figures and journalists to 'expose' and explain the centralization of economic, social, and political power concomitant with urbanization-industrialization. Among the former were the two Adams brothers (Charles Francis and Henry), Hamlin Garland, William Dean Howells, Edward Bellamy, Henry George, and Henry Demarest Lloyd. Novelists depicted the struggle between farmers and railroads, the character of grain speculation, the stockyards, railroad high finance, and oil corporations, for instance. The emerging ('muckraking') journalists exercised their influence through the new mass circulation magazines (e.g., Lincoln Steffins, Ida Tarbell, Ray Stannard Baker). They probed political corruption (both state and national), big business, child labor, vice, religion, the newspapers, fake advertising, and impure food – to mention only a few of the domains investigated.

A last sector of the movement was comprised of persons associated, on the one hand, with charities, relief, and philanthropy (and out of which professional social work emerged), and on the other, with higher education and especially the newer social sciences (and particularly sociology). They were the men and women who devoted their efforts to the amelioration of the conditions of the disadvantaged and exploited newly arrived 'poor' in the urban communities. Initially, persons with these interests had had a common affiliation with the American Social Science Association, which in turn became the pregenitor of more differentiated and specialized professional social science associations. Begun in 1874, the National Conference of Charities and Corrections evolved into the professional organization of social workers. The specialized social science associations emerged from 1884 up to 1905 (the latter the year of the establishment of the American Sociological Society). Among the important reform-oriented figures in social work were Robert A. Woods, Jane Addams, Florence Kelley, and Edward T. Devine. Such persons as Edward Bemis, Richard T. Ely, E. A. Ross, and President Van Hise of the University of Wisconsin were representatives of higher education and especially the social sciences with a major commitment to social reform.

These were the persons who articulated an interest in social problems. They directed attention to the problems of pauperism, charity, philanthropy, relief, unemployment, migratory labor, child labor, women wage-earners, the labor movement, dependent children, sanitation, housing, living standards and costs of living, crowding, insanity, illness, crime, juvenile delinquency, family instability, temperance, immigration, and race relations. These were the phenomena whose study became more or less the distinctive province of sociology. They became problems in terms of the core values of progress and humanitarianism-reform.

Emergence of modern universities

Higher education is the second context to which sociology was importantly oriented. Emerging as an academic discipline during the 1880s and 1890s, sociology found its place in the curricula of colleges and universities in an era in which higher education itself was undergoing dramatic modifications.[5] The size and character of student bodies, faculties, and administrations, curricular offerings and orientations, and physical plants and facilities changed substantially. The small denominational college, with a faculty of often five to eight clergymen, few buildings, a paucity of books in its library, a relatively undifferentiated curriculum emphasizing mental discipline and religious piety, and of apparent relevancy only for law, medicine, and the ministry, was gradually displaced from its central position in academia.

College enrollments altered.[6] In 1870 and 1880, the number of graduates from colleges and universities numbered only 9,371 and 10,353 respectively. But in 1890 the figures spurted to 14,306; then to 25,324 in 1900 and to 34,178 in 1910. Just who these younger persons were and what their social backgrounds and aspirations might have been has provoked speculation. Veysey suggests (1965, p. 265) that between 1885 and 1890, significant numbers of sons and daughters of upwardly mobile self-made men in the new industrial America came to construe the academic degree as a symbol of the mobility of their parents and of their own aspirations for further social advancement. 'The magic of the degree, which had lost some of its potency under the [earlier] impact of Jacksonianism, now reasserted itself more beguilingly than ever before' (Veysey, 1965, p. 265). It may well be that these new ascendant Anglo-Saxon families felt a newly pronounced need to distinguish themselves from those who were below them (i.e., the more recent immigrants).

Manifestly, such expansion in enrollments could be accommodated only if finances were available for enlarging faculties, programs, and facilities. Accumulating after the Civil War, surplus (private) wealth was directed toward education as the earlier antagonisms and objections of men of substance toward education waned or disappeared. The 'prominent academic donors before 1890, Ezra Cornell and Johns Hopkins, were Quakers who were motivated by an uncommon humanitarianism'; only after that year did 'benefactions toward higher learning become widely fashionable' (Veysey, 1965, p. 3). The sums of money were incomparably greater than any ante-bellum contributions. According to Hofstadter (and Hardy, 1952, p. 32), they ranged from 'Ezra Cornell's $500,000 (which was supplemented by large amounts from the sale of New York's land script allotted under the Morrill Act), through Vanderbilt's $1,000,000 and Johns Hopkins' $3,500,000 to the $20,000,000 that ultimately came from the Stanford estate and Rockefeller's munificent $30,000,000 for the University of Chicago.' Such sums were not only important for the new private institutions established, but also for the competitive stimulus provided to some of the State universities in the Midwest and on the Pacific Coast.

Through intentional reform and expedient accommodations, the university evolved from the traditional college to become relevant to the life of the emerging urban, industrial and (more) secular society in general and to the interests of practical, wealthy men in particular. At first slowly and then more rapidly, 'education began to be identified with material success, bringing it into the notice of those whose financial backing was necessary for its widespread growth' (Veysey, 1965, p. 3).

Changes occurred in the boards of trustees, presidencies, and in faculties. The predominance of clergymen waned (Hofstadter and Hardy, 1952, pp. 33–6). Boards of trustees came increasingly to be dominated by businessmen and men from other non-academic professions. Eliot at Harvard 'believed that the ideal trustee was just such a "business or professional man," "successful in his own calling," albeit "highly educated" and "public spirited"' (Veysey, 1965, p. 350).

Backgrounds of the presidents do reflect some sectional or regional variations (Veysey, 1965, pp. 69–70). Originating in banking and mercantile backgrounds, Presidents Charles W. Eliot of Harvard and Andrew D. White of Cornell seem to typify the transfer of academic leadership to persons of more secular antecedents. In the East, apparently, men representing established wealth initially managed the transformation of the college into a genuine university, though men of new wealth provided the financial support. Persons of humbler origins took command in the Middle West. William Watts Fowell, President of the University of Minnesota in the 1870s, and David Starr Jordan, who headed Indiana University and then Stanford University, both came from more rural upstate New York. Charles Kendall Adams, first White's successor at Cornell and later also President of the University of Wisconsin, and Charles R. Van Hise, who followed Adams as educational chief executive at Wisconsin, both stemmed 'from undistinguished farm backgrounds in the Middle West' (Veysey, 1965, p. 70). Andrew S. Draper, who developed the University of Illinois in the late 1890s, had never attended college and had earlier been a lumber salesman and a school super-intendant (Veysey, 1965, p. 70).

Veysey's inquiry (1965, pp. 300–2) into the backgrounds of more than one hundred of the prominent professors in the last three decades of the nineteenth century indicates similarly secular characteristics. The largest number (amounting to about 23 per cent) had fathers who were merchants, bankers, or manufacturers; the second largest number (around 20 per cent) had fathers who were religious leaders (ministers, missionaries, or rabbis); and the third largest category of fathers (about 15 per cent) were farmers. In addition, the bulk of the professors he studied (over 70 per cent) derived from Old New England families and Anglo-Saxon antecedents.

But perhaps the most important feature of all the changes involves the reform of the (undergraduate) curriculum and the acceptance of graduate study and research as parts of university structure. It was especially the utility-oriented reform of the curriculum which provided the basis for the enlarged enrollments of undergraduates (Veysey, 1965, pp. 57–120). Utility-oriented reform seemed to be two-fold. On the one hand, utility seemed to mean that the college world should become more accessible to those outside (elimination of gender and ethnic restrictions, abandon-ment of classical language requirements, facilitation of dissemin-ation of knowledge to society at large, gearing college itself to people's needs). On the other hand, it seems to have meant especially a restructuring of the curriculum to be more relevant to vocational possibilities and aspirations of modern urban, in-dustrial, secular life. Utility thus signifies service to society through one's calling, the conception of which was extended to 'include a wide number of practical occupations requiring specialized skill and hence technical preparation' (Veysey, 1965, p. 66).

This concern with vocational preparation had direct consequences for the undergraduate curriculum with the possibility of exercising choice among courses. Although few institutions carried the principle of choice as far as Harvard did under President Eliot, the elective system generally won acceptance at the expense of traditional prescribed studies from 1865 until about 1903. The turn of the century brought especially noteworthy changes both in the adoption of the elective system and in the relaxation or abandonment of traditional classical requirements. Cornell, Columbia, and Yale Universities and the Universities of Michigan and Wisconsin were prominent in the movement.

In addition, specialized subdivisions and professional schools were developed under the utility ideal. Admittedly, the Morrill Act itself was a powerful incentive, with agricultural and engineering colleges resulting. Schools or colleges of pure and also applied sciences emerged (e.g., at Columbia University in 1890). The younger professions of engineering, schoolteaching, and academic scholarship itself were elevated. With the introduction of professional schools in conjunction with the elective system at the undergraduate level, the possibility of genuine undergraduate preparation for a professional career opened up (e.g., biological sciences for medicine).

Utility was also construed as social utility and the efficient conduct of public affairs. The universities, it was envisaged, would aid in the achievement of this goal both by making each of its graduates a force for civic virtue and by training persons for political careers. In addition, scientific scholarship might itself be organized into special units in the university to promote efficient public service. Accordingly, semi-autonomous 'schools' of political science were established at Columbia University under John W. Burgess in 1880, at the University of Michigan in 1881 (because President Angell was interested in political science and because Columbia was the example), and at the University of Wisconsin in 1892.

The incorporation of graduate study and research is the last major change in the emergence of the modern American university which is significant for sociology. Undeniably, a certain congruence exists between enlarged undergraduate enrollments, the elective system, departmental and curricular differentiation, specialized schools, on the one hand, and graduate study and research on the other. The necessity for specialization which is associated with research (and graduate study) tends to impact on departmental and curricular differentiation and specialization and thus supports and indeed promotes the range of selection for the undergraduate.

Adoption of research-oriented graduate education by American universities, which seems to have proceeded in two 'waves,' issued from the model of the German university, the German professor, and German 'Wissenschaften,' along with graduate fellowships, the laboratory, and the seminar. The first wave was initiated by the founding of the graduate school at Johns Hopkins University under President Daniel Coit Gilman and a 3.5-million-dollar endowment in 1876. Faculty salaries were substantially increased while the teaching load was decreased. Research was emphasized. The German university seminar method was used especially in the social sciences, among whose leaders was Herbert Baxter Adams who had studied at the Universities of Berlin and Heidelberg. The developments at Johns Hopkins apparently stimulated Columbia University to permit John W. Burgess to proceed with his plans for a School of Political Science in 1880. Burgess had also studied in German universities (Göttingen, Leipzig, and Berlin).

The second wave of research-oriented graduate education encompasses the founding and early development of Clark University and the University of Chicago, together with the autonomous emergence of graduate schools at Harvard, Columbia, and Wisconsin during the 1890s. Based on the endowment of Jonas C. Clark and promises of further gifts from his fortune, Clark University opened as the first and only important all-graduate institution in the United States in the fall of 1889. Under the presidency of G. Stanley Hall, who had been educated under Wundt (and several other physiologists and philosophers) at Leipzig and had taught first at Johns Hopkins, the major aim of Clark was to be the promotion of pure research. But by 1892 Clark lost his enthusiasm, withdrew, and made no further contributions. Eventually, Clark University was compelled to adopt a more conventional educational organization.

As the institutions in both waves of expansion indicate, the usual pattern was for researchers to form an enclave within the large institution of higher learning which was substantially devoted to other purposes. The men who operated such institutions as Harvard, Columbia, Chicago, and Wisconsin often developed 'facilities for research largely as a means of gaining or retaining an "up-to-date" reputation' for their academic establishments (Veysey, 1965, p. 171). Graduate training at these places had greater future significance than at the two pioneering institutions. Research could expand at these larger universities because their resources were more bountiful and secure.

Manifestly, the emergence of the research-oriented university with graduate education as a context for sociology was of signal importance. Small himself received one of the first American doctorates under Adams at Johns Hopkins, studied in Germany, and had his career at the University of Chicago, which emerged as a major center of graduate work. Ross had also received a doctorate under Adams at Johns Hopkins, studied in Germany, and was conspicuously associated (along with Ely and Commons from Hopkins) with the University of Wisconsin, another center of graduate work. Cooley's life-long career at the University of Michigan warrants comment because that institution also acquired a reputation for its graduate education and research. Giddings's association with Columbia University is similarly significant. Sumner had the earliest graduate training in German universities and whether Yale's primarily undergraduate commitment constituted an obstacle to Sumner's intellectual development might be debated. Ward's career and certainly his subsequent influence in American sociology did suffer from his failure to develop an academic base until the end of his life (at Brown University).

It does seem important that sociology emerged concurrently with – rather than subsequent to – the crystallization of the university as a formal, bureaucratic, large-scale social system. By 1910 the major attributes of the university system had appeared (Veysey, 1965, pp. 263–341). Boards of trustees, presidents, faculties with a system of ranks and organized by departments and schools or colleges, separate business staffs with their own internal gradations, graduate assistants, ordinary graduate students and (a larger mass of) undergraduates, and custodial staffs had substantially emerged. Formal registration procedures, transcripts of students' grades, and athletic stadia had also appeared. Six universities already had enrollments of over 5,000 (and another just under) by 1909. Graduate studies were characteristic and five universities had graduate enrollments of about 400 or more. Large undergraduate lecture courses (e.g., of 400 or more) had developed. Student behavior already evidenced symptoms of alienation.

Differentiation of the social sciences

The related social sciences provided the most immediate context for the emerging sociology of the 1880s and 1890s. Differentiation of the disciplines from one another was still partial and incomplete, even though it may have been incipient as early as the 1860s. The base out of which the social sciences arose was moral philosophy, which had separated into different sections (represented in courses) apparently in response to the new problems occasioned by industrialization of the Civil War era (Bryson, 1932a, 1932b). By the 1870s, courses in moral philosophy were beginning to disappear as more secular (or less religiously oriented) courses in 'social science' appeared in many academic institutions, e.g., Pennsylvania, Yale, Missouri, Columbia, Michigan, and Cornell (Becker and Barnes, 1952, pp. 954–5). Most of these courses dealt with what would now be termed 'social problems,' i.e., race, immigration, poverty, crime, alcoholism, divorce, etc. Apparently the American Social Science Association – established in 1865 with a heterogeneous membership drawn especially from lawyers, physicians, ministers, businessmen, humanitarian reformers, and educators – was too amateur in outlook and too practically oriented to social problems phenomena to retain the loyalties of the emerging professionals in the restructured universities in the early 1880s (Haskell, 1977). Led by incipient professionals (especially Herbert Baxter Adams from graduate-oriented Johns Hopkins), the American Historical Association was formed in 1884. The next year (1885) the economists followed and established the American Economics Association. In 1892, the American Psychological Association was organized. Other social science professional organizations followed in rapid succession just after the turn of the new century: the American Anthropological Association (1902), the American Political Science Association (1903), and the American Sociological Society (later Association, 1905). In the two decades before and the one after the beginning of the twentieth century, the several social science fields had differentiated, formed separated departments (in many cases), started their own journals, and organized themselves professionally.

Significantly, the inclusion of general social science courses and specific social science courses in the revised and expanded curricula of higher education – but independently of any outside organizational connections – did apparently have the consequence of strengthening and emphasizing the scientific concerns of social science, on the one hand, and of weakening and de-emphasizing to some extent its reformist aspirations and enthusiasm, on the other. Eventually the non-academic pursuit of social science declined and was eclipsed because it was obviously amateur and normative in character (Brandt, 1974, pp. 76–81). But the academic social science(s)-scientists were interested in the promotion of peaceful, rational progress within a unified, cohesive social order through the establishment of appropriate science(s). To an 'even greater extent than amateur social science,' the scientific and professional stance of academic social science 'acted as a check on popular zeal for panaceas and partisan schemes of total reconstruction' (Brandt, 1974, p. 68).

The fields which later came to constitute the social sciences appeared independently in the 1870s under scholarly auspices. Some of the men who had begun their careers within clerical or public settings started to teach these subjects without religious limitations in colleges. Positions in these fields were also opened in part as groups of trustees and alumni applied pressure to the colleges to introduce modern knowledge into their curricula. At Harvard, for example, William James introduced physiological psychology and Charles Dunbar political economy; and sociology and political economy were taught at Yale by William Graham Sumner and Francis A. Walker respectively; and Andrew D. White offered political science at Cornell. Although Daniel G. Brinton taught anthropology chiefly at the University of Pennsylvania, the major development of anthropology in the 1870s occurred under Powell in Washington or in museums, such as with Frederick Ward Putnam at Harvard's Peabody Museum of American Archaeology.

The pioneers of the differentiating disciplines in the 1870s regarded science as systematic knowledge with (an increasingly) naturalistic and evolutionary outlook. They were influenced in their adoption of such an outlook by both major figures and traditions in England and Germany. The works of Darwin directly placed man within nature generally and the animal kingdom particularly. As an organism, man was subject to all of the naturalistic processes. Furthermore, even the main figures and traditions of German idealism with whom American graduate students came into contact in the later nineteenth century were scarcely congruent with the conception of providential interventionism so characteristic of American Protestant orthodoxy in general and fundamentalism in particular. Darwinian biology (-materialism) and German historicism (-idealism) both contributed to a (naturalistic) developmentalism or evolutionism in the various social sciences, though not necessarily equally. Increasing acceptance of Darwinian (organic) evolution facilitated and often fused with an older persisting (pre-Darwinian) social evolutionism (e.g., through Comte, Spencer, Tylor) in American political science,

43

sociology, and anthropology (especially ethnology or cultural anthropology). In certain sectors of American economics, the influence of German historicism led to somewhat similar results.

However, it was the younger generation who appeared on the scene around 1880 who provided the main impetus to professionalization.[7] The older generation was transitional, educated, and certified – if at all – in one of the older branches of knowledge. In contrast, the younger academics had acquired a professional training and often Ph.D. degrees at one of the German universities or at one of the few American universities with a graduate program (e.g., Johns Hopkins). Members of this younger generation took the initiative in introducing new courses and graduate training programs and in founding the journals and national associations of the emerging professions.

But even within this new generation of the 1880s, two different segments can be identified. A first was traditionally oriented, with attitudes toward science and reform similar to those of the older generation. They comprised a substantial number in all of the disciplines and played an important role in multiplying and moderating professional institutions. But they were relatively devoid of the acute sense of difference motivating the second. The second segment is comprised of scholars who adopted a more militantly professional stance. In economics Richard T. Ely became the spokesman for the men trained in German historical economics. In psychology, G. Stanley Hall was in the vanguard of men trained in the new German physiological psychology with its laboratory emphasis. In anthropology it was Franz Boas who assumed leadership in advocating a more historical and critically scientific discipline. In political science John W. Burgess took a position that was both historical and administrative. In sociology Albion W. Small, E. A. Ross, and Franklin H. Giddings were the prominent professionalizers, with diverse orientations ranging through German idealism and Anglo-French positivism combined with social reform concerns.

Ordinarily, the individual social sciences did not immediately achieve organizational autonomy as separate departments in colleges and universities around the turn of the century.[8] By the first decade of the new century, sociology (for instance) had won sufficient acceptance to become recognized in the departmental name with some other discipline – perhaps most frequently political economy or economics. Only in a few instances in the East did autonomous departments of sociology exist. Sumner introduced the first course in sociology at Yale University (then College) in

1876. Yale apparently did have a Department of Sociology during the first decade of the twentieth century. At Columbia, courses in sociology actually began with Giddings's arrival in the Faculty of Political Science in 1892. By the end of the next decade a Department of Social Science existed. In 1893 the first sociology course was introduced at Dartmouth College, which apparently had a Department of Sociology by 1908. At the University of Pennsylvania the first course was offered in 1894 and a Department established in 1905.

In the Midwest, Arthur B. Woodford introduced a sociology course at Indiana University in 1885 and by 1889 that University had a Department of Economics and Social Science (including sociology). Small went to the University of Chicago in 1892 to set up the first and largest Department of Sociology, which in 1893 was officially designated as the Department of Sociology and Anthropology. Also in 1893 the University of Illinois added its first sociology course and had a Department of Sociology by 1910. One year later (1894), the University of Michigan, University of Minnesota, and Northwestern University included their first sociology courses in their curricula. At Ann Arbor sociology had won recognition by inclusion in the departmental name with Political Economy before 1910. At the University of Minnesota, sociology's and anthropology's relationship was acknowledged in the name of the department. But at the University of Wisconsin and Northwestern University, sociology's location within the Departments of Political Economy and Economics respectively was not recognized in the departmental name during the first decade of the twentieth century. The Ohio State University's first (full) sociology course was taught in 1899–1900, although the discipline was officially designated by name in the (separate) Department of Economics and Sociology in 1897–8.

Certainly the social sciences were not sharply differentiated from one another in this early era. The careers of some earlier sociologists are revealing (Odum, 1951). Cooley's doctorate was in economics and Ross entered sociology from economics. Ward's eventual academic appointment in sociology occurred in a Department of Political Science headed by James Q. Dealey at Brown University. Frank Blackmar began his career in history and economics and moved into sociology only later. Ulysses Weatherly was first professor of history, then economics, and finally sociology at Indiana University. George Howard at the University of Nebraska was a professor of history and political science for many years before sociology became his specialty. Although E. C.

Hayes was one of the first to receive a doctorate in sociology at Chicago, he was first a professor of economics and sociology before he came to the University of Illinois in sociology. (Admittedly, these shifts reflect in some cases graduate majors and minors and availability of positions at different times as well as relative absence of rigid disciplinary and professional boundaries in the early social sciences (Odum, 1951, pp. 105–6)).

Within this context it is manifestly illuminating to discover just how early American sociologists endeavored to conceive of their discipline's relationships with the other social sciences. (Interestingly, here also, early sociological theorists were active in performing one of the basic intellectual functions, just as the scheme suggests, II, D, 1.) In comparison with its European antecedents and counterpart, American sociology was fortunate in its emergence in an academic setting which was itself undergoing major modifications. But the recency of its appearance – both in the US and Europe – creates a unique difficulty in defining its distinctive problematics. History, of course, stands in marked contrast. Focusing on major institutions in the modern era, economics and political science also seem to have substantial and irrefutable claims to certain intellectual content and academic legitimacy. Psychology's concern with the organic, behavioral, and psychic aspects of human individuals appeared definite and unchallengeable. The interest in primitive, aboriginal, or native peoples provided anthropology with a similarly unquestioned intellectual realm. Not unsurprisingly, sociology might readily seem to be a discipline of the 'leftovers,' such as the social problems. However, early theorists advanced a much more commanding and comprehensive claim.

Their conception of the place of their discipline in relation to the other social sciences was commensurate with the generic conception of sociology itself. Ward, Sumner, Ross, Small, and Giddings presented sociology as the basic, general, comprehensive, or inclusive social science (see Scheme II, D). Admittedly, Sumner's arguments were least fully developed, but it is evident that he also construed (1927, pp. 2213–14) his science of society (sociology or societology) as a generalized social science embracing political economy and political science as branches.

According to Ward, sociology is the primary social science, under whose rubric the special social sciences fall on the classificatory principle that lesser, secondary sciences should be arranged in synoptical form under the primary science. But each field – such as ethnography, ethnology, technology, archaeology, demography, history, economics, jurisprudence, politics, ethics – contributes its data to sociology as the general discipline (Ward, 1898, p. 136). Each is an element entering into the new general, or to use Ward's own term, synthetic, whole. Neither separately nor together can they 'be said to form sociology, but sociology is the synthesis of them all' (1898, p. 136).

Both Ross and Small regard sociology as the general, generic social science with a holistic approach appropriate to the organic, interrelated and interdependent unity of social life. Ross declares that so 'far as social life is one, there will be one master science of social life' (1919, p. 15). Sociology is this 'single comprehensive science of social phenomena' and eventually its necessity will be recognized. Since sociology investigates a social phenomenon in its organic unity, it should rightfully occupy the dominant place among the social sciences. For Ross (1919, p. 27) the fit symbol of the relation of sociology to the special social sciences is the relation of the trunk of a tree, a banyan tree, to its branches.

Small and Giddings conceive of sociology (1905, p. 5, and 1896, p. 32) as a general social science with relations to the special social sciences similar to the relations of general physics, general chemistry, and general biology, each to their special and subordinate divisions. Yet the arguments they advance seem to vary considerably. To Small (1905, p. 6) the advantages of such a relationship in the social realm include: enhanced 'coherence to the details observed,' a focus on common interests among scattered workers, a disclosure of previously undiscovered meanings in phenomena, promotion of further investigation of phenomena, and an increasing respectability of the sciences. Most importantly, the partial perspectives of the several (specialized) social sciences can be surmounted (1905, p. 104).

For Giddings, the emergence of sociology as a general social science signifies the possibility of a coordination of the special social sciences into a larger whole. As a general social science of social phenomena, (general) sociology can contribute a 'common basis' and provide the foundational postulates for the social domain because it deals with the attributes of the class of phenomena, i.e., social phenomena, 'that are common to all of its sub-classes and not with the particular attributes of any sub-class' (Giddings, 1896, p. 31). These common attributes are elementary. Its general principles are fundamental. Sociology is thus 'the science of social elements and first principles' (1896, p. 33). It studies 'exhaustively the elementary and generic phenomena of . . . [its] vast subject, and . . . leave[s] the endless forms of

47

combination to other' fields of investigation (1896, p. 33).

Because it is not 'concerned with every aspect and grouping of social phenomena,' (general) sociology 'is intermediate between the organic sciences on the one hand, and the political and historical sciences on the other' (1896, p. 33). The 'special social sciences are differentiations of sociology' (1896, p. 33). These disciplines, including political economy and politics, cannot claim logical precedence over sociology. Each 'builds on assumptions that are, demonstrably, deductions from more elementary social truths' (1896, p. 34). Both fields 'frankly assume without explanation the phenomena of human association' (1896, p. 34). Nor does any one of the recognized special social sciences investigate 'the origin of the motives that are assumed to account for all that occurs in the social life of mankind' (1896, p. 38). And no one of them can claim to be the primary science of society, 'either as an objective or as a subjective explanation' (1896, p. 39). For Giddings as for Ward, Sumner, Ross, and Small, sociology was both the general and primary social science.

Sociology as a discipline

Undoubtedly it seems logical to suppose that just as the social sciences constituted a context for sociology (and theory), so sociology as a total discipline might provide a context for theory. But in this instance logical inference and fact are at variance. The various fields within sociology had not yet become clearly differentiated and demarked from one another, with theory one of several realms within the field in general. Interestingly, theory is indeed the very core of sociology, for theory was the fundament of general sociology so often contrasted with special sociology in early discussions about the field. Both Giddings and Small used the terms to designate different domains within the discipline. For both sociologists the distinction between general and special sociology involved a contrast between a 'theoretical' and a 'practical point of view.'

Despite the similarities between Giddings's and Small's conceptions of sociology as the general social science in contrast to the specialized social sciences and their common acceptance of 'general sociology,' they did state their notions in different ways. According to Giddings (1896, p. 31–3), 'general sociology' designates the 'scientific study of society as a whole,' of social elements, first principles, essential facts, causes, or laws, the fundamental phenomena of social life under its varied forms. In Small's view (1912, p. 200), general sociology is the 'study of the conditions (physical and psychical), elements, forms, processes, results (at given stages), and implications of human association.' But whether the focus is on the more structured society or processual association, general sociology is to reveal the general, common, invariant, or universal in social life.

Admittedly, differences do exist between Giddings's and Small's notions of special sociology. Involving the practical point of view, special sociology for Giddings entails (special) courses in 'pauperism, poor laws, methods of charity, crime, penology, and social ethics' (quoted by Tolman, 1902, p. 806). Giddings leaves no doubt that such social problems courses represent phenomena 'met in their most active form' in the city with its 'poverty . . . mendicancy . . . intemperance . . . unsanitary surroundings, and . . . debasing social influences' (quoted in Tolman, 1902, p. 806). In Small's understanding (1912, p. 200), special sociology is the 'procedure on the basis of a presupposed general sociology, particularly upon the presumption of certain ascertained social values and corresponding purposes, to work out feasible programs for societal co-operation which will assure progress toward the ascertainment of the purposes.' Although Small does not necessarily claim (1912, p. 213) that the techniques-technology or programs seeking improvement of particular groups and their situations depart from social problems, Henderson does suggest (1912, p. 215) such programs do aim at the amelioration of social problems.

When L. L. Bernard reported on the teaching of sociology in the US in 1909, his data did confirm that 'general sociology' was the most commonly noted division of sociology for purposes of instruction among some 139 institutions reporting and in terms of catalogues from 166 additional institutions. Descriptive sociology was second, social psychology was third, social technology (including discussions of social problems) fourth, history of sociology fifth, and methodology sixth. Admittedly, these terms do seem to stem from Small, who apparently was offering his own (presumably preliminary) notion of what field differentiation might be. But national recognition of some measure of field differentiation did not come until the American Sociological Society meetings of the 1920s.

Manifestly, general sociology with its central core of theory (indeed, general sociology apparently became equatable with theory) was oriented toward and anticipated 'practical application' to the social problems phenomena of American society. However, early sociologists seemed to have such apprehensions about the possible submergence of their discipline in practical use by amateur reformers that it appears more correct to say that general sociology provided the context for the remainder of the discipline rather than the reverse. Sheer preoccupation of the field with social problems could not have provided intellectual respectability.

European sociological theory – theorists

The last major context to which early American sociological theory responded was the legacy of prior and (then) contemporary European sociological theory. In a sense, this context may be regarded as partially self-selected by early American theorists. But the qualification 'partially' is important. Intellectuals in general and academicians in particular were expected then to be conversant with and oriented to their European predecessors and contemporaries. Both the detailed analyses and the citations offered in the volumes of the early American theorists testify to their European indebtednesses and their recognition of the relevancy of the European intellectual legacy.

Many of the early volumes on American theory do contain chapters explicitly devoted to analyses of European theorists. It seems significant that the first major work in early American theory by Ward begins by essentially acknowledging an indebtedness to the founders of French and British sociology respectively. In the second and third chapters of the first of his two volumes on *Dynamic Sociology* (1883), Ward offers both summaries and critiques of the sociologies of Auguste Comte and Herbert Spencer, the first of which comprises some fifty-eight pages and the second of which constitutes eighty pages. Small's lengthy *General Sociology* of some twenty years later (i.e., 1905) devotes three chapters to Spencer, two to Albert Schaeffle, and thirteen to Gustav Ratzenhofer, to whom Small was most substantially indebted. In addition, Small's volume also offers a critical chapter on Tarde. One of Cooley's chapters in his *Social Organization* is basically oriented to certain of Tarde's ideas. Ross acknowledges Tarde as the major inspiration of his *Social Psychology* (p. viii). But unfortunately some early theorists do not explicitly refer to any of their European predecessors or contemporaries to indicate indebtednesses (e.g., Sumner's *Folkways* (1907)).

American theorists also cited European theorists and their works, on the basis of which rankings of frequencies of citations from the (name) indexes in major volumes might be developed to infer who the more influential European theorists were. But difficulties also arise with this procedure. Unfortunately, Sumner and Cooley did not provide any single unified presentation of their theories in one composite work and thus no one work of theirs can be used for developing a ranking of persons by frequency of citations. However, the author or name indexes of Ward's *Pure Sociology*, Giddings's *The Principles of Sociology*, Ross's *Foundations of Sociology*, and Small's *General Sociology* are useful and did provide lists of the numbers of separate pages on which a given European theorist is referred to (plus, in some cases, the number of pages over which an analysis of the given person or his ideas was conducted).

Because the frequency with which different American theorists cite their European predecessors and contemporaries varies considerably, it is important to consider how many positions or places (e.g., 5, 8, 10, 12, etc.) are involved in the rankings, how substantial the breaks or discontinuities are between different places, and who the theorists in the different positions or places (i.e., their names) were. The highest number of citations to a European theorist was 53 for Ward, 41 for Giddings, 42 for Small, but only 10 for Ross. In Ward's frequency ranking, substantial differences existed between the first and second, the second and third, and the third and fourth positions. For Giddings, the difference between the first and second and between the second and third were substantial. But in the case of Ross, it was difficult to distinguish between a first and second and a second and third. For Small, a major difference between first and second existed, but almost no difference between second, third, fourth, and fifth.

Significantly, Spencer was at the top of the ranking frequency of pages cited for Ward, Giddings, and Small, but he was only third for Ross. He was cited on some fifty different pages of Ward's volume, on about forty different pages in Giddings's and Small's books, but only on eight pages in Ross's *Foundations of Sociology*. (Undoubtedly, the historical record on Sumner indicates the major significance which Spencer had in Sumner's thinking. Cooley also acknowledges (1969, p. 4) that 'for a while,' he had been 'under the spell of Herbert Spencer,' from whom he got his 'first outline of a general scheme of evolutionary knowledge.') Comte held second place in the frequency of citations by page in Ward's *Pure Sociology*, second in Giddings's *The Principles of Sociology*, but only fourth in Small's *General Sociology*, and occupied no major place in Ross's *Foundations of Sociology*.

Tarde, Gumplowicz, and Ratzenhofer were generally the theorists in the next three frequency positions. Tarde was fifth in Ward's list, third in Giddings's, first in Ross's, and third in Small's hierarchy.[9] Gumplowicz was fourth for Ward, fifth for Giddings, third for Ross, but tied for seventh (along with Durkheim and Simmel) in Small's case. Ratzenhofer was third for Ward, ignored by Giddings, fifth for Ross, and second in Small's listings.

The next three places (i.e., sixth, seventh, and eighth) tended to include the French sociologist Durkheim, the Belgian Guillaume DeGreef, and either the Polish sociologist L. Winiarski or the German Georg Simmel. Durkheim was sixth in Ward's, Giddings's, and Ross's rankings and tied for seventh (along with Gumplowicz and Simmel) in Small's case. Presently ignored or unknown, DeGreef was eighth for Ward, fourth for Giddings, sixth for Ross, and fifth for Small. Winiarski, who is also unknown or ignored today, was seventh for Ward and for Ross (but ignored by both Giddings and Small). Simmel was ignored by Ward and Giddings but was eighth for Ross and was tied for seventh (along with Durkheim and Gumplowicz) in Small's rankings. (Albert Schaeffle appeared only on Small's list, on which he was sixth. Interestingly, Cooley remarks that early in his career he devoted more energy to perusing Schaeffle's *Bau und Leben des sozialen Körpers* than anyone else's books and he regarded Schaeffle's volume as offering a more satisfactory view of the social system than Spencer provided.)

Unfortunately the data on analyzed and cited European theorists do not permit inference about the nature of the influence they exerted. The information indicates only that European theorists had some intellectual significance for early American theorists. But the data do not reveal in any way the content of European influences – assumptions, ideas or concepts, arguments or explanatory formulations which American theorists might have been induced to accept or reject. Indeed, many of the citations pertain to specific information or data rather than to basic assumptions or ideas. Thus, the citation data are not helpful in affording cues and clues to the fundamental intellectual predispositions of early American theorists. Beyond the mere knowledge of who the important European sociological personalities were it is impossible to go.

Although it is impossible to establish in advance of the actual analysis of early American sociological theory just what the influence of the several contexts were, they did have an undeniable significance. First and perhaps foremost among them was the changing character of post-Civil War American society itself. Sociology in general and theory in particular developed justifications which demanded that the field be consciously oriented to the social problems phenomena associated especially with the conditions of industrialization, urbanization, and immigration around the turn of the twentieth century. The changing structure of higher education comprises a second context of early sociology and early theory. Unlike its European counterparts, American sociology entered academia in a period in which the organizational structure of higher education itself was undergoing major modification. American sociology did not experience the resistance to its claims that its equivalents in Europe did. The social sciences themselves are a third context of emerging sociology and sociological theory. Although it is evident that the other social sciences differentiated from one another slightly in advance of sociology's own formation, such priority does not seem to have been a major obstacle to sociology's own acceptance and incorporation within the structure of American higher education. Sociology's own definitions of its subject-matter reveal unmistakable sensitivity to the conceptions and knowledge-claims of the other social sciences. Certainly, it would be logical to assume that the discipline as a whole comprised a fourth context for theory. However, such an assumption is at variance with the actual state of sub-field differentiation in sociology. Indeed, it appears that theory itself represents an important intellectual context for the more specialized interest in social problems (which did constitute the focus for later field differentiation in the 1920s). And finally, European theory (as represented by Comte, Spencer, Tarde, Gumplowicz, and Ratzenhofer) also provided a (fifth) context. Singly and in combination, these five contexts provide a perspective within which the application of the scheme to early American theory must proceed and be understood.

3   An overview of the major characteristics of early theory in terms of an analytic scheme

Delineation of the several contexts to which theory was more or less oriented before World War I provides a fundamental perspective that is indispensable to undertaking the analysis of the theory itself in terms of the scheme. But two other preliminary requirements must be met. First, it will be necessary to demonstrate that early sociology is at least in part consciously theoretical and that certain of its literature displays such a focus. (The heretofore unquestioned assumption that the works of the Founding Fathers constitute theory or theories must be subjected to confirmation or disconfirmation.) If confirmed, it will become imperative to investigate the concrete content of their volumes to ascertain what the major themes, issues, or concerns are and how they are organized and presented in order to judge the degree of ease or difficulty in making comparative generalizations about early theory. And on the basis of this judgment, the classificatory-periodicizing scheme can be presented and then used to develop a preliminary profile or overview of the major characteristics of early American sociological theory.

The works of the Founding Fathers as theory

To the fundamental question of whether or not the significant works of the Founding Fathers of American sociology were theoretically conceived, an unequivocally affirmative answer can be given. Their works (and those of many of their students, such as Charles A. Ellwood, E. C. Hayes, John L. Gillin) were consciously and intentionally theoretical. They refer explicitly to the words 'theory,' 'social theory,' 'sociological theory,' 'theoretical sociology,' or 'general sociology.'[1] Clearly, these early figures identified with a field which has now become known and differentiated as general or macro-sociological theory. And, in turn, later generations of sociologists have tended to recognize their contributions as distinctively theoretical.

Furthermore, 'theory' had a prevalent meaning which can be understood in relatively contemporary terms. Unlike the later 1920s when theory was construed categorically-conceptually or empirically-inductively, theory in the founding era was regarded predominantly as a formal, deductive, or systematic enterprise. Either it was or would become a comprehensive, logically closed, deductive, integrative structure. Ward construed his *Pure Sociology* (1903) and *Applied Sociology* (1906) as together constituting a system of sociology (pp. viii and iii respectively). Although Small did not claim that his *General Sociology* (1905) is a system, he did not disavow a logically coherent system as the ultimate aim of his intellectual endeavors (p. viii). Even Sumner's own declaration (n. d. *a*) that 'extended theorizing and ambitious attempts at systematization are not suited to the early phases of a new science' might be interpreted only as a temporary, conditional rejection of theory as a system. Paradoxically, his own vigorous debates with his contemporaries permit at least the inference of the basic outlines of an implicit system. Interestingly, Cooley seems to have admitted (1927, p. 117) that he had his 'own system,' which he found 'tiresome to think of, except at rare intervals,' and which he had presumably insinuated 'in a diet of agreeable details' extending through his several major works. But by contrast, Giddings is direct and explicit in his endorsement of and commitment to theory as a system. Not only does he believe (1896, p. v) that there 'are principles of sociology, and [that] they admit of logical organization,' but he construes his own *The Principles of Sociology* (1896, p. v) as 'an attempt to combine principles of sociology in a coherent theory.' His volume (1896, p. xvi) – he admits – contains some guessing (which, hopefully, is careful and suggestive), involves speculation, and 'is avowedly and without apology deductive as well as inductive.' It 'includes a multitude of logically related subjects [and problems] of research,' which can be systematically stated, presented, and answered.

All of this suggests that the basic works of the Founding Fathers must be envisaged as contributory to a general theory (or theories). It is in this perspective that Ward's *Dynamic Sociology* (1883 but republished in 1969 and so cited below), *The Psychic Factors of Civilization* (1893 but the 1901 printing has been used subsequently), *Outlines of Sociology* (1898), *Pure Sociology* (1903 but republished in 1970 and so cited hereafter), *Applied Sociology* (1906), and his and James Q. Dealey's *Textbook of Sociology* (1905) must be understood. Sumner's *Folkways* (1907 but republished in 1959 and so used below), which was preceded by a series of essays, and his and Albert Galloway Keller's *The Science of Society* (1927) must be regarded as at least implicitly theoretical. In contrast Giddings's many works are explicitly theoretical: his *The Principles of Sociology* (1896), *The Elements of Sociology* (1898), *Inductive Sociology* (1901), *Readings in Descriptive and Historical Sociology* (1906), *Studies in the Theory of Human Society* (1922, the chapters of which were published as separate articles before 1918), *The Scientific Study of Human Society* (1924), and his posthumous *Civilization and Society* (1932). Ross's four volumes of the era, his *Social Control* (1901, republished in 1969 and so cited hereafter), *Foundations of Sociology* (1905, but the 1919 5th edition is used subsequently), *Social Psychology* (1908, but the 1912 printing is noted below), and his *The Principles of Sociology* (1920), are undeniably theoretical. A similar verdict must be rendered for Small's *General Sociology* (1905), *Adam Smith and Modern Sociology* (1907), and *The Meaning of Social Science* (1910). And however camouflaged or concealed his intentions may be, Cooley's *Human Nature and the Social Order* (1902, republished in 1964 and so cited subsequently), *Social Organization* (1909, republished in 1962 and so noted hereafter), *Social Process* (1918, republished in 1966 and used below), his autobiographical *Life and the Student* (1927), and the posthumous *Sociological Theory and Social Research* (1930, republished in 1969 and so cited hereafter) do contain the outlines of his sociological theory.

Variability in the personal formulations of early theory

However, it must be conceded that the central content of early general theory is not immediately evident from an investigation of the principal works. Ward's *Pure Sociology*, Giddings's *The Principles of Sociology*, Ross's *Foundations of Sociology*, and Small's *General Sociology* do reveal extraordinary variation, if not total heterogeneity, in the central problems, assumptions, concepts, arguments, and structure of the field. (Sumner's *Folkways* is so extensively illustrative and Cooley's three (major) volumes are so bulky that they are all excluded from consideration here.)

According to *Pure Sociology*, Ward envisages the discipline as divided theoretically into three major sections: taxis, genesis, and telesis. In taxis, he describes the general characteristics of pure sociology, how science is established, what the subject-matter of sociology involves, and what its methodology is. In genesis, he considers the development of the various levels or domains of phenomena or forces out of one another, their interconnections or filiation, the rise of the subjective faculties, such as mind, feeling, and will in organisms, the nature of human nature and the social forces (as constituting ontogenetic, phylogenetic, and socio-genetic varieties), which are expressed in society as a social mechanics with the two legitimate branches of social statics and social dynamics. He also begins his analysis of telesis with a conception of human nature, especially the objective faculties of mind (and particularly indifferent sensation, intuition, perception, reason and calculation or indirection in several forms). Ward conceives of invention and discovery as direct expressions of individual differences in the development of the powers of human nature as persons seek their own individual advantage in controlling (objective or external) nature. The accumulation of inventions and discoveries constitutes what Ward terms 'achievement,' which has unconsciously and unintentionally become disseminated in a society, but which he believes can and will increasingly become consciously and intentionally oriented to the interests of society (i.e., will become 'socialized').

Giddings's conception of general sociology or sociological theory is perhaps more easily discerned. His *The Principles of Sociology* is divided into four major sections on 'The Elements of Social Theory,' 'The Elements and Structure of Society,' 'The Historical Evolution of Society,' and 'Social Process, Law and Cause,' each of which contains four or five chapters. His first section considers the historical interpretations of society, how it may be known, what the major postulates of social phenomena have been, the conception of social evolution, how sociology is related to the other social sciences, what its methods of investigation and research have been, and what the major problems of the discipline are.

In the division on 'The Elements and Structure of Society,' Giddings examines the problem of how the objective basis of society or the plurality of individuals is constituted ('aggregation'), how it develops awareness (as a form of 'consciousness of kind'). Giddings proposes two main modes of relationships of parts in society (i.e., 'composition' and 'constitution').

His section on 'The Historical Evolution of Society' argues that human association has its beginnings in earlier animal evolution (as 'zoogenic association') and reviews the basic requirements for the development of association among men ('anthropogenic associ-ation'). In this section, he also identifies the two main stages of human social evolution as 'ethnogenic association' and 'demogenic association.'

The final section of 'Social Process, Law and Cause' is devoted to an analysis of several issues. According to Giddings, social change or process involves both physical and psychic causes. In turn, cause is distinguished from law. Finally, he outlines the distinctive end or ends of human society.

Published earlier in the *American Journal of Sociology* as a series of articles on 'Moot Points in Sociology,' Ross's *Foundations of Sociology* is a compact volume of eleven chapters of just under 400 pages. Chapters 1 and 2 consider the scope and task of sociology and elaborate on the subject-matter of the field and its relations to the other social sciences, including economics. Chapters 3 and 4 are manifestly epistemological-methodological in their import. In the former, Ross critically reviews the past application of the notion of social laws to social phenomena and indicates what he regards as a tenable view. In the latter, he examines what unit (or units) of investigation promise(s) to be the most methodologically expedient for achieving the scientific status for the discipline. Like other sociologists, Ross exhibits a major concern with the phenomena of social forces which seem to be basic to the very nature of social phenomena. He is also interested in the problem of the appropriate foundational divisions of sociology and provides an extensive treatment of the factors of social change. His chapters on the mob-mind, the crowd, deliberative assembly, representative body, the public, sect, and corporation seem to reflect his views on groups which have major relevancy for modern life. The last three chapters on recent tendencies in sociology, the causes of race superiority, and the value rank of the American people are presumably included because they possessed (then) significant contemporary popular appeal.

A 'syllabus' of just over 700 pages, Small's *General Sociology* comprises nine major sections. His 'Introduction' of about 100 pages surveys the subject-matter of sociology, considers definitions of the field, probes the major intellectual antecedents in the rise of an interest in sociology, outlines the history of the discipline, and examines the major problems of the field. Over the following 300 pages (i.e., four sections), Small reviews the conceptions of sociology of Spencer, Schaeffle, and Ratzenhofer, who in his view occupy a central position in the cumulative development of the discipline. He believed that sociology would build especially upon Ratzenhofer whose position represents an advance beyond Spencer and Schaeffle. His chapters on Ratzenhofer intermittently include expositions of his own ideas, with frequent references to such other social scientists as Morgan, Tarde, Simmel, Veblen, Ward, and Ross. On the basis of his intellectual analysis, Small concludes (1905, p. 397) that he has reached 'a series of generalization, of concepts, of categories' about human association which under different circumstances assume 'certain typical forms, manifest certain typical contents, and involve certain typical interconnections.' He devotes the subsequent 200 pages (the next section) to an analysis of the contents of the most important 'categories,' such as 'the social process,' 'association,' 'interests,' 'individual,' 'group,' 'social structure,' 'social function,' 'social forces,' 'social ends,' and 'social consciousness.' In sections 7, 8, and 9 he probes the problem of social causation, examines the relation between social process and moral judgment (i.e., between sociology and ethics), and finally suggests the implications which seem to follow for the development of social policy or constructive reform to achieve adjustment and facilitate progress.

Achieving comparability by resort to a classificatory-periodicizing scheme: an overview of early or founding theory of American sociology

The manifest differences among these modes of presenting early sociological theory make evident, on the one hand, just how difficult the task of developing a comparative analysis is and, on the other, how useful some generalizing instrument may be. Initially, the variations among the four works appear substantial, if not almost forbidding. But with a very careful and sensitive use of the proposed classificatory-periodicizing scheme (Table 1) it is possible to extricate and analyze very fundamental similarities which are obscured, if not concealed, by these apparent organizational and expositional differences among the major theoretical works.[2] Early general sociological theory is divisible into a social epistemological-methodological domain and a social ontological domain, as the scheme suggests. Furthermore, the majority of the concerns within the two domains (of the scheme) are treated in the expositions of early American theorists.

TABLE 1 *A scheme for classifying and periodicizing macro-theories in the history of American sociology*

I   Criteria for the analytical classification and periodicization of sociological theory
    A   The nature of theory in sociological theory (implying an expanded concern with social epistemological-methodological theory)
    B   The nature of the social in sociological theory (implying an expanded concern with social ontological theory)

II Theory about knowing – studying the social (social epistemology-methodology)
    A   Bases of knowing the social (social knowledge)
       1   Sensation (empiricism) vs. reason (rationalism)
       2   Feeling – empathy – 'nacherleben'
    B   Methods for studying the social (social methodology)
       1   Similarity-dissimilarity of methods for studying the social
          (a)   Similarity (with the methods for studying the physical and organic realms): positivism ('naturwissenschaftliche' approach)
          (b)   Dissimilarity (or uniqueness of method for studying the social): humanism ('geisteswissenschaftliche' approach)
       2   Focus of the method(s) on:
          (a)   Parts of the whole (methodological atomism or individualism)
          (b)   Whole as such (methodological holism or collectivism)
    C   Explanation – interpretation (predicated on aspects of 'A' and 'B' above and supplemented appropriately by '1' or '2' below)
       1   Positivistic, objectivist explanation – theory
          (a)   Logical-methodological requirements of 'explanation'
          (b)   (Logical or quasi-logical) Structure of explanation (i.e., the notion of theory as:)
             (1)   Categorical – conceptual
             (2)   Empirical – inductive (generalizations)
             (3)   Formal – systematic (hypothetico-deductive)
          (c)   Kinds of explanation (reductive vs. emergent)
          (d)   Modes of explanation (universal-deductive, pattern, probabilistic, etc.
          (e)   Formulae of explanation (causation, interaction, function, etc.)
          (f)   Criteria of 'truth' (correspondence vs. consistency)
       2   Humanistic, (inter-) subjectivist interpretation – theory
          (a)   Interpretation (vs. explanation) as theory
          (b)   (Non-formalistic) Structure of interpretation
          (c)   Kind(s) of interpretation (emergentist – meaningful wholes)
          (d)   Modes of interpretation (hermeneutic, particularist –

essentialist)
- (e) Formulae of interpretation (inter-individual purposive-teleological; social-dialectical-historical)
- (f) Criteria of 'truth'
    - (1) Reality of the social: 'multiple vs. singular'
    - (2) Truth in relation to multiple social reality: translatability into folk or commonsense discourse
- D The functions of theory in organizing and justifying sociological knowledge
    - 1 Cognitive (-intellectual)
        - (a) Critical formulation (-reformulation) of the relationship(s) of the several fields within the discipline and their roles in the total division of intellectual labor in sociology
        - (b) Critical formulation (-reformulation) of the relationship(s) of sociology with other disciplines – fields of knowledge (e.g., philosophy, humanities, natural sciences, social sciences)
        - (c) Critical formulation (-reformulation) of the relationship(s) between the discipline and the total society and the rationales for that relationship offered by the discipline
    - 2 Instrumental (-technical) and/or moral (-evaluative)
        - (a) As a means to ends (in the present socio-moral order)
        - (b) As a program for a new socio-moral order
            - (1) Through social reform
            - (2) Through social reconstruction

III Theory about the (known) social (social ontology)
- A Conceptions of the social (as):
    - 1 (Interpersonal and/or multipersonal) Relation(s) or relationship(s)
    - 2 (Interpersonal and/or multipersonal) Activity(ies)
        - (a) The character of the activity: 'behavior,' 'action,' 'interaction,' 'sociation' (association – dissociation)
        - (b) Forms of the activity: (processes of) cooperation, competition, conflict, accommodation, assimilation, etc.
    - 3 (Persisting, structured) Group
        - (a) Basis: interpersonal and/or multipersonal relations and activities which persist and are structured
        - (b) Kinds: dyad to society
- B Relations of the social to other phenomena and/or realities
    - 1 The social as a domain, realm, or system
        - (a) As a type of object (or object-like) entity in nature (as constituted of distinctive forces, for instance)
        - (b) As a distinctive whole possessing some autonomy from nature

    2 Relations of the non- and near-social to social phenomena
       (a) Non-human biophysical
       (b) Human
           (1) Organic
           (2) Psychic
           (3) Cultural
           (4) Near-social
               (a) Plurals
               (b) Categories
               (c) Aggregates

3 Analogies-models between the social and the non-social
    (a) Materialistic analogies-models ('social mechanism,' 'social organism')
    (b) Idealistic analogies-models ('social mind,' 'social consciousness,' 'public will,' 'concerted volition,' 'social reason,' 'social ego,' etc.)

4 Social as a form of reality
    (a) Preponderantly 'pure' forms (monisms)
       (1) Social – sociological 'materialisms'
       (2) Social – sociological 'idealisms'
    (b) Substantially 'mixed' forms (dualism, pluralisms of 'social materialisms – social idealisms')

5 Social in relation to the (logical-ontological) part-whole or whole-part controversy ('universals-particulars,' 'holism-atomism')
    (a) Social nominalism (and neo-nominalism)/social atomism
    (b) Social realism (and neo-realism)/social holism

C Major problems and their interrelations in the study of the social
   1 Nature of the major problems
      (a) *Genesis* or origins
      (b) *Stasis* (statics, stability, persistence, structure)
      (c) *Dynamis* (dynamics, instability, change, variation, transformation)
   2 Major problems and their relations to social reality (especially *re* structure and change)
      (a) Earlier concern with reality
         (1) Preponderantly 'pure' forms: eternalism (structure), temporalism (change)
        (2) Substantially 'mixed' forms (as combinations of '1')
      (b) Modern concerns involve primarily a differential emphasis (e.g., as on 'genesis' or 'structure' or 'change' or any two in relation to a third)

D Criteria for the analysis of theories of social genesis or origins
   1 Concepts and definitions of genesis-origins and social genesis-origins
   2 Characteristics and dimensions of theories of social genesis-origins

    3 Explanation of social genesis-origins
    4 Distinctive methods of studying social genesis-origins

E   Criteria for the analysis of theories of social structure or stability
    1 Concepts and definitions of structure and social structure
        (a) Definitions of structure and social structure·
        (b) Concepts of social structure (equilibrium, order, organization, etc.)
    2 Characteristics and dimensions of a theory of social structure
        (a) Nature of the structure or unit (e.g., value, norm, role, group, etc.)
        (b) Locus of unit (e.g., value or norm in relation to role, etc.)
        (c) Features of the unit as a separate entity
            (1) Goals, values, purposes, ends, aims
            (2) Size or magnitude (personnel in relation to units or levels)
            (3) Duration (uni-occasional and multi-occasional)
            (4) Complexity of parts and their coordination, e.g., differentials and stratification
            (5) Unity (pattern integration, behavioral conformity, motivational commitment)
            (6) Characteristic social identity

F   Criteria for the analysis of theories of social change or instability
    1 Concept(s) and definition(s) of change and social change
        (a) Definitions of change and social change
        (b) Concepts of social change (change, transformation, evolution, progress, etc.)
    2 Characteristics and dimensions of a theory of social change
        (a) Identity of phenomenon undergoing change (what is it?: norm, value, role, etc.)
        (b) Locus of phenomenon undergoing change in relation to other social phenomena (where is it in relation to other social components, its setting, etc.?
        (c) Inception of change in phenomenon in relation to other events in its setting
        (d) Duration of change (how long does change last from inception to acceptance and incorporation or institutionalization?)
        (e) Rate of change (how fast has change occurred?)
        (f) Magnitude of change (how much has the phenomenon changed?)
        (g) Direction of change (does the change have a direction, e.g., by virtue of evolution, progress, sequence of stages, etc.?)
        (h) Amplitude of change (what else has been changed by virtue of the change?)
        (i) Consequences of change for various levels of the system (eu-, dys-, a-functionality)

3 Explanation of change as a problem and its dimensions (why, or perhaps more accurately, how has the change in the unit and presumably its relation to other units occurred?)
   (a) Analogies or models of change (mechanical impact, organismic growth)
   (b) Nature of sources, origins, factors, variables, or causes
   (c) Location of sources (internal to or external to unit or system)
   (d) Dynamic or processual mechanisms: interaction of sources, factors, etc.
   (e) Phases of change process
4 Methods of studying change (e.g., comparative method)

Division of early theory into two major domains

Implicitly or explicitly, the theory of early sociology involves a general division into epistemological-methodological and (substantive-) ontological realms in accordance with the scheme. Of all the early sociologists, Giddings was most explicit and succinct in his declaration. As a would-be science, sociology is differentiated from other sciences by its methods 'no less than [by its] subject matter' (1896, p. 52). For Sumner (1934, p. 19), sociology as a science is the 'investigation of [the] facts [of its domain] by sound methods.' Although Ross did not elaborate on the implications for sociology, he did observe (1912, p. 290) that 'Science is credible . . . because of its method.' His concern (1919, pp. 2, 3) with the definition of restricted units of investigation and the derivation of regularities and laws in sociology would seem to support this interpretation. Ward and Small also evidence an interest in the theory of (general) sociology which suggests a dichotomy into subject-matter and (epistemology-) methodology, though the latter seems to be construed somewhat ambiguously. As noted above, Ward presents an entire chapter on methodology in his *Pure Sociology*. Small's *General Sociology* (pp. 43, 91) is preoccupied with both defining what the science is to study and with developing an appropriate method (or scheme of inquiry). Cooley was thoroughly convinced that the 'sciences that deal with social life' are separate and distinguishable from the sciences that deal with physical and organic phenomena both in what they study and in the methods used. So sociology and introspective psychology involve 'unique methods' (especially sympathetic introspection) (1966, pp. 396–7, 351–2, 372, 395, 400, 401).

Social ontological theory

Of the two divisions of general theory, early sociologists were obviously much more interested in the social ontological than in the social epistemological-methodological theory. Their theory-theories about the known social (i.e., their social ontology) did treat each of the major portions of the scheme. For instance, their explicit definitions of the discipline of sociology did involve some (one of the three) conceptions of the 'social.' Invariably, their analyses did consider the relations of the social to other phenomena and realities (e.g., the social as a domain, realm, or system, its relation to other near- or non-social phenomena, possible analogies or models, implications of general notions of reality for social reality, and the social in relation to the part-whole or whole-part controversy). Finally, early general theory was oriented to the three major problems in the study of the social in accordance with the scheme. But early theory did manifest a characteristic emphasis in that it was much more prevailingly focused on the problems of genesis or origins and on dynamics or change than it was on stability or persistence. Each of these major features of early theory does warrant some preliminary comment however brief it must be.

Conceptions of the social   Typically, the definition of the field of sociology offered by the early theorists indicate what it studies, i.e., its subject-matter, and thus ineluctably imply some conception or notion of the nature of the social. Fundamentally, these early theorists conceive of sociology as the investigation of society, social phenomena, or the social process. Ward (1970, p. 4), Sumner (1970, p. 167), Keller (1915, pp. 15fn, 29–30, 34–5, 78–9), and Giddings (1898, p. 8) have at one time or another regarded sociology as devoted characteristically to the study of society. As will become evident below, society is a form or type of relatively permanently structured group (Scheme III, A, 3). According to Ross (1919, pp. 6–8), sociology is concerned with the investigation of recurrent social phenomena. Small (1905, pp. 3, 4–5) and Cooley (1966, p. 395) are both inclined to avoid static formulations and thus seem to conceive sociology essentially as the study of the social process. Both Ross's social phenomena and Small's and Cooley's social process are classifiable as forms of multi- and/or inter-personal activity (Scheme III, A, 2). And each of these three terms – society, social phenomena, social process – entails obscurities, ambiguities, or complexities and thus requires further clarification.

Actually, society as the most common of the notions displays four distinguishable meanings in the writings of the early theorists. First, it may embrace all mankind, humanity, or the human race, especially under the designation 'human society.' (See Ward, 1968, I, pp. 16, 30, 210, 454; Giddings, 1896, p. 7; Small, 1905, p. 183; Cooley, 1964, pp. 49, 36.) Second, society is the largest permanent group in which men and women continuously associate, are able economically, socially, and politically to be self-sufficient, and carry on a common mode of life (Ward, 1968, II, p. 397; Giddings, 1898, p. 7; Cooley, 1969, p. 165fn; Ross, 1969, p. 72; Small, 1905, p. 145). Third, and perhaps less frequent, is the identification of society with a group, any group (e.g., Cooley, 1964, p. 38; Giddings, 1896, pp. 3–5). Finally, society might be used to signify a specialized limited purpose group or voluntary association. Each one is part of a more complex differentiation of the general societal functions and structure (e.g., Giddings, 1898, p. 193). Each of these meanings is examined more extensively below.

Of all the meanings of society, probably the most common are the first and second, and the fourth is least common. The range of meanings for the concept is considerable. But, interestingly, Small was the only sociologist who objected to the use of the notion. He indicted the term not only because its meanings and concrete applications were 'too vague and shifting for precise scientific purposes' (1905, p. 405) but also because it presumes a false, static, fixed, or structural quality in human social conduct (1905, p. 183).

The three other theorists, Ross, Small, and Cooley, are explicitly dynamic, processual, and interactive in their conceptions of that which sociology studies, i.e., multi- and/or inter-individual activity (Scheme III, A, 2). After designating sociology as a science studying recurrent social phenomena, Ross explains that social phenomena are social because they arise through multi- and/or inter-individual psychic or mental interaction. Such phenomena may involve both the covert (beliefs and feelings) and the overt (actions).

For Small, sociology is a study of the social process of association and dissociation within the course of human social experience. Individuals' wants and interests constantly converge and diverge, occasioning social relationships, the concert of purposes, the emergence of structure, eventual disagreement and conflict, and finally the dissolution of past structures and the rise of new ones. In Small's view, sociology is to investigate the recurrences, regularities, and uniformities of structure, function, and process in the course of human social activities.

Nowhere does Cooley seem to offer an explicit definition of sociology. But his views seem to construe the discipline as the study of the whole of human social life, with its three interconnected, interrelated, and interdependent unities of personality, group, and idea-systems (or culture). Each unity develops its own types and each is involved in interchanges and reciprocal activity with the others. Each is dynamic and is constantly caught up in the processes of social life.[3]

Certainly, the mere fact that the Founding Fathers' definitions of sociology in terms of subject-matter are subsumable within at least two of the categories or types of meaning of the 'social' in the scheme has little significance in and of itself. But this subsumability in conjunction with early sociologists' notion of the 'social' as a domain or realm of nature (Scheme III, B, 1) and in conjunction with a certain set of problematics (i.e., the emphasis on the problems of genesis or origins and dynamics or change, Scheme III, C) does provide a basis for articulating and conceptually designating the fundamental theoretical orientation of early American sociology as 'evolutionary naturalism.'

To understand just what is involved requires first an explanation of the interrelationship of the more abstract notions of the social as inter- and/or multi-personal relations (relationships), inter- and/or multi-personal activity (or activities), and group (in its various forms) as a structured, persisting set of inter- and/or multi-personal relations and activities. Manifestly, the conception of the social as a group entails both inter- and/or multi-personal relations and activities, though neither inter- and/or multi-personal relations nor activities *must* be conceived as persisting and structured.

Just why the inter- and/or multi-personal becomes a relation (-ship) or an activity is understandable only with the recognition that the very notion of the social forces as a domain of nature (Scheme III, B, 1) involves the needs, wants, desires (etc.) of a common human nature. Early sociologists prevailingly argued that all human beings were endowed with common human nature biopsychic wants, desires, needs, etc., which prompted, induced, or impelled satisfaction (as 'forces') and thus entailed inter- and/or multi-personal contact, relations, activities.

Indeed, it is out of the logical (combinatory) relationship between the social forces, some of which are properly (and intrinsically) human and others of which are non-human (or extrinsic) but do affect association and dissociation (Scheme III, B, 2, a), and the problematics of the study of the social (Scheme III, C) that the bases are provided for deriving evolutionary naturalism as the common theoretical orientation of early American sociology. (Admittedly, the evolutionary formulations in other disciplines and the vehemence of public controversy over evolutionary interpretations of origins and change certainly affected the emphasis on origins or genesis and dynamics or change as problematic in early theory.)

Evolutionary naturalism as the fundamental theoretical orientation of early American sociology   The term 'evolutionary naturalism' is an appropriate designation for the general theoretical orientation of early American sociology by virtue of the primacy and centrality of the problem of social origins in relation to the more usual problems of social structure and by virtue of the particular set of accompanying assumptions and tenets about social phenomena and sociology.[4] As the term suggests, evolutionary naturalism is fundamentally preoccupied with the explanation of the genesis of and orderly change within social phenomena (Scheme III, C, 1). Three pervasive and distinguishing features identify evolutionary naturalism as a distinctive orientation in early American sociology.

(1) It asserts that it is possible and desirable to offer a naturalistic rather than a supernaturalistic explanation of social or societal phenomena. From Sumner and Ward through Cooley, early American sociologists implicitly or explicitly accepted naturalism (e.g., Ward, 1968, I, pp. 411–12). Humankind and social phenomena were construed as being within and part of nature just as the inorganic and organic generally were. Nature was conceived as a series of domains or spheres of forces, each somewhat separable and distinctive from the others (e.g., physical, chemical, organic, etc.) and each with its own regularities and laws. Accordingly, social phenomena were prevailingly regarded as (or at least deriving from) a domain of forces, social forces, which is self-subsistent and self- or internally-regulated, can be studied naturalistically and scientifically, and can reveal characteristic regularities or laws (Scheme III, B, 1). The pervasive resort to social forces is perhaps the single most distinguishing characteristic of the naturalism of this first era of American sociology. Virtually all of the early theorists were concerned with the identification and classification of social forces as the initial central problem of sociology. And except for Cooley, all of them made the social forces a core feature of their very conceptions of sociology.[5]

Basically, three varieties of social forces – as the factors, causes, determinants, conditions, variables, or influences affecting human association, social existence, and society – can be identified.[6] First are the largely (though not entirely) extra-human (or sub-psychic) and essentially biophysical forces, determinants, or conditions. They include features of the environment, topography, climate, soil, physical resources, plants, animals, and human populations as aggregates of organisms differentiated by race, physique, and (some would have said) ethnicity. Whether designated by social forces or not, all sociologists were cognizant of man's needs and wants which could be satisfied only within and by a given surrounding environment. They would have concurred in Small's declaration (1905, p. 408) that 'Life is an affair of adjusting ourselves to material, matter-of-fact, inexorable nature.' Yet, only Giddings disclosed (1922, pp. 147–50, 253–4) some interest in dealing systematically with the nature of the environment, which he classified by bountifulness of its resources and its relative accessibility. The second and by far most common variety of social forces is the pan-human, universal and more or less original (human) nature or biopsychic forces. They embrace a broad range from instincts, innate appetites, needs, wants, cravings, and impulses to inclinations, feelings, sentiments, desires, and wishes. Their form seems to be relatively fixed in the organism by heredity, but they are subject to definition, modification, intensification, elaboration, specification, generalization, expression, adjustment, and orientation by (individual and collective) experience. Linking the organic and the psychic, they imply the psychic unity of mankind just as much as a similar anatomy and physiology imply an organic unity of mankind. Finally, a third set of social forces is also human but is interactionally or societally engendered as (personal) incentives and (impersonal) mechanisms to maintain association in general and a specific, defined set or structure of social relations in particular (e.g., Giddings, 1901, pp. 67–8). Such social forces include formal and informal means of social control and techniques of (and inducements to) social approval and (deterrents to) social disapproval. They also involve both sensitivity to and the actual content of public opinion, traditions, values, ideals, tastes, faiths, creeds, and various kinds of norms (e.g., folkways, mores, laws).

However, most frequently the term social forces tended to be confined to the human realm, generally to human nature, and especially to the psychic. For Ward, Ross, and Small (but not for Sumner and Keller), the social forces are the consciously felt desires of men. But all five of the theorists agree that these forces impel or attract persons to act for or against other individuals. They are basically organic-affective in nature and constitute the true dynamic agents of society. The only major psychic component which Ward and his contemporaries exclude from the social forces is reason or intellect, which is excluded because it is a directive or selective factor rather than a dynamic or activating agent in human conduct. At the psychic level, social forces are desires and as such are conscious, telic, volitional, and motivational. They become organized and oriented by personal and collective experience. And accordingly they may operate more or less reflectively or impulsively, more or less rationally or emotionally. They are manifestations of and derivatives from a more or less biological and genetic stratum of basic wants, needs, instincts, or interests, which are general, implicit, and not necessarily consciously recognized.[7] Small suggests that desires, wishes, sentiments, or feelings are related to the more biological and genetic substratum as attributes to substance or species to genus. (Yet the interests, instincts, wants, or needs can become socially effective and consequential only as they provoke feelings to prompt action toward other person.) The desires in turn function to define ends, goals, purposes, etc. For those thorists who were Lamarckians, these desires are part of human nature, though they are not rigidly and permanently fixed in character. They change and develop in accordance with a notion of interdependent parallel evolution which interrelates the organic, psychic, and socio-cultural realms.

Understandably, early American sociologists tended to model formulations of their discipline as a domain of forces in nature after the accounts offered by such figures as Herbert Spencer. Generally, the Founding Fathers were convinced that sociology could become successfully organized as a discipline to the extent that the ideas and approach to evolutionary naturalism were extended into the realm of social phenomena, just as had earlier been accomplished for organic phenomena by biology.

(2) Evolutionary naturalism is evolutionary in that it holds that the appearance of social phenomena can be accounted for in terms of other more basic, elementary or generic phenomena, states, or conditions, out of which social phenomena arose gradually. Early sociologists thus accepted what might be called the doctrine of genetic filiation. Ward, for instance, characterized the naturalistic genesis of various domains of phenomena appropriately from cosmogeny, physiogeny, chemogeny, and biogeny through psychogeny and anthropogeny to sociogeny. According to him (1970, p. 93), each level of phenomena (beginning with the physical) is a part of 'an ascending unilateral series' in which it possesses 'all the

properties of the one that immediately preceded it' and 'the one additional property by which it is specially distinguished.' Each level is thus an emergent from prior levels in accordance with Wundt's notion of 'creative synthesis' and Ward's own broader dialectical notion of synergy as the systematic, organic, and creative working together of the (prior) antithetical forces of nature (1970, pp. 79, 94–5, 171–84). Applied most immediately to the social realm, the doctrine of genetic filiation means that association or society derives from or is required by the nature of biopsychic human nature (and perhaps also from or by man's more encompassing features as an organism in relation to the conditions of human existence) or from man's descent from higher organisms which existed themselves in a state of gregariousness or association.

As chapter 5 reveals below, a serious controversy did erupt around this problem of social origins. Giddings, Small, and Cooley adhered to the view of man as an intrinsically social creature whose animal forebears also lived in association. But Ward, Sumner, and Ross conceived man's original state or condition as being asocial (if not antisocial) and atomistic (because humankind had been egoistic). Nevertheless, the notion of a core of biopsychic human nature needs – whose basis was pre-human – could be invoked and employed in both positions. In the case of Sumner *et al.* it functioned to account for origins (and maintenance) of association, whereas in the case of Giddings *et al.* it was used to explain maintenance or persistence.

(3) Finally, early American sociology in its commitment to evolutionary naturalism is basically indebted to and dependent upon Darwinian (and Spencerian) views of organic evolution. All early sociologists concurred in the view that human association must be explained ultimately as an effective adaptation to the conditions of human existence, which involve an aggregate of individuals who are distributed in relative proximity to one another and who confront similar circumstances of life in a given habitat. Even consciousness itself – which is distinctively involved in and characteristic of human association – may be interpreted as the outcome of such an evolutionary adaptive process. Social structure and social change both finally depend on the persistence or modification of the nature of the conditions of existence in the habitat or situation. Some would contend (e.g., Sumner and Keller) that structure and change must be explained at least immediately (if not also ultimately) by a deterministic organismic model of struggle and survival, whereas others (e.g., Ross, Small, and Cooley) would seem to imply that the biophysical conditions of existence set broad

limits within which alternative forms of adjustment may be more or less consciously chosen. Certainly, early sociologists' emphases on modification, variation, and change in social phenomena seem to have followed Darwin's and Spencer's leads in biology. Most sociologists of the era construed the course of change in accordance with the directional implications in the hierarchy of life: from simplicity to complexity, from less to more differentiation and specialization – as in the transition from primitive to civilized society. One theoretical stance, which was also positivistic and relatively Darwinian–Spencerian, can be identified as 'social evolutionism.' Another, which incorporates more clearly Hegelian elements in its formulation, can be characterized as a 'social process' orientation.

In its simplest terms, evolutionary theorization in sociology proposes that human association in general and human society in particular originated and persisted because they facilitated man's survival under the typical conditions of human existence. Survival, adaptation, adjustment, 'workability,' or 'fit' are the criteria against which association in its various forms must be assessed and interpreted in relation to the circumstances under which human beings exist. Early American 'evolutionary naturalism' endeavored to explain the origins of social phenomena and human societies, structure (i.e., maintenance or persistence), and change (i.e., variation, modification, and transformation) both naturalistically and evolutionarily in accordance with a substantially Darwinian–Spencerian stance.

However, it would be misleading to conclude these preliminary overview comments without any indication that some diversity existed within the general evolutionary naturalistic orientation. Three social ontological positions can be identified and are significant, i.e., a preponderantly behavioristic-materialism, a more or less balanced materialism-idealism, and a more preponderantly interactionist-idealism.[8] Sumner and Keller are champions of the first; Giddings, Ward and perhaps Ross represent the second; and probably Small and certainly Cooley upheld the third position (note Scheme, III, B, 4).

Varying interest in the three basic (social) ontological problems
However, the directness, elaboration, systematicity, and coherence with which these three major (social) ontological problems were considered by the early theorists varied tremendously. Social-societal origin is illustrative. Ward's earlier experiences as a paleobotanist do seem to be reflected in the detail with which he

approaches the problem in his first major sociological contributions. A concern with origins figures prominently in his *Dynamic Sociology*, chapter 6, which is devoted to 'Anthropogeny: Genesis of Man,' and chapter 7, which investigated 'Sociogeny: Genesis of Society.' (However, the treatment becomes much more schematic in the sections on 'Social Assimilation' and 'Social Differentiation' of chapter 10 on 'Social Statics' in his *Pure Sociology*.) Giddings also writes extensively on the topic in his two chapters on 'Zoogenic Association' and 'Anthropogenic Association' in his *The Principles of Sociology* and his chapter on 'The Early History of Society' in his *The Elements of Sociology*. Origins is a direct and conspicuous problem in Small's chapter 16 on 'The Primitive Social Process' in his *General Sociology*. By contrast, the issue appears more fragmentarily, incidentally, and incompletely in the first chapter of Sumner's *Folkways* and in the early chapters of his and Keller's *The Science of Society*, chapters 2 and 3 of Ross's *Social Control*, and in chapters 11 and 22 of Cooley's *Social Organization* and *Social Process* respectively.

Early sociologists' treatments of the problem of social equilibrium, statics, structure or organization, on which chapters 6 and 7 of this monograph are based, exhibit a similar variability. Sumner's basic notions and theory are scattered throughout his first chapter on the fundamental notions of the folkways and of the mores in his *Folkways* and in the first three chapters of his and Keller's *The Science of Society*. Ward's structural ideas are substantially contained in his chapter on 'Social Statics' in *Pure Sociology*. Giddings's basic structural views undergo change between his early *The Principles of Sociology* and *The Elements of Sociology* and his later *Studies in the Theory of Human Society*. His chapter on 'Social Organization' in his *The Elements of Sociology* is especially significant for an understanding of his earlier views.

Ross's, Small's and Cooley's ideas about structure are presented less systematically and elaborately and are scattered throughout their works. True, the last few pages of chapter 4 in Ross's *Foundations of Sociology* are particularly important and Cooley's *Social Organization* is more relevant than his *Human Nature and the Social Order* or *Social Process*.

The best known structural concepts of early theorists tend to be formulated as simple dichotomies or taxonomies of groups, which are not always or necessarily clearly and independently demarked. (Sumner's 'in-group'–'out-group' distinction occurs in conjunction with his consideration of primitive society. Giddings's analysis of

73

the social composition and social constitution are presented as two separate chapters in his *The Principles of Sociology*. Cooley's 'primary group' is offered as a separate chapter by that title in his *Social Organization*, but his 'nucleated group' appears unannounced in the text of a chapter on 'Group Conflict and Modern Integration' in his *Social Process*. Ross's 'community–society' dichotomy is introduced at the beginning of his concluding chapter in *Social Control*.)

But it is manifestly the analysis of the problem of social change – extending through chapters 8, 9, and 10 of this monograph – that occupied major and primary interest among early theorists. (Indeed, many of their major structural notions are actually embedded in considerations of social change.) Social dynamics is the second of the two major explicit divisions of Ward's *Pure Sociology*. Giddings's *The Principles of Sociology* consists of four parts, the third of which is termed 'The Historical Evolution of Society.' In Ross's *Foundations of Sociology*, social dynamics is presented (p. 183) as the second of the two fields of the discipline. This same work divides (pp. 97, 98) the social processes into three varieties with the reconstructive or dynamic as the third. Ross's later *Principles of Sociology* lists five types of social process, including one on 'Progress and Regress.' It is true that Sumner's *Folkways* and Small's *General Sociology* are not formally and explicitly structured so that change appears as a major investigative division of their sociologies. (However, Sumner's and Keller's *The Science of Society* assumes social evolution as its underlying premise. And Small's *General Sociology* focuses on the social process (of human association and dissociation) which is an equally dynamic conception.) Finally, the third of Cooley's three major volumes is *Social Process*, whose title is accurately descriptive of its interest.

Social epistemological-methodological theory

Chapter 4 (as the immediately following chapter) does take as its point of departure Section II of the scheme concerning 'Theory about knowing – studying the social,' i.e., social epistemological-methodological theory. It is based substantially, though by no means entirely, on Ward's chapter on methodology from his *Pure Sociology*, Giddings's chapter on the methods of sociology from his *The Principles of Sociology* and his *Inductive Sociology*, Ross's chapters on social laws and the unit of investigation from his *Foundations of Sociology*, Small's *The Meaning of Social Science*,

74

and Cooley's chapter on social science from his *Social Process* and his 'The Roots of Social Knowledge' from his *Sociological Theory and Social Research*.

Clearly, the adoption of certain views about the nature of social reality and what is construed to be primarily problematic do influence the nature of (social) epistemological-methodological theory (and vice versa, the latter may affect the former). By virtue of the commitment to evolutionary naturalism, the problem of the genesis of different levels of phenomena becomes important and especially the genesis or origins of the social out of prior levels by way of causation (Scheme II, C, 1, e). In turn, the prevailing doctrines about causation tended to imply a theory about knowing which was dualist in the sense that it demanded both experience (empiricism) and reason (rationalism). Consult Scheme II, A, 1 and 2. In spite of their epistemological dualism, most of the early American theorists seemed to be more inclined to a positivistic methodology rather than to a humanistic methodology (in the sense that they emphasized the similarity (and not the dissimilarity) between the methods for studying physico-organic phenomena and social phenomena. See Scheme II, B). Adherents of a more or less prevailingly positivistic methodological outlook include Giddings, Ross, Sumner, possibly Ward and perhaps even Small. Cooley is the only explicit and articulate exponent of a humanistic methodology which is elaborated as part of a more encompassing epistemological idealism (i.e., a romantic or non-rationalistic idealism).

In spite of early theorists' more restricted treatment of the epistemological-methodological domain it does warrant more detailed consideration. Chapter 4 endeavors to provide this more extended examination.

4 Social epistemological-methodological theories

One of the most basic features for distinguishing the theory of a particular period by application of the scheme is the varying emphasis on the social ontological versus social epistemological-methodological domain. Interestingly, the very approach to epistemological-methodological theory through causation reveals the basic preoccupation of early theory with social ontological concerns in general and with the second tenet of genetic filiation of evolutionary naturalism in particular. Knowledge, or more specifically scientific knowledge, was assumed to be causal knowledge, i.e., knowledge of cause-effects. Put simply, the interest in a naturalistic explanation of the various domains and levels of phenomena, including and culminating in social or societal phenomena, is the basis of early American sociologists' concern with causation.

Assuming apparently the existence of some protean undifferentiated force, energy, or matter, each level or realm was regarded as the cause of the next and the effect of the previous one (Scheme III, B, 1). These domains extend from the (inorganic) physical to (organic) life to animals and to man and from the psychic up to the social and the cultural. As Ward observes (1970, p. 94): 'Each product [or level of phenomena] is at once the effect of antecedent causes and the cause of further effects, and the kinds of causes to which these latter belong may also be classified.' Such a conception presupposes natural causation – to use Giddings's term (1896, p. 417) – in which 'every cause is itself an effect of antecedent causes; in which every action is at the same time a reaction.' In somewhat gross terms, the social derives from the psychic, the psychic from the vital, and the vital from the physical

(Giddings, 1896, pp. 7–8, 416). So Giddings declares (1896, p. 417) that 'every social force . . . has . . . been evolved in a physical-organic process . . . [and] . . . is . . . at every moment conditioned by physical facts.' In Ward's case, telic causes as the distinctive development of the human psychic stem from the domain of conative forces which are associated with higher (animal) organisms, i.e., vital forces, which are in turn derived from efficient causes which are identified with the domain of physical forces. Thus, the realms of nature comprise an interconnected, relatively continuous series of cause-effect chains.

Like the other domains, the realm of the social was also a realm of natural forces, with its own distinctive (natural) causes and (natural) laws in accordance with the first tenet of evolutionary naturalism. Ward, Sumner and Keller, Giddings, Ross, and Small all concurred. (Only Cooley was an exception.)[1] As a science, sociology was to investigate both the (natural) causes and (natural) laws of social phenomena. On the basis of what he notes about natural laws generally, a social law for Ward (1970, p. 169) merely 'states the fact that certain phenomena uniformly take place in a certain way.' Sumner's and Keller's natural laws (of social forces) derive (1927, pp. 2175, 2220–1) from 'the nature of things,' become operative 'whenever [certain] conditions are fulfilled,' and are universal and invariable. Giddings remarked (1896, p. 417) that 'Natural laws are simply unchanging relations among forces, be they physical, psychical, or social.' Ross apparently construes (1919, p. 67) social laws as 'the relation between facts of variation' or 'between one set of unvarying facts and another.'[2] Small insists (1905, p. 44) that sociology almost universally endeavors to formulate laws of present and past correlation and sequence.

Science and causation

In agreeing then that a science and its method (or methods) must provide explanation (or interpretation), use deduction, and formulate causal knowledge, American sociologists of the early era were in effect arguing that sociology must aim beyond mere observation, description, and induction or empirical generalization. All of the major theorists used the terms 'cause' and 'effect' in their sociologies (see Scheme II, C, 1, e). 'Social causation' is commonly employed. Giddings's paper on a 'Theory of Social Causation' (which was later published in his *Studies in the Theory of Human Society*) and Small's chapter on 'The Elements of Social Causation' in his *General Sociology* are illustrative. Early sociologists wanted not only generalizations and laws but also explanations or interpretations of such regularities. As Ward remarks (1970, p. 169) a law 'cannot explain anything, but must itself be explained.' A principle alone explains. It 'deals wholly with cause, or perhaps more correctly, with . . . the *modus operandi*' (1970, p. 160). Giddings provides a somewhat different version. According to him (1898, p. 330), 'explanation of any subject must include an attempt to show that laws inductively discovered are deductively inferable from wider principles of cosmic phenomena.' Sociologists were thus not content to observe, describe, and derive inductions or empirical generalizations. They accepted as part of their scientific mandate the necessity of formulating explanations which they prevailingly conceived to be causal in nature.

In spite of the virtually universal concern with causation among early American sociologists, such crucial concepts as cause and causation are neither treated systematically nor extensively. Ward's comments are perhaps the most numerous of all those of early sociologists. And if his views are representative of the field generally, cause would seem to be conceived in prevailingly materialistic, physicalistic, and mechanistic terms. Cause, matter, and force are inextricably intertwined. Every domain of nature is a domain of forces. And virtually every early American sociologist regarded social or societal phenomena as a realm of (natural) forces. According to Ward (1970, p. 19), 'no line of demarcation can be drawn between the properties of matter and physical forces. Properties are forces and forces are properties . . . if matter is only known by its properties, and the properties of matter are forces, it follows that matter possesses inherent powers.' Thus, Ward claims (1970, p. 19) that 'matter is causality' because it 'is power.' It is particularly activated power producing 'contact, impact, collision, and pressure' that constitutes cause (1970, pp. 136, 466).

Manifestly, cause as Ward uses the term is secondary (or natural) cause as opposed to First Cause. Sumner does employ the notion of secondary causes, implying a contrast to a First Cause in *The Science of Society*. First Cause is obviously supernatural; it is an ultimate source of change, a First Mover, which is itself uncaused and eventually unmoved by its own action – like Aristotle's Unmoved Mover, or the One of Neoplatonists. In contrast, secondary causes are natural causes. Men – claims Sumner (1927, pp. 2245–6) – 'have lived on into what they have become' through 'a progressively clearer understanding of secondary causes and their effects.'[3] There 'never has been a time when they have not eventually, if not promptly, seized upon and appropriated what scientists, dealing wholly with secondary causes, have been able to demonstrate' (1927, pp. 2245–6).

More precisely and explicitly, Ward's concept of cause really departs from the notion of efficient cause. (Presumably, the same assertion can be made also for Sumner and Giddings.) Ward refers (1970, p. 46) to 'natural or efficient causes.' He also asserts (1970, p. 120) that efficient causes are the same as 'occasional' or 'occasioning causes,' though it seems unlikely that Ward was adopting the usage of Malebranche. Elsewhere, he remarks (1970, p. 156) that 'efficient causes are physical causes.' An efficient cause consists of a force acting 'upon a body' and impelling 'it in the direction in which the force acts' (1970, p. 466). Interestingly, he typifies the efficient cause by the immediate contact with the effect. Clearly, he does conceive of efficient cause in the common sense of an 'extrinsic motive agent, or external influence producing change' (Bunge, 1959, p. 33). It acts *ab extrinsico*, from the outside. In brief, the efficient cause is 'an external compulsion' (Bunge, 1959, p. 174). If efficient cause is the prototype for cause in general, as it has been in modern science and in Ward's writings, cause will undoubtedly tend to display materialistic, physicalistic, and mechanistic features.

Because none of the early sociologists provides a coherent systematic and extended treatment of the notion of cause, the causal principle, or the doctrine of causation, even the major and central components or characteristics of the causal bond are inadequately and incompletely presented in the literature. Such features as Bunge terms conditionalness, asymmetry (temporal or, more accurately, existential priority), constancy, uniqueness, and efficacy in his *Causality* are not completely and unambiguously indicated in the writings of the major theorists. Presumably, Keller was alluding to what Bunge would have called conditionalness, asymmetry, and constancy in his reference to the notion that (if) similar causes (are present, they) will have similar effects and (if) similar effects (are present, they) are the products of similar causes (1927, p. 2171). Conditionalness asserts that the occurrence of the effect is conditioned by the occurrence of the cause. In the formulation of 'If C, then E always,' the terms 'If C' state the condition(s) for the occurrence of E. Asymmetry indicates the unidirectionality of cause to effect. Such a declaration may signify either the temporal or the existential priority of the cause (to the effect). (Bunge's position, for example, is (1959, p. 39) that the 'cause is existentially prior to the effect – but need not precede it in time.') Constancy means that cause and effect occur invariably. 'If C is the case, E will ensue invariably; this is what the all-operator "always" . . . means' (Bunge, 1959, p. 39). The connection between cause and effect occurs without exception, i.e., invariable regularity. Presumably, Ward's assertion that order or regularity is due to causality (1970, p. 51) is a reference to what Bunge terms 'constancy.' No major sociologist apparently cites the uniqueness characteristic of the cause-effect connection. It signifies a one-to-one reciprocal correspondence 'between the cause and the effect' so that 'the relation between C and E is such that there is a single E for every C and vice versa. The existence of E follows [Bunge adds that follows does not necessarily mean in time] in a unique or unambiguous way from the existence of C; or, again, E is a single-valued function of C' (Bunge, 1959, p. 41). Efficacy indicates that cause has a truly generative or productive capacity. The connection between cause and effect is a genetic connection. Causal agents possess an active and productive nature. An effect emerges from a causal process. Ward (and probably Giddings in *The Principles of Sociology*) was unmistakably committed to the view that any efficient cause was efficacious and productive. His *Pure Sociology* is devoted to the causal analysis of the genesis of social forces from the other kinds of forces (as opposed to telesis). The forces of each domain in relation to other forces exhibit synergy and creative synthesis, out of which the next level derives. As Ward declares (1970, p. 90), the 'more complex phenomena of the higher sciences are the creative products of phenomena of a lower order. The former are *generated* by the latter, and all generation, or genesis, is creative.' Each new level of forces of phenomena, 'while possessing all the properties of the one that immediately preceded it, possesses the one additional property by which it is specially distinguished' (1970, p. 93). Each domain 'is at once the effect of antecedent causes and the cause of further effects' (1970, p. 94). Thus, each realm of forces comprises a category of cause which can be genuinely generative, productive, or efficacious of the next realm as its effect.

Ward's sociological writings do display other features of the doctrine of causation. For instance, his exposition of efficient cause evidences the mechanistic (if not also materialistic and physicalistic) view of Hobbes and Hume that the cause and effect must be spatially contiguous (Bunge, 1959, p. 58). The 'effect is always in immediate contact with the cause . . . There is no "actio in distans"' (Ward, 1970, p. 466). Consistent with a contiguity-continuity conception of cause-effect, he also argues that the 'effect is always equal to the cause' (1970, p. 468). The next sentence suggests that by the equality of causes and effects he means the proportionality of cause and effect (1970, p. 488). (Bunge indicates that 'causa aequat effectum' may indicate quantitative constancy, numerical equivalence, or proportionality (1959, p. 215)). Finally, Ward adheres to a version of the hypothesis of the summation or superposition of causes. In a plurality of forces of different intensities and in different directions, the 'body impressed has a motion of its own and reacts upon the impinging bodies . . . the general effect will always be the exact resultant or algebraic sum of all the forces involved' (1970, p. 466). Actually, Bunge claims (1959, p. 166) that the 'hypothesis of the summation or superposition of causes holds that the factors that make up an effect act independently of one another; that is, even if they act jointly they behave as an aggregate and not as a combination, synthesis, or whole having qualities of its own that had been absent from the separate addends.'

With this background inquiry into the nature of cause and especially efficient cause and its major inferrable characteristics complete, it is now possible and appropriate to examine the basic classes or categories of cause proposed in the literature of early American sociological theory. Ward offers an explicit categorization of causes into efficient, conative, and telic classes. Keller implies a difference between biophysical and social causes. Giddings divides causes into those which are independent and original and those which are dependent and derived.

In Ward's case, the extensive analysis of efficient cause seems to warrant no further consideration. But the categories of conative and telic causes have only been cited. According to him, a conative cause is only a modality of efficient causes (1970, p. 97). It is the form characteristic of life or, more precisely, higher animal life. It involves will and is thus psychic rather than physical in nature (1970, p. 97). The chief differential attribute of the animal is what Ward calls 'feeling – the property of self-awareness' (1970, p. 95). Ward tends to construe feeling, intensive sensation, desire, and will as essentially the same phenomena, which may entail 'instincts, impulses, or motives' (1970, pp. 95, 97, 156–7). Although it is basically a form of efficient cause, it deserves a special designation. Presumably, feeling in various forms leads to movement and thus Ward can contend (1970, p. 156) that basically psychic or conative causes are 'at bottom efficient causes also.' They are also the dynamic agents of society because they denote 'force' (1970, p. 97).

Telic causes are peculiarly characteristic of man because only he possesses intellect or reason. By definition, a telic cause is also a final cause because it is 'more or less remote from its effect' and thus cannot be an efficient cause or a force as such. Basically, a telic cause involves an end envisaged by the mind and a knowledge of some natural property or force which can be and is used as a means to move material things to achieve the end in view. 'This force or property is both a means to the end and an efficient cause' (Ward, 1970, p. 467). In brief, both a telic and a final cause signify 'the rational employment of a means to an end' (1970, p. 467). Accordingly, a 'telic or final cause is not a force, as is every form of efficient cause, but it utilizes efficient causes in a manner wholly its own, and thus produces effects' (1970, p. 97). (Unlike the effects of efficient causes, the effect of a telic or final cause 'is usually wholly out of proportion to the cause, if we mean the personal effort put forth' (1970, p. 468)). Eventually, Ward anticipates telic causes becoming the directive agents of society. Although they have been produced by conative causes in man, they apparently threaten to operate with an unprecedented autonomy. But Ward's emphasis on the continuity or filiation of causal domains perhaps precludes the admission of the duality of causes (i.e., the telic versus the efficient and conative) as seems to appear in the writings of many other sociologists.

Giddings offers a classification of causes which is explicitly focused on social or sociological causes. He divides causes into those which are independent and original, on the one hand, and those which are dependent and derived, on the other. 'The original [and independent] causes of aggregation and of dispersion . . . are physical [or more accurately, biophysical] forces. But the secondary [and derived] causes of social phenomena are conscious motives and are products of social life itself' (1896, p. 363). These derived, dependent causes are volitional and thus psychic factors (1896, pp. 19–20, 416). Sociological causes 'are as much more complex than the merely psychical as the psychical are more complex than the merely physical' (1896, p. 416). Sociological causes are derived from 'simpler phenomena than themselves' and stem from 'processes of the physical and organical world' (1896, p. 416). Although the sociologist affirms that 'the reality of sociological forces . . . are distinctly different from merely biological and from merely physical forces,' he 'is careful to add that they are different only as products are different from factors' (1896, p. 417). Every 'social force . . . has . . . been evolved in a physical-organic process . . . [and] . . . is . . . at every moment conditioned by physical facts' (1896, p. 417).

Original or physical causes operate through the physical or regional environment which sustains, energizes, constrains, depletes, and stimulates a human population. Of course, human beings' 'bodily forms and activities are as strictly physical facts as are the forms and activities of inorganic things' (1898, pp. 330–1; cf. 1932, p. 392).

Secondary causes are evident in society because human individuals are simultaneously minds 'disposed by feelings, passions . . . ideas and trains of thought' (1932, p. 392). Elsewhere, he notes that 'personal influence, conscious motives, and ideas, and the historical tradition' are products of the original responses and react as secondary causes or stimuli on subsequent behavior (1922; p. 117). The major part of all pluralistic behavior is provoked by secondary stimuli (or causes). 'The very arrangement under which we live, the groupings and doings of our fellowmen, their ideas and purposes, their laws and institutions, are ever present, ever potent causes of continuing action' (1922, p. 145).

Thus, the causation and laws of both the physical and the psychic must be invoked in social causation. Human society must reckon with the indestructibility of matter and energy, the tendency for forces to balance or equilibrate, the inclination of all motion to follow the line of least resistance, and the disposition of all activity to assume a rhythmical pattern and to integrate, differentiate, and segregate (i.e., to evolve). 'Physical laws determine the aggregation, the growth, the movements, and arrangements of population; they determine the amounts, the kinds, and the combinations of social activities' (1898, p. 350).

But human society also operates in part in accordance with universal psychic dispositions. Men seek 'a maximum of clearness or of pleasure in some form, with a minimum of exertion or of pain' (the law of least effort, 1898, p. 341), compare others with themselves and make favorable assessments in terms of likenesses, and engage first in impulsive social action (with sympathetic like-mindedness) and only later in rational social action (with formal like-mindedness).

Nevertheless, 'the institutions, laws, and policies that are ultimately incorporated in social organization . . ., are determined, not by conscious social choice, but by a process of survival, which is itself conditioned by cosmic law over which man has no control' (1898, p. 351). Ultimately, biophysical forces and laws become determinative and Giddings's dualistic scheme of social causation assumes a prevailingly materialistic or physicalistic emphasis.

Although Ross's, Small's, and Cooley's notions of social causation, explanation, or interpretation involve a dualism of the physical and the psychic, they emphasize the latter rather than the former. They stress the subjective, internal, conscious, or imaginative. Social causation entails the attribution of motives at the conscious, psychic level for each of the individuals involved in a social activity. According to Ross (1919, p. 55), sociological inquiry 'should . . . seek the causes, i.e., motivation.' Factors in the external situation (e.g., physical environment) enter into human volitions as their proximate causes (1919, pp. 151–2). Small acknowledges 'all the physical and biological conditions to which men are subject,' but he insists that the distinctive and distinguishing variant in human association as opposed to animal association 'is the influence of mind upon mind' (1905, p. 622). The 'real explanation [of the social process] must be found in the spiritual initiative which is superior to mechanical causation' (1905, p. 639). As an ontological and methodological holist who accepts universal interaction (rather than causation), Cooley regards everything as interconnected, interrelated, and interdependent. The material and the mental must thus operate in conjunction with one another. Cooley finds 'no warrant in observed fact' for assigning the originative impulse either to material things or to mind (1966, p. 48). He even cautions that 'will is as much effect as cause' (1966, p. 43). To Cooley (1927, p. 151), 'outside and inside,' 'consciousness and behavior, mutually complement and interpret each other. They cannot be disjoined without denaturing both.' Still, he claims (1964, p. 120) that 'the social and moral reality is that which lives in our imaginations and affects our motives.' Although he was a dualist, he was predominantly an idealist.

Dualists also, Sumner and Keller represent the opposite of the position which Cooley adopted. They were predominantly (behavioristic-) materialists in their views. (See below.) Although they resembled their colleagues in differentiating non-social or non-societal forces from social or societal forces or causes, they employed different arguments. They recognized consciousness, but they made it dependent on and subordinate to the material-physical-organic. They did not emphasize it as differentiating and distinguishing features of social causes. Perhaps more than others of their era, they admit the 'break in the biological series of transitional forms between anthropoid and man' and the futility of trying 'to make direct and simple connection . . . of particular human institutions with their animal prototype . . . from one plane of evolution into another' (1927, pp. 2200–1).

According to Keller, societal causes differ from other kinds of causes because: (a) they are less precisely and exactly determinable (1927, p. 2165), (b) cannot be studied simply and directly or simplified by experimental isolation (1927, pp. 2169–70), (c) display different effects (even though they are the same and likewise similar effects may be produced by unlike causes), and (d) their consequences are complex, subtle, elusive, shifting, and contradictory because they (and their causes) are enmeshed in a web of relations.

Unlike his colleagues, Keller is insistent that the purposes and consequences of human actions have no necessary relationship (1927, p. 2175). Though purposes may be important for initiating actions, such activities once started 'produce their own result according to their own laws' (1927, p. 2175). A science of society 'must watch what really happens, that is, consequences as distinguished from purposes or motives' (1927, p. 2175).

Summer and Keller do differentiate between social phenomena, forces, and causes and those of other domains. But they refuse to accord a primary or strategic significance to what Ward termed telic, Giddings psychic, and Ross and Small simply social causes.

For early theorists, causal explanation as the main objective of scientific inquiry into social phenomena reflects their primary concern with the problem of social origins in the doctrine of evolutionary naturalism. The terms 'cause' and 'effect' occur frequently in their writings but no one of them offered systematic and detailed accounts of the technical criteria of causation in sociology. Naturalistic in outlook, they concurred that the causes in which they were interested were secondary (as opposed to first or primary) causes. Such distinctions as Ward's efficient, conative, and telic causes and Giddings's independent-original and dependent- (or derived-) secondary causes reflect their ontological-substantive conceptions much more than their epistemological-methodological notions. Early sociologists were prevailingly dualistic, varying only in the extent to which they stressed the distinctiveness and primacy of materialistic or idealistic features in social causation.

A prevailingly dualistic conception of epistemology and a conception of science as the study of the general

The epistemological and methodological views of early American sociologists presupposed the tenability of causation as the objective of scientific inquiry. But the doctrine of causation was so conceived as to entail both empiricist and rationalist components of epistemology. Both the actual experience of antecedent-consequent relations and the reasons accounting for such relations are presupposed. Early theorists thus manifested both empiricist and idealist inclinations and, accordingly, supported epistemological claims based both on sensory experience and rational consistency – or even the congruity of (emotionally) felt wholes (see Scheme II, A, 1).

Sumner, Keller, Ward, Giddings, Ross, and Small are essentially unanimous in insisting that knowledge must start with something variously characterized as observation, description, or fact. Clearly, such terms as observation, description, or fact do refer to sensation, experience, or sensory experience as a necessary basis of (scientific) knowledge. Keller, for instance, constantly emphasizes (1927, pp. 2163, 2168) that science begins with the 'collection and assembly of facts' stemming from 'experience or observation.' Faulty as the senses may be, their reports about objects 'are the best we have . . . [and the] race has got where it is by depending upon them' (1927, p. 2173). Ward agrees (1970, pp. 9, 4, 508) that science is based on 'observations' and the possession of a 'domain of fact.' Giddings's preoccupation with the fundamentals of induction in his *Inductive Sociology* reveals a substantial commitment to empiricism as the basis of acceptable scientific knowledge. Science commences with (the collection of) 'fact' which 'is the close agreement of many observations or measurements of the same phenomenon' (1901, p. 13). In turn, a class (or category) is 'a plural number of facts that resemble one another in some given point or number of points' (1901, p. 13). (Note the atomism so often associated with induction and empiricism.) Ross's direct quotation from Tarde leaves no doubt that the basic observations or descriptions of fact which are demanded in any science are 'sense-given data' (1912, p. 322). Small's descriptive phase of the scientific process is concerned with displaying facts as such (1910, p. 186). Basically, this insistence by early sociologists on the use of fact, description, or observation (and induction) as the point of departure for sociological inquiry reflects their adherence to naturalism and their rejection of the metaphysical, mysterious, and the supernatural.

But a rationalistic component necessarily was present in their epistemology because they believed that the nature or reality which science studied was characterized by the recurrent, persistent, common, typical, permanent, uniform, general and universal. In effect, early sociologists concurred with the verdict of eighteenth-century Cartesian science that the diversity and particularity of the data of concrete, specific experience must be excluded from inquiry. Abstract reason or reasoning is the key. By abstraction, it becomes possible – so they held – to separate out and exclude the individual, concrete, particular, peculiar, abnormal, accidental, exceptional, and unique – all of which are associated with the dated and the sited, i.e., the domain of traditional history. Understandably, therefore, early American sociologists continued to accept – except for Ross – the tradition of earlier social philosophy that mankind, humanity, the human race, or human society in general is the bona fide, legitimate whole or universal which is to be studied. Specific, concrete, existent societies are construed as parts or particulars of the (imagined) whole or universal of human society generically. But in this view, an induction from present and past existent societies never seems to (and cannot) achieve the comprehensive level of generality of human society as a whole. The (general) structural features, properties, units, relations, regularities and causes which early sociologists really sought are not inferrable from the concrete, specific, particulars of sensory experience and induction. Ward, Small, Keller, and Giddings are illustrative.

Ward claims (1970, p. 49) that in 'a field so great as that of human society, a wide induction becomes unmanageable. The number of facts to be dealt with is so great that they bewilder the mind. Something must be done besides accumulating facts, and drawing conclusions from them.' Generalization is the process of combining and recombining categories of facts and associated conclusions into ever more complex and abstract orders up to the most general or universal level of the phenomena, i.e., human society in general.

Small displays an illuminating ambivalence between empiricism (particularism) and induction and rationalism (universalism) and deduction. He does assert (1905, pp. 45, 371, 642) that human experience is to be understood by inductive investigation, that sociology should rest on valid inductions from the actual social process, and that the problem of regularity in the operation of motives should be pursued by inductive investigation. Conversely, he was concerned (1905, p. 103) that sociologists may 'have conceived of people and their activities under so many categories of contrast, and separation, and disjunction, that similarity, and unity, and community have been overlooked.' Sociology 'is [or should be] essentially an effort to find more adequate categories with which to conceptualize social details, and to organize the contents of these categories into a universal conception' (1905, pp. 89–90). In Small's (as in Ward's) case, conceptualization, abstraction, and generalization are interlinked.

Keller (with his mentor Sumner) is unique in endeavoring to minimize the role of reason and deductive logic in epistemology and methodology. Both Sumner and Keller insist that a science of society must begin with a mass of facts, abjure abstract reasoning, and avoid dependence on analogy. Keller does define a science of society as necessarily 'general in both place and time,' aiming apparently at a vision of 'human society as a whole' (1927, pp. 2206, 2208). He concedes (1927, p. 2203) that classifications contain 'an element . . . contributed from the mind of the . . . maker, not from fact.' Furthermore, the effort to find uniform 'bonds of connection' as first and causal explanations eventually from classified facts also requires rational inference which must be tested against a wider range of experience or observation.

Significantly also, Giddings's recommendation (1896, p. 63) for acceptable classification in sociology presupposes that human society displays characteristics 'that normal differentiation has produced' in the course of societal evolution as a whole. By developing categories and sub-categories in accordance with the degree of evolutionary differentiation, the investigator will be able 'to distinguish primary from secondary characteristics' and to 'mark off the general from the special' or the 'permanent and essential relations' from 'temporary or adventitious relations' (1896, p. 63).

Clearly, sociologists tended to be epistemological dualists who accepted both sensory experience (or empiricism) and deductive inference of mind or reason (rationalism). But they varied in their emphasis. Ward and Small seemed most inclined to rely on mind, reason, or deductive logic, and accordingly they appear to be preponderantly rationalist (or rationalistic-idealist). In contrast, perhaps Giddings but certainly Sumner and Keller are inclined to restrict the role of reason and deductive inference and to emphasize sensory experience. Accordingly, they seem to be preponderantly empiricist.

But Cooley was distinctive. An epistemological dualist also, he was much more inclined to idealism than to empiricism. He held (1969, pp. 297, 306) that all knowledge is ultimately mental, a work of the imagination, a construct that the mind is generally developing as a system. As 'knowledge that is verifiable and accumulative,' science – beyond precise and easily repeated experiment – involves interpretation that is never unquestionable in its verification (1927, pp. 148, 149). It is provisional and must always be renewed to meet the general advances of thought (1969, p. 306). It persists as a general set of ideas, theories, and arguments only because it has gained the assent of an expert group (1927, p. 148).

Like their epistemological positions, the methodological positions of most early sociologists can be understood only in relation to their conception of nature or the reality which science studies. Early theorists showed a seemingly ambivalent and contradictory attitude toward induction. They accepted it as the necessary point of departure for research but depreciated the concreteness, specificity, and especially the particularity of the results achieved by rigorous adherence to the procedure. Ward, Small, and Cooley, for instance, condemned inquiries of historians and the German school of historical (or institutional) economics for just the reasons cited (e.g., Ward, 1970, pp. 47, 49). Simultaneously, sociologists employed the term 'generalization' with considerable latitude. It incorporates abstraction, classification, and the attainment of logical universals in a way that exceeds the circumscriptions of empirical induction. Generalization tends to conceal the prevailing direction of logical operations between the level of particulars and that of the universal. The term seems to suggest movement from specific, particular societies to society as a whole, whereas in operating practice it departs from an assumed notion of human society in general and moves to particular societies. In actuality, human society in general is arrived at by a process of abstraction which arbitrarily strips away or excludes what is presumed not to be general or universal. In turn, social or sociological classifications presuppose and begin with such an assumed abstract universal entity of human society in general or the social in general. Thus, generalization is not strictly inductive (e.g., Ward), but is in effect deductive, for it departs in actual practice from an *abstract generality* or universal.

Early sociologists accepted the Aristotelian–Cartesian view that science studies the normal or natural in phenomena; i.e., that which happens for the most part, recurrently, persistently, commonly, typically, uniformly, generally, or universally.[4] Their conception of the domain of the human social or society reflects this assumption. Manifestly, Ward's method of generalization presupposes that the social is a natural domain of the recurrent, general, and uniform, in which details and particulars are to be ignored (1970, pp. 55–6). Sumner and Keller claim unmistakably that a science of society is to be concerned with what 'is general in place and time' (1927, p. 2208). It 'arranges its materials irrespective of time and place' (1927, p. 2190). By use of comparison, it endeavors to divulge the general and typical in human societies. The natural laws which their science seeks 'follow an unchangeable sequence in all times and places and for all men' (1927, p. 2221). In Giddings's view, sociology as a general science is 'a study of the universal and fundamental phenomena of societies' (1901, p. 8). It is to be concerned with 'permanent and essential relations' (1896, p. 63). It 'investigates only the facts and correlations found in all societies, the types of society, the stages of social development, the general laws of social evolution' (1901, p. 8). All the irrelevant, accidental, incidental, or occasional features must be eliminated in preference for the simple, elementary, and persistent (1901, p. 9). Ross adheres to essentially the same position, insisting (1919, p. 84) that the sociologist 'cancels out the particular' and 'has no use for the fact that occurs but once, unless, by driving out of it that which is individual, he can break it up into familiar components.' Since sociology 'is one of the abstract sciences,' the 'sociologist aims to rise from particular cases to general terms which he can employ in formulating generalizations and laws' (1919, p. 81). What he seeks is 'not unique facts, but recurrent facts, for which he can frame a concept that shall neglect details and emphasize common properties' (1919, p. 81). Small also concurs, declaring (1905, p. 48) that without recurrence, regularity, or uniformity 'in societary events, there is no possibility of the rudiments of . . . science.' According to him (1905, p. 15), sociology is not interested in discrete, unconnected events or 'in facts as such. It is interested only in relations . . . in which facts reappear in essentials.' Sociology should be concerned with the constant and general in social relations, with the nature of forces in human association and the conditions, modes and laws of their action (1905, pp. 101, 105). Indeed, its very reason for existence is the discovery of the universal in social relations (1905, pp. 87, 89). It was the prevailing opinion of early sociologists that their discipline was concerned with the general or universal in social relations and entities as might be expressed in social regularities, laws, and causes.

Admittedly Cooley, who explicitly accepted an idealist epistemology and an appropriate humanistic methodology, displays little evidence of a commitment to this view of the domain of social life. He is interested in generalization, general facts, and enduring principles of human nature and social process, and in the personality, the social, and the cultural as types, but apparently not in abstract generalities or uniformities (1966, pp. 402–3, 198, 201,

30; 1962, p. 32). Cooley tended to dissociate himself and his position from the then present or past conceptions of sociology as a natural science.

Early sociologists' prevalent endorsement of this notion of science and of the social as a domain of natural phenomena also finds its confirmation in their antagonism to history as the study of events.[5] For early sociologists, history was the realm of the knowledge of the individual, particular, concrete, non-recurrent, rare, exceptional, peculiar, accidental, and unique, which was dated and sited. Sociologists tended to conceive of science and history and their modes of inquiry as distinctively different and opposed.[6] Sumner and Keller commented that science contrasts with history which 'is a picture of what happened at a time and place. It [history] has but one course and does not admit of comparison' (1927, p. 2206). History 'deals with localities and definitely marked times' (1927, p. 2206). 'True to its origin in chronicle, history is written about chronology and makes much of dates' (1927, p. 2206). It 'is the name for the flow and sequence of events in time' (1927, p. 2205). Ross also viewed the sociologist and the historian in contrasting terms and characterized the latter as one who 'clings to the particular,' who studies events, i.e., the dated, sited, specific, concrete, unique, and personalized occurrences (1919, pp. 84, 82). Small noted that 'history, as usually written, exhibits facts in all their accidental form' with 'the accidents of time, place, personality' (and Vincent, 1971, p. 64).

A positivistic methodology: a majority view

Although the methodology of early American sociology was unmistakably based on a combination of induction and deduction, the comments of early theorists indicate that much more was involved. Some of their statements were explicitly and systematically formulated (e.g., Sumner and Keller, Giddings, Small, Cooley), whereas others were not (e.g., Ward, Ross). In Ward's case, it is evident that generalization (in conjunction with classification and abstraction) is the key to an understanding of his position. Small's *The Meaning of Social Science* (pp. 186, 192, 202, 203, 210, 211, 220, 222, 224, 232, 242, 259, 263–5) proposes four 'chief methodological divisions' or phases of the scientific process: description, analysis, evaluation, and construction. Sumner declared that 'Analysis, comparison, generalization, and deduction are operations of scientific method' (1927, p. 2212). (Keller provided an elaboration of his understanding of Sumner's views

(1927, pp. 2168–9).) In his *Principles of Sociology*, Giddings expounded (pp. 52–69) at length on observation and retrospection, classification and generalization, induction and deduction. He also makes the chapters on the logic of the moral sciences from John Stuart Mill's *A System of Logic* 'the solid foundation of sociological method' (1896, p. 52). Although Giddings's inclinations to a positivistic and statistical notion of scientific method are already apparent in *The Principles of Sociology*, they become increasingly conspicuous in *Inductive Sociology* (1901) and *Studies in the Theory of Human Society* (1911).

Giddings was the leading advocate of the positivistic methodological orientation in early American sociology. This position claims that the methods, procedures, and techniques of the physical and biological sciences (i.e., the natural sciences) can and should become the basis for the study of social phenomena without any major modification or supplementation (Scheme II, B, 1, a).[7] The prevalence of this orientation can be understood in terms of early American sociologists' pervasive enthusiasm for the beneficial consequences of natural science and their inclination to construe social phenomena as a domain of phenomena or forces which can be investigated for regularities or laws as other domains or phenomena or forces have been studied in nature. Adherents of a more or less prevailingly positivistic methodological outlook include Giddings, Ross, Sumner, possibly Ward and perhaps even Small. Interestingly (at least to their later successors), they failed to recognize that their insistence on the psychic nature of social phenomena represented any significant problem or obstacle to their basic methodological inclination.

Perhaps the most general or common indicator of a positivistic commitment is an acceptance of the comparative method. Such other features as the demand for a more or less exclusive reliance on empirical observation, induction, precision, objectivity, and quantification-mensuration seem to have evoked some disagreement. Ward certainly did use the comparative method as part of his method of generalization. Keller and Giddings do employ the comparative (or comparative-historical) method, which presumably derives from biology as it did in Comte's case originally.

Neither Giddings nor any of his colleagues seems to have recognized that the comparative methods (or, more accurately, the comparative-historical methods) actually presuppose that all mankind has been unified as a great society which has been undergoing change in accordance with the principle of (organic) differentiation. The comparative-historical methods assume that all mankind is comprehended in a vast, single developmental unity whose general course and component stages in sequence modern social science can and should reconstruct. Basically, the methods identify the development of humanity with the abstract outlines of the historical experience of Western European societies. All shades and degrees of social and cultural differences are assumed to be arrangeable between the poles of primitivity and modernity. At or near the former pole are to be found traditionalism, backwardness, primitivism with an emphasis on kinship, a sacred or religious view of life, corporatism, hierarchy, localism, handicrafts, or rurality. At or near the latter pole are to be found a complex technology, industrialism, democracy, secularism, individualism, equalitarianism, or socialism (Nisbet, 1969, p. 191).

In simple terms, the comparative method (to use a more convenient, abbreviated designation) was the procedure used to arrange socially and culturally distinct peoples – who were often widely separated in space or time – in a graded series of similarities (and dissimilarities) from simplicity to complexity which was believed to be temporal and developmental.[8] Simplicity was more or less equated with earliness or primitivity and complexity with lateness or modernity (e.g., Keller, 1927, p. 2190). Evolutionists held that existent peoples in the ethnographic present (in the late eighteenth and nineteenth centuries) and in the historical records of the (Indo-European) past broadly embodied various stages through which mankind as a whole had passed (and would pass).[9]

Up to this point, exposition has not distinguished the comparative and the historical methods, both of which are known in logic as forms of the method of concomitant variations, so Giddings remarks, and each of which 'is a systematic observation of coherence among phenomena, combined with an inference that phenomena that persist together, or that change together, are cause and effect, or are effects of a common cause' (1896, p. 64). The comparative method affords a way of dealing with coexistence and the historical method is a way to deal with sequence. Giddings defines the comparative method as 'an observation of identical coherences of social phenomena in two or more places, or in two or more populations' – presumably at the same time (1896, p. 64). Again in Giddings's words, the historical method 'is an observation of coherences through periods of time' (1896, p. 64).

What Giddings does indicate is that the coexistent (relatively) contemporary inter-societal series can be transformed into a sequential series by invoking the assumption equating simplicity with earliness in time (or primitivity) and complexity with lateness in time (or modernity). Thus, the results of the comparative method can essentially be translated or transformed into the results of the historical method. Different societies become types of stages (or ages) in the evolutionary development of mankind or human society. Admittedly, the actual names of the stages vary considerably among sociologists.

Obviously, actual historical differences (or chronological sequence) and geographical (or spatial) distances were ignored. As Keller remarks (1927, p. 2190), the 'approved method in science – approved because it verifies – [is] to arrange its materials irrespective of time and place.' He and his contemporaries assumed that scientific generality is the consequence (not of rigorous time and place inductions) but of abstraction. So, for instance, contemporary primitives are regarded as socially and culturally equivalent to our remote ancestors. 'The savages of nowadays are under pressure to adjust to conditions not dissimilar to those of our remote ancestors and with the same lack of accumulated knowledge of facts and forces' (1927, p. 2191; cf. Giddings, 1896, p. 209). (Keller documents his argument by quotations from Montelius, Nilsson, and – significantly – from Tylor, the father of the comparative method in anthropology (1927, p. 2191).) But each societal type as a typical age or stage in sequence is abstract and thus a simplification of empirical reality. Probably, no 'purely pastoral people was ever observed; but there is a distinctly pastoral type' (1927, p. 2202). Although no people actually ever experienced the reality of the types in the series of stages, the construction of such a series from phenomena 'presented in many societies, set in order and sequence of development,' is necessary to achieve 'the best command of the whole' (1927, p. 2203). A unity of mankind or of human society is thus assumed even though the actual history of any specific society may present 'gaps, inversions, or transfers in the order set down' in the constructed series (1927, p. 2203).

But more disagreements become evident as other (contemporaneously identified) features of positivism as a methodological orientation are examined in early American sociology. Although positivism tends to argue that the social realm is phenomenally distinct, it argues that social phenomena are sufficiently similar to other natural phenomena to warrant use of the same type or types of method. Like Comte, Ward and Keller indicate that social phenomena are complex. Ward notes (1970, pp. 57, 568) both complexity and subtlety. Keller declares that social phenomena are less concrete and positive and their relations more complex, shifting, and elusive than those of physical phenomena (1927, p.

2165). In both instances, the other adjectives employed cast some doubt on just how similar social phenomena are believed to be to other phenomena. In Keller's case, the doubts are substantial, for he remarks (1927, p. 2165) in the paragraph following his characterization of social phenomena: 'It is quite idle to pretend to treat societal phenomena strictly by the methods of natural science; such pretense issues in mere affectation.'

Positivism has also asserted that as part of the realm of nature social phenomena should be studied with objectivity, detachment, or impersonality. Ward insists (1970, p. 4) that (pure) sociology is pure diagnosis, concerned only with 'the effort to determine what actually is,' with 'the present and the past.' It does not preoccupy itself 'with what society ought to be, or with any social ideals' (1970, p. 4). It refrains from moral approval and disapproval, 'from all praise or blame, as wholly inapplicable to that which exists of necessity' (1970, pp. 4–5). It neither extols nor condemns facts or defends 'nature's methods as necessarily the best' (1970, p. 5).

Keller reaches a similar verdict. Passing moral judgment is (1927, p. 2187) to 'measure things and men by our own code,' to be ethnocentric, and to vitiate 'all our [scientific] results.' It is as scientifically inappropriate or impertinent to be a pessimist or an optimist or to pass moral judgment 'in a theoretic science that has to do with the evolution and life of society' as it would be in chemistry or entomology (1927, p. 2187). The investigator must eschew the use of 'ought' and 'must' and instead speak in terms of 'is' and 'can' (1927, p. 2187). Despite difficulties, he would endeavor to maintain 'unwaveringly as impersonal an attitude as he can' (1927, p. 2170). What occurs in society must be regarded as historically expedient – as necessary in terms of evolution or adaptation to life-conditions (1927, p. 2240). 'Moral judgments, therefore, are idle' and 'vain' (1927, pp. 2241, 2242).

Another common feature of positivism is the association of objectivity and detachment with precision, quantification, measurement, and statistical analysis. Interestingly, Ross, who condemns the 'vice of exteriority' and insists on studying motivation, urges that the units of sociological study be small-scale and circumscribed. 'The bane of sociology has been the employment of large units, the comparison in lump instead of comparison in detail' (1919, p. 74). Sociologists 'ought to generalize on the basis of numerous and minute and exact resemblances' (1919, p. 75). They will 'never make headway until' they renounce 'the comparison of a few huge and only superficially integrated complexes of phenomena – such as nations, epochs, and civilizations' (1919, p. 75). According to Ross: 'The more minute the fact or relation we study, the more frequent will be the cases of its occurrence, and the more likely they are to be so similar that they can be treated as equivalents. The adoption of petty elementary units will therefore hasten the advent of the day when . . . we can [genuinely] measure' (1919, p. 80). He concludes enthusiastically that the 'statistical method, which enables us to measure social phenomena exactly and to substitute quantitative truths for qualitative, constitutes an instrument of precision, which certainly is destined to be applied to sociological problems in ways yet undreamed of' (1919, pp. 80–1).

By contrast, Ward, Sumner and Keller, who seem to accept certain features of positivism, object strenuously to quantification, measurement, and statistical analysis of social phenomena. Ward warns sociologists (1970, p. 48) against the effort to reduce the broader domains of social activity to 'exact notation' and to formulate or state 'the laws of society . . . in equations' by citing the alleged 'failure of the old-time political economy,' which reduced man to an over-simplified abstraction. The essentials of a science are uniform laws or processes; their expression in mathematical formulas 'is not essential' (1970, p. 48). Sumner and Keller expressed their objections more extensively. Because the relations of social phenomena are 'more complex, shifting, and elusive' than those of the physical world, their 'relations can seldom or never be expressed mathematically except as an academic exercise; they are highly contingent and are qualitative rather than quantitative' (1927, p. 2165). But the 'great difficulty,' according to Sumner, is the inability to derive theoretical law from statistical data in the absence of any 'routine [i.e., set or standardized] process' (1927, p. 2210). He indicts statistics because they 'are static only' and do not say anything about development (1927, p. 2211). They 'contain no secrets, in the way of laws, which can be extracted from them; much less do they reveal anything by their own voice. They only describe what is, either as data or as tests to be used in verification' (1927, p. 2212).

Of all the theorists of the first era, Giddings was the most evidently inclined to the positivistic features of objectivity, precision, measurement, quantification, and statistical analysis. Even in his *The Principles of Sociology* he notes that both the comparative and historical methods can be made more precise when they become statistical, i.e., when the social phenomena involved admit of numerical or quantitative statement. His

Inductive Sociology transforms the comparative and historical methods, the two specific, inductive methods of research, into forms which accord with his positivistic and quantitative conceptions. Categories, with their data, are further subdivided into class-intervals or magnitude-classes. Means, medians, and modes are to be calculatcd. Like all natural phenomena, social phenomena can be counted on to 'show a normal range of variation from the mode and a standard deviation' (1901, p. 22). Determination of standard deviations will allow classes or series of figures to be compared in order to ascertain whether they vary directly or inversely with one another or not at all. If they vary directly or inversely, a coefficient of correlation can be computed. Giddings regards a coefficient of correlation as 'equivalent to a generalization or a law' (1901, p. 22). But he refuses to abandon deduction entirely, for it is necessary as a complementary or supplementary method in 'extended or complicated inductive research' (1901, p. 26).

With the publication of a series of essays as *Studies in the Theory of Human Society* (1922), Giddings's commitment to a positivistic and quantitative view of science and sociology as a science was essentially complete. John Stuart Mill, Karl Pearson, and Ernst Mach became his authorities. Physics was the model of science and method in sociology. And as a science, sociology will more and more involve the accurate and reliable description of facts, their accumulation, inductive treatment, and statistical analysis. Giddings anticipated that sociology will have an increasingly quantitative character, with its chief theorems probably admitting of 'quantitative statement, solution, and correlation' (1922, p. 121).

A humanistic methodology: a minority view

Cooley is the only explicit and articulate exponent of a humanistic methodology which is elaborated as a part of a more encompassing epistemological idealism (i.e., a romantic or non-rationalist idealism). Curiously, Ross's declamation against the 'Vice of Exteriority' (or objectivism-behaviorism) does not lead to a humanistic methodology at all; he adheres to positivism. Interestingly, Giddings's method of psychological synthesis which he had proposed in his *The Principles of Sociology* is simply ignored in subsequent publications as he moved to a more explicit and consistent positivism. Furthermore, Small's suggestion (1910, p. 224) that in the methodological phase of evaluation the investigators place themselves 'in the position of the actors' and 'look forward from their standpoint into their problems' is not actually offered as a way to understand the evaluations of the actors, but instead as a means to judge the adequacy of their evaluations! Thus, Cooley stands alone as an explicit and articulate exponent of a humanistic methodology (see Scheme II, C, 2).

As just noted, Cooley's methodological stance is associated with a broader adherence to epistemological idealism.[10] He defines knowledge explicitly as a 'construct of the mind,' as mental and subjective (1969, pp. 297, 306). He challenged the usual criterion of scientific knowledge as exact measurement 'in small units of space and time' and suggested instead 'conformations, patterns, systems,' or wholes (1969, p. 314). Although he refused to separate science, philosophy, and art sharply from one another, he did distinguish a domain of knowledge of the social from a domain of knowledge of the physical. His method of the 'instructed imagination' or 'sympathetic introspection' is Cooley's own characterization of a humanistic methodology which is appropriate to a distinctive domain of the study of social or dramatic knowledge.

Both his epistemology and methodology are revealed by what he rejected as well as by what he accepted. Unlike the positivists, he refused to separate science and art. In both, men 'occupy themselves with a precise study of facts,' seek 'to interpret and reconstruct nature after patterns' of their own, and 'rise above the tumult of the hour to serene and lasting aims' in the 'the pursuit of truth' (1927, p. 144). Both science and art abstract from and illuminate concrete objects, though in their own distinctive ways. Workers in both fields seek, out of the multitude of facts at their disposal, the one 'that will illuminate their idea' and both 'find that it is rarely to be had without research' (1927, p. 146). Both fields involve authenticity as a test of truth.

For Cooley, science contains a component of art. All science becomes art when it passes from facts, theories, and arguments to the construction of a system of ideal truth (1927, p. 145). Indeed, all 'science may be said to work by a dramatic method when it takes the results of minute observations and tries to build them into fresh wholes of knowledge' (1966, p. 395). Sociology itself can be a science 'only as to detail' (1927, p. 145). When it interprets life 'largely' it is an art (1927, p. 145). In the *Social Process*, Cooley intimates that sociology resorts to art in selecting the more universal facts which enable 'us to discern underneath the apparent confusion of things the working of enduring principles of human nature and social process' (1966, p. 403).

Conversely, Cooley rejected the major characteristics of positivistic methodology as inapplicable to the human social domain. He declared that there is 'no reason to think that . . . [exact] prediction or control,' which is a 'false ideal inconsiderately borrowed from the provinces of physical science,' will 'ever be possible' in sociology (1966, p. 398). Admittedly, social life in large aggregates may have currents of mechanical movement whose mass and direction can be measured and the course of whose conjuncture can be predicted by statistics (1927, p. 157). But only in some limited respects is human behavior generally mechanical, repetitive, or habitual. Therefore, any encompassing external, mechanical determinism is precluded (1966, p. 401). Except in subordinate degree, the numerical method is apparently not the right method in sociology (1966, p. 401). The true aim of social science is 'not . . . to bring society within the sphere of arithmetic,' however important precision may be in preparing data (1966, p. 398).

But it is the very nature of social data which prompted Cooley's apprehensions about relying on the physical measurements of psychological laboratories and his declaration that the 'sooner we [in the social sciences] cease circumscribing and testing ourselves by the canons of physical and psychological science the better' (1964, p. 121; 1966, p. 397). Human conduct involves both exterior and interior domains, 'outside and inside, consciousness and behavior, [which] mutually complement and interpret each other. They cannot be disjoined without denaturing both' (1927, p. 151). To restrict a human science only to the 'study and measurement of behavior, the outside of life . . . without sympathetic observation of the mind, is . . . only mystification' (1927, p. 151). To 'dodge the mental and emotional processes in which society consists, to circumvent them, find them superfluous, arrive at social truth without them' is to make social science a pseudo-science (1927, p. 154). Originative or creative mental synthesis, which distinguishes human life from mere physical processes, does not appear to be subject to exact prediction (1969, p. 305). Thus, the appropriate technique for studying human conduct must be one predicated on consciousness and will, so basic to the ontological and epistemological idealist.

Cooley's technique of the 'instructed imagination' or 'sympathetic introspection' is, accordingly, proposed as the distinguishing methodological feature of the humanistic disciplines, including sociology, within the realm of personal, social knowledge in contrast to the realm of spatial material knowledge.[11] Each branch of knowledge has its own characteristic object, approach, and method corresponding to the dualism of matter and mind. Knowledge of things in extension (matter) depends principally upon the sensory perception of space and time and is readily subject to mensurative techniques. Man functions only as a mediator in the measurement of material objects in terms of other material objects. Thus, spatial knowledge is categorically different from social knowledge. But material knowledge enters the realm of social knowledge and becomes subject to the general movement of thought when interpretative hypotheses are introduced to discover what men judge to be true.

Personal, social knowledge concerns minds, consciousness, imaginations, and feelings – the internal and the subjective. It is a form of knowledge requiring that the researcher engage in interpretation using the unique technique of sympathetic introspection (see Scheme II, B, 1, b). Less precise, verifiable, cumulative, and susceptible to measurement, quantification, and statistical manipulation, its data are to be treated emergentistically, synthetically, and typologically.

Cooley believed that its technique of the 'instructed imagination' or 'sympathetic introspection' was peculiarly adapted to understanding or interpreting valuation, choice, and the creative synthesis of individuals' wills. It employs the dramatic experience of the investigator through his own idea or feeling of the 'I' as actor in the situation. He embraces the situation of some subject within his own mind and, by an act of creative intelligence, anticipates the outcome – as 'you would anticipate the conduct of an individual by putting yourself wholeheartedly in his place' (1927, p. 157). You understand 'another's consciousness by the aid of your own' (1969, p. 300). The conduct of other men, including their language, is interpreted by 'ascribing to them thoughts and sentiments similar to our own' (1969, p. 300). When we observe overt activities and hear words of others, we understand them by recalling in our own consciousness how we thought and felt under similar circumstances of word and deed. We impute the same thoughts and feelings to others and thus gain 'an insight into their minds' (1969, p. 298). Through communication, contact with the minds of other men 'sets going a process of thought and sentiment similar to theirs and enables us to understand them by sharing their states of mind' (1969, p. 290).

Sympathetic introspection is fundamental to social knowledge. It entails a subjectivist procedure for knowing others which can lead to knowledge because all men are one biopsychically: all men are endowed with a common human heredity and a common primary group socialization (and thus have similar instincts, drives, emotions, and sentiments). Cooley seems to hold that social knowledge, like its material counterpart, appears early in the development of the child and the race. The child's first overt responses to facial expressions, gestures, and the spoken word assume a covert emotional reaction. Furthermore, it appears to be part of man's nature and consciousness to ascribe a similar inward experience to others in like circumstances (1969, p. 293). What makes human words and actions social is their accompaniment by sympathy, sentiments, and ideas having meaning and value. Social knowledge thus comprises mental-social phenomena sympathetically introspectively derived: innermost thoughts, feelings, and meanings communicated through gestures, voice, words, and writing and known only through consciousness.

Cooley was relatively distinctive in his epistemological-methodological stance in early American sociological theory. Epistemologically, he was an idealist, albeit a romantic (rather than a rationalistic) idealist. Knowledge for him was essentially a construction of the mind rather than a derivative of sensation or experience (as empiricists held). Although he refused to separate science, philosophy, and art sharply from one another, he did distinguish a domain of knowledge of the personal-social from a domain of knowledge of the spatial-material. His method of the 'instructed imagination' or 'sympathetic introspection' is the core of his humanistic methodology which insists on a distinctive approach to the study of the personal social realm.

But Cooley's colleagues of the first era cannot be accurately characterized as mere empiricists. They were epistemological dualists, with some seeming to emphasize sensation or experience (e.g., Giddings, Sumner and Keller) and others to stress reason and logic (e.g., Ward and Small). Undeniably, they accepted the basic importance of sensation (in the form of observation), description, and fact. But none of them argued for an exclusive reliance on induction. For all of them, deduction was also necessary. Reason or mind was imperative to achieve the abstract generality of generalization and law which they believed science demands. For Sumner and Keller, Ward, Giddings, Ross, and Small, science was pre-eminently a (Cartesian) concern with the study of what happens normally and naturally, generally, commonly, for the most part, recurrently, or persistently. Reason is important in separating out

101

and excluding the individual, concrete, particular, peculiar, abnormal, accidental, exceptional, or unique. Accordingly, science and history come to have antithetical objectives for Sumner and Keller, Ross, and Small.

Except for Cooley, the major theorists of the first era were more or less disposed to a positivistic methodological stance. They were firmly convinced that sociology could and should become a science with the discovery of its own generalizations and laws. Thus Giddings, Ross, Sumner and Keller, possibly Ward and perhaps even Small tended to hold (though with varying emphasis) that the methods, procedures, and techniques of the physical and biological sciences (i.e., the natural sciences) can and should become the basis for the study of social phenomena without major qualification or supplementation. Perhaps the most conspicuous common indicator of this positivism was their resort to the comparative method (which – as Comte had noted much earlier – derived from biology). Although they did invoke observation and induction, they also used inference and deduction. Objectivity, detachment, or impersonality was also a common feature. But quantification, measurement, and statistical analysis provoked disagreement. Ross and Giddings were their proponents, whereas Ward, Sumner and Keller were their opponents.

Although causation was probably the most central methodological concern of early American theorists, it was not extensively or commonly subjected to analysis. Only Ward, Keller, and Giddings can be readily examined in terms of Bunge's more recent treatment of causation. Indeed, causation is presented more frequently as an ontological rather than as an epistemological or methodological notion. It appears as part of the doctrine of genetic filiation and thus reflects the dominance of the ontological domain of early theory, to which attention must now be directed.

5 Theories of social origins

Although early American sociological theory evinced certain epistemological-methodological concerns and distinctive views, it was more substantially oriented to problems of a social ontological nature. Early theorists were primarily interested in explaining human association, social phenomena, or (human) society. Even within this domain of theory, they were not equally interested in all basic questions. They were especially preoccupied with the problems of (social-societal) 'origins' and 'change,' toward which they adopted a stance characterizable as a sociological expression of evolutionary naturalism.

What this designation means is that their efforts to explain human association, social phenomena or (human) society were both naturalistic and evolutionary. Indeed, 'naturalistic' tended to signify 'evolutionary' in the late nineteenth and early twentieth centuries. Prompted positively by the success of the physical and organic sciences and negatively by the claims of a threatened supernaturalism of a rural and prevailingly agrarian small-town outlook of the era, early sociology was characteristically concerned with the problems of social 'origins' and 'change.'[1] To imply, of course, that all interest in (social) structure was missing in the era would be patently false. But the popular and scientific definition of problems of the times did ascribe a priority or primacy to questions of origins (and change) and only a secondary or derived interest in structure (or stability).

Conception of social origins as a sociological problem

Clearly, the second tenet (of genetic filiation) of evolutionary

103

naturalism accounts for the genesis of one level of phenomena by derivation from the prior level(s) of phenomena. Ward had precisely this possibility in mind in envisaging the derivation of the social, the human, and the conscious from life itself (i.e., sociogeny, anthropogeny, psychogeny out of biogeny). Giddings's distinction between zoogenetic association and anthropogenetic association (in the chapters by those titles in his *The Principles of Sociology*) is also based on the same possibility.

Unfortunately, early theorists offered no systematic conception of origins, genesis, or beginnings as a general problem (Scheme III, D, 1). Ward noted only (1970, p. 198) that in 'nature there is no first, there is only an eternal becoming.' The problem in sociology 'is to explain the origin and genesis of human society' (1970, p. 199). Sumner remarked (1959, pp. 7, 8) that 'All origins are lost in mystery' and thus 'any conception of the "beginning"' of a social phenomenon can be formed 'only by analysis and inference' (e.g., from biopsychic human nature needs). Giddings alluded (1896, p. 71) simply to the 'problems of the origins of society.' Small also acknowledged genesis as one category of the problematics of human association–dissociation (1912, p. 212). For many of the early theorists, the problem of social origins or genesis became a matter of offering a naturalistic evolutionary account of the development of more or less permanent association or society out of human organic evolution and universal biopsychic human nature needs in relation to the aboriginal conditions of human existence.

To provide such an account, early theories were compelled to infer and reconstruct the origins of humankind organically, psychically, geographically, and geologically. They resorted to such data and conjectures as the geology, biology, anatomy, paleontology, physical anthropology, archaeology, and ethnography-ethnology of their era could provide. They did generally accept the comparative method (Scheme III, D, 4), which assumed both temporal and developmental continuity between the earliest known conditions of historic Western peoples, 'primitive,' 'savage,' or 'simpler' peoples existing in the then ethnographic present (of modern times), and the earliest, aboriginal, or original condition of humankind and association inferrable on some factual basis. But, even so, origin might be defined in two ways – depending perhaps on what constituted tenable or reliable evidence. On the one hand, origins might be taken to mean a more or less conjectural, remote, or ultimate beginning. On the other, it might mean a proximate or near origin as could be represented by the simplest discovered (or discoverable) condition of existing primitive societies. Both views were present in early American sociological theory.

Ward and Giddings represent the first position. Neither in *Dynamic Sociology* nor in *Pure Sociology* did Ward display any hesitancy about conjecturing about the biopsychic and social (or anti-social) condition of earliest man. Giddings's chapter on 'Anthropogenic Association' in his *The Principles of Sociology* accepts the legitimacy of the task of reconstructing the condition of early, if not earliest, 'primitive human society' on the basis of the data of biology, geology, archaeology, and ethnography.

But Keller (and presumably Sumner) seek(s) explicitly to disavow any concern with ultimate social origins and thus advocate the second position. Since the origins of human societies are lost in mystery, our starting point must become 'the earliest state of human society of which positive knowledge can be obtained' i.e., evidence from 'prehistoric societies' or 'contemporary societies of primitive men who have no history in the strict sense' (1927, pp. 2184, 2183; Sumner, 1959, p. 8). Inferences 'as to societal origins . . . are untrustworthy because they are largely speculative, and [thus] . . . not verifiable' (1927, p. 2186). However, it is also true that Sumner in his earlier writings did infer what the social (or actually, antisocial) condition of early or primeval, if not earliest, man had been (Sumner, 1914, pp. 120–1; and 1927, pp. 62–3, also pp. 11–19).

However, even more determinative of the conception and explanation of the problem of social origins is the argument over whether more or less permanent association was prior to human organic origins or whether the human species (as an organic form) had arisen before more or less permanent (human) association occurred. If association had developed before the human species had evolved, human association is then at least in a basic sense derived from prehominid forms (even though it may have developed a distinctive hominid expression). But if human association is argued to have evolved only after humankind emerged organically, the original condition of mankind must have been entirely different (i.e., asocial) and the explanation of social genesis must be entirely *ab initio* or *de novo*. Both positions were expounded in early American sociological theory.

Sumner and Keller, Ward, and Ross are representative of the view that the human species emerged first as a distinct organic or biological unity and only later did (human) association evolve.[2] All of them agreed with Ward's declaration (1898, p. 90) that man was not and 'is not naturally a social being.' As Sumner and Keller insisted (1927, p. 11), man was not 'outfitted with any innate quality of sociability implanted in his germ plasm' (cf. Ward, 1968, I, p. 451). Exponents of this position (e.g., Ward, 1898, p. 91) rejected the 'Aristotelian idea that man is a gregarious animal and the Comtean doctrine that he is by nature a social being' – just as the other viewpoint accepted these ideas (cf. Sumner and Keller, 1927, p. 11; Ross, 1969, p. 14).

As champions of the other position, Giddings, Small and Cooley are thus not compelled to account for the (independent) origins of permanent human association and structured social life after the appearance of humankind organically. Mankind has descended from a species which had become social before it had become human in the anatomical-physiological genetic senses.[3] Accordingly, Giddings asserted (1898, p. 236) that 'society originated ages before man appears on the earth.' The 'earliest human beings [probably] lived in rather large bands or communities' (1898, p. 238). Small's analysis of Baldwin Spencer's and F. J. Gillen's study of the Australian Arunta and Warramunga (1905, p. 211) – which are probably the best cases of the 'quasi-original condition' of early man – evidences a recognition of permanent association and the elements of a tribal structure. Cooley also insisted that early man lived in many small societies and he certainly agreed with Small's claim (1905, p. 208) that human life 'is always and necessarily social life; i.e., life in a group, the members of which influence each other.' Cooley's position on social origins is consistent with his argument for the necessary interrelation of individual and society and with his articulate rejection of the four major varieties of individualism (1964, pp. 38, 37, 42, 43–7).

Manifestly, the two explanations advanced to account for social origins involve substantially different components and inter-relations. The post-hominid or post-organic origins account, for instance, emphasizes the (alleged) considerable differences between the organic and/or biopsychic traits of earliest man and his habitats and modern man and his environments. It tends to stress the imperiousness of hunger and the scarcity of resources or the niggardliness and inhospitability of early environments. Sumner and Keller, Ward, and Ross conceived early humans as egoistic, individualistic, selfish, atomistic, solitary, quarrelsome, suspicious, prone to violence. The transition from an atomistic and an a- (if not anti-) social condition to continuous, permanent social existence is explained in accordance with the assumptions of evolutionary naturalism. In particular, Darwinian evolution is invoked, with an interplay between the needs-wants of the original nature of (human) organisms whom changing circumstances and environments throw into contact. Such contact necessarily entails recurrent conflict, struggle for existence, selection by survival of the fittest. Permanent social life emerges because it functions to secure adaptation – survival under prevailing conditions of human existence. Interestingly, this evolutionary process does involve the sequential emergence of the social in all three senses: inter- and/or multi-personal relations, inter- and/or multi-personal activities (or processes), and (finally) continuous, permanently structured association or the group.

The pre-hominid or pre-organic explanation tends to place less emphasis on the possible differences between early and modern men in terms of their organic constitutions, their dominant biopsychic dispositions, and their environments. Giddings, for instance, alleged (1896, p. 225) that 'Human nature is [characteristically and] preeminently social nature.' Furthermore, it is fallacious to argue that early man was peculiarly subject to a harsh life and scanty subsistence on the basis of the circumstances and characteristics 'of the lowest hordes of human beings now living in . . . remote [and marginal] regions' (1898, p. 238). Cooley urged (1966, p. 245) that early men were not irresponsibly disposed to brute force, 'but then as now the man fit to survive was a moral man, a "good" man in his relation to the life of the group.' Living in groups, the earliest human beings would also have effectively internalized the moral-social sentiments engendered in primary group relations. For all three sociologists who adopted the second conception and explanatory stance of social origins, aboriginal humankind was substantially social, sympathetic, and altruistic in nature. Antagonism and opposition in varying degrees and kinds might and did occur, but they were not construed so typically to eventuate in the unmitigated struggle of the Darwinian interpretation. Certainly, Small and Cooley seemed to endorse a more Hegelian-dialectical view of conflict.

For the adherents of this second perspective, the problem of social origins is basically to indicate what is distinctive about the human social and to formulate (especially for Giddings and Cooley) just how these distinguishing factors in human association, such as speech, language, and communication, arose and developed. And, finally, the intellectual commitments of members of this second position meant also that no one of the forms or meanings of the social was temporally prior to any other one and no one could be understood apart from the other two. Inter- and/or multi-personal relations necessarily could be comprehended only in relation to the actual activities of persons which in turn were predicated on some existing structure of some group. Similarly, any other one of the meanings of the social implicated the other two.

The pre-organic social origins theory

The sociologists who adopt the position that humankind descended from prehuman (animal) ancestors who were substantially social do agree substantially on speech, language, and (symbolic) communication as conferring a distinctive quality on human association. Both Giddings and Cooley endeavor to explain the genesis of speech out of the prehuman circumstances of interaction-association and both, in turn, outline the significance of speech-language for human association. Yet, they do display some major differences (e.g., Giddings in his concern with the impact of physical environment, shifts in habitat, isolation, contact and diffusion in the emergence of distinctive human association and the impact of that association on human mental development, and Cooley in his vigorous rejection of instinct and his rigorous assertion of plasticity, learning, and communication in human social conduct). Their differences do warrant separate inquiries. In addition, Small and Cooley draw a distinctive significance from man's association and sociability for the place and character of conflict in early human conditions. They accept an essentially Hegelian as opposed to a Darwinian view of conflict.

Environment, the sociability of human nature, learning and speech

Giddings is unique in attempting to account for the transition from and the conversion of anthropoid groups into human groups. In particular, he notes the consequences of alternate periods of isolation and endogenous autonomous development and of contact with exogenous, heteronomous development in the transition and conversion of anthropoid into human groups. Both genetic and congregate groupings were involved. 'At times small bands, dwelling long in secure, more or less isolated environments, and maintaining exclusiveness of association, developed distinctive traits' (Giddings, 1896, p. 220). But at other times perhaps 'the distribution of food, the occurrence of floods or fires, or the movements of enemies' might cause shifts in habitation, occasion contact, provide for exchange of sociocultural traits, or even result in the formation of new groupings (1896, p. 221). 'In such disturbances of life unstable variations quickly perished; stable, helpful variations were communicated from each center of origin to every horde and individual of the species' (1896, p. 221). Giddings concludes (1896, p. 220) that 'no one small group of intermediate creatures contributed all of the acquisitions and that no one place or environment' was the source of all developments. The modifications 'which converted the anthropoid into man were made, exchanged, and multiplied' through 'innumerable minglings of peoples, mixtures of bloods, and blendings of traditions, by means of which the mental and physiological gains made by each group have been communicated to a thousand groups' (1896, p. 220).

In fact, Giddings claims (1896, p. 221) that the 'chief cause of the mental and moral development, and of the anatomical modifications that transformed a sub-human species into man,' was association, which was 'more extended, more intimate, more varied in its phases, than the association practiced by inferior species.' That significant differential is itself due to unique development of speech in the human line of organic evolution. Although he indicates that animals 'use gesture, grimace, tone, utterance, and to a slight extent, articulation, indicatively and denotatively'; and only occasionally do they 'use vocal or other signs connotatively,' man is unique in employing signs denominatively and predicatively (1896, p. 224). Interestingly, Giddings locates (1896, p. 225) the source of this unique human capacity for (true) speech in early festal celebrations involving 'bodily play movements in imitation of actions, rhythmic beating, some approach to song, and social interest.' The mental exultation of such occasions fixed attention 'upon vocal sounds' which were used as signs as distinct from 'the things signified' (1896, p. 225). (Thus, they were employable denominatively.) Conventionalized as names, these signs became the 'movable types of speech,' i.e., they were utilized predicatively.

The acquisition of speech had a profound significance for humankind and typically human association. First, it permitted the development of a human nature which is 'pre-eminently [a] social nature,' though by no means has the 'primordial animal trait' of self-interest been displaced (1896, pp. 225). Second, human consciousness of kind has become 'more profound, more inclusive, more discriminating, more varied in its colouring' than that found at the animal level (1896, p. 225). Third, the primary elements of desire, which 'originate in the fundamental physiological processes of nutrition and reproduction,' can become infinitely multiplied at the secondary level; i.e., by thought (1896, pp. 226, 227). Fourth, individual differences can be elaborated into inequalities and become the bases of desires to excel and to emulate (1896, p. 228). Finally, mental activity is itself enhanced and the bases of primitive life are expanded to provide for the development of a differentiated culture or tradition; i.e., the economic, the juridical, the political, personal, aesthetic, and religious (1896, pp. 239–54).

However, Cooley was unique in emphasizing the dependence of human beings on groups, the antiquity of human society, and the indispensability of communication for (human) group life. He unmistakably associated the plasticity of the behavior of the (neonate) human organism with the (learned) acquisition of specific modes of conduct in conjunction with communication in human societies. Although Cooley explicitly recognized the existence of the inherited bases of race and inherited individual differences in capacity, aptitude, disposition, temperament, and psychic dispositions, he emphasized the *in*applicability of the word 'instinct' to 'most human behavior' (1964, pp. 24, 4, 18). Animal behavior is distinctively determined by (innate) instincts (1966, p. 199). However, the most conspicuous general feature of man's evolution is the plasticity, modifiability, or teachability of the responses of the (early) human organism. Humans acquire or learn their conduct from society. Most importantly, humankind is subject to universal socialization in primary groups in conjunction with the learning of verbal communication and the acquisition of a social human nature which is constituted of such primary ideals or sentiments as moral unity, loyalty, truth, service, kindness, rightness, and freedom.

Cooley was apparently convinced that communication was characteristic of the group life of man's ancestors. Pre- or non-verbal communication, including 'facial expression, in-articulate cries and songs, and a variety of imitative sounds and actions' arousing sympathy 'permitted the simpler kinds of general ideas to be formed' and became the medium for the early development of tradition and convention (1962, pp. 67–8). The purposeful reproduction of instinctive motions and cries or of the sounds, forms, and movements of the exterior world in order to recall associated ideas is the basis of all kinds of conventional communication. Indeed, artificial gesture language was probably well organized before speech had developed significantly. Cooley suggests (1962, p. 68):

> Even without words life may have been an active and continuous mental whole, not dependent for its unity upon mere heredity,

but bound together by some conscious community in the simpler sorts of thought and feeling, and by the transmission and accumulation of these through tradition. There was probably cooperation and instruction of a crude sort in which was the germ of future institutions.

Furthermore, a context of primary relations would seem to provide the setting, e.g., some primitive form of assembly, in which 'speech itself . . . [was] born. Just as children invent words in the eagerness of play and slang arises among gangs of boys on the street, so earliest men were perhaps incited to the invention of language by a certain ecstacy and self-forgetting audacity, like that of the poet, sprung from the excitement of festal meetings' (1962, p. 109). Speech and language do involve, 'almost from the first, a conventional development of communication, springing out of spontaneous signs but soon losing evident connection with them, a system of standard symbols existing for the mere purpose of conveying thought' (1962, p. 62). This 'achievement of speech is commonly and properly regarded as the distinctive trait of man as the gate by which he emerged from his pre-human state' (1962, p. 70).

Although speech-language, words-ideas, and thinking were elicited initially by association, they in turn exercised a significant influence on the nature of early association itself. 'Ideas regarding the chief interests of primitive life . . . were defined, communicated, and extended' (1962, p. 71). Public opinion came to be crystallized into current sayings which served as rules and they in turn were enlarged and interrelated as institutions (1962, p. 71). Preserved in words or other symbols, ideas could be 'stored up in a continuing whole, constantly growing in bulk and diversity' (1962, p. 69). The experiences of the mind were 'foreseen, mapped out and interpreted by all the wisdom of the past,' so that a mind 'has not only its own experience but that of the race' (1962, p. 70). Formulated verbally as projections of the mind, ideas immediately react upon the mind to further fix, stimulate, and develop some thoughts and not others (1962, p. 64).[4] This circumstance affected the 'natural capacities of man, perhaps by the direct inheritance of acquired social habits and aptitudes, certainly by the survival of those who, having these, were more fitted than others to thrive in social life' (1962, p. 71). A more 'rational and human kind of thinking and feeling arose' (1962, p. 70). If man 'was human when speech began to be used, [he] rapidly became more so, and went on accumulating a social heritage' (1962, p. 71).

Process (es), relations, and structure in the nature of the social

This conception that human association actually had its origins in a pre-human (or animal) social existence prior to human organic origins does involve some notions about the social as inter- and/or multi-personal relations and as activities (or processes) which diverge substantially from the companion views of the conception and explanation of human social origins after human organic origins. Manifestly, the notion of social as relations is predicated on a view of human nature as substantially other-oriented and other-regarding, i.e., social and sociable, if not also amicable and to some extent capable of altruism. Accordingly, too, the assertion of the temporal priority or precedence or of the basic pre-dominance of one inter- and/or multi-personal process over others is not accepted generally. Small and Cooley rejected any exclusively Darwinian conception of conflict or struggle. Cooley agreed with Small's denial (1905, p. 369) of the Social Darwinist thesis that the social process is simply struggle mitigated by acceptance of the inevitable and cooperation merely stifled conflict. And Small concurred with Cooley's insistence (1966, pp. 36, 39) that 'both conflict and cooperation have their places' in the social process and, indeed, both are 'phases of one process which always involves something of both.' (Although Small conceded that 'conflict is the active factor' in the earlier stages of the social process, he insisted (1905, pp. 200, 203) that 'some measure of conjunction of interests' did exist (cf. Cooley, 1962, pp. 200, 201). However, Giddings seemed willing to accept a Darwinist view of conflict and, therefore, he resembled Ward and especially Sumner and Keller in many contexts.[5]) Small and Cooley disputed the occurrence of absolute and implacable hostility and the frequent termination of disputes by violence and extermination of the losers among earliest human aggregates. Physical and social differences are not believed to be constantly extinguished as the Darwinian version of struggle for existence and survival of the fittest might suggest. Instead, they are retained in some accommodation and are incorporated in a new relationship, a new synthesis. Small and Cooley are substantially committed to a dialectical Hegelian view of conflict (see chapter 9, pp. 239–41).

For Small and Cooley, conflict was only one of several processes, each tending to be followed by another in the general social process. Small basically differentiates a relatively intensive *conflict* or struggle over dissimilar and divergent interests, subsequently a lessening of hostility occurs, then gradual *accommodation* of egoistic interests, their *harmonization*, the emergence of some common interest(s), and thus *moralization*, and finally *socialization* of interests, a recognition of common welfare, and outright *cooperation*.[6] Cooley's delineation of processes includes *competition, conflict* (embracing clash and struggle), some accommodation or *compromise*, with the achievement of a *synthesis* of divergent viewpoints (through pragmatic *selection* and *valuation*), and culmination in *organization* as a whole and *cooperation*. (Giddings also distinguishes more severe and mild forms of *conflict* (whose participants are respectively unlike and unequal versus those alike and equal), *toleration, accommodation, assimilation* (or reciprocal accommodation), *socialization* (of differences), and *cooperation*.[7])

Manifestly, these sociologists do conceive of the relationship of processes to relation and structure differently from Sumner and Keller, Ward, and Ross. The three pre-organic social origins theorists do envisage inter- and/or multi-personal activities or processes (and also relations) as more or less conditioned by the prior existence of some elements of structure.

The post-organic social origins theory

In contrast, Sumner and Keller, Ward, and Ross offered a post-organic account of social genesis of origins which construes the social as evolving sequentially from inter- and/or multi-personal relations, to (inter- and/or multi-personal) activities or processes (with severe conflict eventually transformed into recurrent, structured cooperation), and finally to the relatively permanent group or society. Each later form (or meaning) of the social depends upon the preceding one. The first or earliest, the social as relations, especially derives its character from the nature of biophysical human nature within the prevailing habitat or environment in which earliest human beings had emerged. All three of the theorists agreed in conceiving early man as naturally egoistic, individualistic, selfish, suspicious, fearful, quarrelsome, and prone to violence. (But they were in some disagreement about the location and features of the earliest human habitats and the principles by which human organic evolution and social genesis occurred.)

Environment, scarcity, and the egoism of human nature

Sumner and Keller avoided speculations about man's pre-human ancestors and instead restricted their conjectures to contemporary

113

primitives as a basis for inferring the biopsychic characteristics of early humankind. They did insist that selfishness, egoism, fear, suspicion, impulsiveness, hostility, and bellicosity were characteristic of (early) primitives. But whether these features are to be ascribed to biopsychic human nature as such is open to question. The only psychic capacity with which Sumner and Keller endowed human nature was the capacity to discriminate between pleasure and pain as men and women endeavored to satisfy their basic needs-wants (e.g., hunger and sex). Ordinarily, consciousness-reason had a negligible role in human behavior, for it was only substantial recurrent pain which would evoke consciousness and reflection (on past experiences). Presumably the characteristics of selfishness, etc., stem from early humankind's responses to endemic and exacerbated hunger in relation to scarce resources and the niggardliness of nature, the inhospitable climate, an unfriendly topography (of the early marginal environments), along with an ineffectual technology and the absence of any interpersonal organization. Organic evolution and social genesis are a consequence of the Darwinian processes of individual organic variations, (scarcity and the) struggle for existence, and selection-adaptation by survival of the fit(test).

By contrast, Ward employed a broad base of speculations for inferring the nature of early biopsychic human nature. He endeavored to establish the kinds of biopsychic characteristics which man's simian or anthropoid ancestors had possessed, the nature of the earliest human organic forms, the geological eras of their origins, and the habitats in which they were found. On the basis of morphological and taxonomic evidences, Ward concludes (1968, I, pp. 451, 452) that 'nothing could certainly be more reasonable . . . than that the human race has descended by a very long course of gradual modifications from the family of apes which it resembles in so many respects' and which he regards as devoid of substantial 'innate social sentiments.' The pre-human animal probably appeared in Southern Asia, possibly Central Asia, and certainly somewhere in the Old World (1970, p. 202; 1968, I, p. 444). An animal-ancestor of man such as Pithecanthropus was already widely distributed by the late Tertiary or the early Quaternary (geological) era (1970, p. 196; 1968, I, p. 444).

Ward seems to emphasize especially the equipment with some means of attack and thus the capacity for injuring others, the ability to eat all types of food objects including organisms, the frequency and intensity of the expression of the passions (e.g., hunger and sex), and the considerable development of reason (but especially in the service of passion) for characterizing the ancestors of and early members of mankind. Presumably the descent to terrestrial existence is involved in the biopsychic modifications of early humankind which are required for the development of association. Certainly, the shift to a terrestrial life does promote a tendency to erect posture, enhances manual dexterity, induces bipedal locomotion, provides for the development of the double curvature of the spine, stimulates brain development, increases cranial capacity, expands intelligence or reason, which is linked in turn to augmented flexibility in the use of the vocal chords and the acquisition of speech (1968, I, p. 429–38). The 'development of the cerebral hemispheres, of speech, and society must have gone on simultaneously, each mutually reacting in a favorable manner upon the others' (1968, I, p. 454). But the 'cause of causes' (the *causa causarum*) was the antecedent human mental superiority (1968, I, p. 455).

In Ward's case, selfishness, egoism, fear, suspicion, impulsiveness, hostility, and bellicosity are characteristic of early human nature and early inter- and/or multi-personal relations (1968, I, p. 454; 1970, p. 556), although he does distinguish between a condition of earliest solitariness (and autarchy) and a subsequent early condition of recurrent struggle and conflict (or anarchy). These psychic dispositions are part of the inherited legacy which early man had received from his animal ancestors. Ward's own comments do suggest change (and/or inconsistency) in his views about the scarcity or abundance of resources and the harshness or complaisance of early human habitats. He does invoke the Darwinian principles of organic variation, (scarcity and) struggle for existence, and selection-adaptation through survival of the fit(test). However, he makes even more prominent use of the Lamarckian principles of use and disuse (in relation to the inheritance of acquired characteristics through persistent environmental stimulation of organs and their functions or the lack thereof) which permit him to emphasize the development of the brain and the enhancement of reason in the evolution of permanent association. (Indeed, the very nature of biopsychic human nature forces undergo gradual modification so that the essential (or physical or ontogenetic-phylogenetic) forces are increasingly supplemented and complemented by the non-essential (or spiritual, socio-genetic, or moral-aesthetic-intellectual) forces.)

Ross seems to subscribe to the same conception of the nature of biopsychic human nature and inter- and/or multi-personal relations among earliest humankind. Ross does, for instance, claim

115

(1969, p. 8) that early human males were prevailingly quarrelsome, savage, bloodthirsty, warlike, and solitary. Presumably these features are derived from an earlier animal inheritance as are certain elementary motor and emotional reactions. His Darwinian evolutionism is revealed in his declaration that such features of individuals in relation to others in the same or different aggregates are advantageous or disadvantageous relative to their recurrent biophysical environmental circumstances and that they survive or perish accordingly. Ross does propose that such early environmental circumstances do change and that, therefore, the males with previously adaptive characteristics gradually fail to survive because association itself becomes conducive to survival. Selection in society puts a premium on the more amiable type of man. Gradually, the 'disorderly and blood thirsty spirits are drained away and devoured by the sword, while the more peaceable elements of the population gain a steadily increasing preponderance' (and betake 'themselves to group life sooner than the rest') (1969, p. 8). This shift is accompanied by the increasing prevalence of persons in the population with the several natural (social) sentiments, e.g., sympathy, sociability, a sense of justice, and a fear of resentment. Accordingly, association results primarily from a deterministic, non-rational Darwinian process which paradoxically culminates in increasing sensitivity-awareness induced with the possession of the particular natural social sentiments.

Significance of conflict as a process in the early human condition

Significantly, Sumner and Keller particularly, Ward (especially in his *Dynamic Sociology*), Ross, and even Giddings (sic!) envisaged earliest humankind as existing in a condition of recurrent, internecine conflict because the earliest humans were fundamentally organisms involved in a struggle with organic and inorganic nature for survival. All of these earliest sociologists adopt a more or less materialistic-objectivist-Darwinized outlook which departs implicitly if not explicitly from Hobbes. Inter- and/or multi-personal conflict tends to begin as an extension of organic conflict, especially the struggle for existence. Some of the antagonists may be pitted in a death struggle with extermination the outcome for the losers.

Sumner's views were unmistakably clear. All life, including that of humankind, requires maintenance 'by a struggle against nature' and by 'a competition with other forms of life' (1970, p. 173). Like other organisms, men are implicated in the struggle for existence against a nature which is both physical and organic. But men are also involved in a competition of life with all organic forms – e.g., 'beasts, reptiles, insects, and plants' – and with members of their own kind (1970, p. 173).

Accordingly, Sumner and Keller contend that early humankind and nature are parties to a common struggle for existence, in which climate, topography, resources for supporting life, the flora and fauna of the habitat, the level of technology available, and the relative population density of the human aggregate, or more precisely the land–man ratio, were all crucial factors in determining who lived and who died in the struggle. The greater the number of persons, the more niggardly nature is in providing support, the less efficient or more primitive the technology; the more predominant and imperious hunger is likely to be in relation to other basic human nature forces and the more intensive will be the struggle for existence generally. Thus, early humans who had emerged in (or soon came to live in) an inhospitable environment of a niggardly nature, under conditions of natural scarcity, severe physical and organic perils and monstrous calamities, and possessed only a rudimentary technology, were necessarily preoccupied with sheer physical survival, especially satisfaction of their hunger and sex appetites. Necessarily, they came into conflict over the scarcity of the food supply and turned to the method of the organic world at hand: violence (Keller, 1927, pp. 373, 19; Sumner, 1959, p. 116).

Ward's views on the relative involvement of prehuman and early human creatures in conflict appear contradictory. In one passage in *Pure Sociology* (p. 202), he referred to the earliest prehuman stage of biopsychic development as a 'halcyon' era with conditions of 'natural abundance' in which human collisions 'could be avoided by migration.' But in another passage of the same work, he noted (1970, p. 511) that the prehuman being was caught in 'a struggle for existence like the rest' of the organic world and held in the grasp of the 'iron law of competition' as were 'all other organic beings.' Apparently, this circumstance prevailed because 'Everywhere and always the environment . . . has withheld the necessary supplies, has doled out its resources in a niggardly way, and has starved to death by far the greater number of all the creatures that have been born' (1970, p. 511).

In *Dynamic Sociology*, he indicated that earliest man (rather than his animal ancestors) had increasingly developed his rationality which allowed him to deal effectively with the physical and organic hazards of existence and thus to augment in numbers. With this expansion of population, the possibility of encroachment and conflict increased both from within a given aggregate and from without. Consequently, the likelihood of more frequent and intense hostilities arose for early humankind.

Ross's early remarks in *Social Control* (especially p. 8) indicate that he assumed a recurrent condition of conflict and struggle among aboriginal human beings. In his view, the preponderating strains of early males were bellicose, quarrelsome, of savage and solitary mood, and likely to be disorderly and bloodthirsty. The implications for a condition of early conflict and struggle are evident.

Interestingly, Giddings also adhered to similar views on the prevalence of conflict among early humankind, even though he did insist that it had been social from its very origins and before. However, an inheritance of egoism, the persistence of 'instincts of conflict which are kept alive by the necessity of destroying life to maintain life,' the presence of 'original differences of nature and habitat that have not yet been blended or neutralized' in the emerging aggregate, and the threat of natural crises or calamities (e.g., starvation) provoked conflict among early men (1896, p. 113). Indeed, Giddings declared (1896, p. 123) that the 'exceptionally weak have been killed off by the strong, and the exceptionally strong have been killed off by their own rashness or by a combined resistance of individuals of average power.' From Giddings's arguments, it would be difficult to infer that opposition in general or conflict in particular was substantially less frequent or intensive in its consequences in his conception of early human existence than it was in Sumner's or Ward's views of the earliest human condition.

Toleration, compromise, accommodation in the cycle of processes

Interestingly, all early sociologists distinguished between severe and mild forms of opposition, the emergence of some form of modus vivendi or equilibrium, and finally the appearance of collaboration with more or less structured cooperation (the group or society). Sumner and Keller recognize (the more severe) 'struggle' (i.e., struggle for existence) and the (less severe) 'competition of life,' from an implied equilibrium, and the appearance of ('antagonistic') cooperation (with organization and specialization). In Ward's view (1970, p. 175), the more intense phases are collision, conflict antagonism, and opposition and they are followed by the milder phases of antithesis, competition, and interaction. Equilibrium seems to be the relatively immediate sequel of accommodation and compromise following opposition in any of its more extensive and intensive forms. (Achievement of an equilibrium (via equilibration) is not the same as or immediately equivalent to compromise, for Ward lists (1970, pp. 212, 215) 'conquest, struggle, compromise and equilibration' as the states in the evolutionary process.) For Ward (1898, p. 170), 'Society itself [is a] . . . state of equilibrium.' In Ross's case (1919, pp. 96–8; 1920, pp. x-xvi; 1969, p. 250) it is virtually impossible to ascertain just at what phase the 'equilibrium of interests and balance of egoisms' occurs, i.e., at what point it emerges following the processes of toleration, compromise, and accommodation. Each sociologist provides his own somewhat distinctive explanation for the gradual shift from relatively unmitigated struggle and severe conflict to some form of equilibrium, balance, or accommodation.

Although Sumner and Keller are pervasively mechanistic-materialistic in their formulations, they do ultimately invoke consciousness-reflection. They indicate (1927, p. 751) that individuals living in the same environment, experiencing the same conditions, sharing the same problems of life policy, subject to the same 'ills of life,' and oriented by the same organically or neurally-based pleasure and pain considerations would be prompted to reflect, 'however rudimentary' it might be. Pain occasioned by the errors of experience will stimulate reflection. Thus, experiences of an individual in a given habitat may lead him to perceive that he can avail himself of a particular source of food only with help from others. Or, presumably, he may recognize that his own survival against natural calamities or beasts of prey within the ambit of his own environment or threats from external human invaders require a combination of efforts of several individuals whose interests are similarly menaced. Under such jeopardy, men may at least temporarily submerge their differences and antagonisms in order to combine and cooperate to secure their own individual survivals. Sometimes, the several individuals who are distributed throughout the same environment and for whom the conditions and problems of life policy are the same will be confronted by a common alternative. Any individual 'and the others may so interfere with each other that all shall fail, or they may combine, and by cooperation raise their efforts against nature to a higher power' (1959, p. 16). Failure means failure to survive in the struggle for existence, i.e., elimination.

Although their reflection attendant upon the experience of pain does resemble the operation of Hobbes's egoistic rationality, it is not a reason prior to but posterior to experience (1927, pp. 13, 14, 18, 19). Men did not consciously and deliberately choose association as such; they merely combined and antagonistically cooperated for a given occasion (e.g., to secure food or protection). Sumner and Keller claim that primitive men recognized that association requires an unacceptable restriction upon liberty. Still, the necessities of the struggle for existence were inexorable. Recurrence of critical situations thus repeatedly demands that isolation and solitariness – which are consonant with individual liberty – must be abandoned in some instances and association accepted, even with its limitations, for survival. Men need protection and so they are compelled to associate irrespective of whether or not they had so willed (1927, p. 20). Powerless separately, men in association acquire an augmented strength with organization (1927, p. 14). 'The offensive against nature can be managed better under organization, and so can the defensive, against both nature and fellow-men' (1927, p. 15).

Apparently, recurrence of such crises demanding antagonistic cooperation tends to make association itself habitual and thus relatively permanent. Men in a given habitat, especially when threatened externally by others, develop organized relations as a society. They become what Sumner calls a 'primitive society,' whose size was determined by the conditions of the struggle for existence.

Even more a Lamarckian than he was a Darwinian in his exposition of evolutionary mechanisms, Ward stressed the enhancement of reason which changing environmental conditions stimulated and which eventually led to the resolution of the severe conflict prevailing among early mankind during the second stage of its development. That conflict was itself the result of an expansion of human populations made possible by reason and its effective surmounting of the physical and organic hazards of existence. However, men's increasing rationality must have enabled them to perceive the advantageousness of mutual defense or protection to be afforded by association. Still, such association was only temporary and intermittent and embodied 'none of the elements of permanency' (1968, I, p. 467). Relatively permanent association can develop only as each individual agrees 'to rules for his own protection' and ceases 'commissions of violence' (1968, I, pp. 513–14). Association comes to be a desired end – as 'the desire of each [individual] to protect himself by sustaining the community came to exceed the desire to gratify immediate personal wants which were incompatible with the existence of society' (1968, I, p. 394). (Note the implicit social contract.) The shift to permanent association and society is identified by Ward with the transition from the anarchic to the politarchic stage, i.e., with the appearance of the state or polity. Human society is distinctively a product of man's 'reason and arose by insensible degrees pari passu with the development of his brain' (1898, pp. 90–1). It is 'the result of the perceived advantage which it yields' and comes 'into existence only in proportion as that advantage was perceived by . . . intellect' (1898, p. 91).

Ward also envisaged the permanent group as requiring a sustaining emotional bond which derives jointly from affection or love, on the one hand, and altruism and sympathy, on the other. The basis of such emotional bond stems from mother–child and from sibling–sibling affection and they are in turn involved in the expansion of familial into kinship relations (e.g., horde, gens or clans, phratry, and tribe). Mother love is the foundation of consanguineal love which is limited to persons of the same blood or kin (1970, p. 427). In turn, 'altruism begins with the blood bond' and extends outward from the horde and beyond (1970, p. 427). Altruism is itself the foundation of sympathy, which involves a peculiar linkage of reason and emotion (1970, p. 423; cf. 1968, I, p. 396). Because sympathy is the basis of morality, it is indisputably consequential for the full evolution of permanent association or society. And thus for Ward, reason and emotion are important in decreasing hostility-conflict and in increasing amiability-cooperation and the appearance of enduring or permanent association.

Like Ward, Ross also envisages the biopsychic evolution of humanity and the genesis of association as occurring concomitantly in and through response to a variety of environments according to Lamarckian principles (even though he disavows these). Gradually, changing conditions of existence, selection, and heredity decrease the numbers of egoistic-individualistic-aggressive individuals and increase those with altruistic-social-amiable proclivities so that by the time historically existent primitive peoples have emerged, mankind has acquired a human nature with social sentiments and a prevailing inclination to associate naturally. Thus, Ross stresses emotion.

It was in the family that selection operated first to preserve more 'sociable' women. Those who did not possess 'the feeling of tenderness for the helpless [i.e., the young]' were gradually eliminated (1969, p. 8). And so because they were less quarrelsome than men, women 'learned to associate' first (1969, p. 8).

Changing conditions and the operation of selection also eventually affected the prevailing type of males. The bullies tended to kill one another, to be extinguished by the combined action of the peaceable, or to be 'disposed of by the agents of authority' (1969, p. 8). A predominance of males 'of savage and solitary mood' became disadvantageous because it tended to prevent cooperation within the aggregate in the event of contact and conflict with other aggregates. Other things being equal, the larger and better-knit the aggregate, 'the better its chances of success in conflict' (1969, p. 8). With the possibility of 'choice between warfare and peaceful industry, those inclined to be disorderly and bloodthirsty are gradually eliminated and those disposed to be peaceable become predominant in the population' (1969, p. 8). Thus, selection tends to increase the number of individuals who are endowed with several natural social sentiments conducive to association.

Each sentiment – sympathy, sociability, the sense of justice and fear of resentment – has its function or functions in facilitating association. The essence of most social relationships, sympathy prompts beneficence, restricts excessive discipline and subordination, and engenders a sensitivity to the conditions of others. Sociability fosters 'friendly interest, spontaneous helpfulness, and a sense of solidarity' (1969, p. 14). Complementary in nature, the sense of justice and the fear of resentment both operate to induce or preserve equitable rights and duties of individual members. The former inclines a person voluntarily to recognize the rights of another and presumably one's obligations to him. The latter involves a fear of a possible reprisal from a second person if his rights are not observed.

Acting under the spontaneous and unreflecting prompting of these natural inclinations, early primitive mankind came to live under conditions of a natural (social) order – without any social imperatives, arbitrary codes, traditional requirements, conventional standards, social institutions to be protected, or any 'vague corporate welfare' to be safeguarded (1969, p. 47). Under appropriate conditions, these natural sentiments – which bear a remarkable resemblance to Cooley's primary ideals or sentiments – induce an increasingly permanent association with a natural social orderliness.

Interestingly, Giddings – who insisted that man who had always been a social animal but displayed considerable tendencies to conflict in his earliest conditions – does offer a purely naturalistic account of the emergence of an equilibrium, i.e., the termination of conflict. An equilibrium is developed because the exceptionally weak and the exceptionally strong have been eliminated (1896, p. 123). The survivors 'are too nearly equal in strength for one to hope to vanquish the other; and they are obliged to live on' in terms of an equilibrium of toleration (1898, p. 52). The human organisms who remain thus are more or less objectively similar or alike (which, in turn, becomes the basis for subjective similarities, e.g., reason and feelings in the consciousness of kind).

By contrast, Small – who also argued for the constancy of association and the frequency of conflict among early human beings – seems to have endowed the species with an expediential, pragmatic, or utilitarian rationality by which conflict would eventually be terminated. Apparently, men do judge utility or calculate consequences or costs which, in turn, leads to the weakening of (exclusivist) egoistic antagonism, the emergence of a type of modus vivendi, and an advance towards the recognition of equal value in other individuals (1905, pp. 328–32).

Cooperation and the emergence of structure

In Ross's case, the transition from equilibrium or balance to outright harmony and cooperation is so gradual that it is virtually impossible to separate and distinguish the one process-phase from the other. It may not be as even and gradual for Ward and Sumner. But ultimately, the effect of equilibrium and the cessation of active, intense, and/or pervasive conflict is to introduce the process of cooperation so that the members of the aggregate more or less can and do act together, become a whole, or find themselves permanently associating. The process of cooperation is explicitly invoked by Sumner and Keller, Ward, and Ross. The two Yale sociologists do contemplate conflict as culminating eventually in cooperation, even though the residue of conflict persists in the term 'antagonistic cooperation.' (Initially at least the implication of unwillingness is present and equilibrium is merely the suppression of outright, active struggle or conflict in the face of impending disaster and failure to survive.) Ward does manifestly view (1970, p. 175) what begins in 'collision, conflict, antagonism, and opposition' as leading through the intermediate processes eventually to a 'modus vivendi, or compromise, and ending in collaboration and cooperation.' Ross unmistakably indicates (1919, pp. 96, 98) cooperation as a type of process too. Of course, differences among the three cannot be ignored, as, for instance, the role of consciousness-reason and/or emotion in the gradual diminution of hostility-conflict and in the emergence of amiability-cooperation. Yet, these differences must also be understood in relation to other differences.

Varying social ontological positions and the explanation of social origins

Sumner and Keller, Ward, and Ross do differ from one another in several ways in their efforts to account for the transition from relatively unmitigated struggle and harsh conflict to some sort of equilibrium and balance and eventually to (a) relatively permanent, fixed, or patterned cooperation, i.e., society. They disagreed over whether social origins should be construed and explained more broadly or more narrowly (whether accounts should begin with conjectures about more remote animal ancestors and transitional humanoid forms and their environments (as Ward proposed and Ross implied) or with the simplest contemporary primitives and their habitats (as Sumner and Keller argued)). They were in opposition whether both Lamarckian and Darwinian or only Darwinian interpretations of the principles or mechanisms of evolution were to be invoked (e.g., Ward and Ross versus Sumner and Keller). And, finally, they were in dispute over just what weight and significance should be attached to factors in the deterministic-indeterministic, involuntary-voluntary, or matter-mind controversies (e.g., extrinsic biophysical conditions – intrinsic instincts versus consciousness – reason – feeling). Actually, this last dispute is perhaps the most consequential, for it permits a comprehensive, systematic, and integrated restatement of the varying components and relationships in the post-organic theory of social origins, along with their continuities-discontinuities with the pre-organic theory of social origins. In essence, then, the recognition of the sociological relevance of the (ontological) traditions of materialism and idealism has pervasive implications for explaining the origins of the social as inter- and/or multi-personal relations and activities (or processes) and, finally, the social as a relatively permanent, structured entity.

Applied to the social realm, the philosophical (or more accurately, ontological) traditions of materialism and idealism yield two sociological counterparts, a 'social materialism' and a 'social idealism.' (Each can be understood most readily if it is conceived as a diametrically opposite view of the nature of social reality, i.e., as contrary exclusive monisms (see Scheme III, B, 4).) 'Social materialism' asserts that human social existence and its various forms (e.g., inter- and/or multi-personal relations, activities or processes, and relatively permanent groups) are essentially explicable as a form of matter, matter in motion, or energy, i.e., as something physical, chemical, or biological (e.g., electrical impulses, gland secretions, reflexes). In direct opposition, 'social idealism' asserts that social existence and its various forms derive from mind, soul, spirit, conciousness, feeling, will, intention, purpose, attitude, and/or meaning. The former position tends to assume an objective and the latter a subjective stance toward social phenomena (their reality stems from their being constituted as a type of object versus their being constituted by human beings' distinctive capacity to be subjects).

However, early American theorists adopted a dualistic rather than a monistic viewpoint toward the nature of social reality: their conceptions embodied both (social) materialism and idealism. Not one of them (not even Sumner or Keller) was exclusively a 'social materialist' or (for instance, Cooley) exclusively a 'social idealist.' They were all patently dualistic in their accounts of social origins. (However, their arguments about social structure and especially social change do reveal varying emphases. Sumner and Keller are predominantly materialistic and Cooley a predominant idealist. Ward, Giddings, and perhaps Ross occupy a more intermediate position or a relatively balanced materialist-idealist place. See below.)

Sumner's and Keller's dualism does seem substantially materialistic in their theory of social origins. They view human beings essentially as forms of organisms whose behaviors are to be explained as an adaptation to (consciousless, purposeless) biophysical conditions of existence. The social as relation(-ship) begins as the material-objective likeness of two or more individuals occupying similar or contiguous points in space and time; i.e., it involves similarity in the biopsychic nature of the human units (e.g., needs–wants and a disposition to seek pleasure–avoid pain) in an aggregate existing at a common point in time and so distributed throughout a common or similar habitat that they confront essentially similar conditions of existence. Because these needs (e.g., hunger) are so imperious and impel a 'blundering' or impulsive effort at satisfaction in relation to scarce resources, they tend to transform the merely multi-individual relationship of coevality (in time) and contiguity (in space) into activity (or behavioral process), which tend to assume the form of struggle or conflict. Thus, men's behaviors are 'like products of natural forces . . . unconsciously set in operation' (1959, p. 4). Men do not tend to think or reason first; they act or behave impulsively. Only as they recurrently fail to achieve gratification of their needs and/or experience pain do they respond consciously, subjectively, reflectively. Under these circumstances and with a series of threats arising within or on the periphery of their habitat, men restrain their antagonisms, associate, and cooperate – even though it is antagonistic cooperation. Thus, reflection is invoked to prompt association but it is manifestly hedged by considerations of pleasure–pain – just as are the adoption of common modes of behavior so necessary to (persisting, effective) cooperation.

In marked contrast, Ward and Ross ascribe to consciousness a much more prominent function in the beginnings of association and the relatively permanent group. Ward's explanation confers a direct, explicit, and substantial importance to both reason and emotion. Subscribing to the Lamarckian view (in opposition to Sumner and Keller), Ward did envisage an expanding role for reason, which was stimulated by favorable environmental circumstances and which itself prompted the rise of permanent association. What reason initiated emotion solidified and sustained. Thus, the social as relationship and as activities (or processes) does presuppose consciousness or the recognition of mutual advantage (and disadvantage).

But Ross envisages earliest (and thus 'lowest savage') man as a 'creature of appetite and propensity,' who is 'anything but rational' (1969, p. 180). In his account of the rise of association, consciousness is included but it emerges as an accompaniment of the changing emotional nature of human nature in response to changing conditions of existence.[8] An endowment with natural social sentiments is a concomitant of the increasing appearance of more amiable males. Apparently, the acquisition of permanent association is a gradual process which is not necessarily directly conscious (except that at some point those more amiable and sociable males might be inclined to eliminate the 'bullies'). Yet consciousness, feeling, and sensitivity are associated with the increasing effectiveness of the social sentiments as individuals interact with one another. (Admittedly, Ross's explanation virtually precludes an explicit separation of the social as inter- and/or multi-personal relationship, activity and (increasingly permanent) group or society.)

Significantly, the three early sociologists who accepted the pre-organic theory of human social origins are at least relatively balanced materialists-idealists or predominantly idealist in their outlook. Giddings seems to fit the former category and Small and Cooley display features appropriate to the latter designation.

Still, Giddings manifests some seemingly paradoxical characteristics. On the one hand, he contends that human beings as descendants of pack-living anthropoids had always lived in a social condition. On the other, he apparently argues that the earliest condition among men did involve considerable inter-personal antagonisms and hostility – much in the fashion of Sumner! Inter- and/or multi-personal relations do apparently presuppose a basis of inter-personal similarities, though Giddings actually refers both to awareness of likeness between self and others and to the similarity between the (immediate) environments of self and others in the aggregate. Existing as part of a common habitat, the individuals in the aggregate are subject to the operation of the process of struggle for existence, elimination of the unfit, and survival of the fit(test). Individuals in the aggregate, therefore, come to possess objective (physical) likenesses, which in turn become the bases of subjective likenesses!

Such like-mindedness and like activity (or behavior) emerge reciprocally in the situation. On the one hand, persons in the aggregate evolve from multi-individual reaction to a common situation or stimulus, to inter-individual stimulation and response, and finally to co-individual behavior. On the other, an inherited sensory or organic sympathy (with which all members of the aggregate are endowed because they are hereditarily alike) becomes reflective sympathy as contacts lead persons to perceive and discuss their likenesses regarding both themselves and their situation (Giddings, 1901, pp. 91–9). They come to like their likenesses (i.e., to like one another). What had been an aggregate of objectively (organically) like organisms becomes a subjective unity of like-minded and consciously like co-acting selves and others (i.e., an organized group). Their activity in concert is more action (in the technical sense) than it is behavior, though Giddings is thus in a paradoxical situation. He has explicitly committed himself to a pre-organic theory of social origins but the implicit structure of his argument concurs with the post-organic theory of social origins.

Even though consciousness may have its beginnings in simpler forms of life, it is for Small and Cooley the (actually or potentially) distinguishing feature of human association. Small concedes (1905, p. 211) that the influence of instinct may be at 'a maximum' under conditions 'in the lowest tribal state,' but he does not exclude all relevance of consciousness. Although it may be at a 'minimum,' consciousness is still present (1905, p. 211). That which 'at last separates human association from the associations of other animals . . . is the influence of mind upon mind' (1905, p. 622). Manifestly, that influence is exercised – at least to some extent – consciously among early human beings. To claim that the human plane is encountered when 'choices, as distinct from physiological cause and effect, begin to modify individual action' is also to assert the presence of consciousness (1905, p. 207).

For Small (and for Cooley), the fact that humankind has always lived in a more or less permanent state of association means that (inter- and/or multi-personal) relations, activities or processes, and structure cannot be rigidly and sharply separated. Each one is linked with the other two. A relationship always arises within some prior structure and tends to entail some activity or process. And similarly for each of the others. Most importantly, some modicum of consciousness is always more or less present in relationship, activity, and structure.

Denying that humankind ever had its prevailing bases of behavior or conduct in innate, specific, instincts, that it was predominantly antisocial in its dispositions, or that suggestion, habit, and impulse are radically and sharply separable from consciousness, will, and choice, the logic of Cooley's position is (1964, pp. 52–3) that earliest mankind did have a psychic life that was fundamentally – and certainly potentially – similar to the mental activity of its modern counterpart. Manifestly, earliest human beings were not reducible to material atoms or their activities to the collision of inert masses. Both by virtue of their (plastic) natures and the universality of socialization within primary groups, inter- and/or multi-personal relations and activities involve some orientation of individuals to one another's feelings and sentiments. Social relations and activities are necessarily based on and involve a socially acquired human nature whose formation in each individual is necessarily accompanied by the development of those social sentiments (1962, p. 28). Because sentiments and ideas are substantially interconnected, interrelated, and interdependent, self-feelings will tend to elicit self-ideas and self-consciousness; and because such self-feelings are stimulated in relation to feelings about others, social feelings will tend to evoke social ideas and social consciousness. Basically affective, inter- and/or multi-personal relations and activities are even for early human beings at least rudimentarily self- and other-conscious.

Once the total social ontological positions of Ward, Ross, Giddings, Small and Cooley have been fully developed to include their views on social-societal structure and change, their adherence to a more or less balanced materialism-idealism or substantial idealism will become more evident. Admittedly, their notions of social origins only render such social ontological developments

128

potentially possible. No one of them seems to argue for a substantial – much less a primary or predominant – role for consciousness, reason or reflection, and selection or choice in the biopsychic nature and the social life of earliest human beings. All of them ascribe a major importance and, indeed, predominance to the material constraints imposed by the biophysical conditions of existence on early humankind and its modes of social existence. Still, all of them are convinced that early mankind and its earliest inter- and multi-personal adjustments or adaptations do exhibit the rudiments of consciousness, reason, and choice. Their involvement in the various features of (social-societal) structure now warrants consideration.

6 The theory and characteristics of primordial social structure

Irrespective of whether early American sociologists endeavored to explain relatively permanent association as originating before or after the appearance of humankind as a definite form of life, they were concerned with the nature and characteristics of social structure. A theory (or theories) of the origin of relatively permanent association is (are) necessarily a theory (or theories) of the origin of society, which must have had a structure or organization. Thus, a theory (or theories) of the origin of relatively permanent association is (are) also a theory (or theories) of the origin of primordial social structure. Clearly, this chapter is logically a continuation of the inquiry of the previous one. Earliest human societies develop a certain number of features of structure, the genesis of which requires examination. But because early sociologists oriented their analysis of social structure toward more general notions and models of structure in the physical and biological sciences, the present chapter begins with a consideration of these more general views.

Generic notions and models of structure

Early theorists did employ the more generic notions of structure from the physical and biological sciences, often in conjunction with machine, mechanism, organism, or an equilibrium of forces. Ward and Cooley are illustrative of the general use of machine, mechanism, and organism as a model of structure generally. Ward, for instance, conceived of a structure as 'an organized mechanism for the storage and . . . expenditure of energy' (1898, p. 48; cf. p. 171). A structure is a machine in that it is a device for 'reducing . . .

130

forces . . . to a state of equilibrium' (1898, p. 171). For Cooley, the organism is the appropriate model for structure or organization. As such, the organism is a system of activities, the parts of which influence one another 'so that they are bound together as an interdependent whole' and can afford an adjustment, adaptability, or workableness to the conditions confronted (Cooley, 1962, pp. 19, 383).

But social structure is conceived even more frequently – if not also more basically – in terms of a general structure, which is the outcome of some sort of adjustive or adaptive equilibrium of forces (e.g., social forces), whether construed as a mechanical equilibrium or an organic equilibrium or as akin to the latter in being an approximate, partial, or moving equilibrium. (See Cynthia Russett, *The Concept of Equilibrium in American Social Thought*, pp. 78–81.) Ward is copiously illustrative of the use of both models of equilibrium in the derivation of structure in general and of social structure in particular. In *Dynamic Sociology* (1968, I, p. 178), he regarded structure as comprising an equilibrium, which is essentially physical and statical, as 'the universal tendency of all forces of the universe to approach the statical condition.' He suggests in his later *Pure Sociology* (p. 183) that structure is the consequence of the mutual checking, constraining, and equilibrating of forces with one another. But in this later work, he also essentially resorts to the model of an organic equilibrium (in Russett's sense), with its accessibility, openness, relevance of external as well as internal factors, time, and the possibility of change. Once created, institutions as units of (social) structure tend, if they persist, to have their equilibrium converted 'into a moving equilibrium' and to be able to adapt 'to both internal and external modification' (Ward, 1970, p. 230).

Giddings is even more explicit than Ward about rejecting a complete, static, or unchangeable-changeless equilibrium (what Russett terms a mechanical equilibrium) as a point of departure for construing social structure. Both living organisms and societies are – according to Giddings – variable systems, in which internal forces reach an approximate (or partial) equilibrium but are prevented from achieving a perfect (or complete) equilibrium by the action of external forces (1896, p. 59). More precisely, any such system represents 'a moving equilibrium' (or in Russett's terms, an organic equilibrium) (1896, p. 59).

Ross and Small also substantially subscribe to organic equilibrium as the most apt model of the phenomenon out of which social structure is generated (Ross, 1969, p. 250; Small, 1905, pp. 580,

597, 595). (Interestingly, Cooley refused to employ the equilibrium notion in interpersonal relations.) And it is entirely evident in Ross's and Small's statements about equilibrium (just as it is also clear from other aspects of Ward's and Giddings's positions) that they do not regard an interpersonal equilibrium as arrived at only through a process which is natural, automatic, deterministic, unconscious, and unintentional (1969, p. 61; Small and Vincent, 1971, p. 336). For Small and for Ross and certainly for Ward and Giddings, the potentiality of change stipulated in the organic, partial, moving, or labile equilibrium presupposes the possibility that both the equilibrium and the related structure derive from some degree of consciousness and the exercise of choice and intentionality on the part of the individual persons involved. Any assumption of a monistic materialistic social ontology is precluded.

Thus, the six basic features of social structure in early American sociology do tend, more or less, to presuppose the social ontological dualism (of materialism-idealism) elaborated at the close of the previous chapter. These features include: (1) evidence of some social identity (either objective or subjective); (2) a common set of desires, interests, purposes, ends, or objectives; (3) a more or less organized or structured activity of the social whole; (4) rules and values reflecting and defined by a notion of the common good or welfare of the whole; (5) a requisite integration, cohesion, or solidarity; and (6) a process of orienting and mobilizing structured action (which for some theorists was prevailingly deterministic but for most of them predominantly voluntaristic) so as to adapt or adjust to the peculiar circumstances of the situation or the conditions of existence.

On the basis of the analysis just offered (above), it is also apparent that these six features, directly or indirectly, reflect the main characteristics of the section of the scheme for the analysis of theories of social structure (see Scheme III, E, 2, c).

Of course, the primordial social unit whose structure is to be considered and analyzed is 'earliest' or 'aboriginal' society originating out of the relatively permanent interpersonal association either before or after the human species appeared as a distinguishable, distinctive organic form. Early theorists suggested only that such a group might resemble the most simple primitive society in *size*, would be sufficiently large to be self-sufficient (economically, socially, politically), to perpetuate itself across the generations, and to carry on a common mode of life, and thus would be relatively permanent or exist over an extended period of time (i.e., without a *necessarily* limited *duration*).

Characteristics of primordial social structure

Of course, the six characteristics do presuppose the analysis of origins offered in the last chapter and the model of structure considered above. They do depart from the basic tenets of evolutionary naturalism. They are predicated on the assumption, therefore, that society is adaptive and thus provides for the satisfaction of the biopsychic needs and wants of its member human organisms in terms of the resources and conditions (both hindrances and opportunities) in the situation, habitat, or environment.

(1) Persistent association and aggregate adaptation which are signified by organization presuppose first that the social entity has acquired a definite, distinguishable social identity (but which the differing theoretical orientations construe variously). The predominantly idealists (and subjectivists) from Cooley and Small through to Giddings and Ross employ 'social consciousness' (or some related notion) as the basic concept.[1] (However, basic differences do exist.) Sumner's (and Keller's) predominant materialism (and objectivism) find(s) expression in the distinctive implications of ethnocentrism in relation to the in-group/out-group phenomenon.

Small and Cooley are noticeably similar in their stances. Small declares that at some time or other, and with some degree of clarity or other, 'members of every group perceive that the group exists, that they condition it and are conditioned by it,' that 'individual interests are more or less bound up with the affairs of the group, and that the existence and prosperity of the group are dependent upon the conduct of its . . . members' (1905, pp. 547, 548). In Cooley's perspective, social consciousness is reciprocally associated with self-consciousness and public consciousness. Social consciousness is 'a sense of . . . [one's] relations to other persons, or other persons to one another,' i.e., their sense of relation to each other (1962, p. 5; 1964, p. 119). This social consciousness emerges through communication, discussion, and understanding with each person developing an awareness of others, their personal traits, modes of thought and feeling. And out of this process is likely to arise a public consciousness, 'a group state of mind which is more or less directly aware of itself' (1962, p. 10). Included in this public consciousness is not only my awareness of myself (i.e., personal or self-consciousness) and my consciousness of others (i.e., social consciousness), but my awareness of ideas of others which they hold of me and others (and their awareness of my ideas of them and others) as arise through discussion.

Unlike Small and Cooley, Giddings adopts a conception of social consciousness (and social self-consciousness) which is predicated on the similarity of the contents of the consciousness of the members of an aggregate. Both social consciousness and social self-consciousness are aspects of Giddings's broader notion of the consciousness of kind and associated types of sympathy. Subject to relatively similar stimuli from the relatively similar habitat and characterized by relatively similar organisms (due to selection under similar conditions of existence), members of the aggregate will exhibit multiple simultaneous similar states of consciousness or social consciousness. In turn, such social consciousness will tend to become social self-consciousness because persons as speaking creatures will communicate their states of consciousness and thus will become conscious of the similarity between and among their states of consciousness. Each individual will tend to make both his and others' feelings, thoughts, and judgments the objects of reflection, will judge his and others' mental contents to be similar if not identical, and will act 'with full consciousness that his fellows have come to like conclusions, and will act in like ways' (Giddings, 1896, p. 137).

Ross accepts and endorses Giddings's notion of the consciousness of kind and by implication, social consciousness. But Ross's presentation is especially notable because he emphasizes that consciousness of kind or similarity may also result (dialectically) in relation to consciousness of the dissimilarity with other groups or societies. Such perception of differences can awaken 'a positive antipathy' (1919, p. 263). Interestingly, Ross juxtaposes the sense of like and unlike with what Sumner terms in- and out-groups and the pejorative manifestations of ethnocentrism so directly and intimately that he approaches a recognition of the dialectical relationship between a society's self-consciousness and its consciousness of other societies. For instance, 'Just as the ego attains self-consciousness – so we are told – through the non-ego, a nation "finds" herself through her awareness of other nations' (1919, p. 287).

Sumner's own notion of a social identity is predicated on an objectivist, Hegelian (dialectical) formulation of ethnocentrism in the polarizing, antithetical, and dichotomizing consequences of in- and out-group conflict.[2] Manifestly, Sumner does not tend to conceive of early human societies as being in or remaining in isolation for long periods of time. Contact and conflict will tend to generate objectively a differentiation and polarization of one society vis-à-vis another as in-group versus out-group. Each presumably will develop an ethnocentrism or a 'view of things in which one's own group is the center of everything and all others are scaled and rated with reference to it' (1959, p. 13). To assert that the characteristics of the relationship between the in-group and out-group, the we-group and the others-group, 'are correlatives to each other' seems to mean not only that the characteristics of the others-group are conceived negatively in relation to the we-group but also that the features of the in-group are envisaged positively in relation to the others- (or out-) group (1959, p. 12). For Sumner, therefore, the salient features of the social identities of different earliest societies are thus not to be ascribed to subjective motivation or intention but to the determining objective (and often historical) circumstances which happen to bring the two societies into contact and conflict with one another.

One of two approaches to social identity, Sumner's position does reflect his materialism-objectivism through adapted Hegelian dialectical conflict. The other more idealistic-subjectivist approach invokes the notion of social consciousness – either as the consciousness of selves and others in association (Cooley and Small) or the similarity of states of consciousness of persons in the group (Giddings and Ross). But invariably social identity does presuppose that any society is based on something more or less universal in biopsychic human nature.

(2) More precisely, the social whole that is organized is predicated on a common set of desires, interests, purposes, ends, or objectives, which derive from the various catalogs of social forces or biopsychic human nature needs-wants (but as modified and elaborated by shared, collective experience). In terms of the tenets of evolutionary naturalism, organization or structure must be intrinsically adaptive in the sense that it provides for the satisfaction of the requisite shared needs-wants of the aggregate in relation to the resources, opportunities, restrictions, and hazards of the conditions of existence as given by the habitat or environment. Whether characterized as collective desires, common interests, social ends, etc., they tended to imply that biopsychic needs-wants have been defined, modified, and elaborated by collective experience and learning and oriented to common objects in the society's habitat or situation. They 'pull' or 'attract' action rather than 'pushing' or 'impelling' behavior as the more unmodified social forces do.

In most instances the various catalogs of social forces do provide for or permit classification of such collectively or socially defined desires, ends, or purposes. Ward's five types of social forces, Sumner's and Keller's four varieties of socializing forces, Small's several categories of interests, and Cooley's distinction between human nature and institutional values afford a scheme of classification. In more abstract terms, such purposes might be economic, political, religious, moral, aesthetic, or intellectual, etc.

Early American sociologists tended to refer to the common conational orientation of an aggregation in common abstract or generic rather than in varying, concrete, specific and especially historic terms. In some instances, separation of the innate and acquired was – understandably – virtually impossible. Ward, Small, and perhaps Ross exemplify this predicament, whereas Sumner and Cooley did distinguish broad innate cravings, appetites or inclinations from specific, historically particular (and culturally defined) interests or purposes.

Terminology varied. Sumner and Keller employed (more objective) 'interests.' Ward referred to collective desires, Ross to cultural desires and interests, and Giddings to like purposes or concerted volitions. Small employed a notion of social ends and common purposes, which were based on his categories of interests (1905, pp. 540, 286, 245, 247, 251, 373). Cooley designates 'social ends' and 'general ends' (1962, pp. 133–4, 399).

Yet it is precisely because such desires, ends, or purposes are not automatically or unproblematically satisfiable in relation to the conditions of existence that organization or structure in its most immediate sense(s) is required. Activity in concert or coordinated behavior of the members of the aggregate must occur.

(3) Although early sociologists did employ the terms organization or structure with reference to the common ideas, ideals, notions, feelings, sentiments, values, attitudes, preferences, aversions, etc., prevailing in the society, they applied the terms especially to the activities, behaviors, actions, or interactions of members. Desires, ends, or purposes can be successfully or satisfactorily realized only if members act in a certain way(s) under given conditions of existence of the habitat. Survival demands behavior(s) which is (are) adaptive to such conditions (as the tenets of evolutionary naturalism stipulate). Quite significantly, the various senses or meanings of organization or structure derive from the fundamental presupposition of the necessity of aggregate adaptation. For instance, Ross observes (1969, p. 183) that organization entails adaptation to the requirements of existence. Cooley asserts that organization is per se adaptation. With organization, 'activities [have become] fitted to the conditions' (1966, p. 19; cf. 1962, p.

243). Less rigorously Darwinian than some of his colleagues, Small defines structures as adjustive arrangements which people have wittingly or unwittingly developed as 'devices, tools, instruments to serve purposes of some sort that could not be as conveniently accomplished, if at all, without such arrangements' (1905, p. 149).

Of the four major meanings of organization and structure, the first in the sense of definiteness, uniformity, stability, and regularity is among the most readily and extensively documentable in early theory. It is evident in Ward's *Pure Sociology* (p. 184), Ross's *Social Control* (p. 2), and in Giddings's *The Principles of Sociology* and *Studies in the Theory of Human Society* (pp. 4, 269). Sumner's *Folkways* directs attention (p. 34) to the 'more or less fixed positions . . . and more or less established sequences and methods of interaction' as characteristic of organization or structure. In Small's *General Sociology* (p. 149), structure is the 'arrangement of individuals into somewhat permanent relationships.' Significantly, Ross's *Social Control* (pp. 12, 11) perceives that organization in the sense of regularity also means reliability, which is 'the cornerstone of . . . organization,' and predictability or the trust 'that others will do certain things, at certain times, in certain ways.' Organization in this sense signifies that activity has become established, accepted and required, institutionalized. All of the early major theorists used the term 'institution.'

A second meaning of organization as the consistency, compatibility, and supportiveness of individual activities one with another is more implicit than explicit in the writings of early sociologists. Obviously, the notion of an equilibrium implies the cessation, if not the elimination, of unrestricted conflicts in the interest of more paramount holistic considerations, which are important for Small and Cooley. Both of them link coordination and organization. Indeed, Cooley defines (1966, p. 19) organization as a process resulting in a 'system of co-ordinated activities.' Associating coordination with organization, Small seems to construe (1905, p. 587) coordination as the 'operation of interacting spiritual energies and material devices, as consistent and constant after their kind as the principles of military tactics [are].' Writing more explicitly, Ross specifies (1969, p. 11) that the orderliness of organization means that each individual confines himself 'to his appointed work' and 'interferes with no one else.' Sumner declares (1959, p. 35) that in social structure, custom has produced (a discernible) 'coherence and consistency' in 'the fabric of relations and prescribed positions' sufficient to warrant the use of the word 'structure.' Perhaps less directly and frequently

137

encountered, evidence for this second meaning of organization does exist unmistakably.

In contrast, the third meaning of organization as division of labor, differentiation, and specialization of tasks of member individuals seems to be the most frequent and conspicuous of the four. Ward, Keller, and Ross are incontrovertibly explicit, though Small and Cooley are somewhat more indirectly and inferentially associated with this meaning (Ward, 1898, p. 45, cf. 47–8; 1970, p. 184; Keller, 1932, p. 14; 1927, p. 144; Ross, 1969, p. 218; Small, 1905, pp. 607, 147; Cooley, 1966, p. 28). Keller does ascribe the bases of differentiation and specialization to individual differences and warns that true specialization 'is not clearly recognizable until certain individuals devote all or most of their time to a single activity' (1927, p. 144). Ross is noteworthy for his conceptualization of the differentiation of activities as a system of places or positions (1969, p. 218). Each place or position has its requirements involving 'particular activities and forebearances' (1969, p. 219). What the incumbent does 'can be looked upon and discharged as duties' demanding also that he 'assume certain definite relations to other persons and to other parts of the system' (1969, pp. 218, 219). His refererences to son, lover, father, friend, neighbor, partner, businessman, teacher, servant, policeman, citizen as illustrations of places (and associated types or patterns of conduct and character) seem clearly to anticipate what are now termed roles.

Apparently following Spencer's leads, early American sociologists did distinguish between differentiation of structure and of function occurring rather reciprocally, coordinately, and concomitantly. Of course, such differentiation is assumed to ensue because aggregate adaptation is evolutionarily enhanced. Their notion of structural differentiation is understandable but their view of function basic to functional differentiation contains unresolved difficulties. Function for Ward, Giddings, and Small meant activity, activity that is purposive, and especially activity that is purposive in fulfilling the needs, wants, and desires of the social forces (Ward, 1970, p. 15; Giddings, 1896, p. 172; Small, 1905, p. 528; Ward, 1970, pp. 15, 175, 180–1; Giddings, 1896, pp. 257–8; Small, 1905, pp. 174–5). To hold, as Ward and Small did, that the successful or satisfactory performance of function consists in precisely those activities gratifying the human wants, needs, or desires of the social forces implanted in human nature is to identify (or confuse) the satisfaction of the functional prerequisites for structured association with the requirements for organic survival of the individual and/or the species.

The fourth meaning of organization as leadership–followership, hierarchy, inequality, stratification, superordination–subordination, and differential authority seems to derive from the problem of coordination which is associated with increasingly complex differentiation of structure and function. Ward declares (1970, pp. 184–5) that the social order, which 'is the product of organization,' is 'high in proportion as . . . [its] structures are differentiated and multiplied and still perfectly integrated, or reduced to a completely subordinated and coordinated system.' Keller contends that as organization becomes more complex, it requires not merely differentiation and cooperation, but also authority (leadership–followership) and discipline (1927, p. 9). For Ross (1969, p. 2), increasing complexity of organization brings hierarchical relations and persons share 'unlike burdens' and receive 'unequal benefits.' As individuals in relations become more numerous, authority is needed apparently because the effectiveness of their performances is more delicately poised. Small seems to view (1905, p. 525) structure intrinsically as an arrangement involving superordination–subordination, leaders and led, bosses and bossed.

Even though early sociologists did occasionally use the word 'instinct' or 'instinctive' to apply to the organized or structured activities of early human societies, they were still reticent to ascribe unqualified genetic fixity or invariant determination to such behavior. Whether early organization means definiteness, uniformity, stability, or regularity; or systematic coordination, coherence, or consistency; or differentiation and specialization of tasks; or primordial hierarchization or inequality in activity, it could not be construed as entirely constitutionally dictated or innate. It is not wholly animalistic because human beings were prevailingly believed to be more than mere animals. Possessing the fundamentals of culture, they communicated by rudimentary signals or symbols.

(4) Indeed, human social activity was organized or structured because it was more or less regulated by one or more rules (and values) which reflect and embody a notion of common or general good-will, good of the whole, a common weal, or societal welfare. As a heritage of successful adaptations or adjustments to the conditions of existence (or to recurrent situations) is transmitted across successive generations, aboriginal mankind invariably associated and endowed the instrumentally effective past practice with a sense of an appropriateness, propriety, desirability, approval, imperativeness or obligatoriness. The 'is' is invested with 'ought.' Morality develops. All theorists from Ward to Cooley

reflect the view that what works, adapts, or permits survival for the aggregate of individuals necessarily defines and involves the common good.

Admittedly, sociologists varied markedly in the simplicity-complexity of their normative terminology. Ward and Small alluded only to institutions to designate established and accepted practices.[3] Sumner offered the most elaborate set of notions: folkways, mores, fads, fashions, laws, and institutions. Later in his career Giddings obviously borrowed from Sumner in proposing (simple) folkways, mores (or superior folkways), themistes (as the most important mores), stateways, and values. Ross refers only to social uniformities, imperatives, and institutions. Cooley designates rules, principles, values, and institutions.

Ward's and Small's institutions are a type, kind, or category of related collective responses, which have become definite, permanent, established, and fixed, and are accepted, expected, and more or less obligatory because they are instrumentally effective adjustments to satisfy a need or needs (social force or forces) in relation to the situation or conditions of social existence. Less Darwinian than Ward, Small construes institutions as having behind them a definition of common interest which involves a notion of the good as a whole as a judgment of utility for all (1905, pp. 668–9).[4]

Ward – who accepted the prevalence of a struggle in early human organic and social evolution, but argued that it was a struggle for structure rather than a struggle for (simple individual) existence – refers to the emergence of a group instinct or sentiment of safety as the primordial basis of all social institutions (1970, pp. 185, 419).[5] Morality as founded on (a) *mos* is a derivative of this sentiment (1970, p. 185).[6] Manifestly, the establishment of a set of responses (an institution) by virtue of its presumed contribution to the safety of the social whole is a definition of collective or societal welfare. Survival is, of course, the factual requisite of a definition of safety.

Sumner, Keller, and Giddings adopted similar views. Shared practices or collective behaviors arise because they are more or less effective modes of adaptation for satisfying needs under common conditions of existence. Judged in terms of hedonistic criteria (i.e., actually the absence of pain), they are all more or less appropriate to circumstances. But not all of the behaviors are equally significant. Certain of the folkways come to be distinguished by the addition of a more imperative normative stipulation of adherence for the sake of societal welfare.[7] Later in his career, Giddings also adopted the Sumnerian categories with slight variations: folkways, mores, themistes (as superior mores), and stateways. Presumably, they do involve a definition of the good as a judgment of the 'safety of the group.' By virtue of the sanctions attached to deviations, a range of likeness within (Giddings's consciousness of kind in a particular environment tends to be preserved. (Giddings presumably followed Sumner in offering the most extensive analysis of the function of sanctions for social control in early American sociology.)

Ross proposes a typology of social uniformities, imperatives, and institutions which also seems to join adaptation to the conditions of existence with a sense of the welfare of the whole. By virtue of imitation or influence of a common environment, uniformities of common ideas, beliefs, desires, valuations, and opinions may arise (1919, pp. 89–90). When these uniformities become sanctioned actions or beliefs, they are designated imperatives (e.g., mandates, injunctions, rules, conventions and dogmas). And once the imperatives involve relations sanctioned by coercion, they become institutions (1919, p. 98).[8] Most importantly, Ross argues that in the process of transmission, the criteria of social approval tends to prompt the suppression of egoistic and aggressive notions and the retention of more altruistic, cooperative, and solidary views (1969, p. 343). Thus, a selection of normative components occurs such that only those 'felt to comport with . . . [social] welfare' are retained (i.e., survive) and become disseminated (1969, p. 327).

As the most unqualified idealist with the greatest stress on holism, Cooley does employ the term 'the good of the whole' and does allude to 'a general moral sentiment . . . underlying [specific] standards of right,' the 'moral unity' of the group, and the unsatisfying character of an 'aggregation of merely individual good' (1966, p. 129; 1962, pp. 132–3; 1966, p. 417). Certainly, Cooley's insistence on the function of sympathy in socialization, the notion of 'moral unity' as one of the primary ideals or sentiments, with its merging of members 'into a whole' by 'intimate association,' along with the emergent synthesis from the process of valuation in interaction emphasizes the development of a common good that *is not* simply a distributive notion like 'the greatest good of the greatest number' (1966, p. 417). Nevertheless, Cooley's notions of rules, principles, values, and institutions do not constitute an elaborately differentiated terminology.[9]

Manifestly, social structure or organization for early American sociologists is not merely adaptive behavior but rule-oriented and rule-governed activity based on a common notion of the welfare or

141

good of the whole. Some early theorists had only a minimally developed terminology (e.g., the institution of Ward and Small). Others had a somewhat more elaborately differentiated vocabulary (e.g., Ross with social uniformities, imperatives, and institutions, or Cooley with rules, principles, values, and institutions). Undeniably, Sumner offered the most elaborate set of notions (e.g., folkways, mores, fads, fashions, laws, and institutions). But because the organization of parts of a social whole involves the non-genetically determined activity of physically discrete or separate organisms rather than the activity of accrete or organically determined and physically connected units, organization or structure might be beset by certain problems whose resolution could never be taken for granted.

(5) To be persistent or continuous, the organization or structure of society must display a requisite minimum of such features as cohesion, solidarity, and integration. Early American theorists did use these terms with the more modern meanings of (personal motivations) to resist inclinations to division in and secession from the group, of readiness to act in concert for group purposes (even in the face of personal disadvantage or peril), and of the (structural) operation of various mechanisms by which the parts can enhance the stability of the social whole.[10] Admittedly, all of the notions can be found with all of the terms. But still other meanings can also be identified. For instance, both Giddings and Ward do resort to Spencer's evolutionary conception of integration to derive somewhat different views. Giddings conceived (1898, p. 121) of integration as the subjective process by which a consciousness of likeness among minds gradually evolves into group formation and action in concert (so that subjective likeness supplements and complements mere objective organismic or environmental likeness). By contrast, Ward (and occasionally Giddings and Ross) regarded integration as the gradual evolutionary tendency of societies to consolidate and enlarge (Ward, 1970, pp. 202–3; Giddings, 1896, p. 274; Ross, 1919, pp. 69, 231, 261–2).

However, it is evident that early theorists were concerned with the problem of the development of motivations to resist tendencies to division or secession in the group and of motivations to act in concert to achieve group purposes. The prevailing stance was idealist and subjectivist, with sympathy adopted as the most frequent analytic point of departure. Ward, Giddings, Small and Cooley do employ the notion or an equivalent. The term is very useful because it suggests the psychological beginnings of a social bond which is both negative (resistance to division or secession) and positive (action in concert for the whole). It possesses both emotional and rational features and implications. Ward's analysis is illustrative. He is explicit about the presence of feeling and reason. He indicates that sympathy is evolutionarily engendered out of family affection and thus the basis for (perhaps a less particularized) positive identification and commitment and loyalty is provided through an expansion of altruism.

It is clear that sympathy is the fundamental basis of the unity which Giddings's consciousness of kind entails and is thus foundational to his notion of social cohesion. For Giddings (1896, p. 148), social cohesion is revealed by a group's tendency 'to make any sacrifice that may be necessary' when 'its integrity is threatened.' 'Natural [or spontaneous] means' of social cohesion include 'spontaneous sympathy, agreement in opinion,' and 'loyalty.' When they fail or are lacking, such 'artificial [or contrived] means' as 'bribery, patronage, and coercion' may be resorted to (1896, p. 148; 1898, p. 166).

Admittedly, the connection between Small's notions of 'vicariousness,' which assumes and is to some extent an approximation of sympathy, and 'solidarity' or 'community' is not made explicit by the Chicago sociologist. Vicariousness apparently exists if – on the basis of mutual sympathy among members – each feels toward others a 'just' proportionality or reciprocality in the mutual exchange of activities or services with one another in the group. Solidarity or community is 'the common relation to all parts to certain conditions which may at first appear to be wholly external [to the group], or to influence only a certain select few within the association' (1905, p. 582).

Cooley's analysis does reveal an explicit relationship between the emergence of sympathy and the broader conditions on which solidarity rests. He construes solidarity as 'a fundamental harmony of forces resulting in effective cooperation' (1962, p. 330). His acceptance of the modern notion of solidarity appears to be signified when he claims (1962, p. 331) that the 'only adequate proof of a lack of solidarity is inefficiency in total action, such as disabling conflict within the group.' And of all the sociologists of this era none was as perceptive of the social psychological components and auxiliaries of social solidarity as was Cooley. His expositions of personal discipline and emulation in service have no counterparts.

Personal discipline concerns not merely the willingness of individuals to aid others in seeking the goals of the whole despite personal hazards, but also the steadfastness and persistence of that action. Requisite to this condition is the identification of the individual's 'very self with the whole he serves' (Cooley, 1966, p. 145). He must be motivated to 'control and guide his wayward impulses' in the interests of the ideal of the whole (1966, p. 145). Only then will cooperation occur voluntarily in a 'spirit of loyalty and service' (1966, p. 146).

Within limits, emulation in service facilitates solidarity. It does require a 'conscious loyalty and service to a common idea,' a 'sense of devotion to a larger whole,' a preference for 'the good of the whole' over the individual's personal glory, a 'sense of service to some public and enduring idea,' which limits (accompanying) self-assertion, personal display, and rivalry (Cooley, 1966, 128–9). On the one hand, the individual must feel that the group and its ideals are more worthwhile, larger, and more enduring than he is, and on the other hand he must be able to feel a sense of creativity and self-expression and be able to recognize and assess his contribution in relation to others (Cooley, 1966, pp. 138–43).

Manifestly, social solidarity is an accompaniment of, if not a derivative from, the commitment and loyalty associated with the sympathy and 'we-feeling' which are engendered by social participation and experience in what Cooley terms the 'primary group' and Ross the 'community.' If participation in the life of the whole are as personally direct, 'intimate and cooperative as possible,' members will identify with one another and should 'get the group feeling and become accustomed to act in view of group purposes and ideals' (Cooley, 1966, pp. 148–9). Ross would stipulate that membership in the group should be no more numerous than is possible in terms of personal ties, with the 'circle of obligations' being as wide as 'the circle of relations.' Attachments must be many, close, diffuse, and long lasting. People must be capable 'of feeling keenly with one another' (1969, p. 433). They must live, labor, and share pleasure and sorrows together. Presumably the individual will then meet the most searching test of solidarity: He 'will cherish . . . [the social] whole in his heart and do his duty to it in contempt of terror or bribes' (Cooley, 1962, p. 335). Cooley envisages cohesion as a necessary accompaniment of solidarity, for the latter 'react[s] upon and control[s] destructive forms of activity' (1966, p. 248, cf. p. 143).

As a materialist and objectivist, Sumner assumes an entirely different stance towards social solidarity (and integration). He emphasizes external conditions. Yet his objectivism also includes a Hegelian dialectical formulation in construing the solidarity of one (i.e., in-) group as arising reciprocally through antagonism and conflict with another (i.e., out-) group. Admittedly, other sociologists, such as Ward, Ross, and even Cooley, recognized the same phenomenon in intergroup conflict (Ward, 1970, p. 428; Ross, 1919, pp. 242–3; Cooley, 1964, pp. 209–10).[11] However, Sumner's analysis was unique in its exclusive concern with objective, external conditions, its dialectical emphasis, and its resort to primitive societies in which obligations were defined by kinship and goblinism.

According to him, the murder of one person from one set of kinsmen by another from a different kin under mutual beliefs in goblinism would require that the spirit or ghost of the deceased be appeased by blood-revenge exacted from the murderer or his kinsmen. The efforts of the victim's kinsmen to secure such redress and the reciprocal attempts of the murderer's relatives to prevent blood-revenge led to inter-kin conflict, which transformed and solidified the two aggregates of kinsmen into genuine, operative societies reacting to one another as in- and out-groups. Recurrent tension, friction, threats, hostility, and actual conflict of in- and out-groups provide the basis for their cohesion and solidarity (1959, p. 507). Sympathy and antipathy, concord and discord, solidarity and hostility are reciprocal. Polarized by blood-revenge, the kinsmen were thus divided and each simultaneously unified in relation to the other (1959, p. 499).

Sumner also uses the term 'integration' in the modern sense as 'system integration.' He is concerned with the pervasive use of the same pattern, or its equivalents, as one of the structural mechanisms by which parts of a structure can enhance or increase the stability of the whole. (Cf. Cohen, 1968, pp. 149, 151.) Sumner argues (1959, pp. 5–6, 102) that the parts of a structure (especially the mores) are subject to a strain toward consistency because consistency represents enhanced efficiency and such efficiency in turn increases chances for survival (cf. Cohen, 1968, p. 151). Achievement of relative consistency and harmoniousness throughout the various parts of the society in relation to common life conditions is designated as 'integration.' (Ross seems to subscribe to a similar view, 1912, p. 364, and 1919, p. 229.) Sumner remarks (1959, p. 36) that 'India, Chaldea, Assyria, Egypt, Greece, Rome, the Middle Ages, Modern Times, are cases in which the integration of the mores upon different life conditions produced [total] societal states of complete and distinct individuality (ethos).'

Admittedly, cohesion, solidarity, and integration do refer to problems which have somewhat overlapping and variant definitions in early American sociology. But they point to the fact

145

that the different theoretical (or more precisely, social ontological) stances reflect a major controversy about the character of organization or structure: it cannot be taken for granted and it must be constantly renewed (if not also reviewed).

(6) Organization or structure tends to involve the problem of the mobilization of action, or its orientation to, the peculiar circumstances of the situation or conditions of existence. Individual variations or periodicities in the human organisms or changes in the situation, habitat, or environment render the nature of the needs-wants-desires-ends or the presumptively relevant adaptive-organized behavior or action somewhat problematic. Here the different theoretical stances of early sociologists directly and unmistakably intrude. The more predominantly materialistic theorists (e.g., Sumner and Keller) construe the process as operating primarily and substantially deterministically, i.e., as dependent mainly on the objective nature of the human organisms in the aggregate, the accumulation of past collective experience as embodied in the culture (folkways, mores, etc.) and on the objective state of the environment or habitat (scarce resources, etc.) and only secondarily on the more minimal, intermittent, and capricious intrusion of consciousness and reason as pain is encountered by members of the group. But the bulk of early American theorists (i.e., the more balanced materialists-idealists and prevailing idealists) tended to conceive of the process as potentially (and increasingly) entailing more or less consciousness and choice, i.e., social decision, public will, or concerted volition. Still, the present emerged out of the past and the future will emerge out of the present. Collective decisions or judgments were thus only minimally variant from the past and continuous into the future. Organization is continuously adaptive. It does, indeed, represent an organic or moving equilibrium – as the general model proposes.

Any suggestion that early American sociologists had developed a relatively elaborate, unified, systematic, and integrated theory of the emergence of the six features of social structure would be substantially at variance with the actual state of their writings. Rather these features appear fragmentarily, incompletely, haphazardly, often separate and isolated from one another. But – directly or indirectly – they reflect generally the basic tenets of evolutionary naturalism and specifically certain aspects of the three positions stemming from the dualistic social ontology of early theory. First, organization signifies that the aggregate has become an adaptive unity with a distinguishable, distinctive social identity, which could be defined either through idealism (-subjectivism as social consciousness) or materialism (-objectivism via ethnocentrism and in-group/out-group relations). Second, organization or structure is defined by and in terms of a common set of desires, interests, purposes, ends, or objectives deriving from the various catalogs of social forces or biopsychic human nature needs-wants (but as modified and elaborated by shared, collective experience in relation to the conditions of existence). Manifestly, the adaptation out of which organization results indicates that needs or wants are not unproblematically satisfied within the situation. Activity, action, or behavior is required on the part of the human organism in the aggregate. Thus, in the third place, organization or structure must finally be organized or structured behavior in several senses. It is organized or structured in the sense of: (a) having become definite, uniform, stable, and regularized; (b) comprising a system of coordinated, coherent, consistent activities; (c) entailing a division of labor, a differentiation and specialization of tasks; and (d) finally producing leadership-followership, hierarchy, inequality, stratification, superordination–subordination, and differential authority. Because structure is not automatically and innately given, it entails, fourth, the emergence of norms defining the common good or welfare of the whole. Fifth, the peculiarly physically discrete character of the particular human entities who are unified also means that such terms as cohesion, solidarity, and integration are distinctively relevant to the organization or structure of human societies. Early theorists were concerned with the problem of the development and inculcation of motivations to resist tendencies to division or secession in the group and of motivations to act in concert to achieve group purposes (e.g., the phenomenon of sympathy, identification, emulation in primary group, community, or in-group as against out-group, etc.). At least one of them was explicitly interested in integration as a system condition involving the consistency of parts as conducive to increased chances for societal survival. Because some change occurs incessantly – either it originates within the human organisms of the aggregate or intrudes from the environment – organization can never be an entirely fixed or static condition. It is, in the sixth place, a continuous process. Here also the effects of different theoretical positions are evident. The more predominantly materialistic theorists (e.g., Sumner and Keller) construed the process as operating relatively deterministically and objectively. But the bulk of American theorists (i.e., the more balanced materialists-idealists and the prevailing idealists) regarded the process as potentially entailing increasing consciousness and choice, i.e., social decision, public will, or concerted volition. Thus, the meaning of organization reflects an organic or moving equilibrium.

By no means was the interest of early theorists in social structure confined to the theory of the genesis of societal structure or the characteristics of primordial societal structure. Their concerns did lead them to propose a variety of types of social structure.

7 Toward theories of social and societal structures

Undoubtedly, early theorists' interest in structure was much broader than merely the problem of its origins. Still, their attention to structure was secondary to change. Structure was, after all, only a temporary adaptation to the conditions of existence, an adjustment to a situation, an equilibrium of forces whose persistence is contingent or problematic. Structure is subject to change and often it appeared in the larger context of the study of change (as will become evident in chapters 8, 9, and 10). Yet, paradoxically, much of the transmitted legacy of the early theorists consists of concepts of structure (which understandably but regrettably have become detached from the context of relevant theory).

But recognized or not, the influence of early theory was present. For instance, the better known (and frequently encountered macroscopic) notion of 'institution' and the lesser known (and less frequently encountered microscopic) concepts of 'status' and 'position' are thoroughly embedded in the tenets of evolutionary naturalism and especially in the doctrine of social forces. Admittedly, such other notions as Sumner's 'in-group' and 'out-group,' Giddings's 'social composition' and 'social constitution,' Cooley's 'primary group' and 'nucleated group,' and Ross's 'community'– 'society' dichotomy may seem to be less directly involved in the theoretical matrix of the era. Still, it is the current ignorance of the past rather than the past itself which is being displayed. Sumner's 'in-group' and 'out-group' do reflect his materialistic objectivism and determinism joined with a Hegelian dialectical conception of conflict, Giddings's 'social composition' and 'social constitution' bespeak the role of consciousness of similarity and of difference which are fundamentally operative in adaptive structuring (and selection) of an aggregate. But it was Ross who offered the most complex typology of groups, the theoretical background of which seems equally complex and remote.

Of all of their structural notions, institution seems to have been most conspicuously and frequently employed in early theory. Sumner, Ward, Giddings, Small, and Cooley had more or less explicit conceptions of an institution.[1] For all of them, institution is basically a type, kind or category of related collective responses which have become definite, permanent, established, and rigid, and are accepted, expected, and obligatory (if not compulsory) because they are instrumentally effective adjustments to satisfy a need or needs (i.e., social forces) in relation to the conditions of existence. True, early theorists were vague about the precise mechanism of the demarcation and differentiation of one sphere or type of institution from another – apart from the general view of evolutionary change. They were convinced that the institutions of a society tend to become and, indeed, disclose at any point in time an interrelatedness, consistency, congruency or harmony with one another.[2]

Early theorists did attempt to construct taxonomies or at least typologies of groups, although many of these efforts are now ignored or forgotten. Giddings, for instance, proposed several types of groups (or societies): 'natural society,' 'integral society,' 'component society,' 'constituent society,' 'social group,' 'multitude,' and 'societal group.' Ross distinguished 'fortuitous groups,' 'natural groups,' 'likeness groups,' 'interest groups,' 'functional groups,' 'authorities,' and 'hierarchies.' But by contrast some other typologies or dichotomies have become part of the intellectual legacy of American sociology, e.g., Sumner's 'in-group' and 'out-group,' Cooley's 'primary group' and 'secondary (or more correctly, 'nucleated') group,' and Ross's 'community–society' differentiation.

Finally, the most comprehensive structural notions involve societies, of which 'primitive societies' and 'modern societies' are designated most often. Although the two types of societies are viewed synchronically or coexistentially, they are more frequently construed diachronically or sequentially. They are part of general theories of social change – as the two following chapters indicate.

150

Major social dichotomies

It is appropriate to begin the analysis of the more prominent social structural dichotomies in early theory by a consideration of Sumner's major contributions. Although he did not exclusively restrict the application of the concepts 'in-group' and 'out-group' to societies, he did use them primarily in that context in accordance with his Darwinian (or Malthusian and perhaps also Hegelian) views about social change, in which scarcity and struggle and dialectically reciprocated conflict are important explanatory factors. The paired concepts signify the correlative and reciprocal interconnection, interrelation, and interdependence between two groups or sets of groups involved in a struggle for existence with limited resources in the same environment. Each group or set of groups develops a unity, coherence, integration, or solidarity in relation to (reciprocal) opposition, competition, hostility, and conflict with another group or set of groups. The one becomes differentiated from the other. The 'insiders' are a 'we-group' or an 'in-group,' and everybody else, or the other-groups, are out-groups. Comradeship, sympathy, peace, order, mutual rights, law, government, and industry characterize the relations of insiders with one another in a we-group. But with outsiders or others-groups, their relation is (1959, pp. 12, 496) one of suspicion, hostility, war, plunder, and even subjugation – unless some accommodating agreements are worked out between the in-group and out-group.

Sumner explicitly notes (1959, p. 13) that the 'relation of comradeship and peace in the we-group' is a correlative of 'hostility and war towards others-groups.' Successful conduct of war with outsiders requires (1959, p. 12) 'peace inside, lest internal discord should weaken the we-group for war.' The exigencies of belligerency (1959, p. 12) 'also make government and law in the in-group, in order to prevent quarrels and enforce discipline.' Accordingly, war and peace react on one another and develop one another, the latter within the group and the former between it and another group. Sumner also argues (1959, p. 12) that the 'closer the neighbors, and the stronger they are,' the more intense will be the warfare. In turn the more severe the hostilities, the stronger will be the internal organization and discipline of both. Appropriately correlative sentiments are also developed from the same situation. Loyalty to the group, sacrifice for it, and brotherhood within, arise as hatred and contempt for outsiders, and warlikeness without, occur. Together, these 'relations and sentiments constitute a social philosophy,' which 'is sanctified by a connection with religion'

151

(1959, p. 13). The ghosts of the ancestors of the we-group who also fought with the ancestors of the out-group will be delighted to see their descendants continuing the fight, and will assist them. To kill, plunder, and enslave outsiders is virtue.

As conflict constitutes a group (an in-group against an out-group or out-groups), it also elicits in each group a conception of itself and its basic characteristics which is different from others. Indeed, its conception is antagonistic and – presumably as conflict becomes more severe – polarized against the other(s). Each group develops an appropriate ethnocentrism in which its social and cultural characteristics are assumed to be central and normal, 'and all others are scaled and rated' accordingly (1959, p. 13). So Sumner remarks (1959, p. 13) that each 'group nourishes its own pride and vanity, boasts itself superior, exalts its own divinities, and looks . . . on outsiders' with contempt. Correlatively, it 'thinks its own folkways the only right ones, and if it observes that other groups have other folkways, these excite its scorn' (1959, p. 13). Such differences stimulate opprobrious epithets. Itself a consequence of conflict, ethnocentrism seems further to accentuate conflict by prompting a people to exaggerate and intensify everything peculiar and different in their folkways. Thus, ethnocentrism 'strengthens the folkways' (1959, p. 13).

Concerned especially with primitive societies, Sumner endeavors to show how the inclination to blood-revenge is organized to make a group an in-group. Manifestly, blood-revenge within a group would mean self-extermination. As Sumner comments (1959, p. 498):

> It would serve the interests of the enemies in the out-groups. Hence the double interests of harmony and cooperation in the in-group and war strength against the out-groups forces the invention of devices by which to supercede blood revenge in the in-group. Chiefs and priests administered group interests, especially War and other collisions with neighbors, and they imposed restraints, arbitration, or compensation in internal quarrels.

Inside the in-group, justice was administered by precedents and custom, wrongs were composed by payments or penalties, breaches of order or violations of petty taboos were punished by authorities or discretionary fines, and exile took the place of retaliation. The individual who had murdered a member of his own in-group 'had to fear the ghost of the murdered' (1959, p. 499). But he could be protected from their ghosts, gods, or the furies who demanded revenge by religious rites. 'Cities of refuge and sanctuaries secured investigation and deliberation to prove guilt and determine compensations' (1959, p. 498). But basically the 'custom of blood revenge was a protection to all who were in a group of kinsmen,' for it 'knit them all together and served their common interest against all outsiders' (1959, p. 499). Accordingly, Sumner declares (1959, p. 499) that 'it was a societalizing custom and institution.'

Certainly, Sumner suggests that changing social and historical circumstances can change in-group and out-group definitions and relations. The emergence of some threat which is external to both groups and mutually threatening may prompt some accommodation and conciliation. Indeed, Sumner tends to conceive (1959, p. 12) of a society as embracing at least two or more groups, i.e., as a 'group of groups with some relation to each other (such as kin, neighborhood, alliance, connubium and commercium) which draws them together and differentiates them from others.' Mutual defense, assistance, and offense develop. The two groups can eventually become an in-group and peace group.

With the emergence of modern states, the component (and compounded) groups must necessarily become a peace unit. Every part of the 'same civil body' must be 'united by a peace pact' (1959, p. 503). Imposition and eventual acceptance of law (e.g., Roman law in the Roman Empire) becomes the peace pact of the peace unit. Presumably, sympathy, ideas, and ideals may supplement and facilitate but never be entirely a substitute for a central authority with adequate coercive force. Inability to suppress local wars and internal conflict render the state liable to disruption and disintegration. In turn, a union of two or more states, 'even for the purpose of aggregating more force for war . . . will necessarily be a peace union when regarded from within' (1959, p. 503). Presumably, a peace union is functionally an in-group.

Patently, Sumner was not the only early American theorist to emphasize the significance of conflict in intra- and inter-group relations. Giddings was also sensitive to the functions of opposition. Both early sociologists were indebted to Darwin and Spencer. But Sumner's in-group/out-group analysis reveals a distinctively contextual and dialectical (and apparently Hegelian) foundation which is not present in Giddings's social composition – social constitution dichotomy. In contrast, it rests on interpersonal and inter-group subjective-objective similarities and dissimilarities.

Giddings's effort to develop a typology of the bases of organization, which seem to reflect the influence of both Spencer and Durkheim, displays his theoretical commitments just as did Sumner's 'in-group' and 'out-group' analysis. Giddings's two basic types of organization by social composition and by social constitution manifestly exhibit his preoccupation with the consciousness of likeness (similarity, resemblance) and unlikeness (dissimilarity, difference). Social composition is organization established on the basis of similar or like units, whereas social constitution is organization predicated on the foundation of dissimilar or unlike units. Significantly, the two types are cast in an evolutionary formulation which assumes an inherent tendency for societies to expand. When the like is translated into homogeneity and the unlike into heterogeneity, the presence of Spencer's influence can be readily recognized. But the indebtedness to Durkheim seems even more important, for the two types of organization are obviously Giddings's interpretations of the characteristics of mechanical and organic solidarity. Giddings is unmistakably explicit about the absence of a genuine division of labor in social composition and its presence in social constitution.

Organization by social composition entails the creation of larger social entities from the combination, addition, or aggregation of similar or like groups. Each component unit is accordingly a 'component society' (or in the terminology of contemporary sociology, a component group). Giddings illustrates the phenomenon of social composition in his posthumous *Civilization and Society* by citing (pp. 35, 396) the unification of families into kindreds, tribes or neighborhoods into towns, little scattered towns into cities, cities into federal states, states into nations, and nations into empires.[3] Now obviously resemblance is a relative matter and the only minimum that can be accurately asserted is that the members of a component group 'are more like one another than they are like the individual members of any other [component] group' or the totality of members of the next larger encompassing social entity (1898, pp. 182, 181). To a considerable extent, the enlarging organization by social composition beyond the family and horde arises consciously and deliberately from a judgment of utility, especially the advantage of combination for defense or offense against external threats (1898, p. 191). Usually the few far-seeing persons who propose this form of organization 'have a good deal of trouble to persuade other people to adopt it' (1932, p. 36). But once accepted, the mutual attraction of like with like and the emergence of a consciousness of kind tend to preserve the relationship beyond the demands of the immediate circumstance. People discuss the arrangements which have resulted. Analysis, criticism, and finally approval occur. Out of the process of sifting and segregating, the potentially alike are brought together, potential resemblances are converted into actual resemblances and inconsistencies are eliminated or rejected (1898, p. 183). Each component group in the social composition is moulded into conformity with a type evolved from the consciousness of kind. Expansion of the group by social composition, by the addition of like units, brings an increase in mass and power.

In addition to likeness of type, each group in the social composition is alike in function. It can 'live an independent life and perpetuate human society if it were cut off from relations with all other communities in the world' (1898, p. 176). It contains all of the requirements for perpetuating the species: it is bi-sexual and bi- or multi-generational. Each component group is thus capable of providing for an increase of population and for an evolution of social relations.

By contrast, the parts or units in the social constitution are interdependent rather than independent. Organization by social constitution entails addition, aggregation or combination of groups, each of which is unlike others, has become specialized and differentiated, and provides a distinctive contribution to the whole within a division of labor. The effect is more than an increase in power or mass; functional coordination has occurred. Thus, the constituent groups can have no independent existence for they 'depend on one another, and they presuppose the social composition' (1898, p. 193). They are alike only in their acceptance of the purpose or objective of the larger social whole, in their exertion of effort to achieve an objective, and in their dependence on one another. But each constituent group differs from others in the special end sought, the particular activity performed, and in the specific or specialized work or function contributed to the whole. According to Giddings, members of a constituent group typically resemble one another mentally and/or morally, whereas members of a component group resemble one another in blood kinship, descent, race, or nationality and in insistence on potential likeness. Basically, constituent groups are voluntary, purposive, associations. Affiliation is consciously and deliberately requested and granted. Finally, each purposive association or constituent group involves the combination of individuals as persons and categories (i.e., a composition) and a plan of organization (or constitution) by which its function may be effectively performed.

At best, organization by social constitution among primitive or nonliterate societies is rudimentary, incomplete, and subordinate to

155

social composition. Much cooperation exists but such peoples possess no specialized cooperative groups for systematically carrying on particular, circumscribed activities. Specialization is more a matter of occasion for the particular group than of its personnel or their roles. Constituent groups do not tend to become separate or distinct from component groups but rather remain incidental and subordinate to component groups. Barbaric or tribal societies do show 'slight beginnings of purposive association and a few simple constituent societies [or groups]' (1898, p. 195). The household, the clan, secret associations, and the council of chieftains who preside over the tribal military organization are Giddings's illustrations (1898, p. 198).

In demotic or civilized societies the social constitution is completely developed and is relatively separated from the social composition which has become subordinate. The chief purposive association of civil society is the state. Public in character, it 'prescribes the forms and obligations for all minor purposive associations and shapes the social composition' (1898, p. 199). These private purposive associations are of narrower range and more specialized functions. Giddings identifies four types: political (e.g., parties), juristic (e.g., boards of arbitration), economic (e.g., partnerships, corporations, labor unions), and cultural (e.g., religious, philanthropic, scientific, educational, aesthetic). Life in modern societies is possible only as these associations supplement and complement one another. Any withdrawal or disruption of a specialized activity also presents a threat or danger to the whole.

Both like and unlike are necessary to organization. The former or homogeneity is maintained in society's composition and the latter or heterogeneity is tolerated or promoted by its constitution. Psychologically, these two types of organization (and their bases) are opposites. Organization by constitution requires that individuals be alike mentally or morally for the purposes of the association but otherwise they may be different. But as wholes, constituent groups are functionally specialized or differentiated in relation to one another so that they together constitute a coordinated whole.

Undeniably, aspects of Giddings's dichotomy are similar to features of other early theorists. As constituent groups, (voluntary) associations have their counterpart, for instance, in Cooley's secondary (or more correctly, 'nucleated') groups. However, by no means are all groups in the social composition necessarily or even typically primary groups. Generally, Cooley's (implicit) polar types can be understood more accurately within Cooley's own theoretical stance rather than by comparison or contrast with others such as Giddings's.

In turning to the primary and secondary group typology attributed to Cooley, certain initial warnings must be issued. A first concerns their association with developmental change. Like the component and constituent groups which form the bases of Giddings's typology of social (or societal) organization, the pair of concepts attributed to Cooley can be related to primitive and modern societies. Some but not all primary groups are primitive. And even though primitive society is constituted basically and pervasively of primary groups, certainly not all primary (and most obviously not all secondary) groups are societally comprehensive in their inclusiveness. In Cooley's usage, primary and secondary seem to refer to a characterization of total groups, although modern applications of the terms have often tended to focus on aspects, qualities, or characteristics of relationships rather than on groups as wholes.

A second caution pertains to the originality and accuracy of the designation. Cooley was not the originator of either 'primary' or 'secondary' and he did not actually propose them as an interrelated pair, polar type, or dichotomy. Albion W. Small and George E. Vincent introduced the term 'primary social group' in their *An Introduction to the Study of Society* in 1894 (reprinted 1971). In fact, the term 'primary group' did not appear in the first edition of *Social Organization*. Cooley never did use the notion 'secondary group,' although he did propose the 'nucleated group' (albeit inconspicuously in *Social Process*) with a meaning that embodies certain features of the term popularly attributed to him. His analysis of 'institutions' and 'formalism' seems to suggest 'institutional groups' and 'formalized groups' as terms which would include other facets of the meaning of 'secondary group.'

As a pair of concepts, primary group and nucleated group do reflect Cooley's fundamental commitment to romantic idealism. They emphasize – directly or indirectly – the role of mind and especially imagination in the social, the emotional quality of relations, the necessity of some sense of unity, the indispensability of variegated individual response and expression, the part of both conflict and cooperation, and the varying amenability to stability and instability.

In endeavoring to understand the meaning of both primary group and nucleated group, it is necessary to recognize that Cooley's own personalized commitment to romantic idealism was at variance with rigorous, systematic exposition of his ideas. Both what he said and what he implied must be examined. Accordingly, it is imperative that analysis go beyond the mere definition of the primary group and the enumeration of the senses in which a primary group is primary. Fundamentally, the primary group is 'characterized by intimate face-to-face association and co-operation' (1962, p. 23). It is primary in the sense of its basic importance in forming the social nature and ideals of the individual (1962, p. 23), in its priority in providing the individual experience with social unity (1962, pp. 26–7), and in the comparative stability of relations (1962, p. 27) and universality (or prevalence) of its existence (1962, p. 24). Cooley cites 'the family, play-group of children, and the neighborhood or community group of elders' as concrete illustrations of primary groups. However, he does not attempt to provide a systematic elucidation of the term as a concept.

Analysis of the implications of the several related chapters on the primary group and primary ideals in *Social Organization* in contrast to the chapters on institutions and formalism in the same work and on the nucleated group in *Social Process* suggests that a primary group tends to be characterized by six distinguishing features (Cooley, 1962, pp. 23–57, 313–14, 319–20, 342–3, 349; 1966, pp. 249–53; 1969, pp. 185, 186). Yet nowhere did Cooley actually enumerate the characeristics of the primary group in an explicit, serial manner. Some of these features are implicit whereas others are explicit. Some concern the size of the group, the nature of its goals, objectives, or purposes, the quality of its relations, and the features of its communication networks. Others pertain to its overall structure, its unique solidarity, and its function in the formation of human nature and personality. Above all, Cooley's frequent references to the quality of association or interaction with illustrative groups suggests that a primary group is defined by the nature of its relations rather than the structure defining the relations.

First, the primary group seems to have comparatively few members. Cooley uses the adjectives 'intimate, face-to-face,' which imply restricted, identifiable members who – because interaction is relatively durable or permanent – become personally known. His illustrations (the family, play-group, etc.) do reflect this feature of comparatively few members. And, most importantly, he refers to 'small groups' in an early passage in *Social Organization* (p. 54). Second, the primary group entails commitment to a set of values, beliefs, and goals which are distinctively diffuse, general, enduring, and universal. They are the primary ideals or sentiments and human nature values, which the primary group develops in each individual in the course of socializing his instinctive emotional dispositions. For all men everywhere, despite some variation, the basic ideal of moral unity is acquired from common participation and experience in the primary group.[4] And from this basic ideal, Cooley derives in turn certain other sentiments and ideals: loyalty, truth, service, kindness, rightness, and freedom (1962, pp. 24, 20, 32–56). What they involve is not narrowly and specifically defined; it is rather vague, broad, diffuse, and general. In addition, these values tend to retain an enduring validity, to arise in one form or another across the range of mankind, and to be the source of other derivative, secondary values. Third, and perhaps most distinctive of all, the primary group tends to involve direct, durable, stable, face-to-face, intimate, personalized, inclusive, and emotional relations. Cooley is undeniably explicit about the directness, durability, stability, intimacy, and face-to-face character of the relations (1962, pp. 23, 24, 27). In turn, these features imply a personalized relationship in which individuals become known to one another across the range of their personalities. Presumably, the nucleated group is the antithesis of the primary group and Cooley notes that it is 'depersonal' or impersonal (1966, p. 252; 1969, pp. 185–6), with most persons investing only small and apparently superficial or peripheral parts of their personalities. By logical (and antithetical) inference, the primary group entails a personalized relationship in which many or most aspects of members' personalities are involved. Because persons interact frequently with one another and in a variety of contexts, they are involved as whole personalities and the relationships involve them rather inclusively or completely. And these non-specific, non-specialized, inclusive personalized relationships will tend, in turn, to be emotionally freighted. Cooley's entire analysis suggests pervasive affectivity. Sympathy is a dominant feature of the primary group, though competition, 'self-assertion and the various appropriative passions' also intrude (1962, p. 23). Actually, the primary ideals – in whose formation and inculcation the primary group virtually functions alone – are in no sense prevailingly cognitive or intellectual. Feeling and sentiment are powerfully involved. In addition, warmth, poignancy, incisiveness, spontaneity, authenticity, and individuality are aspects of the pervasive emotionality of primary relations. (Relations with such characteristics are intrinsically rather than extrinsically or instrumentally satisfying to participants.) Fourth, communication among members of primary groups is deep and extensive, as is appropriate to the aforementioned

159

character of the relations. For Cooley (1962, p. 54) communication is 'full,' relatively unrestricted and marked by the 'give-and-take of suggestions.' Gesture and other nonverbal behavior become important in expressing and influencing feelings. Presumably, they supplement and amplify speech in the achievement of unity in the group. Fifth, the (total) structure of relations in primary groups is, according to Cooley, simple and undifferentiated (1962, p. 54). Intimate face-to-face associations presumably means that everyone knows everyone else and that communication can 'be full and quick in order to give that promptness in the give-and-take of suggestions upon which moral unity depends' (1962, p. 54). For Cooley, simplicity of structure signifies per se that the basic or primary ideals and human nature needs, sentiments, or values can be readily and fully satisfied. Sixth, the primary group is characterized by an incomparably powerful and compelling solidarity. Presumably this unity is a consequence of the small number of members, the diffuse, general and relatively permanent and universal human nature values of the group, the direct, durable, stable, face-to-face, intimate, personalized, inclusive, and emotional relations and especially sympathy and identification, in conjunction with a stable simple structure permitting full expression of human nature. Primary group members can ordinarily find 'common ground,' have communion, enter into and share the minds, partake of the ideas and sentiments of one another. Each person tends to include in his imagination each other person as a point of reference for thought and action and to discipline himself voluntarily in the relationship to the 'we' of the whole. Everyone feels bound and obligated to the common whole, so that his 'very self, for many purposes at least, is the common life and purpose of the group' (1962, p. 23). Members conceive of themselves as an 'indivisible, though various, "we"' whose parts desire that it be 'harmonious, happy, and successful' (1962, p. 33). Seventh and finally, the primary group has an exclusive function in forming and sustaining a (social) human nature and personality in each individual (1962, pp. 23, 28–31). Without the primary group, man would never acquire that generic human nature of feelings and sentiments that each individual shares with all others of his kind. And removed from the influence of the primary group, that nature 'decays in isolation' (1962, p. 30). This human nature consists of 'sentiments and impulses that are human in being superior to those of lower animals' and in belonging 'to mankind at large, and not to any particular race or time' (1962, p. 28). Through the common discipline and common experience within primary groups which are universal in all societies, men acquire a universal but socially developed human nature.

Once acquired, these components demand an appropriate structure and setting for continuous satisfaction. Yet Cooley argues that only the simple structures of primary groups can afford the necessary opportunity for gratifying human nature needs. Only primary groups can provide the humanness, breadth, adaptability, spontaneity, flexibility, plasticity, and range of variation for individual responses (as demanded by Cooley's romanticist conception of human nature). By contrast, participation in modern nucleated groups tends to impede or hinder gratification of human nature needs and values.

It is perhaps an unflattering commentary on the casual and unsystematic consideration of the texts of the Founding Fathers of the American discipline that Cooley's concept of the nucleated group should have remained so long unknown to or ignored by contemporary sociologists. It is true, of course, that Cooley's analysis of the nucleated group – 'that most characteristic form of modern organization,' the voluntary association – is contained in his *Social Process* (p. 252), which has not attracted the attention of modern theorists to the same extent as have *Human Nature and the Social Order* and *Social Organization*. As in the case of the primary group, so here also the meanings of the term must be inferred both from what Cooley has actually written and from what he implies.

In all essential respects, the seven distinguishing features of this type of group are the antithesis of those of the primary group. First, the nucleated group is composed of a large number of members who have voluntarily affiliated themselves with several such groups in accordance with their talents, inclinations, and interests. Second, this type of group is a differentiated and specialized mechanism for narrow, specific, and particular purposes or goals. Third, in contrast to the primary group, this term signifies that only one or a few of a large number of members is or are devoting the main parts of their personalities to the actual operation of the organization. Typically, most members involve only a small part of their personalities in restricted face-to-face participation and communication within a larger more complex and formally organized structure. Fourth, nucleated groups resemble the institutions of which they are parts in tending to become more or less mechanical, routinized, and fixed in their operations; impersonal and rigid in their procedures; specialized and organized in their purposes, activities, and involvement of personnel. Fifth, the values which these groups and their institutional systems represent are relatively transient, special, historically limited, fixed, impersonal, and complex. Nucleated groups thus tend to loose humanness, breadth, and flexibility. Sixth, they become – to use Cooley's own characterization – formalized. Consequently, their members tend to become frustrated because they are impeded, hindered, or limited in satisfying the broader sentiments and freer and larger impulses of human nature which were acquired earlier in primary group experience and which can only be partially and segmentally expressed in nucleated groups. Seventh, the personality of the individual member is no longer enlisted and disciplined internally. The demand for conformity seems to come from external sources. The individual no longer feels an abiding sense of loyalty. In modern terms, he has become alienated. Conformity tends to be a matter of expedience and deviance a recurrent possibility.

Interestingly, many of the features of Cooley's primary and nucleated groups have their counterparts in and are consistent with the main characteristics of Ross's less known community–society dichotomy which was explicitly constituted as a set of polar types in Ross's *Social Control*, pp. 432–6. It coincides only partially with the 'primitive–modern' classification, as is the case also for Cooley's 'primary–nucleated' conceptualization. In addition to primitive societies, 'community' also refers to (modern) rural neighborhoods and village communities. Furthermore, the 'community–society' designation is obviously applicable both to the (total) societal level and sub-societal level.

Considerable ambiguity surrounds the meanings of Ross's concepts which he acknowledged to be similar to the contrast 'made by Tönnies in his "Gemeinschaft und Gesellschaft,"' but which 'was worked out long before' he 'became acquainted with Tönnies's book' (1969, p. 432). (However, Ross's comment does not indicate whether or not he selected the *terms* subsequent to contact with Tönnies's work and to what extent the characterization as published was influenced by or relied on Tönnies's dichotomy.) Nowhere did Ross explicitly define either 'community' or 'society.' Apparently, the terms refer not so much to specific or particular concrete groups but to certain aspects, qualities, and characteristics of social relationships.

Community seems to imply a social existence which entails a feeling of unity, a sense of solidarity, a conception of a common life within which members 'love and understand one another . . . yield to one another,' and exercise mutual 'forbearances' (1969, p. 433). It apparently refers to a group or series of groups within which social relationships have (predominantly?) primary or primary-like characteristics and persons can 'put themselves in the place of one another' (1969, p. 51). The ties make the group (or groups) rather than vice versa. Natural and spontaneous rather than artificial and planned, the social bonds are many and firm in a realm of small and simple groups whose members are describable as 'mates, kinfolk, neighbors, and comrades' (1969, p. 432). Kinship has a sacred significance. Marriage is a sacrament. The family consists of more than parents and the young. Spatial adjacency means social intimacy. Strong locality feelings exist because frequent change of domicile does not occur. People live, labor, and enjoy one another's company over an extended period of time and, consequently, develop close and lasting attachments. They are keenly sensitive to one another's circumstances. To the extent that social stratification and differentiation exist, they do not preclude the operation of the feelings and conception of community. Concord and reciprocal constraint make possible a natural order and essentially remove the necessity for organized social control. Apparently, these conditions prevailed especially when the 'rural neighborhood or the village community was the type of aggregation' (1969, p. 433).

By contrast, society seems to signify a social existence carried on increasingly in voluntary associations, the newer, more 'narrow gauge,' loosely-binding, and utilitarian affiliations, which have become 'huge and complex aggregations' and are 'founded on affinity and [a] selective choice' or 'a preference for some persons over others' (1969, pp. 434, 433). To quote Ross directly (1969, p. 433), 'society' designated a type set of relationships in which

Kinship has lost its old sacred significance . . . the family now consists of only parents and young . . . marriage has become a contract terminable almost at pleasure. Nearness of dwelling means less in the country and nothing in the town. For the intimacy of the countryside the city offers only a 'multitudinous desolation.' Frequent change of domicile hinders the growth of strong local feelings. The householder has become a tenant, the working-man a bird of passage. Loose touch-and-go acquaintanceships take the place of those close and lasting attachments that form between neighbors that have long lived, labored, and pleasured together. The power of money rends the community into classes incapable of feeling keenly with one another.

Local groups such as the parish, commune, neighborhood, or

village are decaying or 'developing beyond the point of real community' (1969, p. 433). Social differentiation, relational and organizational complexity, economic specialization, private property, social stratification, the extension of relations by conquest and the coercive activity of the state, and the growth of the cities are all apparently characteristic of the realm of 'society' as opposed to 'community.' This society requires a system of (artificial, deliberate, planned) social control with an essentially impersonal and formally organized set of sanctions.

Ross's conceptualization of the 'community–society' dichotomy virtually necessitates a concern with the total character of the relationships existing among all groups in the most comprehensive sense possible. It requires that attention be directed toward society in the sense of the largest permanent group in which men and women continuously associate, are able to be economically, socially, and politically self-sufficient, and carry on a common mode of life. (Admittedly, society was employed in other senses in early theory, but it is this meaning that is significant here.) Undeniably, 'in-groups' and 'out-groups,' 'component groups' and 'constituent groups,' 'primary groups' and 'secondary groups' can be and were identified at a sub-societal level. But the dominance or predominance of the relationships or groups implied by one or the other of the social dichotomies does require interest in the broadest structured social context in which persons ordinarily interact, i.e., society. And it is certainly no less the case for Ross than it is for Sumner, Giddings, and Cooley.

Major societal dichotomy

Patently, a wide variety of adjectives might be prefixed as qualifiers of society. Such terms as 'early,' 'primitive,' 'simple,' 'savage,' 'barbaric,' 'tribal,' 'ancient,' 'patriarchal,' 'feudal,' 'medieval,' 'caste' or 'class' (-organized), 'modern,' 'civilized,' 'civic,' 'developed,' 'complex,' 'differentiated,' 'composite,' 'embryonic,' 'stationary,' 'changing,' and 'European' are only illustrative. But probably the most common designations were 'primitive society' and 'modern society.' The former is typically a kin- or descent-organized society, with hordes, or gens or clans and tribes as subsidiary units. The latter is a typically politically and territorially-organized society, involving nations, peoples, and states.

Some early theorists were extensively preoccupied with the more specific varieties of primitive or modern societies. Sumner and

Keller, Ward, and Giddings provided extensive commentaries on the characteristics of hordes, horde-organized societies, gens or clans, or gens- and clans- (or in more recent terms, sib-) organized societies, and tribes or tribally-organized societies.[5] Their analyses considerably illuminate the general features of primitive societies and, most significantly, point toward the evolutionary process believed to characterize even primitive societies. In addition, many of the early theorists were also concerned with the development of the state, territoriality, and political organization as important bases of modern society.[6]

However, it is the basic distinction between 'primitive society' and 'modern society' as structural categories which require extended consideration here. This dichotomy did appear in many forms in the literature: 'uncivilized' (or more specifically, 'savage,' 'barbaric') versus 'civilized,' 'tribal' versus 'civic' or 'civil,' 'kinship-organized' versus 'politically-organized,' and 'ethnic' versus 'demotic' societies. And understandably sociologists varied in terms of whether primitive or modern societies occupied more of their attention. Ward, Sumner and Keller seem to have been concerned more with primitive societies. Giddings and Ross appear to have been interested virtually equally in primitive and modern societies. Small and, most certainly, Cooley were considerably more preoccupied with modern societies.

Primitive societies

Admittedly, the details and specificity of treatment accorded to 'primitive societies' varied considerably. Giddings's *The Principles of Sociology* contains a chapter on ethnic (ethnical or ethnogenic) association or society, which seems to have a substantial counterpart in his *The Elements of Sociology*. Sumner provided a paragraph on 'primitive society' in his *Folkways*, but many additional details were scattered throughout the book, as was the case with Ward's treatment in *Dynamic Sociology* and *Pure Sociology*. Small included a chapter on the primitive social process in his *General Sociology*. Cooley accorded tribal society a half chapter (11) in *Social Organization* and offered a few pages on prehistoric tribal conflict (of chapter 22) in *Social Process*. Ross's 'community–society' dichotomy is a scant four pages in *Social Control*, although relevant comments are scattered throughout the volume.

A series of generalizations can be drawn from the views of these early theorists. Accordingly, nine major features of primitive societies can be distinguished:

(1) One of the most evident features of primitive societies is the comparatively small size of their populations which have become definitely associated with a particular habitat or territory. Cooley, for instance, remarks that man formerly lived in many small societies (1966, p. 246). Sumner declares that primitive society consists of 'small groups scattered over a territory' (1959, p. 12). Its size is determined by the conditions of existence within the habitat. And Giddings suggests that the range of consciousness and identification of the group were limited by its boundaries and common territory.

(2) A second characteristic is the prevalence of suspicion, distrust, animosity, hostility, and open conflict between such societies. Sociologists believed that the niggardliness of nature and the attendant severity of the struggle for existence made such collisions inevitable. Cooley commented that relations among primitive societies were comparatively external and mechanical (1966, p. 246). Struggling for similar ends in a similar manner, they often came into conflict, albeit local in character and small in scale (1966, p. 247). Sumner especially believed that the culture of each group – its folkways, mores, institutions, and distinctive ethos – constituted a whole that distinctively reflected its past hostilities with other societies. Presumably also notions of a common territory, common interest in mutual aggression and defense, acceptance of leadership and allegiance to the group – which characterize primitive groups, according to Giddings – would be influenced by conflict (1898, p. 249). Conflict was the foundation for its differentiation from others by which it becomes a we-group or in-group, and adjacent groups, they-groups, or out-groups. Each group 'nourishes its own pride and vanity, boasts itself superior, exalts its own divinities, and looks with contempt on outsiders' (Sumner, 1959, p. 13). Conflict engenders, strengthens, and structures the nature of its ethnocentrism. Accordingly, Ross observed that each society exhibits a moral or ethical dualism, with one set of codes for itself and another for outsiders (1969, pp. 345, 348).

(3) Primitive societies accord a sacredness to age, to the traditional, and to the archaic (1969, p. 185). What ought to be is what is and what is is what was. Precedent is overwhelmingly important. Legend and myth have a universal attraction to primitive men. Old age also brings deference, prestige, and veneration. What the elders decide is authoritative. Broadly speaking, age is one of the social

criteria in terms of what tasks, responsibilities, decisions, esteem, and authority are distributed throughout the life cycle in primitive society.

(4) Sex (in the sense of gender) is another characteristic criterion by which members of the society are divided and arranged in rather sharp and exclusive categories. Many of the early sociologists alluded to the importance of gender demarcations but no one of them offered a direct, extended, or systematic interpretation (cf. Small, 1905, p. 211).

(5) Secret societies and clubs are not common throughout the full range of primitive societies but they are sufficiently frequent to evoke comment. Both the secret association and the club are unisexual. Small cited 'systems of secret rites' among the rudimentary structures of primitive tribes (1905, p. 211). Giddings (1898, p. 198) refers to tribal societies as containing 'many secret associations which have religious functions.' Sumner and Keller contend that both the secret association, which always are more or less religious in character, and the prevailingly non-secret clubs, which are secular in outlook, have important age-grading, educational, and regulatory functions (1927, pp. 525–59).

(6) Except for Small, all of the major theorists recognized the centrality of kinship and kin groups in the social structure of primitive societies. Sumner, for instance, observed that kinship was the basis for primitive conceptions of societal rights and duties, societal institutions, and societal organization (1959, p. 493). However, he and his colleagues varied considerably in the fullness of their treatments. Sumner examined incest, noted that among earliest primitives the mother was a more pivotal point for reckoning kinship than the father, distinguished the mother- and father-family as systems of reckoning descent and kinship in terms of mother-females or father-males (matrilinealism or patri-linealism), alluded to the prevalence of what was later termed the classificatory system of kinship among primitives, defined the sib as the extended consanguineous family, but allowed its relation to the horde, clan, and totemic groups to remain unspecified, and explained the regulative efficacy of kin-group membership largely in terms of belief in ghost-spirits as evidenced in blood-revenge. Ward emphasized the fundamental basis of the blood-bond among primitive peoples, but he did not systematically examine kinship as such. But he does conceive of hordes, clans, and tribes as essentially kin-organized social units. In fact, clans are derived from hordes and tribes are derived from clans and each successive unit is increasingly more complex than the prior originating one.

167

But among early sociologists it was Giddings who offered the most systematic and comprehensive exposition of kinship and kin-units. He proposed the distinction between matronymy and patronymy to signify the association of naming, kinship, and descent with mother-female and father-male figures (i.e., matrilinealism or patrilinealism). He related each to exogamy and endogamy and eventually explained the implications of the two systems for the integration of society as a whole. In turn they were related to such kin-based or kin-linked social units as hordes, clans, totems and totemic groups, phratries, tribes, tribal feudalism, and tribal confederations (or ethnic nations).

Sociologists scarcely moved beyond generalizations of the main features of kin groups in their studies. What might be called functional analysis today was only broached incidentally. Cooley observed that the 'group of kindred was for many purposes (political, economic, religious, etc.) a corporate unit, acting as a whole and responsible as a whole to the rest of society' (1962, p. 110). Giddings's general observation that among 'the lowest bands of savage men, there . . . is much cooperation but there is no specialized cooperative group for systematically carrying on any particular activity' is applicable in particular to kin groups (1898, p. 195). They are not differentiated and specialized by activity; although the kinds of activities in which they engaged were limited, they were altered by the nature of the occasion. Nevertheless, sociologists were widely cognizant of the broad regulative function which kin groups performed. A few of them attempted to account for how it was possible for kin groups to provide this function. But their analyses will be presented below because they also involve certain typical features of primitive belief systems and social participation which should be understood first.

(7) Primitive societies were pervaded by a preoccupation with the dispositions of the powers of a personally conceived nature, which moderns might broadly interpret as essentially comprising religion and magic. But to modern students Giddings's notion of ghost spirits, Sumner's goblinism and demonism, or Keller's animism, eidolism, daimonism, and fetishism may not entirely communicate this basic primitive view of the varying beneficent and maleficent powers of nature surrounding and participating in the world of men. Ross construes (1969, p. 140) religion as a 'blend of nature myths, legends, rules for interpreting dreams, notions about good and bad spirits, recipes for exorcism or propitiation, traditions about charms, omens and sacred places.' Yet Sumner's analysis of uncleanliness does point to the common fact that contact with the

extraordinary powers of both the sacred and holy and the evil and impure or unclean were similarly threatening to men. In some instances of such contact, ritual cleansing – de-sanctification or de-contamination – might be possible but in other instances, death might be predestined. Obviously, too, the non-human affects the human and the human affects it, as is evident in primitive efforts to influence, by acts of renunciation or self-discipline (e.g., abstention from food, drink, or sex activity), ghosts or demons who can intervene to produce luck. Totemism, along with other beliefs and practices observed by clans (and by gentes), is illustrative of the personalized relationship between humans and non-humans among somewhat more complex primitive peoples.

For Sumner and Giddings, the beliefs in ghost spirits were central to primitive religion. Everywhere primitive men believed that the dead lived 'on as ghosts in another world just like this one. The ghosts had just the same needs, tastes, passions, etc., as the living men had . . . The living had duties to the ghosts, and the ghosts had rights; they also had power to enforce their rights' (Sumner, 1959, p. 29). The surviving spirits of the dead could come 'back to their bodies or wander through the air,' or enter 'into plants, streams, or other objects' (Giddings, 1898, p. 252). Accordingly, Giddings notes that man had 'to propitiate not only living beings who were more powerful than himself, but also ghosts of the dead which, if not well treated, might become malevolent, and work all manner of mysterious mischief' (1898, p. 252). Perhaps the most significant of the ghosts of the dead were those of expired kinsmen of both the distant and near past. Their spirits were powerfully influential on the conduct of the living. Ancestral ghosts required contemporary kin descendants faithfully to adhere to the beliefs and practices of the past. The ghost of a murdered kinsman demanded that his relatives secure blood compensation by taking revenge on the culprit or one of his kin. Thus, beliefs about ghost spirits had important social consequences.

(8) Primitive social life entails frequent and extensive participation in public assemblies, meetings, and in ceremonial and ritual observance. Lacking indirect means of communication, only direct face-to-face contact through public assemblies, feasts, and games can evoke – to use Cooley's words – 'social excitement and . . . the higher phases of consciousness' (1962, p. 109). Cooley describes these situations as 'the occasions of exultation, the theatre for the display of eloquence – either in discussing questions of the moment or recounting deeds of the past' – interwoven 'with dancing, acting, poetry, and music in one comprehensive and communal act' (1962,

169

p. 109). Thought and feeling were vividly interchanged, sympathy, loyalty, and honor were expressed, intercourse was congenial, and the moral unity was compelling (1962, p. 107). Out of suggestion and discussion, leading and following, conformity and dissent, a primitive public opinion arose (1962, p. 107). Individuality, personality, self-feeling and self-assertion entered, with the display and evaluation of individual characteristics (1962, pp. 108, 110). Eventually, the 'growth and consensus of ideas upon matters of general and enduring interest, such as religion, marriage,' etc., produced a tribal opinion 'of a slow, subconscious sort' (1962, p. 113).

(9) Characteristically, primitive societies possessed a uniform, homogeneous culture (especially religious-moral beliefs) and a comparatively undifferentiated structure of personalized, informal relationships which permitted kinship systems effectively to fulfill a regulative function. Sumner, on the one hand, and Ross and Cooley, on the other, were primarily important in developing appropriate sociological analyses. The former essentially explained conformity in terms of the specific cultural content of (kinship) norms, whereas the latter pointed especially to the distinctive relational qualities of primitive (especially kinship) groups to account for the inducements to conformity and the deterrents to deviation.

For Sumner, it was essentially the common and unqualified adherence to a belief in ghost spirits which was the key to the effectiveness of kin groups in regulating conduct. Each individual was entirely dependent on and committed to his kin group and within that kin group, he was necessarily concerned with avoidance of any offense to the ghosts of his ancestors, which any major departure from ancestral ways might occasion. The penalty of such deviation was especially severe and serious because it threatened not merely him but all his kinsmen; it was categorical. He could bring down the avenging wrath of ancestral ghosts 'on the whole group of which he was a member' (1959, p. 235). The violator thus aroused a sentiment of vengeance and 'united all the rest in a common interest against him' (1959, p. 235). If 'any misfortune befell the group,' its members 'turned against any one who had broken the taboos' (1959, p. 235). He might be permanently banished and, in effect, condemned to death outside the society. In the reaction of the primitive kin group, it was the deed that was important and not any intention (1959, p. 118). In murdering a fellow kinsman – whether accidentally or intentionally – the individual had to fear the ghost of the murdered one. But he could avail himself of religious rites to absolve and save himself from the vengeance of the spirits. For less severe breaches of order or violations of the rights of others in his kin group, the individual would be treated in terms of customary precedents, penalties or payments, and possible amercements by authority.

An individual would in all likelihood be deterred from serious infractions of rules involving members of other kin, such as murder, by the certainty of revenge from the kinsmen of that group (e.g.., a gens or clan). In primitive society, the injured person or aggrieved individual attempts to gain redress himself. But if he fails he can call on his fellow kinsmen. Any individual knows that the ghost of a murdered man will hold his kin responsible for seeking blood-atonement and that members of the kin group will seek to find the murderer in order to appease the ghost spirits (and who in turn can only be satisfied by blood) and thus save themselves from the wrath of the spirits. Any member feels obligated to aid in seeking vengeance for the injury of a fellow kinsman, irrespective of more detached or abstract considerations of right and wrong. Blood-revenge is a solemn duty and obligation involving all kinsmen. (However, increasing societal complexity is likely to be accompanied by restrictions on impulsive reactions and prompt blood-revenge by kin groups. As they become structured within more complex tribal organizations, kin groups are likely to develop councils. Elders on such bodies may regulate member involvement in blood-revenge and retaliation and even attempt to prevent inter-kin disputes or adjust them amicably (1959, p. 506).)

Sumner did not ignore the sympathy, intimacy, comradeship, mutuality, and orderliness among kin groups. However, he regarded these features as effects of prevalent adherence to the rules rather than as causes inducing conformity itself (1959, pp. 496–506). Of course, he recognized that such (in-group) unity and solidarity were also in part a reciprocal accompaniment of the animosity, hostility, and conflict directed toward other (out-group) kinship units (1959, p. 496). Contrarily, Cooley and Ross seemed to regard conformity as especially a function of the qualities of the relationships within primitive (especially kin) social units.

Cooley's many references generally and specifically to the villages of uncivilized, savage, and primitive peoples in his chapter on the primary group (and the following ones on primary ideals) indicate that his analysis of the qualities of primary groups are directly relevant to an understanding of conformity within primitive societies. Comparatively speaking, the number of members in family or kin groups is small. The goals, purposes, or objectives of such groups are diffuse, general, and multi-dimensional. Their structures are relatively simple and congenial to the demands of human nature. The discipline of sharing a common, early, and prolonged experience, with direct, quick, and full communication, in face-to-face intimacy and emotionality, along with complete personal involvement, inculcates in each person a common (acquired) human nature. Sympathy, moral unity, loyalty, truth, service, kindliness, rightness, and freedom are the common sentiments and ideals engendered within the common experience of these groups. Each person is able to imagine himself in the position of the others and each tends to include in his imagination the judgments of others of himself. His consciousness of self is oriented to other members, to their approval and disapproval, to a shared view of right and wrong, to their ideals. As part of the distinctive holistic solidarity signified by a 'we-feeling,' the individual is motivated to conform to the rules of primitive (i.e., primary) groups.

Actually, Ross's analysis merits a recognition which it has so far largely failed to receive. Perhaps his contribution has been obscured by the prominence of Cooley and his conceptualization of the primary group. Perhaps, also, it has been somewhat ignored because it was unsystematically offered in *Social Control* and because it was incorporated in a community–society dichotomy which was assumed to be derived primarily from Tönnies. Admittedly, Ross really didn't explain the full significance of the concepts (natural) community and (artificial) society, although he asserts that the dichotomy was elaborated long before he became acquainted with Tönnies's *Gemeinschaft und Gesellschaft* (1969, p. 432, fn).

The important point is that (natural) community makes possible the emergence of a condition of natural (or spontaneous) order and control as opposed to (planned) social order and control among members of the group. Ross observes that its members have a 'lively sense of a common life' which enables them to 'love and understand one another, to yield to one another, and to observe those forebearances and good offices that make associated life a success' (1969, pp. 432–3). The characteristics of the group are such as to make possible a natural order among its members. Men act uncalculatingly, spontaneously, and directly under the prompting of their natural inclinations, i.e., their social sentiments: sympathy, sociability, sense of justice, and resentment. Individual members respond to these dictates of human nature and unintentionally an orderly, harmonious conduct occurs without

172

reliance on elaborate normative regulation.

This natural order is possible in a (natural) community for a variety of reasons. The community has been spontaneously formed, with no more than the few members who can be bound together by personal ties. The group as a whole is constituted by many firm basic bonds. Kinship has a sacred significance, interlinking and associating families in extended networks. Attachments are close and lasting among those who live, labor, and enjoy one another's company for an extended period of time. The range of fellowship and companionship coincides with the scope of economic activity. People are sensitive to one another's needs. Division of labor is simple. Since men act under basically similar conditions, social and economic equality prevails. Property is readily and easily shared (e.g., early human aggregates were communistic). Members have not yet experienced military conquest or the concentration and centralization of coercive force in the state. Neither police nor crime exist as such.

Thus bound together by personal ties, men's relations are direct and personal and their behaviors are spontaneously regulated. The effects of acts on others are readily traceable and personally visible. Effective relations and obligations do not extend beyond those who are personally known and cared about. Few, if any, groups smaller than the whole exist and they do not compete seriously for men's loyalties to the whole. Deviants cannot hide. Nonconformity is directly censured by forfeiture of companionship, exclusion from pleasurable association, and ostracism. (Sanctions are informal, unorganized, diffuse.) Thus, primitive society which is characterizable in terms of Ross's natural community evidences what might be termed an unpremeditated concord or natural control. Governed by their sentiments, men exercise mutual forebearance and reciprocal constraint. Members of a (natural) community exhibit a natural (and unplanned) order rather than a (planned, artificial) social order.

Modern societies

Modern society is the other major structural type with which primitive society is often contrasted. Modern society is a civilized, civic or civil, territorially- or politically-organized form of society. Giddings sometimes used the adjective demotic or demogenic as an equivalent. In Ross's dichotomy of community and society, society represents the encompassing social structure which is associated with the state and displays some degree of rational, purposive, intentional, and voluntary action. Modern society was construed in an evolutionary framework as later, more heterogeneous, differentiated, and specialized.

All of the Founding Fathers in American sociology were concerned with modern society, its structure and change. In some cases its importance was assumed to be paramount and its nature obvious. Cooley's sociology is predominantly and overwhelmingly devoted to the study of modern society, although nowhere does he even attempt to define it. Small's concern lies primarily in the abstract universals of human association, and secondarily in the genesis of modern society. Ross and Giddings are more inclined to provide relatively equal attention to both primitive and modern social life, whereas Ward and Sumner and Keller concentrated primarily on primitive social structure and the genesis of modern social life. Yet Ward, Sumner and Keller, Giddings and Ross offer the most explicit and systematic conceptualization of modern society, which seems to have been most influenced by the European sociologist Ludwig Gumplowicz. The following characteristics are most conspicuous in their notion of modern society:

(1) Modern societies typically involve larger population aggregates than do primitive societies (Giddings, 1896, p. 299). They have been composed by the frequent coercive or infrequent voluntary compounding of larger kinship-, ethnically- or tribally-organized societies. Simple increase of births over deaths alone would never produce these societies. Their larger size affords the possibility of developing other features which have also become conspicuously associated with the designation 'modern society.'

(2) Developed as a product of two or more different societies, they entail a cultural and racial heterogeneity not characteristic of primitive peoples. The population is likely to be diverse in its physical origins and to become genetically mixed by miscegenation and amalgamation. Its culture is a new composite or synthetic entity deriving from a plurality of antecedents which have been unified as the result of social combination from conquest or confederation.

(3) Perhaps the critical and distinguishing feature of modern society is that it is territorially- or politically-organized by the state. Thus, its synonyms are 'civic' or 'civil society,' the antecedents of which are the Latin 'cives' or 'civilis' both pertaining to citizen. In turn, the citizen was originally a member of a city (or city-state). And the developed municipality had become a territorial organization capable of providing the person its protection. At least in Western European experience (in Greek and Roman eras) state,

politics, and city coincided.

(4) Modern societies involve a (true) division of social labor, with a complex differentiation and specialization of social structures and functions. Groups with more delimited objectives and functions appear as do specialized social roles. Political, juristic, military, religious, and economic groups arise, with some sphere for voluntary activity. Giddings classifies associations into political, juristic, economic, and cultural types.

(5) Social stratification is a main feature of modern societies. What had begun as a coerced division of labor established by unequal power in conquest became the basis of an invidious prestige ranking of conqueror and conquered, their social and economic activities, and the distinguishing features of their cultures and mode of social life (Ward, 1970, p. 205; Sumner and Keller, 1927, p. 585). The relative equality of primitive society was superceded by the relative inequality of modern society. However, early American sociologists were not meticulously careful in using terms to describe or characterize different kinds and arrangements of strata. Class and caste were commonly employed but not sharply differentiated. Ward suggested that conquest was followed initially by enslavement and later by some mitigation of circumstance and the emergence of caste (or caste-relationships). He did not refer to both conquerors and conquered as castes. From his comments, it can be inferred that a caste-relationship involves conquerors and conquered who are racially unlike and culturally different and mutually antagonistic and contemptuous of one another (1970, pp. 205–6). Keller employs (1927, p. 566) both castes and classes as terms. Caste involves a distinctive race-color along with occupational, religious, wealth, marriage, and commensal restrictions. Classes are established by common interests and mode of life. Conquest, wealth, trade, and kin connections are some of their bases. But the distinctive feature of a class is a code, 'a standard of behavior, a set of ideals . . . a standard of living which is in the mores' (1927, p. 587). Ross apparently conceived of classes as separated by interests, education, and mode of life, with coercion, superstition, fraud, pomp, and precedent involved in inter-relationships of classes (1969, pp. 380, 386, 388, 390–2).

(6) For Giddings, modern societies depend on mixed economies, with private property, at least agriculture and handicrafts, considerable trade, and the use of money. Conquest brings (pastoral) nomads and sedentary agricultural peoples into an economic relationship. The former migrate and conquer the latter who are dispossessed of ownership and compelled to cultivate the

soil. Eventually, centers of worship and defense emerge and attract artisans and laborers. Markets and fairs develop. Agricultural produce and town wares are exchanged. Trade proliferates, a mercantile class arises, and money emerges.

(7) Giddings also notes that communities in modern societies become differentiated. Agriculture is focused in the village community. Places of worship and defense become administrative centers which are transformed into distinct towns as the economic exchange of foodstuffs and handicrafts associated with periodic fairs and markets comes to be more continuous. Thus, communities become distinguishably rural and urban, each one the focus of certain differentiated and specialized activities.

(8) For many sociologists, the distinctive and characteristic group of modern societies is the (voluntary) association. It is a limited (or restricted) and specific purpose group with varying degrees of rationality, purposiveness, intentionality, and voluntarism. Giddings (1932, p. 388) noted that the earliest meaning of society (from the Latin 'societas') was an association, a combination, 'a partnership in good or evil, or both.' Ward has argued that in the period of concession and resignation, compromise and toleration, following earlier conquest and subordination, men from both backgrounds began to associate on the basis of common interest and personal qualifications (e.g., affability, zeal, skill, talent) rather than in terms of the mandates of tradition, kinship, or race (1970, pp. 192, 210, 547). 'Society' in the 'community – society' dichotomy of Ross refers to the newer, more 'narrow gauge,' loosely-binding, and utiliarian affiliations 'founded on affinity and [a] selective choice' that implies 'a preference for some persons over other persons' (1969, p. 434). It is the secondary group which has been attributed to Cooley in antithesis to the primary group but which he actually terms the 'nucleated group.' Cooley's conceptualization resembles other notions of the voluntary association. He indicates that the nucleated group is characterized by narrow and specific purposes or objectives, involves a more complex structure of relations, and is composed of a large number of members who affiliate with several such groups in accordance with their talents, aptitudes, and inclinations. Members' relations to one another are specific, less emotional, and not necessarily face-to-face. Most of them are likely to contribute little of themselves to the group whereas only one or a few members (the nucleus) will devote their whole personalities to it. Communication may be indirect, formal, and impersonal (1966, pp. 249–52; 1969, pp. 185, 186).

(9) Characteristically, modern societies with their multiform and heterogeneous culture and comparatively differentiated structures of specific, complex, and formally organized relationships have engendered distinctive regulatory problems and require a new type of regulative system. Both Cooley and Ross have extensive inquiries into the deviational predicaments of modern societies. The former offers a series of discerning social psychological analyses of the sources and mechanisms inducing individual nonconformity, without however discovering any social mechanisms for meeting the problem. The latter provides a more systematic examination of the kinds of structural bases for deviation and, in addition, argues that modern society has begun to evolve an appropriate solution, a social control system.

Understandably, Cooley's analysis of the regulative problems of modern society begins with nucleated groups (i.e., voluntary associations). Because such groups have become differentiated and specialized, mechanical and routine, rigid and impersonal, they have necessarily lost their humanness, breadth, and flexibility (1962, p. 320). In Cooley's terms, formalization has occurred. Consequently, their members can no longer adequately satisfy the broader sentiments and freer and larger impulses of human nature which they had acquired from earlier primary group experiences. They feel frustrated and alienated – without any firm, internalized commitment to rules (1962, p. 349). Evaluated in terms of external circumstances, conformity often becomes a matter of expedience. Deviance is a recurrent possibility.

Nonconformity is further encouraged by the lessened emotional impact of member interaction and by the restricted outlook associated with differentiated and specialized roles in nucleated groups. The individual will be less likely to understand his place in the whole and the function of the group in the institutional system. To paraphrase Cooley, the whole will not commonly live in his thought. He will be less likely to see himself in terms of the perspectives of others, to share their notions of right and wrong, and to be bound by a strong feeling of 'we-ness.' He will have difficulty in feeling any imperious moral obligation to the whole. The disjunction between consciousness and understanding of the role-incumbents and the nature and expanse of the whole as it exists will undermine their motivation, particularly their moral steadfastness, lead to the withdrawal of commitment, permit deviation, and gradually allow disorganization of the parts of the social system.

More broadly, regulation in modern society is beset by the

problem of social disorganization, which means a lack of 'general order and discipline,' a loss of 'unity and rationality,' and reciprocal opposition, struggle, and conflict among individuals, groups, and institutions (1962, pp. 330, 347, 351). Cooley was constantly preoccupied with the destruction of specific moral standards, general moral codes, and broad moral traditions as the basic foundation of social disorganization. It may stem, for instance, from the failure to connect new specialized activities (diachronically) with the past traditions of the institutional realm, from the lack of a (synchronic) commonly supported and integrated tradition in the several parts of the institution, from the absence of any renewal of the meaning of the basic symbols of an institution in the present, or their maladaptation to the situation in which the institution must operate, or their excessive abstractness, intellectuality, or complexity, or inconsistency with the symbols of other institutional realms. Institutional disorganization may also derive from the emergence of new power sources which are not adequately restricted and regulated by moral and legal standards, from the undermining of authority by failure to transmit reverential attitudes and by ineffectualization of sanctions at the disposal of authority-holders, erosion of interdependence between paired-roles by reallocation of functions from one or both roles, the destruction of traditional role distinctions, emergence of activities incompatible with older activities in a role, and redefinition of the obligations of a particular role by incumbents of closely related roles. In addition Cooley argued, by implication, that changes in the context of a role which would allow its incumbents to make choices irrespective of and possibly in opposition to the broader social or institutional considerations, to permit them to insist that role obligations be judged in terms of personal advantages to the incumbent, or which would destroy the fixed routines and so infect the role-incumbents with discontent and uncertainty, would engender social disorganization.

Once departures from a relatively established norm have become so persistent and conspicuous as to constitute a 'falling away from the standard,' they may constitute what Cooley terms degeneration (1966, pp. 153, 154; 1964, pp. 402, 406). Such phenomena as crime, alcoholism, prostitution, dishonesty, selfishness, or sensuality are regarded as deriving from the more or less crude (and non-normatively regulated) impulses of primitive emotions rather than as social phenomena embodying counter-standards and counter-organization (1966, pp. 176, 177, 154).

Displacement is itself a distinct and peculiar causal process of degeneration. It denotes the radical alteration in a person's life conditions such that intimate (primary-group) association, which ordinarily functions to maintain moral standards, is destroyed or can no longer operate effectively (1966, p. 180). Without exposure to the constant sense of the group's opinions through interchange of ideas and feelings so that 'standards of right and wrong seem real,' the individual is likely to engage in deviation and become personally demoralized.

Such personal demoralization is associated with moral dis-integration or the undermining of the coherence of relevant standards, which derives from the extensive deviation engendered by social disorganization and degeneration. Although Cooley used the term demoralization frequently, he never directly and explicitly defined it. Presumably, it indicates that the individual no longer possesses stable, integrated moral norms to which he feels obligated to conform in overt action. In some instances, he may endeavor to retain isolated standards from his past and in others, he may attempt to create rules *de novo* from his own reflective resources (1966, p. 181; cf. 1962, p. 352). But without effective social support for his standards, he is likely to be 'thrown back upon his undisciplined impulses' and private reason (1962, pp. 351, 352). He is apt to feel morally isolated, to be rent by severe mental strain, and to experience an 'atrophy of moral sense' (1966, p. 181; 1962, p. 352). Perhaps most likely, his deviation will ensue as a 'confused outbreak of impulses, better or worse' (1966, p. 181).

Unlike Cooley, Ross offers an account of the inducements to deviation which issues explicitly and directly from the main features of modern society as part of the community–society (or communal–associational) dichotomy. No longer is it possible to rely on the relatively unorganized, informal, and diffuse sanctions of natural control in primitive society, operating unreflectively, impulsively, and spontaneously in accordance with the dictates of a set of common human nature sentiments. Ross employs six main characteristics of modern (associational) society to argue that deviation will occur unless social order – a condition of harmonious, orderly, regularized, and conformist behavior in relation to norms – is consciously, rationally, and purposefully maintained by a system of social control, with an essentially impersonal and formally organized set of sanctions:

(a) Social differentiation introduces competing social loyalties among several groups whereas early society has been fundamentally an integral unity. There can no longer be a lively sense of a common life. Spatially separated and socially distant, people are less sensitive to one another's needs. Kinship has lost its central and sacred significance. The various groups become objects of devotion, seek to monopolize sympathies, and compete for loyalty with the whole society. Thus, the society as the all-inclusive group must find some means 'to assimilate and reconcile its members and weaken the ties that bind men into minor groups' (Ross, 1969, p. 52). Conscious regulation is needed.

(b) Relational and organizational complexity – presumably an accompaniment of social differentiation – is another source of possible nonconformity. As the individual enters into relations with many persons whom he does not know or care for, his natural sentiments of sympathy can no longer operate effectively. Relations become fixed and impersonal and the consequences of acts become remote, less readily traceable, and less visible (1969, p. 13). Specialized control is also necessary to avoid chronic intra- or inter-organizational feuds and disorders which might be occasioned if private attempts to redress grievances stemming from personalized resentment were unchecked. In addition, some explicit form of regulation is needed to restrain the (defective, degenerate, or delinquent) personal deviant, who can readily 'prey and inflict damage upon others' in the intricate cooperation characterizing impersonal relations of the complex organization (1969, p. 51). But the ordinary person in that structure, with its 'delicate poise of numerous individual performances,' requires direction in the form of orders from authority so that he will conform to his special task, unthreatened by interferences from others and untempted to disturb them (1969, pp. 12, 50).

(c) Economic differentiation adds to the demands for specific regulation. As economic activities undergo specialization, the range of the division of labor is extended so that it no longer coincides with the local context of sociability, fellowship, or companionship. The local cluster – parish, neighborhood, commune – was once the unit for both social pleasure and the division of labor, but has now split 'up for sociable purposes and coalesces with other clusters for economic purposes' (1969, p. 18). Solidarity and conformity in economic life now require special support and buttressing.

(d) Private property and economic differentiation facilitate social stratification which in turn constitutes another sphere demanding conscious regulation. Private property, 'a great transforming force which acts almost independently of the human will,' aggravates the tendency of economic differentiation to destroy equality and similarity of condition and to introduce difference and inequality of 'reward, possession, and inheritance' (1969, p. 53). In a differentiated society, private property rights become too complex and extensive to be linked with, and justified by, the good of particular persons (1969, p. 20). Money also allows men to be categorically evaluated. They are violently thrust apart and classes arise on 'the different planes of worldly conditions' (1969, p. 53). Nevertheless, inequality is required – argued Ross – to satisfy the strong and to maintain economic differentiation, which, in turn, contributes to evoking the demand for social control (1969, p. 56).

(e) The coerced combination of men by military conquest is another condition necessitating (intentional) control. The 'increasing agglomeration of communities has . . . always [been due] to conquest or to combination for defense' (1969, p. 18). Conquest and the super-subordination of peoples (Ross uses the word 'races') destroy the natural community (1969, pp. 56, 18). 'The violent superposition of peoples on people forbids the establishment of the primal moral bonds between the upper and lower' (1969, p. 56). The resulting social strife and rancor tend to prevent the emergence of interpersonal sympathy, sociability, and justice and to impose instead a rather sullen, categorical resentment. Order must be created and imposed intentionally by the state and law under the threat of coercion. In the consciousness, intentionality, and design of its instruments of regulation the state provides a model of control for the composite society 'where the need of control is most imperious and unremitting' (1969, p. 97).

(f) The growth of cities has produced distinctive circumstances which are fought with inducements to deviation. Neighborliness has disappeared. People are mutually indifferent. They mingle 'without fellowship' and have 'contact without intercourse' in 'loose touch-and-go acquaintanceships' (1969, p. 433). Frequent change of domicile weakens the sensitivity to others in a given locality. Communal opinion is absent. Urban charity is machinal and its philanthropy vicarious. Its contrasts of wealth and poverty are dismal. The city displays a wolfish struggle for personal success. Its 'crimes, frauds, exploitations, and parasitism' can be hidden and do not provoke 'forfeiture of companionship, exclusion from social pleasure, ostracism' (1969, p. 19).

All of these conditions of modern society require the means, methods, agencies, or instrumentalities of social control, e.g., laws, beliefs, suggestion, education, ideals, enlightenment, illusion, and social valuations. Control is achieved primarily by the leaders of society as they consciously, intentionally, and calculatingly use these instruments to promote conformity and deter deviation (i.e., maintain social order).

These arguments of Cooley and Ross regarding the distinctive regulative problems of modern societies point clearly to the potentialities of change apparently intrinsic to the very modernity of modern societies. In Cooley's analysis, it is the nucleated group which is the point of departure, but it is construed as a part of a context characterized by social disorganization, degeneration, displacement, personal demoralization, and moral disintegration. For his part, Ross envisages deviation elicited from modern societies by virtue of the competing loyalties induced by social differentiation, the obstruction of the perception of the consequences of (personal) action by relational and organizational complexity, the non-coincidence of the extended division of labor with the local context of sociability, fellowship, or companionship, erosion of a sense of communality by social stratification, the destruction of natural community by political conquest and the superordination–subordination of peoples, and the destruction of the bonds of intimacy, cohesion, and solidarity by the growth of the city. Accordingly, modern societies as a type seem to be intrinsically dynamic rather than static.

In broader perspective, it is true that primitive and modern societies could be and were viewed by early American theorists as coexisting simultaneously in the then present. But more frequently they inferred more than mere contrast in the social characteristics of primitive and modern societies. It was not merely a matter of small populations versus larger populations; or of sacredness and significance accorded to age, sex (gender), and kinship versus territory, social differentiation, specialization, stratification, and technological elaboration; or of a personalized conception of nature, public participation, ceremony, ritual, a uniform homogeneous culture and a comparatively undifferentiated structure of personalized, informal social relationships versus (the implication of an impersonal nature,) the differentiation-specialization of local communities, the rise of the voluntary association, along with a multiform, heterogeneous culture, a differentiated structure of impersonal and formal social relationships, and distinctive (derivative) regulatory problems. The two sets of characteristics of primitive and modern societies were frequently conceived to signify fundamental change. Simultaneous or coexistent global structural variation was much more likely to be interpreted in terms of structural succession, sequence, or change. The theory of early American sociology was prevailingly a theory of social change. However minimal the adaptation of organization or structure across generations might be, change – in the view of early American sociologists – was ineluctably predestined.

8 An overview of theories of social change and social evolution

To sociologists of the first era, change was the pervasive feature of all phenomena. They concurred essentially with Giddings (1922, p. 230) in the view that the 'first law of life is a law of motion.' Both this general premise and the more specific insistence that change is the dominant fact of social life are expressions of sociologists' commitment to evolutionary naturalism. Understandably, Cooley could declare (1966, p. 396) that any 'real study of society must be first, last, and nearly all of the time a study of process.' As in other major problems, early sociologists began their study by a consideration of change as a general phenomenon and then by distinguishing social development or social evolution and social progress from mere (social) change. In accordance with their commitment to evolutionary naturalism, they regarded change as the effect of a disturbance of a structured (adaptive) relationship between biopsychic wants-needs-desires and their satisfaction from within the environment. Thus, the nature of the social forces, the character of the environment or habitat, the variety and range of individual differences (especially talents) as a basis for creative innovation, the availability of a past repertory of adaptive-adjustive ideas and practices (i.e., the social heritage) are common features in the explanation of change, though inclinations to behavioristic-materialism or interactionist-idealism were important sources of divergence. However, change cannot be satisfactorily explained without a full consideration of all of the fundamental problems which elaboration of the analytic scheme affords (Scheme III, F). Two basic theoretical stances – social evolutionism and social processualism – are thus derived and examined in the remainder of this chapter and the two following ones.

Basic terminological distinctions

Couched generally within the assumptions of evolutionary naturalism, the preoccupation with social change in these early publications did entail the use of certain terminological distinctions which centered on whether or not the relationship between the structure of a society and its environment or habitat was demonstrably adjustive–adaptive or not. Early sociologists did distinguish (mere) social change from social development or evolution and development or evolution from both change and progress (Scheme III, F, 1). Ross, for instance, notes (1919, p. 185) that change means any qualitative variation, movement, or adaptation (as ascertained presumably by study at two different points in time). Keller is careful to restrict (1927, pp. 2190–1) evolution to adaptation, which is apparently objective and demonstrable (in contrast to the ethnocentric judgments involved in assertions of progress and regress). For Cooley (1966, p. 407), too, development is provable, objective, observational, factual. Presumably, Giddings's acceptance of Spencer's position also means (1932, p. 74) that evolution as 'orderly change which shows a trend, a movement in a certain direction rather than some other direction,' presupposes (more or less) adaptation and thus survival. Ward's basic intellectual position suggests that a similar assumption is basic to his assertion that social evolution is objectively evidenced in movement to social structures 'having greater differentiation and more complete integration of their parts' (1970, p. 255). (Undeniably, too, social evolution is assumed to manifest a more or less objectively ascertainable trend or direction in time.)

Progress, which was often conceded to designate evaluation rather than mere description, was sharply distinguished from the other terms. Ward, for example, warns (1970, p. 98) that social dynamics should not be equated with progress, for the word 'dynamic' may 'apply as well to catabolic or regressive phenomena as to anabolic or progressive ones.' Sumner, Keller, Cooley, and Ross observe (1959, p. 604; 1927, pp. 2190–1, 2216–17; 1966, pp. 406–7; 1919, p. 186) that progress entails a judgment based on a subjective standard that change is for the good, for the better, or signifies advance. For Giddings, progress is material and moral betterment which have accompanied the course of social evolution. Keller associates (1927, pp. 2190–1) progress and retrogress with ethnocentric judgments. Unprovable, subjective, non-observational, and non-factual, the acceptance of progress is for Cooley 'an act . . . of faith' (1966, p. 408). Nevertheless, most early

American sociologists accepted progress. It was, indeed, their ultimate concern in and their justification for their discipline. (Probably only Sumner would have joined Ross (1919, p. 189) in recommending that such vague and dubious conceptions as progress and regress be dropped and the simple fact of change be studied.).

Common assumptions

Basic adherence to evolutionary naturalism did provide early theorists with certain common assumptions about the nature of social change in spite of their varying inclinations to emphasize materialism or idealism in their (dualistic) social ontologies. Because the social order is interconnected, interrelated, and interdependent within the hierarchy of domains of nature, it is necessarily subject to strain and to change. Social phenomena are first and foremost an expedient or effective adaptation or adjustment to surrounding nature. Like all forms of life, social life itself must meet the requirements for the (organic) survival of (most of?) its constituent organisms. Both generally and specifically (i.e., as a given particular arrangement of parts), social existence is necessarily responsive to the recurrent demands of the needs-wants of (the biopsychic human nature of social forces of) individuals in the aggregate in relation to the facilities-resources of the habitat. The study of social change must begin basically with the recognition of the precarious relation between the needs-wants of the human aggregate and their environment.

Because change is change in or of something, it presupposes a prior existing adaptive structure. As Ward observes (1970, p. 222), 'no dynamic phenomena can take place until structures are formed' (or originate). Preliminarily, therefore, social change is the effect of a disturbance of a structured relationship between biopsychic wants-needs-desires and their satisfaction from within the environment as evidenced in the words 'maladjustment' or 'maladaptation.' According to Ward (1970, pp. 221–2), a modification in the relationship between a structure (or equilibrium of desires) and its environment elicits social change. Ross alludes (1919, p. 193) to social change as the outcome of a variation in the direction of desires or the framework in which they operate. Small refers (1905, p. 186) to constant changes in individual purposes and attitudes and in the biophysical surroundings as sources of social change. Variations in the folkways occur – Sumner holds – because there are 'variations of character and circumstance' (1959, p. 495).

185

Elsewhere he notes (1959, p. 84) that the mores change as 'conditions and interests change.'

Basic evolutionary naturalism was not, however, limited to an inquiry into the possible alteration in the relationship between human needs, wants, desires, and ends, and their sources of gratification in the surrounding habitat as a point of departure for investigation of dynamics. All early American theorists considered individual differences among members of the aggregate as a major source for innovative (adaptive) responses. Probably, most of them would have insisted that such investigation of individual differences must be joined with a study of the cultural legacy of past adaptations or adjustments as equally important.

Although all early sociologists pointed to the surrounding environment, habitat, or situation as a factor in precipitating change, their analyses were generally casual, fragmentary, and restricted. Interestingly, Giddings is the only one who systematically explored the relationship of different types of environment and potentiality for change. Still, the scattered remarks from Sumner to Cooley indicate a recognition that such factors as geography (including the absence or presence of physical barriers), climate, topography, soil, flora, fauna, natural resources (and even the human population itself) may precipitate social change (Cooley, 1966, pp. 21, 44, 46–8; Small, 1905, pp. 404–17). Change in any one of them (e.g., deforestation, population increase, accumulation of wealth via resources) can presumably affect the satisfaction of wants or desires and thus provoke behavioral variation and eventually stimulate social change. Relations with foreign or external societies also contain potentialities for (intrusive), change. War, conquest, persistent contacts (e.g., travel, trade, transportation) migration, or the exchange of information at a distance by the technologies of mass communications are illustrative (Cooley, 1966, pp. 180–90, 243; Ross, 1919, pp. 243, 245, 355, 357).

Such more materialistically-inclined sociologists as Sumner and Keller along with Giddings were especially prone to conceive of the components of the environment in terms of increasingly favorable opportunities for or increasingly unfavorable obstacles or threats to the physical survival of members of a given society. Manifestly, a change in the nature of the environment means a change in the conditions under which evolutionary struggle for existence and survival occur. In Sumner's view, a disturbance in the satisfaction of the interests (and their related basic wants) provides pain (which is an index of well-being, adaptation or survival among members of the group). Repetition of such experience tends to motivate men to alter their behavior (i.e., change). Population growth and migration are important because they entail by definition a relocation to a new environment with the necessity of (new) adjustments to (new) conditions of existence.

A second factor important in change is the nature and range of individual differences which are the base for individual behavioral variations and innovation(s). Ward recognizes (1970, pp. 488, 243, 35) 'natural differences among men' as part of the phenomenon of organic, fortuitous variation. Those individuals with favored endowments and opportune circumstances also possess a surplus of social energy which can be expended in innovation (1970, pp. 243–6). (Ward's entire *Applied Sociology* (pp. 113, 115, 128, 236) is concerned with the development of institutional means for releasing and using the best potentials of (hereditary) genius so far unrecognized and untapped.) Sumner remarks that although we do not know who assumed the initiative in devising behavioral variations out of which folkways have arisen in the past, the possessors of major talent have been influential. Keller explicitly located (1915, p. 51) individual variation in the physical changes of individual brains. Perhaps no sociologist was more impressed with the significance of individual differences for social change than was Giddings (1922, p. 92) for whom individuals possessing favorable endowments are the *daimones* of the human race. Ross cites (1969, pp. 275, 8, 350) the 'natural inequality of man' in general and the unique capacities, talents, and gifts of the exceptional man or genius in particular. What he terms 'origination, i.e., invention or discovery, is so difficult that it will always be the prerogative of the few [exceptional men or geniuses]' (1912, p. 385).

The more predominantly idealist sociologists were also impressed with the significance of individual differences in the genesis of social change. Small acknowledges (1905, p. 711) the 'exceptional individuals' whose 'marked differences from other men' and 'particular talents distinguish their possessors from others.' (He also emphasizes the importance of an interpersonal and social context for stimulating and developing such differences.) Cooley argues that human nature inclines all of us to be somewhat individualistic, idiosyncratic, or different from everyone else. We 'do everything a little different from any one else' (Cooley, 1966, p. 300). Each person 'as a whole is always more or less novel or innovating' (Cooley, 1964, p. 355). This proclivity apparently varies with differences in energy, initiative, tenacity, intelligence, endowments, or talents, sensitivity, and self-assertiveness. Presumably, such individual differences are primarily attributable to variations in original nature and secondarily to socialization and experience. Many of these variations are imperceptible and minor, often occurring without recognition by their possessors. But it is these deviations that provide the immediate materials for the construction of adaptive change.

Some broader generalizations about the nature and function of individual differences can be made within the two designations of more materialistic and more idealistic theoretical orientations. Within the former, Sumner and Keller tend to construe the social forces as operating relatively similarly in intensity and in form among members of the same society, though organic needs or wants (e.g., hunger and sex as opposed to vanity and ghost-fear) tend to assume priority to others. Apparently, individual differences for Sumner and Keller find their most significant expression in accordance with a rational–emotional dichotomy among men and especially in terms of varying or differential hereditary endowments of reason, intellect, or intelligence in individuals. Sumner and Keller seem to conceive of a few more rationally endowed persons as the source of effective (i.e., pain-reducing) adaptations to changes in the environment. Simultaneously, they appear to depreciate the influence of emotion as ultimately obfuscating and impeding the emergence of more behaviorally expedient responses. But reason is effective only in the guise of diminishing pain (in conjunction with comparisons of successful and unsuccessful behaviors) within a relatively limited temporal and situational context. Once the appropriate innovative behavior has emerged from some more talented individual (i.e., more favorably endowed with 'reason'), its dissemination among other individuals tends to occur automatically (i.e., deterministically, externalistically, behavioristically) because reactions to pleasure and pain are uniform from individual to individual. (Both observable examples and direct personal experience are consistent.) For Sumner and Keller, the conception of an appropriate response is pre-eminently an adaptive behavior which is ultimately conducive to survival as dictated by a given set of biophysical conditions of existence.

By contrast, the more idealistically-inclined theorists are more prone to envisage the expression of individual differences in both the intensities and the forms which men's common desires and purposes (i.e., the social forces) manifest. Such sociologists as Small and Cooley (and also Giddings and Ross) discern not only individual variation in reason but also in affect, volition, choice, and in displays of energy, temperament, courage, resolution, initiative, self-assertiveness, imagination, and sensitivity. Small and Cooley do not counterpose or differentially emphasize reason and emotion in social change. Indeed, each person's individuality inclines him to be innovating. Thus, the differences of the great mass of people in interaction – rather than only the talented few or elite – are consequential in the emergence of the new and in its acceptance within society. Both nature and nurture contribute to the basis and development of individual differences and innovations. Certainly, Small and Cooley would refuse to base the incentive to social change primarily or substantially on the experience of pain or deprivation of organic wants. Innovation arises as a mode of problem-solving which involves the more internalistic, psychic, and voluntaristic attributes of consciousness, volition, and choice. It signifies an adjustment in behavior and also in sentiments, beliefs, and ideas. Neither Small nor Cooley would deny the necessity of adaptation to the biophysical conditions of existence but for them change entails a much more holistic adjustment within and between any one or more of a variety of levels or modes of social existence.

For many sociologists, unusual capacity or ability can become the basis of innovation only if access to (the past) fund of adaptive ideas is afforded. Social change can occur only if unusual capacity and ideas are joined. Interestingly enough, neither Sumner nor Giddings, both of whose orientations are congenial, explicitly commits himself to the view.[1] In Giddings's case (1896, p. 112), he acknowledges – but without endorsement or adoption – that Tarde's notion of invention 'is the creation of a new idea and a new practice, by a combination of familiar ideas and current practices.' Ross appears to have followed Tarde directly in asserting (1912, p. 360) that an 'invention is not an out-right creation, but, in most cases, a fresh combination of known factors' or 'ideas.' He also invoked (1912, pp. 359, 360) a Tardean formulation of laws on the ease or readiness with which inventions derive from an existent culture base and unusual intellectual capacity.[2] Ward's conception of the genesis of social innovation is generally idealistic, more especially Tardean and Wundtian, and ultimately (apparently Hegelian) dialectical in character. His fundamental concept of creative synthesis explicitly derives from Wundt (and finally from Hegel) (1970, p. 79). Small envisages the efforts of a given generation in achieving ends (i.e., civilization) as leaving a residue of means (or culture in his sense) in the tradition which the following generation can use as a base for innovation (1905, pp. 345, 632).

However, it was Cooley who provided the most direct and extensive analysis of the indispensability of the social heritage for innovation. His comment that 'novelty always consists, from one point of view, in a fresh combination of habits' is consistent with Tarde, if it is not an adaptation of his view (1964, p. 368; 1966, p. 17). Accordingly, the socially new must derive from a prior or existent social structure or repertory of activities, which can be described as having a past historical character or complex of tendencies to change (Cooley, 1966, pp. 19, 12, 17). Any innovation must be derivable from the present social system with its antecedents or past historical experiences. Prior adjustments, adaptations, or organization provide the components for deriving the new from this repertory by combination and recombination. The past also limits the range of possibilities for new adjustments, adaptations, and organization, with a new differentiation and specialization of parts and functions.[3] Deviant tendencies of members must articulate with the innovative potentials afforded by the possibilities for combining and recombining parts or aspects of the repertory of ideas and activities.

Cooley's explicit argument for the derivability of social change from the fund of past social experience, i.e., the social heritage (or social intelligence, as he was sometimes inclined to call it), points more generally to the acceptance of the thesis of social continuity and the accumulation of the social heritage by early American sociologists. Ward was unusually direct in his adherence. Although he recognized the possibility of loss, he emphasized the preoccupation of sociology with 'that great line of social development in which there has been no break in the transmission of development' and in which 'every increment . . . [has] represented a gain and an advance beyond all that had been accomplished before' (1970, pp. 34, 520; cf. pp. 572–3). He quoted Pascal's aphorism approvingly (1970, pp. 34–5). Other early sociologists were careful to qualify the acceptance, adoption, and dissemination of social innovation, including its transmission across generations, by an insistence that it enhances adaptation, adjustment, 'fitness,' or 'workability' of the society in relation to its (social) situation.

However, this broad agreement that social change involves modifications in a given habitat or situation which affect the satisfactions of needs-wants-desires of the human aggregate, requires appropriate mobilization of individual differences in relation to the heritage of past-present social adaptations-adjustments, and tends to be continuous and cumulative, does not in itself actually constitute an explanation of the genesis and institutionalization of innovation as such. The effort to formulate an explanation seems unavoidably to introduce disagreement about the mechanisms involved. For instance some sociologists such as Keller (and perhaps Giddings) would be inclined to emphasize individual differences in relation to scarcity of resources and the survival of the fittest (– adaptation) out of conflict. Others such as Ward would be disposed to add and perhaps stress the Lamarckian thesis of use and disuse. Still others, such as Cooley, would emphasize the uniqueness of each social situation and the slight shifts in interpersonal adjustment relative to the situation and individual differences as the foundation of a constant process of (more or less minor) innovation. (Note, incidentally, that these disagreements about the mechanism may well be associated with varying inclinations to 'behaviorism-materialism' versus 'interactionism-idealism' among early sociologists.)

Of course, an additional complication arises in that it now becomes necessary to distinguish between the possibility of rather constant minor variations and less frequent major innovations. Furthermore, the problem of explanation becomes further complicated because both the genesis of variation-innovation and the broader acceptance, adoption, and dissemination of innovation within the group or society must be acknowledged and systematically considered.

But as the task of explanation becomes more complicated so also does the very intellectual perspective within which change itself is envisaged. The question of social change includes not merely the problem of explanation but other problems as well. But not all of the possible problems were considered by early theorists (see Scheme III, F). Those treated – either explicitly or implicitly – include what the appropriate social unit for the study of change is, the kind of analogy or model which is to be invoked, the possibility of a distinctive method for studying change, the issue of the rate and magnitude of (normal, natural) social change, the question of the directionality of change, and of course, the problem of explaining change, i.e., the causal mechanisms or modus operandi, with which the analysis of change has so far largely been concerned in this chapter.

Within this broader perspective of a plurality of problems actually involved in the investigation of social change, two considerably divergent stances can be identified in early American sociological theory. The first of these can be designated as 'Social

Evolution' (or 'Social Evolutionism'). Its adherents include especially Ward, Giddings, and Keller (though not his mentor Sumner). A second or anti- (social) evolutionary position can also be discerned and involves Sumner, Ross, Small, and Cooley. Their objections are significant and must be examined. But such objections do not in and of themselves indicate the nature of their positive commitments. Interestingly, Sumner appears to adopt a singular position which warrants separate inquiry. Ross, Small, and Cooley do more or less subscribe to a 'Social Process' conception of change.

Social evolution

As a conception of social change, social evolution has characteristically assumed certain answers toward certain questions within the general domain of dynamics. It has been oriented toward a particular unit of study, a certain kind of analogy or model, a distinctive method, a particular notion of rate and magnitude of change, a certain kind of directionality, along with particular features associated with the causal mechanisms or modus operandi of change[4] (see Scheme III, F, 2).

The unit

Like their counterparts in Europe, the social evolutionists among the founding generation of American sociology assumed that the ultimate social unit undergoing change is human society, society, mankind, men, the human species or the human race. Giddings's view must be inferred whereas Keller's is explicit. The titles of the major sections (or 'books') of Giddings's *The Principles of Sociology* indicate the comprehensiveness of his concern. Section 2 on 'The Elements and Structure of Society' is followed by section 3 on 'The Historical Evolution of Society.' In no sense does Giddings intimate that any concrete human societies are to be excluded from his analysis of the common evolutionary trend from an ethnogenic to a demogenic stage. In *The Science of Society* (pp. 2216, 2200, 2215) Keller emphasizes 'Mankind,' 'Human Society,' and the experiences and the history of 'the race' as the unit of study. Human society can be construed as a whole or unity because humankind everywhere is substantially similar and the variability of the life-conditions under which it exists is limited (1927, p. 29). Exceptions and irregularities may be found, but they appear, 'often upon reflection, to be due to local circumstances' (1927, p. 29). For

Keller, the evolutionary process is effective 'on the grand scale, in the life of human society as a whole' and it 'must be viewed over a long perspective' (1929, p. 320; 1918, p. 71).

Basically, all social change is to be approached as fundamentally one common process because all men are assumed to be one organically and psychically and their conditions of existence substantially similar (i.e., at least variability is limited). Ward supposed that he was stating the obvious when he noted (1970, p. 54) that ultimately we 'reach a plane on which all mankind are alike,' with the 'great primary wants [and passions] . . . everywhere the same and . . . supplied [or satisfied] in substantially the same way the world over.' Certainly, Giddings and Keller agreed that humankind is fundamentally alike in its possession of similar (organic) needs and wants and in its (biopsychic) affective and/or cognitive responses (e.g., in liking likeness and in seeking pleasure and avoiding pain). It was in the relationship between that common biopsychic human nature and the reaction to possible changing conditions of aggregate existence that a fundamentally common approach to the study of social change – evolution was to be made. Mankind's biopsychic oneness in relation to limited environmental variability (in the conditions of existence) justified an integral or unified inquiry into social change.

Ward's admonition (1970, p. 32) that the 'human races do not belong to one and the same series of cultural development' must not be misunderstood. It is apparent, on the one hand, that such cultural divergence appears only with the emergence of civilization, which is, however, preceded by an earlier series of common stages of savagery and barbarism. On the other hand, it is evident that Ward was a Lamarckian who does *not* assert that different civilizational series are intrinsically dissimilar, incompatible, or divergent. He proposes (1970, p. 431) that the very early civilizations of Western Eurpoe, such as Stonehenge, 'would have eventually worked up towards the present state.' Furthermore, the pre-Columbian New World had taken steps in civilization which 'were practically the same as those taken in the Old World so long before, and there can be little doubt that with sufficient time the New World would have substantially repeated the history of the Old' (1970, p. 518). Manifestly, Ward does resemble – more than was initially apparent – his colleagues who by and large rejected any basically pluralistic view of human society and culture. Their object of study was (all) human society undergoing development or evolution.[5]

Both indirect and direct influences operated to guide sociologists' attention to all mankind. As sociology emerged in the 1880s and 1890s, it necessarily confronted the still-powerful claims and traditions of religious supernaturalism. God had created all humankind (i.e., monogenism) and ultimately all members of the species (as biopsychically one) had a common social existence and social destiny. The emerging evolutionary naturalism was compelled to dispute in terms of units defined by its opponent. Biology with its evolutionary naturalism endeavored to explain life as a whole and man as a whole organically. Following biology and psychology, sociology also endeavored to account for all human association and social existence in terms of evolutionary naturalism.

The analogy or model

Although the three early American social evolutionists did not use the growth model or analogy (which is, of course, an aspect of the organismic model or analogy) as conspicuously or frequently as their European predecesors did, they still occasionally did employ the notion. Perhaps this feature of social evolutionism is the most significant because it provides the nucleus of all the features. From it, they can all be derived. It reinforces the unity of all mankind or society in general undergoing a vast change, with its empirical particulars finding their places in that whole through resort to the comparative method. But perhaps the most evident feature is the stages notion, which is fundamental to the directionality of evolutionary change. Human society is thus characterized by a series of stages of growth like the stages of growth in the life-cycle of the organism. As is well known, Pascal's aphorism was an important intellectual link in the transmission of the organismic-growth analogy from medieval and classical sources to modern thought. But Ward is the only one of the three American social evolutionists who invoked Pascal in quotation: 'the entire series of men during the course of all the ages is to be considered as if it were one and the same man who has always lived' (1970, pp. 34–5). Ward himself subscribed to a botanical model of growth in suggesting that social change resembles the growth of certain plants (e.g., the grapevine) in which 'the main stem or trunk rises to a certain height and then gives off a branch [or sympode] into which the majority of fibro-vascular bundles enter, so that the branch virtually becomes the trunk' (1970, p. 72).

The organismic-growth model is also evident in Giddings's Sumner's, and Keller's writings. Giddings compared (1898, p. 290)

194

the stages of social evolution with 'stages in the growth of a tree . . . or . . . the seven ages of man.' Sumner's influence on Keller is a matter of record. He commented (1914, p. 331), for instance, that change in American social structure 'has been a life-process, a growth-process, which our society had to go through just as inevitably as an infant after birth must go on to the stages of growth and experience which belong to all human beings as such.' In *Folkways* (p. 78), he did observe that the mores 'seem to grow up, gain strength, become corrupt, decline and die, as if they were organisms.' Although Keller acknowledges the dangers that are inherent in the use of analogies (1927, p. 2181; 1929, p. 308), he did not refuse to utilize the organismic-growth analogy. He declares that society should be conceived of as a 'living whole' (1927, p. 37), certain of whose institutions display 'a distinct life cycle' (1927, p. 36). In general, 'the phases of evolution are necessary like the stages of growth of a man' (1927, p. 2241). Keller cites (1928, p. 308) two reasons to justify use of the analogy: (1) because human beings are themselves organisms, organic and social life 'are not merely contiguous but interpenetrative,' and (2) many obvious similarities between the lives of organisms and societies exist. Accordingly, Keller proposes that society be regarded as 'living a life analogous to that of an indivisible organism,' with 'growth under law' (1915, p. 123; 1916, p. 477). Of the three social evolutionists pre-eminent in the generation of the founders of American sociology, Keller seemed to provide the most conspicuous and frequent use of the organismic-growth analogy.

The method

The comparative method is a particular procedure used by nineteenth- and early twentieth-century anthropology and sociology to implement and to confirm the evolutionary view of mankind as a whole, totality, or unity undergoing change in accordance with the notion of an organism involved in a growth process. It assumes that all mankind is comprehended in a vast single developmental unity whose general course and component stages in sequence modern social science can and should reconstruct. Basically, it identifies the development of humanity with the abstract outlines of the historical experience of Western European societies.

All shades and degrees of social and cultural differences of peoples who were often widely separated in space or time are assumed to be arrangeable between the poles of primitivity and modernity. In particular, comparison is to be used to abstract out a series of likenesses or resemblances as stages in (more or less of) a continuum from simplicity to complexity which was believed to be both temporal and developmental. Simplicity was more or less equated with earliness or (relative undifferentiated) primitivity, and complexity with lateness or (differentiated) modernity. Thus, the degree of social differentiation is more or less the implicit or explicit criterion used. Ward, Giddings, and Keller all believed that the coexisting (or then present) series of spatially separate concrete human societies, some of whom were historical and others of whom historyless, could be transformed into a single unified developmental series of abstract stages.[6] Actual chronological or historical differences are ignored so that, for instance, contemporary (historyless) primitives are regarded as socially and culturally equivalent to our remote ancestors. As Keller remarks (1927, p. 2191), 'The savages of nowadays are under pressure to adjust to conditions not dissimilar to those of our remote ancestors and with the same lack of accumulated knowledge of facts and forces' (cf. Giddings, 1896, p. 209). He documents his arguments by quotations from Montelius, Nilsson, and – significantly – from Tylor, the father of the comparative method in anthropology (1927, p. 2191).

This intentional, calculated ignoring of actual historical (or chronological sequence) and geographical (or spatial) differences is justified in the very name of science itself. Keller argued that 'science . . . is interested in genetic series rather than in sequence in time or proximity in space' (1927, p. 2189). The 'approved method in science – approved because it verifies – [is] to arrange its materials irrespective of time and place' (1927, p. 2190). He and his contemporaries assumed that scientific generality was the consequence (not of rigorous time and place inductions but) of abstraction. Socio-cultural reality presents only 'variety, individuality' (1927, p. 2203). Actual form 'passes into derived or related form by gradations that are almost imperceptible' (1927, p. 2201). Thus, the student of society, so Keller argues, 'needs concepts with firm outlines; he cannot get on without them' (1927, p. 2203).

He must, therefore, abstract out a range of likeness to create a type. Viewed in a sequence or range from simplicity to complexity, a type becomes an age or stage. But each type (or stage) is abstract and thus a simplification of empirical reality. Manifestly, such terms as 'ages' or 'stages' are simply categories of classification which are 'useful for purposes of analysis and exposition; they refer to types of social life, and to types only ' (1927, p. 2201). Probably, no 'purely pastoral people was ever observed; but there is a distinctly pastoral type' (1927, p. 2202). Although no people ever experienced the reality of the types in the series of stages and although the series 'contains an element of arrangement contributed from the mind of the series-maker,' the construction of such a series from phenomena 'presented in many societies, set in order and sequence of development,' is necessary to achieve 'the best command of the whole' (1927, p. 2203). A unity of mankind is thus assumed even though the actual history of any specific society may present 'gaps, inversions, or transfers in the order set down [in the constructed series]' (1927, p. 2203).

Basically, two kinds of stages were proposed through the use of the comparative method. One involved total societal stages (e.g., Ward's 'Protosocial, metasocial, and social' stages; and Giddings, 'ethnic or ethnogenic' and 'demotic or demogenic' stages). The other kind of stage is demarked in terms of the development of a given institution (e.g., technological, economic, governmental, religious, familial, etc.). Ward and Giddings employ a total cross-sectional view of societal stages, which includes a characterization of certain institutions at various stages in the whole. But Ward's and Keller's expositions emphasize a taxonomy of institutions, each tending to have its typical stages of sequence. No American social evolutionist uses the criterion of social differentiation-complexity rigorously, though Ward does display some concern with compounding and recompounding (1970, pp. 212–16).

Whether societal or institutional, the important and indispensable feature of stages is their necessarily sequential or successive character in a developmental whole. Frequently, complete sociocultural data in the sequence in the case of specific societies are lacking. Hence, the comparative method also endeavors to use 'parallels,' 'parallelisms,' and 'survivals' to aid in the reconstruction of developmental sequence. Keller alludes (1927, p. 2190) to resemblances among primitive peoples as constituting 'instructive [ethnographic] parallelisms, to be promptly seized, appropriated, and set in their proper [i.e., similar] places in an evolutionary series'. Earlier in the first edition of *Societal Evolution* (pp. 259–60), Keller had referred to similar kinds of socio-cultural adaptations which have arisen independently in isolated societies and presumably indicate a similar stage of socio-cultural development. Giddings conceived (1896, p. 209) of parallels as features which are similarly characteristic of an early (or primitive) stage of modern civilized peoples and contemporary savages. Ward defines (1970, p. 53) E. B. Tylor's ethnographic parallels as 'the occurrence of the same or similar customs, practices, ceremonies, arts, beliefs, and even games, symbols, and patterns, in peoples of nearly the same culture [i.e., same stage] at widely separated regions of the globe.'

Survivals are features of modern societies which have persisted from an earlier stage of development. Giddings noted (1896, p. 209; 1898, p. 245) that 'beliefs and customs of civilized people contain survivals of beliefs and practices that are still in force in savage communities.' According to Keller (1927, p. 2199), survivals are 'persisting [socio-cultural] items which had their expediency once, have it no longer, but still remain.' He suggests that socio-cultural and organic survivals provide a similar function in evolutionary reconstruction. As in organic evolution, so in socio-cultural evolution survivals 'afford links with phases of the evolutionary far past' and have a significance like 'the rudimentary and aborted organs of which Darwin speaks' (1927, pp. 2194, 2199).

Among sociologists, Keller seems to be unique in urging the use of frontier societies as part of the comparative method. The frontier society is a 'child society' providing an opportunity to observe a summary or abbreviated developmental recapitulation of 'the course of evolution traversed by the adult society' (1915, p. 275). Frontier conditions 'represent a return, in some measure, to the primitive' (1927, p. 2199).[7] Under favorable subsequent conditions, 'there ensues . . . a rapid rehearsal or recapitulation of stages of societal evolution culminating in the attainment' of the state (stage) of the older parent societies (1927, p. 2199).

Rate and amount

In accordance with a growth model of change, early American social evolutionists tended to conceive of the rate of change as naturally slow, gradual, continuous, by degrees, and the amount as relatively imperceptible, infinitesimal, or small. Accepting the possibility of some variation in the rate of change, Ward indicated (1970, p. 222) that change is a 'differential process' occurring in terms of 'infinitesimal' amounts. Indeed, dynamics is by definition 'gradual change . . . in the type of . . . structures' (1970, p. 221). Giddings concurs (1896, p. 375; 1898, p. 340) with Spencer that the social evolutionary process goes on 'slowly', cautions (1922, p. 191) that modes of voluntary cooperation have been 'modified only with incredible slowness throughout generations' and advises (1922, p.

240) against forcing 'the rate of [social] transformation.' In Sumner's opinion, 'constant, gradual, smooth, and easy readjustment is the course of things which is conducive to healthful [normal, and natural social] life' (1959, p. 97). Effective change will involve 'slow,' 'long-continued,' and 'minute variations' (1959, p. 97). Keller endorses similar views. The evolutionary process is an 'unhurried action' with 'unhurried deliberation' (1918, pp. 111, 176). Change 'takes time, but there has been plenty of that, if nothing else, in human history; and if time is given, the result is sure' (1947, p. 40). Change stems from 'slight departures' from the mores, consisting of 'successive small improvements' (1918, p. 42; 1947, p. 49). Elsewhere he remarks that 'form passes into derived form or related form by gradations that are almost imperceptible' (1927, p. 2201). Institutional change (e.g., government and language) is the result of a slow, gradual, growth process (1927, pp. 467, 161). The general process of differentiation is continuously 'growing gradually with the mores' (1927, p. 129). Man 'attains to a successful adjustment' by 'gradual steps . . . accumulating small experiences and fitting them together until he arrives at what might be called a real invention' (1947, pp. 52–3). Generally, 'successful readjustment is attained by small alterations rather than [by] turning the world upside down. Revolutions are not the sudden happenings which some people take them to be' (1947, p. 41; 1927, p. 2216).

Probably, social evolutionists would have agreed with the dictum: 'Natura non facit saltum' (Ward, 1906, p. 232). Nature does not jump or leap, i.e., change sharply, spasmodically, or disruptively. Again, this view has much older historical and philosophical foundations, but American sociologists' constant struggle with a still-powerful supernaturalism tended to confirm their equation of naturalism and a slow, gradual rate of change. Catastrophic or cataclysmic change was unnatural either because it was associated with providential intervention in the affairs of men or with (an anti-progressive) irrationality and violence of political revolutions. Saltigrade change was unnatural. Only pedigrade change could be accepted within a naturalistic perspective.

Directionality

For many early American sociologists, mankind or human society is conceived to experience growth through several stages (of increasing differentiation-complexity) and so manifests directionality just as does the individual in passing through stages of growth in its life-cycle. Social stages in sequence imply a direction, whether the unit is an institution, a more or less concrete society, or human society or humanity as an abstract whole. Stages were assumed to exist in some general sequence, even if then current knowledge of their distinguishing features, precise order of succession, or laws of transformation might still be in dispute (cf. Small, 1905, pp. 222–3). Social evolutionists tend to regard mankind as having moved uni-directionally rather than bi- or multi-directionally. They construed change as having a linear, i.e., unilinear or rectilinear character, although cyclical or repetitive features might be present in the form of repeated processes in the overall linear trend.

Ward's trichotomy of societal stages seems to be based on the degree of structural differentiation. His protosocial, metasocial, and social stages appear to be only an adaptation of Morgan's savagery, barbarism, and civilization through a terminology deriving from a geological analogy (1970, pp. 273–4). Both social aggregates of the protosocial stage and the unicellular organism of the protozoic age are comparably undifferentiated, whereas society of the metasocial stage and the multicellular organism of the metazoic era are comparably differentiated (1970, pp. 273–4). The protosocial designates the stage of aboriginal, primitive, savage, non-historic. Metasocial refers to a stage of intermediate trans-formed primitivity or archaism which is just preliterate and near historic. Social indicates a stage of literate, historically conscious peoples who possess a developed civilization.

Giddings invokes a distinction between an ethnic, ethnogenic, or predominantly kinship-oriented stage of human society and a civic, demotic, demogenic, or prevailing territorially-politically oriented stage of human society. His sub-stages within the earliest type, the ethnic society, are themselves manifestly societal in character (e.g., hordes, clans, gentes, tribes, nations), but his sub-stages within the demotic society are differentiated primarily by institutional changes (e.g., the military-religious, the liberal-constitutional, and the economic-ethical or democratic). In the later *Studies in the Theory of Human Society, The Scientific Study of Human Society*, and *Civilization and Society*, Giddings appears to adopt societal criteria for periodicizing the demotic type of society.

Nevertheless, the characteristics of the stages of the two sociologists are markedly similar. Blood-bonds, consanguinity, kinship and descent are as much a part of Ward's first stage as they are of Giddings's ethnic stage. In turn, this earliest stage of Giddings's scheme implies relative social homogeneity or lack of differentiation. Ward's metasocial stage signifies the emergence of

200

civilization, political bonds, territoriality, the state and citizenship as much as Giddings's demotic stage. Conversely, Giddings's own description of his second stage testifies to the appearance of social differentiation and complexity as much as does Ward's metasocial stage.

For social evolutionary theorists of the first era, the use of both societal and institutional stages of change implies generally a rectilinear direction. Ward's protosocial, metasocial, and social stages and Giddings's ethnic and demotic stages involve a shift from small, relatively homogenous or undifferentiated, blood-related, kinship-organized social units to larger, more hetero-geneous, differentiated, territorially- and politically-organized social units. Whether it be the family-marriage, economic-technological, political-regulative, or religious institutions in Ward's or Keller's analyses, the sequences seem to suggest a rectilinear directionality.

Ward conceives of a main trunk of social development which is constituted of Western European peoples (with Asiatic and others representing variations). His declaration that particular concrete social developments of society display a somewhat sympodial (or zigzag) pattern may seem to deviate from rectilinearism. But as a microscopic view it can be assimilated to a more general or macroscopic linearity. According to Ward (1970, p. 228), 'development never goes backward, retracing the steps it has taken.' It is thus generally irreversible, although specific cases of degeneracy or regression may occur (1970, pp. 228–9).

Both in Keller's earlier writings and in *The Science of Society*, society is regarded as moving 'ponderously on, under laws of its own, through a succession of phases [or stages]' (1918, p. vii). It is evident that 'form [arises] out of form' so that what is subsequent is conditioned by what is antecedent in evolution (1929, p. 304). Each of the major institutions displays its own typical stages of development. The economy proceeds through the collection, hunting, pastoral (horticultural), and agricultural stages. Govern-ment extends from an informal council of elders or vague chieftainship, through definite chieftainship, hereditary monarchy, to democracy. Property begins with a communal stage and passes to family holding, ownership by chief, and to various shadings of private property. The marriage series comprises monandry, group marriage, polyandry, polygyny, monogyny, to true monogamy, or pair-marriage. Religion manifests a series starting with animism, then eidolism, daimonism, fetishism, and deism of several varieties (polytheism, henotheism, and monotheism).

In *The Science of Society* the similarity between the phases of evolution of a society and the stages of growth of a man is explicitly recognized (p. 2241) and the indebtedness to Spencer in formulating a conception of social evolution is acknowledged (p. 2194). Admittedly, a trajectory is used to describe the course of change (p. 2184). However, this allusion seems to be more for the purpose of justifying the use of ethnographic and historical data from less than the whole of human development than it is for asserting that the course of change is curvilinear, cyclical, or spiral. Directionality entails irreversibility, for 'there is no possibility that societal evolution will turn back upon its course' (1918, p. 134).

Based on Herbert Spencer's ideas, Giddings's conception of social evolution manifestly incorporates a directionality which explicitly proceeds from the processes of social differentiation and integration and departs from both physical and psychic levels. The directionality of physical processes involves the redistribution of matter and motion between a society and its environment in accordance with the four processes of social integration, social differentiation, social segregation, and social definiteness and coherence. When the mass increases more than motion in a population in relation to its environment, social integration occurs. (It may be based on genetic or congregate aggregation, i.e., through natural increase of members within a group or by the combination of two or more societies (Giddings, 1896, pp. 60–1).) As the parts of the integrating mass become unlike, the second process of social differentiation begins. New activities, occupations, and professions arise (Giddings, 1898, p. 338). A third process of segregation draws like units or arrangements of units together from among the different kinds and arrangements of units. Similarities of race, nationality, ability, occupation, politics, and religion bring men together (1898, pp. 338–9). Finally, counter-processes (in relation to the integration of matter or the dissipation of motion) further complicate the evolutionary process, introduce new differentiations and segregations, and produce 'increasing definiteness of both differentiation and segregation' (1898, p. 340). At this point, social evolution has become compound. In brief, physical 'laws determine the aggregation, the growth, the movements, and arrangements of population; they determine the amount, the kinds, and combinations of social activities' (1898, p. 350). But emerging from these activities is the social structural trend signified by the term 'social constitution,' with the purposive, specialized association as the core of social differentiation and specialization.

Within the limits of this primarily physical process, psychic laws also operate to produce a certain directionality. Giddings endeavors basically to derive this psychic directionality from what he calls the law of least effort: 'Consciousness endeavors to attain painless clearness, or positive pleasure, with a minimum of difficulty' (1898, p. 341). Because he also believes that each individual tends to make comparisons with himself, Giddings argues (1898, p. 343) that the individual will tend to be most sympathetic and affectionate toward those who resemble him (i.e., consciousness of kind). In 'its entirety, the consciousness of kind is seen to be a consequence of the persistence of mental activity along the lines of least difficulty' (1898, p. 345). (Incidentally, the social passion for homogeneity is the psychic equivalent to integration (1898, p. 348).) Giddings also contends that societal or social action tends to be sympathetic and impulsive in character because 'sympathy and impulse are less difficult than rational self-control' (1898, pp. 345–6). Unless controlled by the reflective process, sympathetic like-mindedness 'commonly results in impulsive social action' (1898, p. 125). Conformity 'to a course of conduct once entered upon, critical obedience to authority, uncritical acceptance of belief, are all far easier than independent judgment' (1898, p. 346). Thus, formal like-mindedness and conformity to an established order tend to occur before rational like-mindedness and rational (chosen) social action.

Only as sympathetic and formal like-mindedness come to yield diminishing returns do persons change their behavior. 'Impulsive social action frequently proves to be enormously costly and destructive' (1898, p. 346). Once this situation arises, 'further activity in line of least effort is necessarily rational' (1898, p. 346). But this process 'begins subjectively in individual minds before it becomes an objective organization of social cooperation' (1898, p. 346). It will begin in 'those most highly developed minds' in accordance with the law of least effort (1898, p. 346). Presumably, they can also more readily envisage remoter utilities. Because these persons are the comparatively few, such functions as 'rational choice, the formation of true public opinion, and the rational leadership of social activity' will always be restricted to their initiative (1898, p. 346).

Finally, it is apparently the law of least effort which also accounts – as will be explained more fully below – for the replacement of primary physical conflict by secondary intellectual-moral conflict. 'On the psychological side, primary conflict . . . is a rapid discharge of motor impulse. Its external expression is a use of physical force in warfare and persecution' (1898, p. 346), but again at some point physical strife will become ineffective, wasteful, or misery-producing (1898, p. 350). Intellectual strife will then tend to replace physical strife. With the 'supremacy of intellectual over physical strife . . . the higher and finer results of social evolution can be attained' (1898, p. 350). Intellectual strife is conducive to 'rational, and ultimately . . . [to] ethical, like-mindedness; it makes for peace, prosperity, and happiness' (1898, p. 350). It is, of course, important that many other sociologists shared Giddings's view that physical strife would be superceded increasingly by intellectual strife and by more pacific forms of interaction as social evolution proceeded. (Manifestly, social progress accompanied social evolution for Giddings.)

However, the crucial core of the directionality of social evolution is the increasing differentiation of function and structure, which is attended by increasing integration. Social evolution is associated with increasing complexity as adaptation and survival are enhanced. Ward does acknowledge increasing structural differentiation and specialization as characterizing all evolution, including social evolution, though he also warns (1970, pp. 77, 255) against the possibility of excessive specialization. Giddings seems to locate the structural center of evolutionary direction in the emergence of what he terms the 'social constitution,' with its specialized and purposive associations, each contributing to the division of labor (1896, pp. 171–5, 194–6, 275–6, 199). It is equally evident that for Keller social evolution manifests a trend from early primitive simplicity to late modernized complexity. Such a trend is essentially a matter of 'advancing organization,' for 'groups showing favorable variation toward such organization [i.e., specialization plus cooperation] . . . survive and grow strong where unorganized groups' perish (1927, p. 150). Function differentiates first and then appear the 'invention of appropriate new structure, adaptation, perfection, cooperation, and rhythmic effort under command and discipline' (1927, p. 9). As organization becomes more complex, inequality is increased, managerial roles elaborated, performance demanded, discipline made more rigorous, and power concentrated and magnified (1927, p. 9).

Causal mechanisms or modus operandi

Typically, social evolution is conceived to operate through a causal mechanism or modus operandi with certain distinctive characteristics. For its European exponents, it was a consequence of causes,

204

factors, or processes which were natural-necessary, internal, and uniform (or constant through time). Ward, Giddings, and Keller were incontestably committed to a naturalistic (as opposed to a supernaturalistic) account of the origins, structure, and change in human social phenomena. Their views of social evolution were predicated basically on Darwin's notion of mankind as organisms involved in a struggle for existence within the domain of nature. All of them elaborated a system of arguments in which social change more or less necessarily, i.e., logically, derived from the premises established. Social change was natural because humanity was basically enmeshed in the processes of nature and thus its behaviors were subject to modifications as the conditions of existence altered. Manifestly, the first requirement of social existence is to maintain life itself, the lives of the members of the aggregate. And although the precipitant of social change may reside in alterations in the conditions of aggregate existence (including contact with and incursions by external societies), the source of change is primarily internal for Keller and Giddings. The source is basically the biopsychic make-up of the members of a given society, e.g., pain or perceived physical danger along with individual biopsychic variations as the bases of an appropriate response. Interestingly, the tendency to envisage all specific concrete societies as members of an abstract, comprehensive total human society based on a common human nature tended to minimize the significance of the external-internal question of concrete cases.[8] Finally, for all of them, the causes or at least the major causes of social change were regarded as operating uniformly (or constantly) through time, given the presence of necessary conditions. Changes in the social conditions of existence (including shifts in the scarcity-abundance of resources), alteration in the biopsychic needs-wants-desires of the human aggregate, and the cumulative of adaptive experience and its transmission to successive generations as the cultural legacy seem to be illustrative of the presence of such factors. As Keller declared, the 'same forces remain always at work' (1927, p. 2189). The congruity between this socially applied doctrine of uniformitarianism (the constancy of the powers of nature, i.e,, 'social nature' in this case) and the enthusiasm of Ward, Giddings, and Keller for a positivistically conceived science should be evident.

The genesis of social innovation   All of these early sociologists are among the more materialistically- and Darwinianly-inclined of the early American theorists. Presumably, social change must be reflected in change in aggregate behavior which must prove to be instrumental or adaptive to the conditions of human existence. Survival or at least enhanced adaptation within a given habitat is the ultimate citerion. All three of these early theorists approach change in terms of (a) alterations in the biophysical (and social) conditions of existence, especially as the scarcity–abundance of resources for satisfying the needs-wants-desires of the human aggregate is concerned, (b) the emergence of conflict and struggle, (c) the presence of biophysical variations among the members of the human population out of which an adaptive response can emerge, and (d) the testing and selection of such behavioral variations associated with (biopsychic) individual differences through struggle in relation to the changed conditions of existence.

Giddings and Keller are prevailingly social Darwinists. For them, survival – adaptation can be tested only by (a more or less) intense struggle for existence under prevailing conditions. Climate, topography, resources for supporting life, (including the) flora and fauna of the habitat, the level of technology available, and the relative population density of the human aggregate, or more precisely, the land–man ratio, are important factors in determining the intensity of the struggle.

Interestingly, only Giddings endeavored to develop a typology of societal environments or habitats as potentially obstructive or conducive to change. His initial formulations involved (1922, pp. 84–5, 144–50) both a classification of environments and populations. The criteria for categorizing environments are the varying riches of resources and accessibility to outside populations (e.g., 'poor and inaccessible,' 'poor and accessible,' 'rich but inaccessible,' and 'rich and accessible'). Later, he attempted to modify his classification so that it could comprehend basic stages of societal evolution. Each stage was represented as a type of social system of some degree of simplicity-complexity. Together, the stages comprise 'a succession of types, each of which is associated with a characteristic situation or habitat' (1922, pp. 84–5). (However, he actually specifies the habitat for only the first and second types or stages: forest and bush, and grasslands. The third is implied to occur wherever simple agriculture is possible. Significantly, he ignores any intimation of a typical habitat for the fourth type – the common base of civilized societies!) However partial and unsuccessful Giddings's endeavors may appear, they are important because they underscore sociologists' conviction that a change in environment, habitat, or situation must affect a society's structured adaptation and elicit a new behavior or behaviors which can become the basis for a new adaptation.

In spite of the fact that social change was construed to be finally a response to an altered relationship between the habitat of a human population and the wants-needs-desires of that population, even the early more materialistically-inclined theorists tended to place the primacy in the etiology of innovation on the biopsychic variations (or individual differences) in the population. Environmental change without the development of appropriate responses from the human aggregate would mean its failure to survive, i.e., its elimination. Understandably, therefore, the early Darwinian theorists emphasized the role of (biopsychic) individual differences, which might be said to constitute internal as opposed to external factors in social change.

This inclination is reflected both in Giddings and Keller. Based on Sumner's conviction of differential talent, strength of mind, practicality, and perseverance (1959, pp. 19, 40–2), Keller suggests that the emergence of superior behavioral variations reflects fundamentally differences in the structure and functioning of individual brains (1915, p. 51). Giddings contended that certain individuals possessed more intelligence, imagination, courage, resolution, initiative, energy, promptness, persistence, and effectiveness of reaction (1922, pp. 90, 92, 180, 267; 1932, p. 35). Both early sociologists insisted that the bases of individual differences are (favorable) inherited variations (e.g., Giddings, 1922, p. 68).

Presumably Keller agrees with Sumner that invention is not the completed work of merely one exceptional man. It is rather subject to a process of alteration and improvement in the 'give and take' and suggestion and imitation between man and man (Sumner, 1959, p. 19). The process is 'one of development,' with new suggestions coming in 'at point after point,' being carried out and combining 'with what existed already' (1959, p. 19). Each 'new step increases the number of points upon which other minds may seize' (1959, p. 19). Sumner *denies* any peculiar power of emergentism of association so that the aggregate has 'a mystic power in it greater than the sum of the powers of its members' (1959, p. 19). But interaction (as in the model of the crowd) only brings 'cooperation and constant suggestion which is highly productive when it operates in a crowd, because it draws out latent power, concentrates what would otherwise be scattered, verifies and corrects what has been taken up, eliminates error, and constructs by combination' (1959, pp. 19–29). Accordingly, various actions arise and develop unconsciously, spontaneously, and without coordination, but only one will tend to persist (1959, p. 19).

Only one will tend to persist because only one will tend to reduce pain most effectively, produce survival, or effect adaptation. Indispensable thus to this Darwinian interpretation is the operation of (the process of) selection, which is the outcome of (pain,) scarcity and struggle operating on individual variations. More precisely, opposition, struggle, and conflict provide tests of fitness among existing and emergent variant behaviors. As Keller remarks (1927, p. 36), selection results from 'conflict and competition, which are furnished primarily by the struggle for existence, and then by the struggle for a better quality of existence'. Through conflict, 'codes and institutions go down to destruction along with the men who practice them' (1927, p. 36). But fundamentally it is the individuals whose behaviors are 'fit' or adapted to the conditions of existence who survive, whereas those whose behaviors are not fit or are maladaptive are eliminated, i.e., fail to survive. Keller is emphatic that 'it takes a conflict to secure selection and the survival of the fit' (1918, p. 156).

Giddings holds (1896, pp. 111–12) that the multiplicity of individual variations, which will tend to be evoked by new circumstances of existence, will necessarily be subject to 'a struggle for existence' until one or two become 'almost universal.' In some cases, however, 'the conflict results in a combination, as when two synchronous waves unite in a complex and stronger wave' (1896, pp. 111–12). The result is the essence of innovation (or invention) (1896, p. 112). Giddings's indebtedness to Tarde is evident and acknowledged (1896, p. 111).

However, some Darwinists were apparently uneasy about the possibility that selection has not been operating effectively in more recent social evolution. Keller conceded that conflict, through which selection had occurred within and between earlier societies, is no longer as extended and intense. As societies have become more complex and civilized, wars have decreasingly entailed extermination. Harmful mores, such as those physically or numerically weakening an isolated group or impairing its organization (e.g., polyandry, the mother-family, cannibalism, incest of the past) are less likely to be revealed and eliminated (1915, pp. 63–4). And within (as opposed to between) more modern complex societies, the process of selection is also less intense. An artificial environment (of technology and economy) is interposed between society and its natural environment (1915, p. 67). The infrequency of death from famine, cold, physical conflict between individuals, and the unrestricted birth rate tend to minimize natural selection (1915, p. 67). Presumably the demand for consistency between past and present folkways and mores, the more manifest and demonstrable expediency (or inexpediency) of the societal self-maintenance mores (those pertaining to the economy and technology), and the strain toward consistency between the self-maintenance mores and the other domains of society tend to exercise some selective effect (1915, pp. 87–8, 132). But the possibility of counter-selection and non-adaptation or maladaptation is very real in modern societies.

Giddings even seems to suggest more fundamental reservations about the operation of selection generally. He contends that, if possible, men and animals will tend to move away from habitats where the struggle for existence is intolerably harsh or ominously severe. Of course, the very fact that humankind maintains a collective existence means that it does develop a cultural and a social organization which shields or removes individuals in aggregates 'from destructive environmental influences,' diminishes thus the 'adverse pressure of environment,' and 'enhances [the individual's] well-being' (1922, p. 117).

Fundamental to the argument of the Social Darwinist evolutionists about the mechanisms of social change is just how (social) adaptation can be defined and established independently of selection. Adaptation may presumably be inferred by decrease in the hazards of existence, greater certainty of or added efficiency in survival, and a decrease of pain (perhaps also an increase of pleasure). If it can be shown that a folkway or mos has persisted continuously and has become settled, it will necessarily be a 'tried and preserved variation.' Its continuous subjection to the process of trial and retention or selection indicates – so Keller argues – that it is an adaptation to the conditions of societal existence (1915, p. 251, cf. p. 249). It thus also represents an effective means to achieve an end, the satisfaction of interests (or needs) with less pain or without pain (1915, p. 160).

In the analysis so far pursued, Ward occupies a peculiar and distinctive place. Seemingly, he was committed to the view that social change must be adaptive ultimately. But he was not solely or even predominantly a Darwinian in his view of the mechanisms of social evolutionary change. Admittedly, he appears to have accepted the major role of struggle for existence and survival of the fittest (or elimination of the unfit) in early human social evolution. But he certainly rejected any such view for the later stages of social development. Furthermore, he opposed the notion of hereditary superior and inferior strains of individual differences. Ward was a Lamarckian (which also accounts for his pervasive enthusiasm about the potentialities of education in later social evolution). He displayed an unswerving faith in the (Lamarckian) thesis of use and disuse (or exercise and non-exercise) of biopsychic characteristics, the accumulating enhancement of acquired capabilities, and their hereditary transmission to offspring, i.e., the inheritance of acquired characteristics.[9] (The use and disuse (or stimulation versus non-stimulation by opportune or inopportune circumstances) was apparently the primary and major cause of individual differences within a human aggregate and of differences between aggregates.) Certain of these variations then become advantageous or adaptive (or at least non-disadvantageous or non-maladaptive) in relation to the changed conditions of existence. Thus, they become more effective means to control nature (as new methods, ways, principles, devices, arts, systems, institutions) (1970, p. 25). Whether mental or physical, they are inventions in the Tardean sense, presumably are based on prior social heredity, achievement, or civilization, and can be imitated, repeated, and perpetuated as an increment of that social heredity, achievement, or civilization.

Ward's principle of conation in social change also operated in accordance with Lamarckianism (1970, p. 253). Conation refers to the exercise of social effort to satisfy social desires (social forces) under given conditions of social existence. If environmental circumstances are modified, the efforts of a human population to satisfy desires (as based on or derived from common biopsychic needs) may lead to a change in the intensity and quality of desires and in the exertion of effort and, consequently, to (an incidental and accompanying) change in the devices or instrumentalities associated with social structures.

Nevertheless, Ward also subscribes to some minimal operation of (Darwinian) selection (or elimination of the unfit). Just as the 'weaker species go to the wall and the stronger persist' in the organic world (the defective are eliminated and the fittest survive), so on the 'social plane' it is the same (Ward, 1970, p. 184). The peoples and societies who are the stronger, i.e., who have the 'best structures' in the sense of adaptation, survive (1970, p. 184).

Acceptance, adoption, and dissemination of social innovation
For Ward as for Giddings and Keller, social evolution does ultimately entail adaptation and adaptation, in turn, requires that a particular idea, belief, sentiment, or behavior is in effect tested and confirmed by extensive acceptance, adoption, and dissemination within a society. No one of them could conceive that an innovation could be regarded as adaptive if it remained confined to its originator(s) or even to a small elite segment. However, only Giddings and Keller offer explanations of this last and important

phase of social change, which reveal their varying intellectual commitments. Giddings insists that conspicuous or 'dynamic men . . . become models to thousands or millions of their fellows' (1922, p. 220). Their 'choice is spontaneously copied and their course of action is uncritically followed' (1922, p. 220). The multitude thinks and does as they think and do. They are the models or examples who are followed because they react more promptly, persistently, and effectively. Fundamentally their actions – which are copied and repeated to become habits in individuals and folkways in the society – are adaptations to the conditions of existence.

Tarde's influence is evident in Giddings's further remarks. He remarks (1896, p. 110) that an innovation will spread imitatively from one individual to another so long as 'the act imitated is pleasurable and is obviously conducive to development and survival.' Such repetition of the innovation constitutes a wave of imitation and it will presumably continue until it meets a wave of equal force, 'is shattered by a counter-wave or is combined with a synchronizing wave' (1896, p. 109–10). By inference, such stronger counter-waves will be more attractive, more pleasurable, more adapted to survival.

Presumably, Keller would agree with Sumner's observation that men 'notice each other's efforts and select the attempt which satisfies the need best with the least pain or exertion' or provides (objective) success in well-being or living well (1970, p. 149). More broadly, the innovation will be accepted and adopted as it decreases the hazards in the conditions of existence, increases the certainty of or the efficiency in survival, reduces pain (or increases pleasure), and is in accord with the strain of the (folkways and) mores toward consistency (Sumner, 1959, pp. 94–5, 5). (The mores are more efficient when consistent (1959, p. 102).) Inconsistency provokes friction and antagonism which may be disruptive of social unity and threaten survival (1959, pp. 5–6). In general, the new behavior must maximize adaptation.

By use of Keller's distinction between primary and secondary societal forms (the former concerning folkways and mores of societal self-maintenance and the latter all other types), it is possible to extend the range of applicability of the strain toward consistency in explaining the diffusion of an innovation. Keller concedes that the secondary societal forms come into consistency with each other, 'and there are doubtless minor mutual harmonizations upon the form taken by the mores of societal self-maintenance' (1915, pp. 141–2). However, the mores and institutions providing for preservation (feeding, clothing, sheltering, and protecting) of the society are 'in a very real sense fundamental' and primary and constitute a 'foundation' or substructure from which 'the form of the superstructure cannot vary except in detail' (1915, p. 142). If the secondary forms do become maladjusted with the primary, they will eventually be 'forced . . . into better adjustment' with the latter (1915, p. 150). Anticipatory of Ogburn, Keller insists that the secondary forms will have to 'catch up, so to speak, with the' primary forms (1915, p. 150). Thus, Keller plainly contends that the extension of an innovation within secondary societal forms will clearly have to reckon with some limitations of internal consistency and in turn ultimately with some minimum of consistency demanded by the primary forms.

Now the increasing dissemination of a new form of thought, feeling, or action – which confirms the adaptive function of the trait – is not confined merely to the members of one generation of a group or society. It must be diachronic as well as synchronic. To use Keller's process, transmission across generations must be involved. Thus, the change has become thoroughly accepted and incorporated within the social legacy, social heritage or culture.

This inculcation across generations is extraordinarily important because it signifies continuity and cumulation across time so that linear or rectilinear directionality of change can be asserted. It means that social-cultural losses are minimal and infrequent. New forms are thus additions or supplements rather than mere replacements or displacements. Both Ward and Keller explicitly confirm the place of continuity and accumulation in the process of evolutionary social change. Accordingly, Ward refers (1970, p. 34) to the 'great line of social development in which there has been no break in the transmission of achievement.' It has never had its 'continuity with the past cut off or interrupted' (1970, p. 214). Keller also notes that 'form passes into derived form' (1927, p. 2201). Recent increasing differentiations of function and structure are based on and derive from more rudimentary earlier (or past) differentiation and specialization as demanded by adaptation and survival. Social continuity and accumulation are thus conceived to be a part of the mechanisms of social evolutionary change.

Viewed now in its entirety, the social evolution of Ward, Giddings, and Keller is a conspicuously macro-conception of social change. It characteristically invokes the organismic growth analogy and the comparative method. The social units undergoing change are assumed to be comprehensive or macrocosmic in nature. Rate and

212

magnitude are regarded as relatively slow and small-scale. Its linear or rectilinear directionality is exhibited in a temporal succession of stages. Like its European counterparts, the American notion of causal mechanisms presupposes that evolutionary change is natural and necessary, internal, and uniform or constant. Giddings and Keller adopt (Social) Darwinist arguments whereas Ward includes both Darwinian and Lamarckian principles in his account. With varying emphases, all three early evolutionists provide explanations both for the genesis and acceptance, adoption, and dissemination of social innovation.

9 Anti-social evolutionism and the social process theory of social change

Bases of the opposition to social evolutionism

Although Sumner, Ross, Small, and Cooley (and also W. I. Thomas) can be characterized as anti-social evolutionists, their opposition varied considerably in terms of its explicitness, directness, vigorousness, and elaborateness. Sumner and Ross seem to stand at one end and Small and Cooley at the other. Indeed, Sumner appears to have been the most explicit, direct, vigorous, and elaborate in his rejection of social evolution. Yet this characterization must sound paradoxical in view of the fact that his younger colleague and successor at Yale, Keller, was such a firm and unqualified adherent of social evolutionism (as the exposition of the previous chapter indicated). The explanation seems to lie in the fact that Sumner's vigorous and extensive indictment was contained in two *unpublished* papers which Keller had retained in his own collection and which have just been located in that collection in the Archives of the Yale University Library.[1] The first of the two papers, the shorter, is entitled 'The Application of the Notions of Evolution and Progress on the Superorganic Domain.' The second and longer one – from which the first twelve pages are missing, including the title-page – is centrally concerned with the question of the tenability of the doctrine of evolution in the socio-cultural realm. These two papers, together with some of the other unpublished Sumner documents and certain passages in the *Folkways*, indicate that Sumner repudiated every one of the characteristic features of social evolution. He concluded that there is no 'stress or strain in any given direction' in the superorganic realm 'as that which evolution shows us . . . [in] carrying up organisms from protozoa to man' (n.d.*c*, p. 23). The conditions of

214

[organic] evolution are not 'fulfilled in human society' (n.d.*b*, p. 10). For Sumner, 'All use of evolutionary terms in regard to . . . [sociocultural] concretions [or phenomena] must be simply metaforical' (*sic*! n.d. *b*, p. 6).

Ross's objections to social evolution seem to be equally direct and explicit, although not as extended or elaborate and more qualified than those of Sumner. They appear as part of Ross's chapter on 'Social Laws' in his *Foundations of Sociology* and extend over nine printed pages. He denies that 'historical facts' and tenable notions of 'social causation' will permit the establishment of determinate sequences of stages of development for given institutions. Institutions are not subject to an internal tendency of 'organic development' or to 'continuous improvement, like a tool or a utensil' (1919, pp. 57–8). Nevertheless, he manifested some inclination to accept the parallel development among those institutions which are most directly and preponderantly dependent upon 'man's thinking' (and thus reflect the fact 'that the human mind is at bottom everywhere the same') and are least responsive to 'outer circumstances' or 'the environment, physical or human' (1919, pp. 60, 61). Even in this instance, the tendency of the human mind to be a unity and for each institution to affect and be affected by all of the others at a given time in the society means that even the more subjectively (or psychically)-derived institutions will tend to be 'tinged with something local [,particularistic,] and distinctive' from the environment of the more or less objectively-derived institutions. Ross concludes that development in a particular type of institution is, therefore, 'in greater or lesser degree, *multilinear*' (1919, p. 62). In declaring finally that efforts to establish 'a single, typical sequence of changes' in the different spheres of social life are 'bound to fail,' Ross does (1919, p. 62) seem to indicate that his objection is to unilinear social evolution and not to all conceivable varieties of social evolution.

Small and Cooley's opposition to social evolution is not stated directly and explicitly. But it can be relatively reliably inferred from their general arguments about social change and especially from their views about Social Darwinism. Initially, Small's objection to social evolution might seem relatively incidental and minor. In referring to variation within types of social structure, Small notes that he might have enlisted 'the term "evolution," if that had not come to be so closely associated with theories of the method of change, rather than with the fact of change itself' (1905, p. 613). Apparently this 'method' is actually the Social Darwinian mechanism of struggle for existence and survival of the fittest. Now both he and Cooley refused to construe struggle, conflict, or antagonism as wholly physicalistic or as totally significant throughout the social process as did the Social Darwinists. Small's position concurred with Cooley's repudiation of 'a simplified and misunderstood Darwinism which unduly exalts conflict and makes the "struggle for existence" between groups almost the sole principle of human life' (1966, p. 244). Certainly, he would have agreed with Cooley's insistence that 'both conflict and cooperation have their places' in the social process and that both are 'phases of one process which always involves something of both' (1966, pp. 36, 39, 34). Both sociologists seem to have recognized many important experientially-derived social and personal bases of conflict as opposed to mere pain and the deprivation of organic wants by scarcity as the primary or ultimate source of that conflict. Both sociologists refused to believe that conflict must always, usually or frequently deteriorate into struggle and mutual extermination. Their bases of optimism included: a faith in the progressive diminution of the frequency and severity of harsh forms of conflict, the presumption that sympathy as universally acquired in primary group socialization will limit hostility, and a conviction that out of the destruction of particular rules by conflict human reason will be able to find more general and permanent principles (Small, 1905, p. 325; Cooley, 1966, pp. 249, 377).

Even though Sumner's, Ross's, Small's, and Cooley's opposition to social evolution varied considerably in explicitness, directness, vigorousness, and elaborateness, it did involve the full range of the typical features of social evolution. Their objections do include the evolutionists' notion of the social unit for studying change, the organismic-growth analogy, the comparative method, the rate and magnitude of (normal, natural) change, its unilinear and rectilinear directionality constructed through a succession of stages, and the Social Darwinist conception of a causal mechanism or modus operandi of social change. Yet their arguments do differ substantially.

(1) And curiously the greatest divergence seems to appear in connection with their views about the appropriate social unity for studying change. Small and Cooley appear to accept the macroscopic concerns of the evolutionists whereas Sumner and Ross do not. Small and Cooley do assume a holism associated with a broad adherence to (interactionist) idealism which accepts all mankind, humanity, or social life in general as the unit of study. Significantly, Cooley's third volume of his trilogy is entitled *Social Process* rather than social processes (even though it is also true that

the general process comprises subsidiary or sub-processes). Cooley does believe that (human) social life is an interconnected, interrelated, and interdependent whole in which change is constantly occurring. Small also holds that human association is 'a whole developing without break of continuity from its origins' (1905, pp. 90–1). Furthermore, it is a synchronic as well as a diachronic whole, for it 'exists at any given moment as a reciprocity between all of its parts' (1905, pp. 90–1). Manifestly, every 'man is a contributing cause of every other contemporary and subsequent man; and, conversely, . . . every man is a composite product of every antecedent and contemporary man' (1905, p. 570). Within the 'types of association men comprise,' 'change is incessantly taking place' (1905, p. 613). Of course, both Cooley and Small did accept much smaller units of inquiry for change too – but always under the assumption that whatever is is in relation to other phenomena, i.e., in context, up to and including social life as a whole. (However, Cooley's and Small's seeming similarity with the evolutionists' preference for a universal social unit must be qualified by their resort to a different conception of organic growth.)

Sumner and Ross both reject human society in general as an appropriate social unit for the study of change. Admittedly, Sumner's objections must be inferred. He did argue, as noted above, that all human beings are endowed with a similar biopsychic human nature and a few similar needs-wants comprising socializing forces and requiring satisfaction in and through conditions of aggregate (or social) existence. However, these adjustments can involve *different* modes of social existence and thus seem to deny the appropriateness of lumping all human societies into a unity. He does differentiate between earliest mankind's existence in hordes (which do entail a struggle for existence and selection through survival of the fittest in relation to scarce resources) and all subsequent modes of social existence based on the development of culture (which provides a buffer mechanism between individual human lives and the processes of nature and which thus prevents struggle for existence and selection among the human organisms themselves). In addition, he also seems to suggest a separation and demarcation of primitive peoples and (modern) civilized peoples. (*Folkways* is overwhelmingly concerned with a primitive mode of social existence. Presumably, Sumner's own societology or science of society would have dealt with humankind's civilized or civilizational existence, but we do not actually know. *The Science of Society* as it was actually published was predicated on Keller's

217

and not on Sumner's notion of social change.) Furthermore, the most encompassing social units he accepted in *Folkways* were societies sharing or possessing a common ethos. And the significance of Sumner's insistence on a detailed and meticulous study of socio-cultural similarities and dissimilarities among and between specifically identifiable peoples must be recognized. This pre-occupation was uncharacteristic of other founding figures in the discipline and was incompatible with the assumption of any notion of the unity of mankind as a whole and the comparative method as it was practiced in his era.

Ross takes the position that the use of global, comprehensive, or macroscopic units of investigation for any purpose, including change, is inconsistent with the exactness and reliability of scientific generalization. He declares that efforts to 'establish laws of succession based on a parallelism in all societies of any special development . . . taken in its *entirety*' are futile (1919, p. 73). It is necessary 'to generalize on the basis of minute and exact resemblances' rather than on the 'basis of a few gross and fanciful resemblances' (1919, p. 75). Civilizations and nations are too gross and vague. 'To reach inductively true laws of succession' it is imperative that 'numbers of small and elementary social facts' from 'little series of [repeated] transformations' be studied (1919, pp. 74, 75). Manifestly, the comparative investigation of small social units is at variance with the older notion of the comparative method associated with social evolution.

(2) Because their holism is actually an organicism, Small's and Cooley's use of growth as an analogy or model of social change follows logically. Both Small and Cooley invoke growth, but not with the same meanings as the evolutionists attach to the term. Writing with George Vincent in *An Introduction to the Study of Society* (pp. 87–96), Small developed a relatively elaborate statement of his notion of the organic analogy, one aspect of which is growth. The organic analogy asserts only a likeness of relations within a society and those within an organism and not an identity (1971, pp. 90, 91). Small and Vincent admonish their readers, therefore, to understand that the growth of society as change does not imply the identical characteristics of actual organic growth. Social growth is thus not to 'be accounted for by the action of the same energies which secure the growth of plants and animals' (1971, p. 91). It involves 'the emergence of the ultra-psychical energies in the reaction of many minds upon each other' (1971, p. 91).

Interestingly, Cooley claims – without acknowledging Ward's

218

views as a precedent – that social forms have a natural tendency to change which resembles the grapevine in continuing to grow only if the tendrils encounter something to provide support (1966, pp. 8–10, 27–8). A 'vine feels its way and has a system of behavior which ensures its growth along the lines of successful experiment' (1966, p. 9). Men, who also have tendencies to act in certain ways, 'come into contact with situations which stimulate some of their activities and repress others' (1966, p. 9). Those who are stimulated have their growth increased.

What is impressive in both the Small and Cooley resort to the organic (or to the organismic) analogy and the related notion of growth is the total absence of any reference to social change involving stages akin to the stages of the life-cycle of the individual. Nor is any intimation of a distinctive intrinsic or internal determinism evident. Apparently, the organic analogy (with growth) is not basically the same as that organismic-growth analogy associated with social evolutionism.

Appropriately, Ross objects to an evolutionary growth conception of change precisely because it entails an organismic notion of society with an exclusively internal dynamic, i.e., because it assumes preformationism. Unlike an organism, 'society has no [genuine] heredity. It is not [an] unfolding [of] what was once folded into it, as the embryo unfolds the predetermined parts and organs' (1919, p. 57). Presumably, Ross refuses to regard 'the succession of social changes . . . [as] predetermined, and . . . accidental, extraneous, and historical events and influences' as lacking in consequence (1919, p. 185). Consequently, he rejects Lewis Henry Morgan's view of institutions as developing from 'a few primary germs of thought' (1919, p. 57).

Sumner also employed the organic analogy with a notion of growth – but with implications hostile to social evolutionism. Society may be considered to be a 'whole made up of parts,' i.e., a system, within which the parts are interconnected, interrelated, and interdependent (1959, p. 49). They manifest a 'strain toward consistency' (1959, p. 5). Furthermore, he does use the word growth to characterize change, e.g., the mores 'seem to grow up' (1959, p. 78). However, he insists that 'the notion that mores grow . . . by virtue of some inherent tendency is to be rejected' (1959, p. 102). He contends similarly that the idea that change in the mores can 'go on of itself, or by virtue of some inherent tendency in . . . [one] direction, is entirely unfounded' (1959, p. 116).

(3) Sumner, Ross, and Thomas are explicitly and vigorously opposed to the assumptions of the comparative method, whereas

Cooley's specific methodological holism or contextualism implies a similar (albeit implicit) rejection. (In effect, Small subscribes to a position akin to Cooley's, though some of his statements are ambiguous at best and inconsistent at worst.) Sumner directly and unambiguously rejects Spencer's use of the comparative method and the logical procedure involved (n.d.*a*). To arrange all phenomena 'in a logical series or on a scale of a determined order' is to put 'a strain on facts which results in error' (n.d.*a*). Developmental or evolutionary order is contradicted by actual temporal or historical sequence of events. 'What seems to us a higher form (e.g., of the family) appeared in one society before a lower form appeared in another' (n.d.*a*).

Ross and Thomas express a similar opposition to the categorical universal quality associated with the stages notion and with the identification of a particular society or type of society with a given stage as determined by the comparative method. Thomas, for example, objects to the comparative method because it tends to consider primitive cultures, societies, and races *en bloc* or *en masse*. He insists that 'There is as much difference between the North American Indian and the Australian as between the Indian and the white man. Between the Australian or the Wood Veddah of Ceylon and the ancient Greek or the modern German, it would be possible to make a rough but continuous classification of culture on the principle of more or less complete control of environment' (1909, p. 133).

Elsewhere, he argues that the comparative method results in a false dichotomy, separation, and distance between the mental, social, and cultural features of savage and civilized peoples. According to Thomas, the 'savage is very close to us indeed, both in his physical and mental make-up and in the forms of his social life. Tribal society is virtually delayed civilization, and the savages are a sort of contemporary ancestry' (1909, p. 13). For Thomas, 'prehistorical man was of essentially the same nature and mind as man at present and . . . this is true also of the savage' (1909, p. 131). The 'mental organization [of primitive peoples] is not defective' (1909, p. 439). The difference between them and ourselves in steadiness and pace of economic activity is a matter of 'social habit on our part, and not a natural disposition' (1909, p. 131). Thomas insists that 'If we make due allowance for the low state of [their] knowledge and the paucity of [their] materials we must admit that . . . [their] ingenuity and interest are of absolutely the same pattern as those of the modern scientist or inventor' (1909, p. 439).

Thomas also would indict the comparative method because it permits the study of cultural elements divorced from their contexts. 'No object can be completely understood when separated from the whole culture of which it is a part, and no culture can be understood when its fragments are dislocated' (1909, p. 857). Presumably, survivals or vestiges should not be employed with the specious logic of Westermarck, who regarded 'certain practices as vestiges of assumed antecedent conditions of whose existence these so-called vestiges are the guarantee' (1909, pp. 532–3).

Ross contends for substantially the same position in asserting that a stage must be referred back to particular, concrete peoples and thus cannot ignore what is contextually relatively specific and unique. He (1919, p. 62) declares that every culture stage must be envisaged as a unity 'in which each element acts upon every other element' and in which institutions 'are sympathetically adjusted to one another,' including alike both the subjectively and objectively oriented institutions. Thus, the institutions oriented to objective conditions – the industrial, domestic, military, political, and ecclesiastical which 'do not follow the same course for all peoples' because they are dependent on variable external or environmental conditions – will also affect those oriented to subjective factors, imposing something 'local and distinctive' (1919, p. 62).

Cooley would certainly adopt the same stance, for he was committed to a comprehensive methodological holism or contextualism. Accordingly, the idea of some social entity or construct, such as a stage, being rigidly determined apart from space and time specificities would have been entirely foreign to Cooley's views. Small also seems to subscribe to a similar methodological holism, though he actually does conjecture about the nature of stages and the necessity that criteria for their demarcation be multiple in character (1905, p. 222). Nevertheless, neither he nor Cooley does indeed use the stages notion in his own research.

(4) The anti-evolutionists qualify their acceptance of the evolutionary notion of the natural rate and magnitude of social change so substantially that their position amounts to a rejection of the evolutionary one. Such figures as Ward, Giddings, and Keller had urged that social change was relatively slow, gradual, and step-by-step and by imperceptible, or barely perceptible, small amounts or increments. The anti-evolutionists did concede that most social change was probably slow and small-scale. Small, for example, does allege that 'the passage of no tribe from savagery to civic order could have been by a leap' (1905, p. 222). But Sumner

and Cooley offer a more complete statement of their views. Both of them indicate that both slow and small-scale and rapid and large-scale forms of social change can and do occur.

True, Sumner did declare that 'constant, gradual, smooth, and easy readjustment is the course of things which is conductive to healthful [normal and natural social] life' (1959, p. 95). Effective change will involve 'slow,' 'long-continued,' and 'minute variations' (1959, p. 97). The mores are 'imperceptible in their growth' (n.d.*a*). Such change is slow and imperceptible because it must arise from within a persisting and fixed structure of habits (and not because it is an organismic-like growth). Sumner also suggests the possibility of slow and minute change as succeeding generations fail to perpetuate cultural forms 'just as they [have] received them' (1959, p. 84). Even if a son 'continues the ritual and repeats the formula [of a mos, he] does not [or may not necessarily] think and feel the same ideas and sentiments as his father' (1959, p. 84).

In addition, Sumner observes that crises and revolutions can and do develop in higher civilizations when old mores persist 'after conditions have changed,' when the mores have become fixed and 'do not conform to new interests and needs,' when 'a great change in conditions' calls for 'new mores' through reform or revolution (1959, pp. 86, 85, 87). 'Great crises' occur when 'great new forces' are changing 'fundamental conditions' but 'powerful institutions and traditions still hold old systems intact' (1959, p. 118). The long genesis of 'protest or revulsion . . . under and within the existing system' produces the 'great leaders of modern revolutions,' for whom the crisis affords an opportunity for personal initiative (1959, p. 118). But a revolution can be successful only in so far as its changes are restricted to meeting alterations in the conditions of existence (1959, pp. 86–7, 118). Dogma alone is ineffective. Manifestly, more rapid and large-scale social change in the form of revolution is neither impossible nor unnatural (or abnormal) for Sumner.

In differentiating 'moderate' from 'radical' change, Cooley seems to be conscious of both the rate and magnitude of change. He appears to have been aware of both slow and small-scale as well as rapid and large-scale change. Presumably, 'moderate,' i.e., relatively slow and small-scale change, is the more normal and natural. Neither stagnation, the cessation of change, nor rapid change is to be regarded as the natural and normal state of affairs. But illustrations throughout his several volumes include various crises, such as eras of ferment, upheaval, rebellion, and revolution. He was obviously interested in the periods of the Renaissance and the French Revolution. However, his commitment to the essential goodness of the social status quo and his adherence to organicism would have militated against any view of the naturalness of sharp, rapid, or violent change. The various organic unities, such as personality, culture, and society, together with such subsidiary types as might be delineated, have their respective, intrinsic tendencies to change. Organic growth, obviously Cooley's model of change, suggests regularity and continuity, with the possibility of a somewhat variable rate of change. Cooley's works also imply that the rate of change may vary depending on whether or not human nature values have been frustrated by prolonged institutional formalism, whether or not the systems of external biophysical nature intrude in the form of crises, and whether or not genius or conspicuous originality is represented in the interaction among members. If these conditions exist, change will be likely to be more rapid; if they do not, it will occur at a slower pace.

(5) Curiously, the anti-evolutionists display what at first glance appears to be a somewhat ambivalent or contradictory view toward the central tenet of social evolution, its linear directionality. On the one hand, Sumner, Ross, and Thomas deny that human experience reveals any consistent directional trend as is entailed in the notion of increasing social differentiation and complexity through a succession of stages. But on the other, Small and Cooley do seem to accept a generally linear directionality of human experience. However, Small and Ross assume that progress has occurred as opposed to the directionality of social differentiation and complexity through time.

For his part, Sumner declares that it is impossible to arrange the mores 'in a logical scale of advance, even if time and place were disregarded' (n.d.*a*). And even if such a series is constructed, it cannot be assumed in any case 'that history has run over the track which is thus laid down' (n.d.*a*). To insist, as Sumner does, that among the great bulk of men in most societies the conditions of social existence are *not* such as to demand struggle, survival of the fittest, or selection is to undermine the basic rationale for the (presumed) directionality of ever-increasing social differentiation and complexity. Under the civilized conditions of modern times, natural selection is precluded because 'the struggle for comfort has taken the place of the struggle for existence' (n.d.*a*).

Accordingly, change in the folkways may be compared to 'a great restless sea of clouds, in which the parts are forever rolling, changing, jostling . . . they do not run forward in time towards some ultimate shape, but they change and change, rise and fall, ebb

223

and flow, without any sequence and purpose' (quoted in Keller, 1931, p. 247). History 'shows us,' Sumner remarks in his recently discovered paper on the application of evolution and progress to the superorganic domain, only 'indefinite variation,' with a 'rolling, tossing, swaying, and endless dissolution of successive forms and stages' – each succeeding each other 'without any connection whatever' – 'in the sequence of all superorganic forms' (n.d.*b*, p. 13). Even in the *Folkways*, his few, inconspicuous references to social evolution (pp. 154–6, 438–9, 140, 118) do not entail an explicit delineation of generalized successive stages or phases.

Both Ross and Thomas urge similarly that the notion of unilinear directionality of social evolution is empirically unsupportable. Thomas asserts that any human activity 'is related to all others' and thus activities in general 'cannot be isolated or arranged according to any fixed order of development' (1909, p. vii). He and Ross both agree that the 'order of emergence of inventions' is not rigidly fixed for all cultures (1909, p. 25; cf. 1919, p. 227). Accordingly, Ross insists that to the extent that inventions control a succession of social changes, the sequence 'is not law-abiding, and cannot be predicted' (1919, p. 227). Although 'the growth of numbers or the accumulation of wealth seems to move all societies through the same stages, their dependence on invention forbids us to look for a single route of development [and direction] traversed [and followed] by all peoples' (1919, p. 227).

In essence Ross concurs with Thomas's insistence that 'a straight and uniform line of development [cannot be assumed] among all races' (1909, p. 25). Ross observes that the empirical sequence of institutional forms 'is sometimes neither "evolution" nor "progress"' (1919, p. 58). He notes, for instance, that the family does not exhibit a uniform evolution from 'the small, incoherent, and indefinite' to 'the large, coherent, definite, and complex' and that a 'steady progress from the ethically "lower" to the ethically "higher"' cannot be found (1919, p. 58). Even in such an important institution as the economy 'there is no fixed order – some hunters skipping the pastoral stage to become tillers, some nomads skipping the tillage stage to become carriers or traders' (1919, p. 58). So Thomas avers that any fixed classification of culture by epochs (e.g., the frugivorous, hunting, pastoral, and agricultural) is doomed to failure if it is 'made too absolutely' (1909, p. 25).

Ross insists that in general laws of succession are necessarily etiologically or methodologically defective. Laws of succession for each aspect of social evolution cannot be accepted because 'an institutional form is not the cause of its successor' (1919, p. 62). To base such laws on the parallelism of entire institutional developments in all societies, moreover, would be indictable because the units are too large. Only one sequence of this kind can exist for a given society and, since known societies are characterized by dissimilar conditions, 'their developments . . . are not sufficiently parallel to yield a valid law of succession' (1919, pp. 73–4). Basically, the 'development of a particular order of institutions is, in greater or lesser degree, *multilinear,* and . . . the endeavor to establish in each sphere of social life a single, typical sequence of changes is bound to fail' (1919, p. 62).

By contrast, Cooley (and Small) do accept some directionality of change in general. Cooley's notion of the growth of the grapevine is suggestive. The grapevine tends to send 'out straight, rapidly growing shoots with two-branched tendrils at the end' (1966, p. 8). But he also implies some degree of randomness in growth which is scarcely compatible with a rectilinear notion of the direction of social change. Any 'improvement in one respect [in social change] is apt to be offset, at least in part or temporarily, by delay or retrogression in others' (1962, p. 55). Furthermore, his objections to the notion of a social cycle or to definite laws of growth and decay for groups or societies because they are mechanical and predetermined would also seem to invalidate the necessity of the sequence of stages in the directionality of change (1966, pp. 31, 33). Still, Cooley does not construe social life as 'a series of futile repetitions, but as eternal growth, onward and upward development' (1966, p. 34). It is, thus, Cooley's own faith in progress which apparently provides directionality. And the same judgment holds for Small. For neither one can directionality be merely equated with increasing social differentiation and complexity through a succession of definite, determined stages of change.

(6) Although anti-evolutionists manifested considerable divergence in their views toward the naturalist-necessitarian, internalist, and uniformitarian features of the causal mechanism or modus operandi by which social evolution was argued to proceed, they showed more agreement in opposing the Social Darwinist and Lamarckian arguments constituting the core-content of social evolutionary explanations of change. Sumner and Ross offered broad indictments of most or all of the main features of Social Darwinism, whereas Small and Cooley centered their objections on the unvarying primacy of violent conflict or struggle which they conceived to be the distinguishing feature of that orientation.

225

Sumner, Ross, Thomas, and Cooley also denied the legitimacy of resorting to the Lamarckian doctrine of the inheritance of acquired characteristics operating through the thesis of use and disuse to account for social evolutionary change.

Sumner and Ross both broadly challenged the Social Darwinism frequently invoked as the mechanism of evolutionary social change, with Sumner offering perhaps the more complete and systematic rejection. Indeed, Sumner explicitly controverted the three basic premises of Social Darwinism: struggle for existence, innate individual variations, and natural selection. Except for the very earliest condition of mankind in hordes, among which extermination and enslavement often followed conflict and conquest, struggle for existence has not genuinely operated among humankind. Certainly, the natural process 'is not the predominant factor' in civilizations in which it has been transformed by culture and (thus) by adaptation through mores, institutions, and science (n.d.*a*). The acquisition of culture has enabled human societies to transcend the characteristic condition of scarcity and struggle among organisms in the natural domain.

Ross was explicit about what remained implicit in Summer's views: the Social Darwinists have committed a 'master error' in equating the (modern) economic struggle with the struggle for existence (1919, p. 340). The 'scramble for money or for place . . . has ceased to be a clear case of life or death' (1919, p. 340). Certainly, there is a vast difference 'between the gaining or losing [of] a rung in the climb for comfort, and the situation Darwin found among animals and plants' (1919, p. 340). Indeed – as Sumner remarks – 'the struggle for comfort has taken the place of the struggle for existence' in modern times, and, in some instances, 'the struggle for luxury has taken the place of the struggle for comfort' (n.d.*a*).

Although cultural change does depend on individual variations, Sumner refuses to restrict the source of those variations to innate individual differences, e.g., the constitution of the brain. It is actually learning in conjunction with the experience with (pleasure but especially) pain in relation to the conditions of social existence that accentuates the original individual differences. Furthermore, the likelihood of the transmission of pain-reducing adaptations from one individual to another and from one society or culture to another de-emphasizes the internality of the sources of change.

Sumner also rejected the notion that natural selection or the survival of the fittest is operative either at the human organic or super-organic levels. In the post-horde condition of humankind, social change does not occur by the preservation of the elite and the elimination of the non-elite. War has no consistent and systematic effect and, consequently, Sumner argues (n.d.*b*, p. 8) that it 'acts unselectively.' Human organic variation associated with the mixtures of populations reveals only 'panmixia,' the absence of any process of selection of the fit or elimination of the unfit. Socio-cultural change following the earliest condition of mankind is the result of diffusion (which may occur through war or other forms of direct and indirect social contacts) and syncretism (which suggests a recombination of cultural items from an outside source with those already present in the society). But syncretism displays no 'directive force to control the movement of selection towards what is [adaptively] better . . . as . . . in organic evolution' (n.d.*b*, p. 25).

Ross takes the position that the economic 'battle of life' is hardly a struggle to exist and but 'little selective' (1919, p. 341). And although the activities within society involve 'social selections,' they 'are by no means of a stripe with . . . natural selections' (1919, p. 342). The difference between what nature and society do is dramatic (1919, p. 343):

> Nature eliminates the unfit; society eliminates the misfit. Nature rejects the defective; society preserves them, but burns the heretic and hangs the criminal. For the most part, though, the social selections do not eliminate anybody.
>
> Social selections . . . discriminate between men on the basis of their volitions, whereas Nature discriminates for the most part on the basis of their bodily traits or their instincts.

Small and Cooley both objected to the unjustified emphasis on violent conflict which Social Darwinism assumed and which seemed to be so intimately linked with explanations of social evolutionism. Cooley repudiated 'a simplified and misunderstood Darwinism which unduly exalts conflict and makes the "struggle for existence" between groups almost the sole principle of human life' (1966, p. 241). Certainly, Small would also have concurred in Cooley's insistence that 'both conflict and cooperation have their places' in the social process and, indeed, both are 'phases of one process which always involves something of both' (1966, pp. 36, 39, 34; Small, 1905, pp. 203, 369–70, 490, 565–6, 502–7). However, Small does agree (1905, pp. 200, 204, cf. pp. 203, 205, 208) with his more Darwinian colleagues – as Cooley does not – that 'conflict is the active factor' in the early stages of the social process. Both sociologists seem to have recognized many important social and personal bases of conflict (e.g., individual variations in reason, affect, volition, choice and in displays of energy, temperament, courage, resolution, initiative, self-assertiveness, imagination, and sensitivity) as opposed (only) to pain and the deprivation of organic wants by scarcity as its primary or ultimate source. Both sociologists refused to believe that conflict must always, usually or frequently deteriorate into struggle and mutual extermination. Their bases of optimism included: a faith in the progressive diminution of the frequency and severity of harsh forms of conflict, the presumption that sympathy as universally acquired in primary group socialization will limit hostility, and a conviction that out of the destruction of particular rules by conflict human reason will be able to find more general and permanent principles. (Small, 1905, p. 325; Cooley, 1966, p. 337; see also chapter 10, pp. 258–9.) Furthermore, they were also disposed to interpret interpersonal and intergroup differences as potentially contributory to the *resolution* of conflict as well as to its *initiation*.

Sumner, Ross, Thomas and Cooley are also explicitly opposed to the Lamarckian assumption that the inheritance of acquired characteristics through use and disuse can affect hereditary lines behind individual differences. Sumner claims that he knows of 'no evidence to support' the Lamarckian thesis – except 'for the most superficial observation on genealogical facts' – that 'the germ-plasm would be affected by all the fysical [*sic*!], mental, and moral habits of man or woman' so that 'heredit[ar]y affects would be produced' (n.d.*c*, p. 30fn). He notes discerningly that Spencer's vigorous reply to Weismann's 'denial that use and disuse could produce hereditary features' shows 'how completely his own evolutionism in society is built on the assumption that such features are hereditary' (n.d.*c*, p. 40). The preponderance of opinion among biologists is moving to support Weismann (n.d.*c*, p. 40). Ross's declarations that 'Thirty centuries of circumcision . . . [have left] no mark on Jewish babies' and that 'Cutting off the tails of mice for many generations does not create a tailless race' presumably constitute the basis for his (socially applied) anti-Lamarckian insistence that 'the moral habit of one generation does not become the instinct of the next' (1969, p. 60; cf. p. 437). Thomas also observes that the 'characters of body and mind acquired by the parent after birth are probably not inherited by the child' (1909, p. 316). And Cooley also concurs that 'no one has been able to produce any satisfactory proof that "acquired traits," that is those due to the mode of life, are ever transmitted through the germ-plasm' (1964, pp. 8–9).

228

Sumner's cultural-historical empiricalism

To recognize that a position has been rejected can only be an intellectual step in identifying what intellectual position is accepted. Such is the case for the anti-social evolutionists whose opposition and rejection of social evolution has just been explained. And of course it does not necessarily follow logically that a relatively similar opposition and rejection will lead to the adoption of a similar positive position explaining social change. Indeed, this logical possibility is actualized in the case of the positive approach to social change. Sumner clearly stands apart from the views which Ross, Small, and Cooley adopt. Perhaps such an eventuality should be expected because Sumner and Keller are generally associated in a position of (proto-) behavioristic materialism (as opposed to the (proto-) interactionist-idealism of Ross, Small, and Cooley), despite Sumner's divergence from Keller on social evolutionism. Accordingly, Sumner's views on social change will necessarily be examined separately from Ross's Small's, and Cooley's commitments.

Certainly both the more incidental particularistic arguments and the more direct and generalized statements of Sumner confirm his rejection of social evolutionism. He clearly regarded evolution or perhaps, more accurately, evolutionism as a 'fashion of thought' of his own era, a 'philosophy of nature about which considerable caution [must be exercised] to avoid an undue tendency to run all things into . . . [its] mold' (1959, p. 194 and n.d.*a.*).

Like his student Keller (and other sociologists of his own era), Sumner construed social change as essentially a response to an altered relationship between the basic human nature needs of the aggregate of members of a society and the conditions of social or aggregate existence (i.e., 'life-conditions'). Any society consists basically of a system of folkways, mores, laws, institutions, through which the basic needs of members were satisfied more or less successfully from the resources of their environment. Thus, the folkways, mores, etc., comprising more or less a system may be said to adapt the aggregate to their conditions of existence. Interestingly, Sumner does not necessarily emphasize the limited variation in conditions of existence, though he does insist on the relative uniformity of the nature of human nature. He refers to the 'range of divergence in the solution of the great problems of human life' (1959, p. 82). Biopsychic human nature does involve the four basic needs of hunger, sex passion, vanity, and ghost-fear. The first two, hunger and sex passion, are original in the organism. They are primary, therefore, both in the sense that they are original in human nature and correspond (or their satisfaction corresponds) to the perpetuation of existence. The other two, vanity and ghost-fear, are derived in the sense that they have emerged following persistent human association and the origin of human society. Unlike vanity which is a 'catch-all' category and plays a more or less minor function for Sumner, ghost-fear is considerably important. It arose in conjunction with the recurring calamities and catastrophies which afflict human existence, and provoke pain, which in turn thus elicits a conscious effort to identify an agency (and more broadly to provide 'explanation'). Ghost-fear tends to evoke a collective judgment (and definition) of what is in the welfare of society and it is that definition that is incorporated in the formation of the mores for Sumner. He regards the entire collection or aggregate of folkways, mores, etc., as modes of adaptation entailing the satisfaction of the four human nature needs in relation to the conditions of existence.

Social change tends to be demanded both by any change in the character of the needs-wants(-desires) and in the resources of the natural environment so that maladaptation rather than adaptation obtains. Actually, Sumner emphasizes that it is in the very nature of folkways and especially mores to become maladaptive over time because they lose their initial elasticity and plasticity and become rigid and fixed. He also seems to suggest that some variability in the conditions of existence will always occur (in population size, resources, climate, weather, etc.) so that some maladaptation seems to be predestined. Increasing strain or discrepancy between the modes of collective behavior and the conditions of existence will produce pain and eventually – as the disparity becomes extreme – a crisis. As individuals experience pain resulting from altered relationship between needs and their satisfaction through the resources of their environment, i.e., encounter difficulties in the struggle for existence, they will be under increasing pressure to find more effective modes of adaptation, i.e., to change.

Unlike the evolutionists who conceive of the source of adaptive behavior as wholly internal (i.e., as arising from individual variations within the society), Sumner recognizes that the constituents of change (or adaptation) may derive from both internal and external sources (from already existing folkways and mores available and accessible from adjacent or external societies). Of course, in either case the stimulus to change is the widespread experience of pain resulting from maladaptive folkways and mores *in* the (given) society. In Sumner's view, such sensation tends to provoke an immediate impulsive, clumsy, and blundering reaction (1959, pp. 3–4). Individuals' responses are not the result of foresight or intention or of 'purpose and wit' (1959, p. 4). The resulting deviations or variations constitute so many trials and errors (to avoid pain and achieve adaptation). However, some persons are more talented than others (they possess superior natural abilities) and can respond more promptly, effectively, or adequately to the changed or changing circumstances than others can. Interestingly, Sumner comments that the powers and abilities of such an elite can be fully realized only in transitional eras when the modes of behavior are jarringly at variance with the conditions of existence, when pain and suffering are severe, when crisis prevails. Unusual individuals have their greatest opportunity in eras of revolutionary upheaval.

However, innovation is not the completed work of merely one (exceptional) person. It is rather subject to a process of alteration and improvement in the 'give and take' and suggestion and imitation between man and man (1959, p. 19). The process is 'one of development,' with new suggestions coming in 'at point after point,' being 'carried out,' and combining 'with what existed already' (1959, p. 19).

In addition, a new or enhanced adaptation may derive from the available folkways and mores of another adjacent or accessible society. They derive from contact with other groups, societies, or cultures. This type of change arises through syncretism which involves a process of mutual 'giving and taking' culminating in the modification of existing folkways, elimination of some folkways and their replacement by others, or the combination of different folkways. Syncretism results either from the diffusion of folkways and mores in the course of cultural contact or from conquest. According to Sumner, 'syncretism of the folkways' occurs 'when groups are compounded by intermarriage, intercourse, conquest, immigration, or slavery' or by virtue of 'contiguity, neighborhood, or even literature' (1959, p. 116). (Conceivably, favorable or unfavorable ethnocentrism directed at a possible donor society or the character of in-group/out-group relations might influence borrowing, though Sumner isn't explicit.)

Acceptance, adoption, or dissemination of the innovating behavior (or the diffused item) will presumably be conditioned by reduction of pain or increase of pleasure, i.e., it provides more certain survival or adaptation to the conditions of existence prevailing in a given habitat. Individuals in an aggregate (group or society) can and do observe the manifest differences in one another's successes or 'well-being' and in the differences in pleasure and pain accompanying behavior (1970, p. 149). Each person in the aggregate profits 'by the other's experience' (1959, p. 2). Because a particular way of acting answers 'the purposes better than other ways, or with less toil and pain,' individuals become (unconsciously?) suggesstible to, or (consciously?) select, imitate, and adopt the successful or expedient 'ways of doing things' (1959, p. 2).

As such adaptive (or more adaptive) behaviors are repeated in individuals, they become habits. And as habits become more or less widely distributed (or shared) and practiced by individuals, they become some form or kind of mass or collective behavior. Currents of similarity, concurrence, and mutual contributions are evident.

Presumably, too, the dissemination of this new mode of behavior would have to be in accord with the strain of the (folkways and) mores toward consistency (1959, pp. 94–5, 5). (The mores are more efficient when consistent (1959, p. 102).) Inconsistency provokes frictions and antagonisms which may be disruptive of social unity and threaten survival (1959, pp. 5–6). Presumably, in view of the heavy emphasis which Sumner laid on the folkways and mores satisfying the hunger interest (and more broadly what may be defined as economic considerations), the strain toward consistency would be substantially influenced by the character of the economic folkways, mores, and institutions – or what later came to be known as the societal maintenance institutions.

Sumner's analysis of social change (after 1899) largely avoids the charges of abstract universalism which could be directed against so many of his colleagues in the discipline. It manifests a 'hard-headed' concern with the specific, time-and-space-bound socio-cultural data of concrete societies. Social evolutionism was apparently to be rejected as a species of evolutionary philosophy of the times. Change is not to be explained by any consistent and systematic operation of the elimination of the unfit or survival of the fittest individuals or societies. It is only a matter of 'expedient' alteration in the folkways and mores of a society.

Committed thus to a kind of historical empiricalism, Sumner avoided easy and loose generalization. He displayed a broad interest in data both from primitive and modern (especially Western European) societies – and so he proposed a 'historical anthropology.' On-going societies were systems or wholes which required appropriate holistic yet meticulous socio-cultural study. He had expelled (conscious) individual teleology and rationalism and tended to retain a residual behavioristic materialism which at times veered toward an (empirical) objective idealism.

Ross's, Small's, and Cooley's social process theory of social change

Ross, Small and Cooley subscribe to what can be characterized as an (interactionist) social process conception of social change. In contrast to the social evolutionary position of Ward, Giddings, and Keller, which in varying degrees shares a proto-behaviorist-materialist foundation, the dynamics theory of Ross, Small, and Cooley is pervasively predicated on an interactionist-idealist basis. Like the accounts of their antagonists, those of Ross, Small, and Cooley do essentially deal with the origins and emergence of social innovation and with its acceptance, adoption, and dissemination. The general designation 'social process' is proposed because innovation and its acceptance are construed to occur within and to require not merely interaction in general but a peculiar or distinctive interrelationship of (interactive sub-) processes together constituting the social process (e.g., competition, conflict, accommodation, etc.). All three of the sociologists do use interaction (and especially its sub-process conflict) as the setting within which the contributions of individual differences are elicited, mobilized, and integrated to construct innovation for adapting the group more effectively to its environment or for adjusting it more satisfactorily to its total situation.

Ross's notion of the social process (and its constituent sub-processes) shows some variation between the writing of *Foundations of Sociology* and *The Principles of Sociology*.[2] The older book divides the processes fundamentally into two basic varieties, the 'social' processes and the 'reconstructive' processes. In turn, the 'social' processes are classified into eleven types (each containing anywhere from two to four specific processes): genesis of society, association, domination, opposition, adaptation, cooperation, stratification, socialization, alienation, individualization, and crystallization (1919, p. 98). Among the dynamic or reconstructive processes are population increase, accumulation of capital, incidental modification of the natural environment, selection, urbanization, migration, diffusion and cross-fertilization of cultures, and innovation. Although almost as many processes are included in the later *The Principles*, they are organized into fewer major types: opposition (seven chapters), adaptation (five chapters), class and caste (four chapters), individual in relation to the group (six chapters), and regress and progress (five chapters).

233

Apparently, change is no longer exclusively associated with one section (as in the 'reconstructive' in *Foundations*), but pervades many sections (though especially 'Regress and Progress') in *The Principles*.

Small's social process analysis of change is envisaged within the interrelationship between the two more or less basic processes of association and dissociation, either one of which is possible following inter- and/or multi-personal contact and the emergence of a definition of 'interests' of the parties involved. If contact is accompanied or succeeded by an awareness of a scarcity of desired objects and competition, the divergence of interests may increase. Antipathy, repulsion, collision, conflict, and violence may ensue. However, extreme violence tends eventually to lessen and wane. Then may follow gradual accommodation of egoistic interests, differentiation, individualization, some harmonization, an emergence of common interests, moralization, and finally social-ization of interest, the recognition of common welfare (along with reflection, coordination, perhaps sympathy and attraction), and outright assimilation, integration and cooperation (1905, pp. 338, 340, 342, 512, 566).

Cooley also suggested a series of subsidiary or sub-processes within the more generic social process, such as opposition, competition, conflict, along with clash and struggle, some accommodation or compromise, with the achievement of a synthesis of divergent viewpoints (through pragmatic selection and valuation), and culmination in organization as a whole and cooperation. He did distinguish many additional social aspects and phases: inter- and intra-societal processes, such as war and international conflict, class and racial conflicts, social disorganiz-ation, social degeneration, and moral disintegration. He also identified many personal aspects and phases: opportunity, discipline, competition, emulation, success and fame, along with personal degeneration and personal demoralization. Perhaps the crux of the general process is Cooley's notion of valuation. Its ultimate criterion and method are a tentative, pragmatic 'work-ability' as opposed to any mere reliance on physical survival of the fittest and impersonal, objective selection.

However, the social process position is not an undivided, consensual whole. Ross does diverge from Small and Cooley and, in turn, they from him on many important points. Small and Cooley, for instance, were inclined to envisage the social process holistically or organically. They believed that social change can be generalized as a relatively continuous, comprehensive and more or less directional process increasingly embracing all mankind in one great whole. In contrast, Ross distrusted analysis which was cast in terms of such a global, encompassing perspective. He preferred inquiry into small social units. In the analysis of individual differences in social change, Ross stressed the place of the great man, genius, or talented individual. By no means do Small and Cooley ignore the role of the unusual person, but their presentation conceives of the usual or ordinary person as also making an input to the process. Ross seems to offer a more inequalitarian or hierarchical conception of the emergence of innovation. He also seems to demark sharply the role of rationality from affectivity in interaction and to emphasize the more positive and lasting features of the former as opposed to the latter in the emergence of social change. By contrast, Cooley stresses the positive contributions of affectivity in interaction. Although the influence of Hegel was present in Ross's antecedents through Tarde's formulation of the process of imitation–counter-imitation (opposition or antithesis) and adaptation (or synthesis), Small and Cooley made much more conspicuous use of the dialectic in their interpretation of social innovation as involving a synthesis which eventuates from opposition, conflict, or struggle. But Ross adopts a position which centers primarily on *adaptation* in relation to the more or less objective conditions of the natural environment (as opposed to Small's and Colley's holistic inter-personal adjustment within the situation). Neither Cooley (and Small) nor Ross entirely rejects and disavows the influence of biogenetic (hereditarian) differences in social change. Of the three theorists, Ross is much more inclined to ascribe considerable significance and prominence to racial differences and inequalities in dynamics. Occasionally, his presentation seems to convey a mechanistic-deterministic tone which Small and Cooley also find in Tarde and condemn. Generally, they rejected and opposed Tarde whereas Ross accepted and supported him.

The origins of social innovation

Interaction – which Ross, Small, and Cooley use as their point of departure for explaining social innovation – is based on an idealist notion of the social as inter- and/or multi-personal activity. It assumes that the activity among and between persons is subjectively oriented. The 'social' thus involves the domain of the mental, subjective, conscious, psychic, intentional, and the volitional. Presupposing interaction, the social process signifies the relatively continuous, persistent, person-to-person inter-stimulation and response, with both social object(s) and social subject(s) always able to assume the initiative and some modicum of creativity. Certainly, Small and Cooley agree with Ross's declaration that whatever is social is so because it arises out of the interplay of minds (1912, p. 3). It is due to psychic interaction. For Ross a social phenomenon has as many causes 'as there are human [minds and] wills involved' (1919, p. 80).

Understandably, then, interaction is the central, crucial, and unifying idealist notion in the explanation of social change generally and innovation in particular. It is true that occasionally such words as 'action' and 'reaction' or 'association' and 'dissociation' may appear, but qualifications are added so that interaction is genuinely signified. Interaction is a characteristically idealist view of change, for it denies the validity of a merely causal notion of mechanical stimulus and response within the human domain. Cooley agrees wholeheartedly with Small in the latter's insistence that when two or more persons come within each other's ken, they exchange influences of some sort or other. They themselves and their relationships are incessantly made, unmade, and remade. Persons and groups are constituted and reconstituted by interaction. Each 'person is what he is by virtue of the existence of other persons, and by virtue of an alternating current of influence between each person and all the other persons previously or at the same time in existence' (Small, 1905, p. 487). Human life is always and necessarily social life, i.e., life in groups, the members of which influence each other (1905, p. 208). Society is composed of the reciprocal adaptations between persons and groups. The 'social is the realm of circuits of reciprocal influence between individuals and the groups which individuals compose' (1905, p. 488). It is the 'reciprocity and the reciprocality between . . . persons' (1905, p. 511). It is 'all the give-and-takeness there is, whether more or less, between persons anywhere in contact' (1905, p. 512).

However important interaction is, it does not occur in isolation from the total situation or environment. The biophysical environment or habitat contains and potentially impinges on or influences the (social) situation and thus becomes a focus for (i.e., 'demands' on) inter- or multi-personal interaction. The aggregate of individuals bring to the situation the (normative) structure of the relevant group and the broader values of the culture – both of which may affect the potentialities for change in interaction.[3] Each person brings his own personal or personality peculiarities and idiosyncracies, aptitudes and inclinations. They include apparently the more or less minor variations of ordinary persons and the more major departures represented by individuals of talent, genius, or unusual endowments. But all of these factors become dynamic only in the context of (social) interaction. The situation – which apparently is always somewhat different on each occasion – is relevant only in relation to interaction. Men must define the situation appropriately to invoke the latent group structure. And personality variation can be transformed from a mere potential resource into the actual substance of change only by the constructive synthesis accompanying interaction.

But Ross, on the one hand, and Small and Cooley, on the other, do construe the eliciting and mobilization of personality differences through interaction to create innovation in very different ways. Ross seems to emphasize differences in rational-irrational proclivities of persons and stresses the role of the rationality of the unusual person in the interactive genesis of the new and its contribution to environment or situational adaptation. But Cooley refuses to separate reason and emotion and is uneasy about any undue elitist emphasis on the contributions of persons of talent.

Nevertheless, Cooley points to the singular positive consequence of emotion or affect in eliciting the development of the new out of interaction. Through interaction, antecedent tendencies are aroused and fresh influences are offered, accompanied by 'a kindred excitement and reciprocation' (1966, p. 16). Individuals feel 'about among the various openings or stimuli offered by one another,' and 'each responds to those which are most congruous with its own tendencies' (1966, p. 9). The range of individual differences in interaction must not be too sharp or too great. Differences must be complementary, just as the ideas elicited in such interaction 'must be different enough' and 'yet cognate enough to suggest and stimulate a synthesis [eventually]' (1966, p. 12). The responsiveness of mind to mind, the communication of ideas and ideals, the interchange of gestures and affects activate, stimulate, excite, and release energy. Non-rational elements necessarily intrude: passions, feelings, and sentiments 'which are sometimes conveyed by words and sometimes by gestures, tones, glances of the eye, and by all sorts of deeds,' enter in, as do 'those qualities of sense and character which underlie insight, judgment, and belief' (1966, p. 357). Interaction, coupled with non-rationality and diversity, produces 'psychical reactions . . . like the kindling of a flame . . . a kind of sexuality of mating of impulses, which unites in a procreative whole forces that are barren in separation' (1966,

p. 17). It mobilizes and synthesizes individual energies and inclinations awaiting on outlet.

Indeed, the energies and inclinations of both ordinary and extraordinary individuals are affected. But if the situation is beset by crisis, the unusual individual will find a special opportunity, if not an insistent demand, to contribute his talents in the course of the developing interaction. Both Cooley and Ross were concerned with the unique characteristics of the person. Cooley acknowledges his (or her) extraordinary heredity, energy, capacity, intelligence, impulses, temperament, initiative, tenacity, and sensitivity. Ross cites (1969, p. 278) the skills, sagacity, experience, talents, gifts, and accomplishments of such individuals. They are likely to possess an impressive physique, strength of will, persistence, courage, faith in themselves, dignity, cordiality, eloquence, generosity, love, and imagination (1969, pp. 277–8). Conversely, they are not likely to be deceptive or self-seeking, for – asserts Ross – they usually possess a 'largeness of caliber,' an encompassing vision, 'soaring ambition, and a passion for large objects, great causes and enterprises of pith and moment' (1969, p. 286). Quite apart from any love of others or devotion to the group, 'a great man is liable to noble enthusiasm for labors which do not terminate upon himself' (1969, p. 286). His renunciation of the rewards and benefits which men conventionally regard as desirable, the uncompromising and categorical tone or quality of his views, and his display of a compelling zeal or enthusiasm do tend to influence others to accept his diagnoses and solutions.

Ross claims that he initiates many impulses and receives few, 'while others receive many impulses and give out few' (1969, p. 102). According to Cooley, he is more immune to the pressures of conformity than ordinary men. Sumner insists that he is a leader because he voices 'the convictions which have become established and because . . . [he] propose[s] measures which will realize interests of which the society has become conscious' (1959, p. 118). Ross notes that he possesses 'unusual insight into the requisites of good personal and social life' and has the capacity to anticipate less direct and more distant consequences of action (1969, pp. 350, 349). In 'no wise a social product,' genius includes the unusual 'intellectual capacity necessary to combine . . . ideas into . . . invention' (1912, p. 360).

Only Cooley endeavors to provide a full explanation of the innovation of exceptional men, though Sumner does observe that such men (and their characteristics), their era, and presumably their social contexts 'react upon each other' (1959, p. 118). Cooley

238

specifies (1966, p. xxxvii) that genius does require a social milieu, such as specialized occupational or professional groups. Through such association, knowledge and skill are transmitted, performance is subjected to criticism, and encouragement and approval are provided. The innovators advance what Cooley terms the public intelligence by consciously, deliberately, intentionally seeking the new. They bring relevant portions of the social heritage of the past to bear on some problem of the present. Their decisions about what may be done effectively is preceded by an imaginative staging, a mental experiment, a constructive vision, of the consequences of the envisaged (plan or) synthesis. They exercise a kind of foresight, anticipating the operation of forces at work and preparing in advance to adjust to these forces. By no means can it be said that their innovations are discontinuous with the past or are in any sense cataclysmic changes. What they contribute is developed by the same process, with the same model, sources and factors, and processual mechanisms, as are involved in the unplanned, unintended, and incidental changes emerging from routine day-to-day interaction.

For all of the importance attaching to the unique characteristics of talented individuals, it is necessary to remember that the social process position holds that the distinctive contribution of such characteristics to innovation can occur only in and through interaction. However, what is even more significant is that it is a particular type or form of interaction (sub-) process, conflict, which to the extent that it is accompanied by certain developments is most crucial in the emergence of innovation for the (inter-actionist-) social process-idealists. But conflict is not conceived to operate strictly, exclusively, or even predominantly as the Social Darwinists had imagined. It is not merely or typically a matter of organic struggle and extermination or annihilation. Conflict among human beings tends to involve more or less the rudiments and aspects of a conscious, *mutually oriented verbal interchange* or discussion, with a common focus of attention on certain issues, the existence of doubt, differences of opinion, argument, dispute (with conflict assuming varying breadth and intensity), denial, criticism, accompanied by some presentation of reasons, and eventually choice or decision. For Cooley and Small, conflict frequently or substantially – and for Ross, sometimes if not often – proceeds in accordance with the dialectic of the Hegelian tradition. Although opposition is assumed as a stage or phase of interaction, it tends to elicit (structural) modification – creativity. Tension, conflict, contradiction, or divergence arises (i.e., as *thesis* and *antithesis*), but

239

some degree of compromise, accommodation, adaptation, or adjustment develops among opposing parties or contestants, with innovation emerging as a concomitant (*synthesis*).[4]

Cooley holds that somehow (interpersonal or intergroup) differences, variety, and contrast in the social situation provoke a development of tension, opposition, contradiction, clash, conflict, and struggle in a variety of forms and in various degrees. Such opposition seems to be necessary fully to evoke, actualize, and mobilize the potentialities for the new lying behind the concrete individual differences. Eventually, a decisive point in the clash or struggle will be reached, as in a drama. As views and opinions divide, 'each side is stimulated by the opposition of the other to define, corroborate, and amend its views, with the purpose of justifying itself before the constituency to which it appeals' (1964, p. 275). To develop the new, some compromise will have to be achieved short of the extermination of one faction by the other.

The two or more parts (or factions) are needed to comprise a new whole. Out of the differences, dispute, and conflict arises an accommodation or compromise in the form of a creative, selective synthesis. All 'points of view are modified and a fresh synthesis is worked out' (1966, pp. 363, 355–6). Opposition is thus formulated in Hegelian dialectical terms, with similar organic consequences. Differences are resolved and integrated (but retained) in a new relation, a new unity. They are not constantly extinguished, as the Darwinian version of struggle for existence and survival of the fittest might suggest. (However, Cooley is laudably cognizant of the possibility that circumstances of conflict can become both pervasive and persistent: they are not easily and rapidly resolved and, therefore, social disorganization, social [and personal] degeneration, moral disintegration, and personal demoralization may occur.[5])

Small also believes that some form and degree of opposition always occurs in interpersonal interaction and evokes something new. Some degree of divergence of interest and purpose is present as individuals attempt to achieve their own ends (1905, p. 325). (An interest is disjunctive if the person finds it necessary to oppose the purposes of others to promote his own (1905, p. 203).) Irrespective of the structure of activities inherited from the past, it is viewed by some persons as favorable and by others as unfavorable to the realization of their own purposes. Opposition in some form and to some degree emerges. Ordinarily, some modus vivendi is worked out with some component or degree of compromise. Small suggests two possible sources for this development. On the one hand, individuals may eventually come to recognize that arbitrary and exclusive pursuit of their own egoistic interests entail excessive costs and so the severity and frequency of conflict are reduced.[6] On the other, some individuals in the course of opposition and its resolution 'reflect upon . . . association [or the consequences for association] itself' (1905, p. 620). They develop an interest in the whole rather than merely in their own purposes. 'These men coin and utter thoughts and feelings and purposes which become current in the group' (1905, p. 620). Accordingly, an interaction of the first and second sources, with a Hegelian synthetic reconciliation of a past definition of the interest or good of the whole with present divergent individual and social interests, provides for the emergence of something new. (Admittedly, Small is not as precise as might be desired.)

Ross apparently adopted Tarde's essentially Hegelian formulation of a social logic of socio-cultural change by conflict and substitution. As in the cases of Cooley and Small, so for Ross change seems to entail initially more or less opposition, conflict, or dissensus, some compromise, and eventually cooperation, consensus, and harmony. He analyzes especially 'silent' conflict and 'vocal' conflict (or discussion). Certain means or forms of the former do lead to the latter. Resort to authority, persecution, example, observation, and trial tend to transform silent conflict into vocal conflict and discussion. When rival authorities appeal to argument, the prosecutor uses reasons because they are more effective with some persons than force, example is reinforced by persuasion, observation elicits formal comparison, and trial is replaced by calculation, the essential ingredients of discussion have emerged. Discussion actually tends to terminate conflict generally only if reasons are involved, if one side tries to win over its opponents, and if facts or empirical data are invoked (Ross, 1912, pp. 311–13). Admittedly, conflict may be terminated by one side being able to defeat, convince, or silence the other, or by both sides being able to find a middle (compromise) ground, or by the two sides eventually specializing and thus withdrawing from direct opposition (1912, pp. 325–7).[7] Compromise is necessary if a group is compelled to take collective action or assume a collective attitude on an issue and thus cannot permit conflict to reach its natural termination. Sometimes, 'compromise is the only solution of an indeterminate discussion, i.e., a *social deadlock*' (1912, p. 339). But Ross regards compromise as more frequently 'a provisional arrangement pending the completion of conflict and the emergence of a real and definitive social decision' (1912, p. 339). Such decision

241

will in turn demand some interpersonal adjustments and concessions, with a new set of relationships emerging.

Yet a considerable difference in emphasis exists between Ross, on the one hand, and Small and Cooley, on the other, in their interpretations of the mechanism of conflict. In spite of Ross's denial of the equation of natural and social selection, he stresses the dialectical aspects of interpersonal and intergroup conflict much less and the Darwinian features much more than do Small and Cooley. His *Foundations* continues to express his conviction of the significance of biogenetic features of human populations for their social behavior, though it is stated less blatantly than in his doctrine of bio-psychic-socio-cultural evolutionism of *Social Control* four years earlier. Claiming in *Foundations* to be much more sophisticated about the operation of racial differences than were his predecessors of a generation earlier, Ross indicates doubt that ideas or beliefs (or feelings, dispositions and conduct depending on them or connected with them) become congenital or fixed racial characters (1919, pp. 335–6).[8] But he does insist that elementary motor and emotional reactions of certain individuals in relation to others in the same aggregate or of one aggregate in relation to other aggregates are advantageous or disadvantageous relative to their recurrent biophysical environmental circumstances and that they 'survive or perish' accordingly. Under the impact of different environments and their consequent winnowings and selections, such differences can and do become characteristic of aggregates of individuals (as breeds and races).[9] (His further unstated premise is that such elementary motor and emotional reactions can apparently become predisposing factors in the emergence or origins of certain beliefs and even ideas.) His chapter on 'The Causes of Race Superiority' in his *Foundations* contains (p. 361) such comments as: 'the men who made their way to the British Isles have shown themselves the most masterful and achieving of the Germanic race; while their offshoots in America and Australia, in spite of some mixture, show the highest level of individual efficiency found in any people of the Anglo-Saxon breed.' (Admittedly, it seems to be difficult to reconcile his list of causes (climatic adaptability, energy, self-reliance, foresight, facility of abstraction and calculation, and stability of character) exclusively with the criteria of inherited motor and emotional reactions to stimuli.)

Ross does believe that certain (individual and aggregate or racial) biogenetic strains are advantageous in relation to a certain biophysical environment and therefore *should be* preserved. He is convinced that 'all social measures, policies, and arrangements . . .

242

must stand or fall by the breed of human beings' who are favored (1919, p. 347). To know the 'kind of people [who] multiply most under' any policy is to 'know whether it is good or bad' (1919, p. 347). Manifestly, any 'practice or arrangement that sifts badly . . . must be given up, be it never so hallowed' (1919, pp. 347–8).

Although Cooley uses Social Darwinist terminology in his analysis of the derivation of innovation from conflict and struggle, he actually introduces meanings for such terms which are considerably at variance with the Social Darwinist tradition. For Cooley, environment for human beings is 'not something fixed but another plastic organism, interacting in turn with still other organisms' in reciprocal stimulation and growth (1966, p. 9). But situation is probably a more accurate word than environment, for situation implies more or less interpersonal awareness of selves and others in interrelationship in a setting (1966, p. 228). Fitness implies a relation to a social situation (1966, p. 228). Among human beings, selection occurs but it is not merely or even preponderantly an objective determination by struggle with the biophysical forces of the natural environment. Brutal struggle is out of place in human society (1966, p. 228). All struggle is relative to 'conditions and standards' (1966, p. 233). Selection is primarily a consequence of interpersonal evaluation and choice among human beings. Cooley insists that struggle is required among human beings, but it is a struggle – with standards – to arouse exertion or to invigorate people to test themselves against difficulties (1966, pp. 233–4).

Clearly, Cooley emphasizes that interpersonal and intergroup selection is more or less conscious, involves communication, evaluation and choice, and occurs in relation to a (whole) situation. Yet he does acknowledge that human life is constituted of fundamentally two interrelated processes, one of which is social (transmitted through communication) and the other organic (transmitted through the germ-plasm).[10] Organic-hereditary types result from the later and social types stem from the former. But the two realms and processes are interconnected, interrelated, and interdependent. Each 'system acts selectively upon the other, determining what will work and what will not. Hereditary types must in some way fit into the social conditions [i.e., meet the social standards of fitness] or they cannot propagate themselves and must disappear' (1966, pp. 201–2). Conversely, 'the biological type acts selectively in determining what social ideas and institutions will work, and how' (1966, p. 202). And he doesn't exclude the possibility of the relevancy of the organic for explaining certain social phenomena. He warns that 'we ought not . . . to ignore the possibility that inferiority of hereditary type may be a factor in' poverty, for instance (1966, p. 231). After conceding that 'we have almost no definite knowledge' about such hereditary divisions as races, except for 'the somewhat superficial traits of color and physiognomy,' he does indicate that he is inclined to accept 'unlikenesses of temperament and [mental and moral] capacity' among races – just as 'family stocks in the same race are so evidently unequal in these respects' (1966, pp. 274, 275). Cooley refuses to accept either an exclusively biogenetic hereditary or an exclusively socio-environmental explanation of alleged racial differences (1966, p. 275). The realms of the organic-hereditary and the social-communicative condition one another. Biogenetic differences as exhibited in organic types among human beings are not currently the preponderant outcome of natural selection but of social selection. Conversely, social types, which do depend primarily on communication and social selection, must also meet the requirements for organic maintenance, although that also is not preponderantly a matter of natural selection among human beings.

What is most distinctive of the Cooley and Small stance is that social creativity or innovation finally emerges in and through the process of valuation which is part of the creative (Hegelian) synthesis following from opposition or conflict. Manifestly, valuation presupposes more or less consciousness, reflection, deliberation, and choice, and accordingly reflects Small's and Cooley's idealism. In association, men are usually conscious – self-conscious if not socially conscious – according to Small. They act for reasons, although not necessarily for socially informed reasons. Their social action embodies 'acts of combined attention, valuation, and choice' (1905, p. 636). By virtue of valuation, the antagonisms of opposition are resolved by some sort of compromise, the differential contributions of individual innovative potential are selectively appraised, divergencies are combined into a synthesis in relation to the group structure, the exigencies of the situation, and the pertinent individual and social, human nature and institutional values. Functioning to permit the individual or the group to make up its mind, valuation involves for Cooley a choice of one or more of several objects offering a workable solution to a problem posed within the situation and defined or interpreted in terms of a scale or hierarchy of values or preferences.[11] Individuals give more or less time and attention to the problem posed by the situation, search their consciousnesses for pertinent ideas and sentiments, engage in discussion and dispute, and then attempt to secure harmony and unity in the presence of conflicting stimuli.

244

The weighing, balancing, and comparing of various outcomes and solutions which so typically characterize valuation are possible because the values in the scale or hierarchy of values are relative and psychically commensurable (1966, pp. 311, 312, 322). (Note the similarity with MacIver's 'dynamic assessment.') In Small's words, social action characteristically requires 'the formation of judgments of value, and a continuous reckoning between persons whose purposes, because of similar or dissimilar judgments of value,' more or less converge or diverge (1905, p. 635). Based ultimately on the constant pragmatic test of 'workability,' utility, fit, or adaptation of objects (or a mode of activity) in the situation, this new synthesis of valuation is the basis of an innovation. A rule, a value, an aspect of social structure has been wittingly or unwittingly modified so that a new organization and a new basis of cooperation are afforded. The whole has become more workable, more adjusted in relation to its parts and in relation to its social and physico-organic environment.

Acceptance, adoption, and dissemination

The differences which occasionally separated Ross's and Small's and Cooley's explanations of the origins of innovation become considerably more evident in the interpretations of acceptance, adoption, and dissemination of the socially new. Ross appeared to show some affinities for certain features or aspects of social evolutionism.[12] His exposition now focuses substantially on adaptation, though he seems to accept more rapid alteration in the environment than evolutionists might be inclined to endorse. (Small and Cooley emphasize the purposes and choices of the actors and the enhanced workability which the innovation brings to the total situation.).

In Ross's estimation, the 'spread or progress of a practice or belief is . . . due to some excellence in that practice' (1912, p. 28). Just as the better adapted survives in the struggle for existence 'between competing structures (gills and lungs), or competing characters (fur and hibernation),' so 'the more useful' of 'conflicting customs' or the 'more reasonable' of 'inconsistent traditions' is adopted and accepted (1912, p. 198). (But he rejects the sheer antiquity of a custom as an index of survival and fitness (1912, p. 203).[13])

Ross's major contribution to the analysis of the dissemination of new practices consists in the use of (the Tardean-derived) rational-imitation and conventionality-imitation. If a practice is judged by 'its apparent fitness' or a proposition by 'its appearance of truth' (or its probability), it will tend to diffuse in accordance with 'rational imitation' (1912, p. 286). Practical arts and science are illustrative. Practical arts adhere to the 'rational' pattern because their fitness can be judged more objectively (and the components can be assessed competitively) and exactly (1912, p. 288). Science and its components spread in accordance with this type of imitation because its doctrines are tested by application to the practical arts and because it employs a method making its statements verifiable (1912, pp. 289 90). If, on the other hand, the novel has prestige in a group or society and thus falls within the irrational-emotional domain, it will tend to follow diffusion by conventionality-imitation. Manners, dress, amusements, and the fine arts are illustrative. New practices (or beliefs) in these fields will tend to diffuse from the socially superior, powerful, successful, wealthy, or urban to the less fortunate opposites. The 'prestige or discredit of those who have [initially] adopted' the new practice or belief, or 'the time and place of its origin' are significant (1912, p. 285).

Ross also accepts the essentials of Sumner's strain toward consistency, though he doesn't use the concept. He believes that in the course of time – aside and apart from the intrusion of additional new components in the culture – 'the incompatible ideas and ideals become fewer, because one of the incompatibles exterminates the other' (1912, p. 363). The 'diversity [i.e., heterogeneity] in the cultural elements . . . becomes less, owing to the march of adaptation' (1912, p. 363). For instance, 'spelling becomes definite; idiomatic flexible speech falls under the tyranny of grammar and of style' (1912, p. 363). Religious dogmas are compared and sifted. Customs and statutes are transformed into a system of jurisprudence. Discrete generalizations about the external world 'are integrated and gaps filled in until there exists a body of articulated propositions called science' (1912, p. 364). Accordingly, culture becomes more congruent, consistent, or unified, but it does so within relatively separate systems. It manifests diversification as a correlate of social differentiation and specialization (as forms of accommodation and compromise). Thus, tendencies toward social complexity, consensus, integration, and cooperation are accompanied by a tendency toward cultural diversification.

Such diversification has its positive functions. 'Just as a developed society partly compensates for the cramping of specialism by offering the individual a greater variety of vocations to select from, so a developed culture affords multifarious opportunities from which each can choose what is congenial to his nature' (1912, p. 365). Because cultural diversity within and between systems 'appeals to the needs of diverse temperaments' by permitting 'a greater number of options,' any spirit of congruency, consistency, or unification will be unlikely to 'bring about the triumph of one [variety] over the rest, or their coadaptation into one form' (1912, pp. 364, 365). Thus, the spread of an innovation in relation to others may be seen to have both its social and cultural consequences.

In contrast, such more idealistically-oriented sociologists as Small and Cooley reject Tardean doctrine and stress the role of purpose and choice in diffusion, and the holistic, integrative function of the dissemination of an innovation. Although both men object to Tarde's ideas, Small argues his case more extensively than did Cooley. Small insists that the subjective process behind the response of a man to an object is uniform, irrespective of whether the stimulus is social or non-social, and that the response does not necessarily bear any resemblance to the source of the suggestion. Tarde is mistaken in locating the essential social factor in a simple, single form of mental reaction. In contrast to Tarde's view, most men are generally conscious of what they are doing and act for reasons. Repeated acts which appear to be externally similar or identical are not necessarily imitation. The 'objective repetition of acts does not prove the subjective phenomenon of imitation as their cause' (Small, 1905, p. 633). Whether the action is autonomously initiated or apparently follows the recommendation of an authority, it is based on a 'judgment of utility pointing to choice of the external acts as a means to an end' (1905, p. 633). Thus, any explanation of the acceptance, adoption, and dissemination of the novel cannot be limited only to the stimulus, or to reflex action, or to subjective change (1905, p. 636). Men's acts – even their apparently externally similar repeated acts – are complex and involve 'combined attention, valuation, and choice' of means to ends (1905, p. 636). Behavior in diffusion is action involving acceptance. It is 'the sign of a judgment,' even if it is 'borrowed, recapitulated or abbreviated, of the value of conduct with reference to an implicit purpose' (1905, p. 632).

Cooley advances an integrative, holistic interpretation of the dissemination of a particular social change. Generally, Cooley observes, 'the determining agent [in the spread of an innovation] is nothing less than the total situation' (1966, p. 371). Acceptance of a new idea, for instance, will depend 'upon the degree and manner of its working in the actual complex state of the mind of the people [or its culture], consisting largely of impulses, habits, and traditions whose sources are remote and obscure' (1966, pp. 371–2). The idea must be capable of 'working in the actual situation'; there must be 'soil in which it can grow,' if the people are to take an interest in it (1966, p. 372). Cooley argues that 'an idea that gets possession of even one individual so that he will formulate and defend it cannot be said to have failed. It takes its part in the larger discussion, and, however contumeliously rejected, it will leave some impress upon the ideas that are accepted' (1966, pp. 373–4). But apparently the given idea can come 'to power only when the situation' is ripe (1966, p. 373).

What Cooley means by propitiousness, congruity, or 'workability' of an idea within the situation is never explicitly explained. Social circumstances must, it would seem, render the idea workable at a given point in time, and over time and idea must be somewhat consistent with the character of the culture of the past. Cooley is clear in his refusal to propose or adopt any sort of mechanical solution, such as Tarde's *Social Logic*, to explain the dissemination of ideas. He asserts simply that over time ideas that have a wide dissemination will evidence adaptability to 'the rest of life' and will afford a 'certain measure of efficiency, or power to meet the struggle' for existence (1966, p. 375). Given sufficient time to experiment, people will tend to form sound judgments and reject 'superficial' (unworkable) doctrines, 'if they are fairly intelligent and their social condition not desperately bad' (1966, p. 374). Furthermore, many ideas are prevented from wide diffusion by their inconsistency with other ideas. Such unwise propositions tend to be eliminated by what may be called cancellation. In general, the new will spread and persist only if human nature values are permitted more effective expression and institutional values are brought into more organic, congruent relationship with the former under the circumstances of existence.

But Cooley does concede that rigorousness of selection is variable through time and, indeed, is determinable only in a negative way! Long persistence means only 'that ideas and practices injurious with reference to the struggle have been kept within limits' so that survival or, better, workability is not precluded (1966, p. 375). The criterion of what continues to exist and of what appears (and disappears?) in society is pragmatic. The concept of workability 'has . . . an advantage over "adaptation," "selection," or "survival of the fittest" in that it gives a little more penetrating statement of what immediately takes place, and also

. . . is not . . . [a] mechanical or biological' conception (1966, p. 18).[14] Cooley does not insist that conditions necessarily establish a rigorous testing such that only one possible idea, standard, or practice, or constellation thereof, is selected out as the exclusive workable formula. A mutual organic sensitiveness, adaptation, or workability of the new in relation to the old seems thus to be Cooley's fundamental explanation for the dissemination of an invention, for what might be termed the extensiveness or amplitude of its adoption.

Irrespective of whether it arises inside a group or a society or outside, an innovation appears to have – so many early theorists intimated – a career of acceptance, dissemination, and adoption which can be more or less envisaged within a social process cycle. It discloses various stages from some degree and form of dis-equilibrium to equilibrium, from opposition (e.g., conflict) to composition, from dissensus to consensus, from disorganization to organization, from disintegration to integration, disharmony to harmony, from disunity to unity. As the social or societal scope of the cycle process expands and the units become more numerous, the spread of an innovation is also associated with increasing social differentiation and specialization and increasing cultural diversification.

10 Social evolution, social process, and social progress in social change: summary

Undeniably, some basic differences exist between the social evolutionary and social processual theorists of social change. But these differences must not obstruct the recognition of other similarities and congruities. Social evolutionists did employ some components of the social processes in their theoretical formulations. And certainly both together accepted and invoked – with few exceptions – the idea of progress as part of their total conception of social change. In any event, their similarities and dissimilarities along with their congruities and incongruities require careful summary delineation and consideration.

Social evolutionists and the social processes

Unfortunately, the differentiation which has just been drawn (in the previous chapter) between social evolutionary and social processual theorists may be exaggerated. It is incorrect, for instance, to infer that the social evolutionists never used the social processes in their theories. Indeed, they did employ the social processes as part of a cycle of processes in the analysis of social change. Ward and Giddings offer a relatively elaborate differentiation of processes, whereas Keller (and his mentor Sumner) resort to a much more limited and simplified set of notions.

As indicated earlier, Ward (1970, p. 171) held that all realms of phenomena were characterized by the operation of synergy, 'the systematic and organic working together of the antithetical forces of nature.' Throughout nature, he (1970, p. 175) discerns (in various forms) a recurrent cycle of collision, conflict, antagonism, opposition, competition, interaction, compromise, collaboration,

250

and cooperation. In human societies, the cycle involves the sequence of conquest, struggle, inequality, resignation, concession, compromise, equilibration, interaction, cooperation, miscegenation, coalescence, unification, consolidation, and solidarization. (Ward readily recognized his indebtedness to Gumplowicz and Ratzenhofer.) His catalog of the processes in the cycle-sequence was perhaps more elaborate than that of any of his colleagues. Like them, he rarely defined the terms. Few of them presented their views explicitly and systematically. But the processes were considered in the context of the analysis of social change.

Giddings's conceptualization of processes begins with a concern with competition and conflict, though their relationship to one another isn't specified. Competition is a process involving like acts directed toward a supply of wanted objects inadequate for all but some part of which is obtainable by individual effort (Giddings, 1922, p. 202). Presumably, competition may be transformed into conflict under certain circumstances. Conflict appears to be conscious and personal (as a form of opposition). It entails impact and attack and counter-impact or counter-attack (Giddings, 1922, pp. 102–3). Since attack leads to counter-action which is similar, it produces imitation. In turn, imitation leads to similarity of structure and, accordingly, conflict becomes milder.

But in its earlier stages conflict tends to result in the elimination of the extremely weak (Giddings, 1896, p. 114). Those who remain are apparently better adapted. (Giddings claims that it is the advantageousness of adaptation plus continued performance which determines survival and not mere advantageousness of adaptation.) Those members who do remain are too much alike and too nearly equal to be able successfully to vanquish one another. Accordingly, some sort of accommodation occurs, signifying that 'new combinations or circumstances make necessary some modification of previous habits' (Giddings, 1898, p. 49). Presumably, for Giddings, accommodation may be both conscious and unconscious. Among the latter are differentiation and specialization (units become unlike and restrict activities to a certain type) and segregation (the like units differentiated out are drawn together (spatially?); 1898, pp. 337–8). Toleration is another form, as is (the conscious) compromise (via discussion). At any point in these developments, accidental, momentary or intermittent cooperation (implying common interest in some object or end leading to a combination of activity) may occur (1898, pp. 77–8). Such cooperation presumably begins in like coordinated acts toward a supply of wanted objects adequate for all but not easily obtained by individual effort (1896, p. 220, and 1901, p. 113). When cooperation becomes systematic, continuous, and habitual, it represents organization (1898, p. 172). Cooperation may also be associated with amalgamation, the physical blending of different physical types through intermarriage (1901, p. 55). Eventually, assimilation may develop. Fundamentally, it involves the diminution of difference and antagonism and the augmentation of likeness (e.g., in ideas and purposes) and of harmony (1898, p. 70). Interestingly, Giddings (1901, p. 101) tends to equate assimilation and socialization in at least one context of analysis. The latter becomes the same as the former as individuals display a growing resemblance to one another, develop a consciousness of kind, show some concern with the welfare of one another, and accept common moral obligations in their interactions with one another. Giddings is apparently not disposed to add such processes as integration, unification, and solidarization, though he refers to harmonization (1896, p. 109).

With the case now made (and illustrated) that the social evolutionists did indeed use the social processes, the basic issue must be confronted as to just what it is that differentiates (and thus justifies) the separation of the social processualists from the social evolutionists. Manifestly, the social evolutionists tend to use a much more Social Darwinist notion of conflict and to introduce the sequence of processes (when completed) within the broader assumption of social evolutionary (structural and functional) differentiation and complexity. Directionality is presupposed in the process.

However, the processualists (Ross, Small, and Cooley) do not invoke social differentiation as a major and crucial means of introducing directionality. Instead, they (i.e., Small and Cooley) achieve directionality by endorsement and acceptance of the idea of progress. Undeniably, Ross, Small, and Cooley do assume some directionality in the shift from primitivity to modern (civilized) societies. But the notion of continuous (adaptive) differentiation was not the focal, supporting process. They recognized that the idea of progress involved a value-judgment that change was for the better, but they accepted that judgment.

Social evolutionists, social processualists, and the idea of progress

Unfortunately, this last statement may convey the impression that a belief in progress was characteristic only of the social processualists. This implication would be manifestly untrue. Both social processualists and social evolutionists generally adhered to the idea of progress. From among the evolutionists, Ward and Giddings conspicuously associated themselves with progress. (Keller, who followed his mentor Sumner, refused to do so, (1915, pp. 15–16, 326).) As processualists, Small and Cooley endorsed the belief in the idea of progress. Although Ross conceded that the 'promotion of progress is, of course, our [i.e., sociology's] greatest practical concern,' he argued that because 'progress is a matter of judgment involving the application of a subjective standard those who desire to see sociology a true science are justified in insisting that social dynamics deal with the factors and manner, not of *social progress* merely, but of *social change*' (1919, pp. 186, 185). Thus, Ross seems to be somewhat more hesitant about committing the discipline as a science to progress than some of his colleagues might have been. But he personally accepted the belief. For him as well as for Ward, Giddings, Small, and Cooley (who essentially justified the very existence of sociology in terms of the idea), progress was a belief that mankind or human society generally has exhibited, does exhibit, and will continue to exhibit during the course of its broad experience a tendency for change to involve improvement, amelioration, and advance.

Fundamentally, progress presupposes that mankind is one biopsychically, socially, and culturally. (Neither social evolutionists nor social processualists disagreed with this basic tenet.) The idea presumes further that as the different generations of different peoples come and go a deposit of experience accumulates in a common linear (or really, rectilinear) direction. That is, the specific experiences of all peoples can be construed as parts of a developmental whole which exhibits a common pattern from primitivity to modernity. In effect, then, history follows a continuous, necessary, and orderly course. (So far, social evolution and the idea of progress accept similar assumptions.) But most crucial to the idea of progress (as opposed, for instance, to 'mere' social evolutionism) is the common judgment that this course of change has brought, is bringing, and will continue to bring improvement in the condition of mankind. Accordingly, the present is better than the past and the future will be better than the present. (In at least some versions, such as Comte's positivistic-industrial state or Ward's sociocracy, an ultimately desirable future state or condition is postulated.) This (third) feature of progress asserts a general optimism about the outcome of human experience and an explicit belief in the increasing happiness of increasing numbers of persons among mankind. In the last (and fourth) place, the crux of the process of progress is the assumption that as human experience accumulates it entails essentially a naturalistic learning process which depends critically on science or the advance of scientific knowledge.

Not always were these ideas directly or explicitly asserted, but they were assumed in the comments about progress made by early American sociologists. Six common features of progress can be delineated in the views of such early American sociological theorists as Ward, Giddings, Small, and Cooley:

(1) Perhaps the most conspicious and pervasive feature of their commitment to progress is the belief in the beneficent efficacy of the extension of scientific knowledge within all spheres of nature and the desirable consequences to its dissemination among members of a society. Basically, sociologists in common with other scientists and intellectuals of the era construe the results of the accumulation of scientific knowledge in the inorganic and organic realms and the practical applications as demonstrably effective and good. Like Comte especially, most early American sociologists assume that similarly desirable results will attend the emergence of genuine social sciences and especially sociology itself. Most of them recognize that the advent of modern industrial society has been accompanied by the appearance of a variety of serious tensions, dislocations, or conflicts which were frequently identified as social problems. Many of them agree essentially with Ward that the continuance of past objective, material, and natural progress in nature is in serious doubt. Improvement can no longer be assumed to take care of itself. Society must undertake a program of artificial progress – involving telesis, active or provisional adaptation, calculation, and the resort to ends through more effective indirect, remote (and scientific) means. To accomplish this purpose, a science of sociology is needed (see chapter 2, pp. 23–4).

Some sociologists, perhaps a majority in the US, were convinced that the experience of the natural, inorganic, and organic sciences can be directly and immediately appropriated to sociology's own purposes. They argue that the realm of the social is a realm of nature, with its own regularities, which can be studied and formulated more or less in the successful fashion of the natural sciences. Presumably the realm of the social forces will also be amenable to prediction and control. Ward, Sumner, Giddings, Ross, and even Small express views aligning them with this position, which may be defined broadly as methodologically positivistic.

Of the major early American sociologists, only Cooley was a

conspicuous dissenter from these views. Although he concedes (1966, p. 401) that the 'possibility of social science rests upon the hypothesis that social life is in some sense rational and sequent,' he denies that any mechanical calculability of social phenomena is assumed. As noted above, he rejects (1966, p. 398) the possibility of exact prediction and mechanical control of the social world as 'a false ideal inconsiderately borrowed from the provinces of physical science.' Cooley's reliance on sympathetic introspection and imaginative reconstruction means that he is methodologically humanistic (or idealistic). However, he does believe that social knowledge can be used by men (as his more positivistic colleagues did) to foresee and diminish the costs of social change by the adoption of appropriate rational measures (1962, pp. 418–19).

Virtually all sociologists were enthusiastic about the prospects arising from the successful establishment of the social sciences and sociology as reliable, useful fields of knowledge. They anticipated the day when these social regularities could be formulated, and systematically made available to education for general diffusion among the members of American society. To a greater or lesser extent, most sociologists shared Ward's zeal for the use of education as a major means of introducing effective social reform. Education was envisaged as an instrument of reform for achievement of social betterment generally.

(2) For early American sociologists, the increasing survival of individuals, the expanding sphere for personal development, and a heightened sensitivity to the fate of one's fellow men are indicative of an augmentation of individual happiness and of human betterment generally within the broad course of social change. Few – if any – theorists questioned the assumption that the enhancement of men's chances to survive through improvements in physical protection and the means of sustenance represents progress. This view is a fundamental component of any conception of social amelioration (cf. Giddings, 1932, pp. 248–9).

However, Darwinian sociologists were inclined to construe progress as primarily dependent on the pool of genetic talent in a population and, thus, they were seriously concerned with the issue of the quality as opposed to the sheer quantity of those who survive under prevailing conditions of existence. Manifestly, science and technology of modern life had mitigated the severity of the struggle for existence. In Giddings's view (1922, p. 286), the survival chances of variates departing from the usual range of physical type in a society had, accordingly, been substantially increased. In *Studies in the Theory of Human Society* (pp. 118, 286) he observed

255

that social control could restrict and/or eliminate anti-social deviants without severely limiting the spontaneity and freedom of the constructively creative variants (cf. 1932, pp. 253–4). Social Darwinism and eugenism were often associated in American sociology.

But a higher rate of individual survival is not in itself a sufficient criterion of progress. Individuals must be able to develop themselves. Accordingly, theorists regarded increasing educational opportunity, occupational competition, the open-class system, and voluntary associations as some of the most important social features affecting personality formation and personal development. These characteristics of modern life enhanced the chances in the society for what some sociologists called individualization or individuation, i.e., the development of unique, special, or distinctive personality traits by which the individual is able to adjust the environment to himself or himself to the environment. According to Giddings, individuation derives ultimately from the individual's distinctive biological inheritance, his acquired nature, and his unique life circumstances (1922, p. 228). Within the individual's personality, individuation is signified by the peculiar constellation of instincts, motor impulses, emotions, beliefs, and ideas. Cooley suggests that the opportunity to associate selectively in modern social life facilitates the operation of this process. Each person can work out his own distinctive system of life by a special choice of influences (1966, p. 249). His personality becomes more and more an organization by itself, less and less identified with any one group, although still dependent on the group system as a whole (1966, pp. 249, 250). Presumably Cooley would agree with Giddings (1922, pp. 119, 205) that individuation increasingly involves intelligence, freedom, responsibility, power, self-determination, and happiness.

However, most sociologists could not conceive of progress as entailing or eventuating in mere amoral egoism. Self-development was becoming – they believed – altruistically oriented. Presumably the educational diffusion of information of social science will entail increasing recognition of interpersonal and social interdependence. Individuals will undergo increasing socialization: they will evince a positive, mutual evaluation of and reciprocal concern for the welfare of the persons or groups involved (Small, 1905, pp. 328, 335). They will conform to social norms, engage in cooperation, be helpful and tolerant of others, be observant of social obligations to and needs of alters, exercise self-restraint and even self-denial (Small, 1905, pp. 334, 353). Giddings notes that such personality traits symptomatic of socialization are acquired by learning rather than from innate endowments (1922, p. 287).

(3) Theorists in early American sociology assumed that a broad range of interaction, a growing societal consolidation and unification, increasing social differentiation, cultural diversification, and moral integration are evident in human experience and represent social progress. According to Cooley (1962, p. 81), the mass publication of newspapers, magazines, and books, modern postal systems, (steamship and) railway transportation, and the telegraph and telephone are exposing individuals to more varied and frequent social contacts. Isolation has been broken. Men's imaginations have been awakened and enlivened.

Concomitantly, the social boundaries within which men think, feel, and act have expanded. The world is becoming one unit (Cooley, 1966, pp. 248, 3). The scope of competition is enlarging and even the systems of struggle interpenetrate with one another (Cooley, 1966, pp. 246–7). Since the same men take part in various systems, the lines of alliance and opposition have become inextricably intertwined (Cooley, 1966, p. 247). Specialized interests of commerce, labor, science, and philanthropy and the informal bonds of literature, art, and public sentiment cross national lines (Cooley, 1966, p. 248). Common interests of some kind unite every sort of man with every other, and, consequently, men may no longer be divided into merely separate, hostile parties. The ceaseless currents of interaction are unifying human life (1966, p. 248).

In Cooley's view, enlarging social systems require increasingly varied and diverse constituent groups. Perhaps most basic to this necessary differentiation is the voluntary association or, as Cooley designates it, the nucleated group (1966, pp. 252, 249–50; 1969, pp. 185, 186, 194, 196). It is characteristically specialized in purpose or interest and composed of a large number of members who affiliate with several such groups in accordance with their talents, aptitudes, and inclinations (1966, p. 252). Most members of any group are likely to contribute little of themselves, whereas only one or a few members will devote their whole personalities to it (1966, p. 252). Competition ordinarily allocates members in the performance of a group's more or less impersonal functions.

Accompanying the trend to social differentiation is a parallel cultural elaboration and diversification. Men have acquired new tastes, desires, and interests, along with newer and more effective means of satisfying older ones. In particular, Ward and Small emphasize the elaboration of new desires and new means of

257

gratification as indicative of progress. Ward avers that in 'both the ontogenetic and phylogenetic development of mankind there has been a series of upward steps, and that at each step on both [the development of the preservative and reproductive forces] the means of enjoyment of the natural faculties has been increased' (1970, p. 431). The trend to diversification of romantic love and conjugal love, on the one hand, and the gradual emancipation of women, on the other, warrant a similar conclusion about phylogenetic wants. Though Ward is less confident about aesthetic progress, he does believe that progress has occurred in the realm of morality (a greater valuation of life, for instance) and in knowledge (e.g., science) and its applications. Accordingly, new desires and their enjoyment have occurred in the sociogenetic realm and will continue in the future. Small is similarly confident about the development, adjustment, and satisfaction of desires in the realms of health, wealth, sociability, knowledge, beauty, and rightness (1905, p. 707, also p. 522).

Indeed, social differentiation promotes cultural differentiation. Groups tend to develop their own specialized standards and traditions appropriate to their own ends and to the performance of their own activities (Cooley, 1969, p. 194; 1966, pp. 364, 366–70).

Yet the same instruments of communication which have broadened social consciousness and increased social unification also favor the growth of common humanity, a moral unity, among races, classes, and nations. Men are being brought into an imaginative understanding of one another, are inclined to look for a common human nature everywhere, and are disposed to demand a common set of principles for the whole world. Thus, Cooley revealed an ultimate optimism about man's eventual moral integration.

(4) Early sociologists held the conviction that men's consciousnesses had become increasingly social, their actions less violent, brutal, or coercive and more rational, cooperative, and interdependent, their personalities more socialized, and their sentiments, ideals, and values more refined and humane. Cooley particularly argued that modern communication and transportation have made groups more and more accessible to one another, added to the range of their interactions and involvements, made them more knowledgeable of one another, and increased their awareness of their interdependence with one another. Together with Giddings and Small (1898, p. 350; 1905, pp. 327–8, 333, 340) he contended that violence, brutality, and coercion have become less frequent (1966, pp. 246–7). Physical conflict has been

superceded often by intellectual conflict (Giddings, 1898, p. 350). Cooley suggests that struggle tends to be restrained in the modern world because systems of conflict and cooperation intersect, overlap, interpenetrate, and became entangled with one another (1966, p. 247). Presumably, reason eventually prompts men to recognize their interdependence and to cooperate. Small conceptualizes a trend from struggle and conflict to moralization and thence to socialization. Sheer violence and brutality tend to be replaced and adjustments bring moralization, the acceptance of a code defining as right and proper the modus vivendi among members of a group or between groups (1905, pp. 296, 328). In turn, moralization provides the necessary condition for the emergence of a common interest and eventually socialization, as explained above.

Manifestly, the categorical and impersonal treatment so symptomatic of mankind's earlier isolation and ignorance becomes less and less possible. In Cooley's words, persons will naturally develop a 'sense of community, or of sharing in a common social or spiritual whole, membership in which gives to all a kind of inner equality, no matter what their special parts may be' (1962, p. 183; cf. Small, 1905, pp. 582–5). This consciousness of community involves what Small would term vicariousness: the recognition of one's dependence on, and the benefits one receives from the activities of others who contribute to one's existence through the division of labor (1905, pp. 592–5). The ends followed recognize the supreme value of the individual persons. Each individual is to be treated – Small asserts and Giddings virtually concurs – as a person or end, 'not a commodity for other persons' (1905, p. 349; cf. 1922, p. 119).

In Cooley's view, values will become more refined and humane because the kind of personalized sympathy which had stimulated the emergence of the primary social sentiments (ideals, or human nature values) in primary groups can and will be gradually extended to non-primary groups. Justice, truth, optimism, brotherhood, kindness, understanding, service, personal usefulness, and personal courtesy – for instance – can presumably become general ideals or values of a common, popular culture (1962, pp. 180–205). All social existence can be brought 'under the control of humane ideals springing from the family and community groups' (1966, p. 249; 1962, p. 178). Thus, Cooley's notion of progress includes 'a tendency to humanize collective life, to make institutions express the higher impulses of human nature, instead of brutal or mechanical conditions' (1962, p. 118).

(5) Early theorists adhered to a conception of progress in which an expansion of the spheres and an increased frequency of the exercise of choice were fundamental components. Cooley notes that the impact of choice is already apparent in the family, education, religion, the arts, economy, the system of class relations, and philanthropy (1962, p. 120). For Cooley especially (but for others too), this expansion of choice is the essence of democracy, by which he means not so much a formal political device as the active participation of the common people in the social process (1966, p. 248). Ward, Giddings, Small, and Cooley employ a variety of terms such as social will, concerted volition, social volition, and public will to designate collective participation in decision-making prior to social action. Out of the exchange of individual opinions arises public opinion, which Cooley divides into general and specialized varieties (i.e., in the society and community versus in specific voluntary associations or nucleated groups (1962, p. 126; 1966, pp. 249–51)). Once public opinion has become so informed and organized as to be an effective guide for the deliberate self-direction of the group, it can be designated as a public will (as Cooley does, 1962, pp. 395, 402). Development of a consciousness of the whole and of the social situation, acceptance of general ends or purposes which are general because each individual member accepts and is aware that others accept them, together with a rationally differentiated and coordinated system of action for rendering the general intention attainable are characteristics of the public will (1962, p. 399). Using social knowledge, such an enlightened will should be able to foresee and diminish the costs of social change by rational measures (1962, pp. 418–19). It should permit the transformation of what had been a blind, subconscious, erratic, and wasteful progress into a conscious, intended, rational, humane, and organic improvement.

(6) Finally, most American sociologists of this era were convinced that progress can and should be made a conscious social objective, which men should seek to implement by specific measures and general policies of governmental action (i.e., melioristic and political interventionism). As the knowledge of regularities or laws in society becomes disseminated, men should be able to facilitate progress by direct intervention. Men can remove obstacles threatening progress or retarding its rate. Basically, sociologists tended to be melioristic interventionists, to adopt an outlook of *faire marcher* (rather than *laissez-faire*), to support social reform, and to recommend political or governmental measures and agencies to effect desirable social change.

Patently, American sociologists of this era did assume the basically desirable moral character of the established American social order. They did not believe wholesale social reconstruction through revolution was necessary or desirable. They supposed that the basic American moral code derived from and reflected a common human nature which remained essentially constant and permanent, though its expression in specific norms and organization might occasionally require reformulation. They did not question the basic values of an earlier social era of small-scale agrarian and commercial enterprise capitalism. Urban industrial life seemed to present only a series of social problems which were presumed to be attackable and resolvable individually without institutional reconstruction. They assumed that social knowledge would permit minor modifications here and there in society. The social order required no more than a program of social reform, to which sociology would contribute basic general principles applicable to the specific problems. Admittedly, Ward seems to be unique in his proposal of a sociocracy, though it did not seem to contemplate any drastic and comprehensive structural reconstitution of society. Giddings's social engineering and Ross's canons of social reform do not seem to anticipate major social change (1932, p. 384; 1920, pp. 549–54). Even Cooley's rational social control – though it consists of 'an intelligence and idealism that understands how the [social] whole ought to work,' and alertness to anything that goes wrong, and a disposition to apply an appropriate remedy (1966, pp. 383, 382) – still assumes intervention only when something goes awry.

Such rational social control will issue primarily, so it seems, from the work of professional experts, social critics, and social scientists. Cooley especially recommends that experts and critics elaborate rational standards of service for various voluntary associations (1966, pp. 390, 393). (He refers to such associations as 'tools,' thus suggesting their place in a rational means–ends relationship in the society (1969, p. 185).) But social science will play an equally important part in rational control. Sociology can aid in the accumulation of social knowledge in the form of rationality that Cooley terms 'public intelligence,' (1966, pp. 351–62). On the basis of conjectural or anticipatory syntheses or constructions of the new out of the old, it may propose, although never entirely successfully, predictions or previsions of forthcoming social change (1966, pp. 400, 395). Presumably it may also indicate alternative courses of action, thus adding to or supplementing 'the results of experiment' which the institutions of society have preserved (1966, p. 355). It should also enable men to trace the outcome of a given sort of action, thus permitting them to take into account wider and remoter results and to ascertain inconsistencies among standards in terms of a broader social perspective (1966, p. 352; 1962, p. 413). Thus, the data of sociological inquiry can be useful in articulating public opinion, in formulating social decision or public will, and achieving social reform (1962, pp. 130–1).

Manifestly, such early theorists as Ward, Giddings, Small, and Cooley did adhere to a belief in progress. That belief basically presupposed that knowledge was good because it had brought improvement in the condition of mankind. Indeed the very establishment of sociology had its justification in the betterment of social conditions which it promised. Increasing knowledge would promote individual happiness in the sense that individuals' chances for survival would increase, their opportunities for personal development would expand, and presumably, also, their sensitivities to one another's fates would be enhanced. Concomitantly, the range of social interaction, societal consolidation and unification, social differentiation, cultural diversification, and moral integration had increased and would increase. Human consciousness was becoming increasingly social; interpersonal actions less violent, brutal, or coercive and more rational, cooperative, and interdependent; personalities more socialized; and the sentiments, ideals, and values of persons more refined and humane. The realms within which choice could operate were enlarging as social actions were the outcome of social or concerted volition or social or public will through an enlightened public opinion. For Ward, Giddings, Small and Cooley, progress could and should be made a conscious social objective, which individuals should seek to implement by specific measures and general policies of governmental action (melioristic and political intervention).

Summary of social change theories: social evolution, social process, social progress

Undeniably, social change or social dynamics was the major problem in early American sociological theory. It had a significance and concern which were far greater than attached to social structure or to social origins as problems. Whether construed evaluatively as progress or non-evaluatively as social evolution or as social process, change was paramount within the hierarchy of intellectual interests in the sociological theory of early American sociology. Both the social evolutionists and social processualist formulations of social change presupposed what has been termed a common, more comprehensive viewpoint of evolutionary naturalism.

To designate the dynamics theory of Ward, Giddings, and Keller as social evolutionist is, of course, to indicate certain intellectual continuities with their intellectual predecessors such as Auguste Comte and Herbert Spencer. Thus, the three American theorists do characteristically invoke the organismic growth analogy and the comparative method. The social units undergoing change are assumed to be comprehensive or macrocosmic in nature. Rates and magnitude are regarded as relatively slow and small-scale. The linear or rectilinear directionality of their evolutionism is exhibited in a temporal succession of stages. Like their European predecessors, the American sociologists adhere to a notion of causal mechanisms which presupposes that the processes are natural and necessary, internal, and uniform or constant. Giddings and Keller adopt (social) Darwinists' arguments whereas Ward includes both Darwinian and Lamarckian principles in his account. With varying emphases, all three early evolutionists provide explanations both for the genesis and acceptance, adoption, and dissemination of social innovation.

Significantly, the almost point-by-point refutation of social evolutionism by Sumner and the processulalists such as Ross, Small, and Cooley suggests that either the conception of change espoused by Ward, Giddings, and Keller was then the dominant interpretation or had been earlier. Admittedly, differences did exist among the processualists, but all of them objected to the bulk of the tenets of social evolutionism. They rejected the monistic and, indeed, monolithic view of the unity of all human societies as one. They controverted the conventional organismic growth analogy. They repudiated the use of the comparative method. They allowed for considerable variation in the rate and magnitude of change, even though slow, gradual, small-scale change might be most common. Directionality might be denied altogether, or the notion of a straight and uniform line of development might be rejected, or some general direction might be accepted in conjunction with progress (as opposed to the necessity of adaptive social differentiation). Finally, Sumner, Ross, Small, and Cooley did attempt to invalidate both (social) Darwinian and Lamarckian notions of the mechanisms of social change.

Admittedly, differences did exist among the processualists. For instance, Small and Cooley did tend to accept comprehensive social

263

units in the study of social change and to endorse the use of the organismic analogy. However, they did deny the operation of any rigid (internal) determinism stemming from the features of human nature. Small seems to have accepted the predominance of conflict in earliest human existence more than did Cooley, but both denied that conflict invariably deteriorated into struggle.

Based fundamentally on interaction, the social process notion of social change is much less rigid and structured than social evolution. It does entail a series of constituent or sub-processes which can vary tremendously in terms of numbers and specificity but which commonly involve conflict and its resolution and transformation. In contrast to the Social Darwinist view of conflict as organic struggle and extermination and annihilation, conflict does not necessarily involve the elimination of the vanquished. Processualists insist that conflict among human beings tends to entail more or less the rudiments and aspects of a conscious, mutually oriented verbal interchange or discussion, with a common focus of attention on certain issues, the existence of doubt, differences of opinion, argument, dispute (with conflict assuming varying breadth and intensity), denial, criticism, accompanied by some presentation of reasons, and eventually choice or decision. For Cooley and Small, conflict ordinarily – and for Ross, sometimes if not often – proceeds in accordance with the dialectic of the Hegelian tradition. Although opposition is conceived as a stage or phase of interaction, it tends to elicit (structural) modification – creativity. Tension, conflict, contradiction, or divergence arises (i.e., as thesis and antithesis), but some degree of compromise, accommodation, adaptation, or adjustment develops among opposing parties or contestants, with innovation emerging as a concomitant (synthesis).

Yet differences among the processualists are undeniably evident. Ross does adopt a more Darwinian-like position in contending that elementary motor and emotional reactions of certain individuals in relation to others are advantageous or disadvantageous relative to their biophysical conditions of existence. Though Cooley invokes the term selection, it is the consequence of interpersonal evaluation and choice, which are – of course – conscious, involve communication, and occur in relation to a whole situation. In both Small's and Cooley's cases, the formations of judgments of value are centrally important in the emergence of (creative) innovation.

Ross tends to analyze the acceptance, adoption, and dissemination of the innovation by resort to (the Tardean-derived) rational-imitation and conventionality-imitation. But Small explicitly objected to Ross's Tardean formulation, insisting that most men are conscious of what they are doing, act with some degree of complexity, and entail attention, valuation, and choice of means to ends. Cooley, for his part, emphasized the propitiousness, congruity, or workability of the new within the total situation. That which disseminates must evidence what he terms 'workability.'

Both social evolutionists and social processualists ascribe a central and pivotal significance to the function of unique individual differences in the emergence of innovation. Evolutionists tend to conceive of a relatively small segment of the population as contributing the biophysical-psychical variations out of which an appropriate adaptive response can emerge and be tested in relation to the (changing) conditions of existence. Ultimately, maladaptive responses it is argued are eliminated because their agents do not survive. The new is assumed to be more adaptive in relation to the conditions of existence. Choice is severely constrained by the conditions of existence.

Social processualists tended to be less elitist, though they also accepted the relevance of unusual biophysical-psychic traits. The new tended to be engendered out of the interaction which also included the less favorably endowed. Selection was more or less conscious and voluntary. Put simply, processualists were substantially or predominantly idealists, whereas evolutionists were substantially materialist in ontological outlook.

11 A basic synoptic characterization of founding theory

The sociology of the Founding Fathers was explicitly and irrepressibly theoretical. They directly referred to 'theory,' 'social theory,' 'sociological theory,' 'theoretical sociology,' or 'general sociology.' For Ward, Sumner and Keller, Giddings, Ross, Small, and Cooley, theory was regarded predominantly as a formal, deductive, or systematic enterprise. Either it was or it could and it should become a comprehensive, logically closed, deductive, integrative structure. Undeniably, theory ultimately had a practical or instrumental justification in terms of contributing to the resolution of social problems and (for most of the early sociologists) to the realization of social progress. But 'founding theory' was indispensable to sociology for it provided a necessary intellectual stature to the discipline and precluded any disposition to a precipitate identification with the practical amelioration of (urban) social problems.

A basic, summary characterization of early or founding theory can be achieved by use of the analytic (i.e., the periodic-izing-characterizing) scheme above. Early theory can be typified by its significance in relation to other concerns and (potential) sub-fields, by the relation of the divisions within theory to one another (i.e., epistemological-methodological division vis-à-vis the social ontological division or vice versa), and by the major features of each of the major realms within theory (i.e., first the traits of social epistemological-methodological theory, and then the characteristics of social ontological theory).

The relation of general sociological theory to other concerns – sub-fields

Because general sociological theory is now regarded as one sub-field or speciality in the discipline, it might logically be inferred that the appropriate point of departure for characterizing early theory would be to examine its significance in relation to other sub-fields or specialties in that period. Unfortunately (for present purposes), sub-fields or sub-areas had not yet become clearly differentiated and achieved such condition only after World War I. Nevertheless, it is true that early or founding theory (as equatable substantially with 'general sociology') had a pre-eminence and stature which have never been re-attained or duplicated in any of the more recent periods of the discipline. It was, indeed, general theory which was believed to confer academic respectability on the discipline and to prevent the field from 'degenerating' into mere practical amelioration of social problems. General theory or general sociology sought to discover the first principles, causes, and laws of the origin, structure, and change of human association, human society, or social phenomena generically and irrespective of variant, particular, idiosyncratic, or unique forms. Irrespective of what they might be or become, all special (or specialized) sociology (or sociologies) were assumed to begin from, contribute, and eventually return to general sociology or general theory.

Social epistemological-methodological and social ontological theories

A second basic feature of early theory involves a distinctive relationship between its two sub-fields (i.e., social epistemo-logical-methodological concerns and social ontological interests), as suggested in the analytical scheme. Admittedly, no self-conscious demarcation between the two divisions was made, but the two divisions are indisputably represented and present in early theory. Interestingly and significantly, founding theory was preponderantly a social ontological theory. This emphasis is revealed in the fact that the concern with social causes and social laws seems to focus on the nature of the domain of the social (and its relation to other domains) rather than on the technical characteristics of causes and laws.

267

Major characteristics of early social epistemological-methodological theory

Still, early theory did manifest a set of epistemological-methodological interests and positions. Early theorists were pervasively epistemological dualists, with some seeming to emphasize sensation or experience (e.g., Giddings, Sumner and Keller) and others to stress reason and logic (e.g., Ward and Small). Undeniably they accepted the basic significance of sensation (in the form of observation), description, and fact. But they all agreed that induction could not be relied upon exclusively. Deduction was also necessary. Reason or mind is imperative to achieve the abstract generality of generalization and law which science demands. For Sumner and Keller, Ward, Giddings, Ross, and Small, science involves a (Cartesian) concern with the study of what happens normally and naturally, generally, commonly, for the most part, recurrently, or persistently. Reason is important in separating out and in excluding the individual, concrete, particular, peculiar, abnormal, accidental, exceptional, or unique. Thus, science and history exhibit antithetical objectives for Sumner and Keller, Ross, and Small.

Except for Cooley's explicit disavowals, the major theorists of the first period were more or less favorably disposed to a positivistic methodological stance. Giddings, Ross, Sumner and Keller, possibly Ward and perhaps even Small tended to hold (though with varying emphasis) that the methods, procedures, and techniques of the physical and biological sciences (i.e., the natural sciences) can and should become the basis for the study of social phenomena without major qualification or supplement. Perhaps the most conspicuous common indicator of this positivism was their resort to the comparative method (which – as Comte had noted much earlier – derived from biology). Although they did invoke observation and induction, they also used inference and deduction. Objectivity, detachment, or impersonality was also a common feature. The desirability of a resort to quantification, measurement and statistical analysis provoked disagreement. Ross and Giddings were proponents whereas Ward, Sumner and Keller were opponents.

Cooley was relatively distinctive in his epistemological-methodological stance. Epistemologically he was an idealist, though a romantic (or emotive rather than a rationalistic) idealist. Knowledge for him was essentially a construction of the mind rather than a derivative from mere sensation or experience (as empiricists held).

Although he refused to separate science, philosophy, and art sharply from one another, he did distinguish a domain of knowledge of the personal-social from a domain of knowledge of the spatial-material. His method of the 'instructed imagination' or 'sympathetic introspection' is the core of his humanistic methodology which insists on a distinctive approach to the study of the personal-social realm.

Although certain kinds of (social) epistemologies-methodologies have had affinities with certain kinds of (social) ontologies (and vice versa) in the history of sociological theory, it must be conceded that such relationships represent only tendencies and not fixed invariancies. Frequently an idealistic epistemology/humanistic methodology is associated with an idealistic (social) ontology (e.g., Dilthey and Weber in Europe) and often an empiricist epistemology/positivistic methodology is linked with a materialistic social ontology (e.g., Spencer and Gumplowicz in Europe). In early American theory, Cooley does exemplify the connection between an idealist epistemology/humanistic methodology and a (prevailingly) idealist social ontology. However, methodological positivism in early American sociology was not always sharply defined or crystallized and thus might be linked with some epistemological and ontological diversity. On the one hand, it might be joined with a dualistic epistemology (an empiricism combined with a rationalism or rationalistic idealism, e.g., Sumner and Keller, Ward, Giddings, Ross and Small). On the other, it was connected with both a prevailingly materialistic social ontology (e.g., Sumner and Keller) and a more balanced materialist-idealist social ontology (Ward, Giddings, Ross, possibly Small). Giddings and Ross do represent interesting cases, for they seem in some respects to be most inclined to a methodological positivism (perhaps especially so in the decade following the close of the founding period (i.e., the 1920s) when Giddings's quantitativism became particularly marked). During the 1920s Giddings displayed some inclination to a more pronounced materialism (i.e., a behavioristic materialism), whereas Ross manifested some disposition to a more or less instinctivistic materialism. Ward died as the founding period drew to a close and Small revealed in many respects considerable methodological and ontological ambiguity such that his position almost approached Cooley's prevailing idealist epistemology/humanistic methodology and predominantly idealist social ontology.

The major characteristics of early social ontological theory

Characterization of early social ontological theory is a complex undertaking. It is based on evolutionary naturalism which links the prevailing ideas of the social to other domains of nature and to the dominant problematics of the era and still incorporates the basic ontological distinctions between (a social) ontological materialism and idealism. It entails three major tenets: (1) it is possible and desirable to offer a naturalistic rather than a supernaturalistic explanation of social or societal phenomena (i.e., the social is conceived of as a domain of nature, a sphere of a distinctive type of force); (2) the appearance of social phenomena can be accounted for in terms of other more basic, elementary or generic phenomena, states, or conditions, out of which social phenomena arose gradually (i.e., the doctrine of genetic filiation is asserted); and (3) Darwinian (and Spencerian) views of organic evolution became the basic point of departure for formulating explanatory statements of and about social phenomena. Although evolutionary naturalism seeks to provide explanations of the three problems of genesis or origins, statics or structure, and dynamics or change, its very name signifies that the first and last problems are of more primary and major interest than the second.

Fundamentally the orientation assumes that the social — irrespective of how it is conceived (as inter- and/or multi-personal relations, activities, or persistent, organized group) or what is problematic (origins, structure, or change) — must be approached as an aggregate of individuals who are endowed with a common set of human nature biopsychic needs-wants (or social forces), who are distributed in relative proximity to one another, and who confront similar circumstances of life or conditions of existence in a given habitat. Thus, the social is ultimately an adaptation or adjustment affording satisfaction of common needs-wants in relation to the conditions of existence, i.e., survival. For analytical purposes of the present study, the extent to which this adjustment or adaptation is worked out unconsciously-deterministically (i.e., materialistically) or consciously-intentionally (i.e., idealistically) is crucial. Furthermore, it is significant that each one of the notions of the social (as relations, activities, or group) can be conceived of as aspects (or even phases) in the adaptive-adjustive process and as entailing varying degrees of materiality-consciousness.

Broadly speaking, early theorists adhered to a prevailingly dualistic social ontology, with the majority ascribing a somewhat greater significance to idealistic as opposed to materialistic components of social reality. Giddings reflected (1932, p. 392) the general position of his colleagues when he observed that the social involves both mind and matter – 'so tied up together that they can never be separated as long as human society lasts.' This dualism is exhibited in the very nature of the social forces concept, which is fundamental to the evolutionary naturalism of American sociology generally, to the notion of origins, structure, and change. As an alleged domain of forces, the social sphere possesses at least a similitude of materiality. Yet – except for Sumner and Keller – the social as a domain of forces is conceived to be ultimately, if not also characteristically, psychic (and even telic). In turn, the psychic derives from the vital and the vital from the organic and the physical. The realm of the social involves more or less consciousness but such consciousness rests on and is contained within an organism, which is itself finally a form of matter. Indeed, the social forces as (conscious) desires are at least minimally prescribed – certainly in the elementary forms of hunger and sex appetites – by the dictates of organic necessity (survival). Men's and women's consciousnesses stem from an organic base which is in turn constrained by the various forces of biophysical nature constituting their environment. Certainly, early sociologists generally concurred with Small's insistence (1905, p. 413) that 'We are portions of matter.' 'Feeling, thought, and volition are tethered to fixed physical conditions' (1905, pp. 412–13). Their basic dualism is important in all of the aspects of the meaning(s) of the social and in the theories about origins, structure, and change.

Manifestly the significance ascribed to materialism and idealism in the dualism varied. Three positions or orientations can be delineated.[1] One was predominantly 'materialistic' and is represented by Sumner and Keller. A second is a relatively more balanced 'materialist-idealist' position. Its exemplars are Ward, Giddings, and perhaps Ross, who sometimes seemed more emphatically materialist and sometimes idealist. Closely approximating the third predominantly idealist orientation is Small, but Cooley is perhaps its most unambiguous protagonist.

As suggested, each of the three positions does offer a distinctive position for viewing the interrelationship of the various components (meanings) of the social. Inter- and/or multi-personal relations and activities and (structured) group acquired a more or less distinctive interrelationship within the positions.

Furthermore, it is illuminating that the positions seem to bear a relationship to the notions of a (proto-) 'behaviorism' and a (proto-) 'interactionism.' Accordingly, the predominantly material-

271

TABLE 2 *The social as conceived in terms of traditional notions of reality*

	Predominantly materialistic	Relatively balanced materialistic-idealistic	Predominantly idealistic
Relation			
Activity			
Group			

ist orientation is in reality a (proto-) 'behavioristic-materialism' and the predominantly idealist stance a (proto-) 'interactionist-idealism.'

(1) Sumner's and Keller's use of the term 'behavior' in 'collective behavior' does apparently imply a (proto-) 'behavioristic-materialism.' External, objective behavior (and surrounding conditions) have a priority or precedence over internal subjective, non-observable consciousness in the nature of the social whole such that the latter is a response to, is determined by, or is even an extension of the former. Sumner contends appropriately (1959, p. 2): 'Men begin with acts, not thoughts.' Most immediately and directly, men's behaviors are unpremeditated, 'blundering efforts' to secure satisfaction of certain elemental human nature needs (e.g., hunger, sex-love, vanity, ghost-fear), which act as stimuli or forces in relation to other types of forces associated with objects in the external habitat or environment. Men look 'no further than . . . immediate satisfaction' (1959, p. 13). The actions of individuals in an aggregate are thus like material bodies set in motion and their behaviors are 'like the products of natural forces' which have been 'unconsciously set in operation' (1959, p. 4).

Consciousness was not, however, entirely denied, though it had at best a secondary and derivative role in accounting for human social activity. Only as men acted and failed to achieve satisfaction of their needs and thus experienced pain did they become conscious and respond subjectively – perhaps deliberatively. As Sumner remarked (1959, p. 29), 'Mental processes were irksome and were not undertaken until painful experience made them unavoidable.' Consciousness offers the possibility of innovating a new response which will be adaptive rather than maladaptive.

Sumner's and Keller's behavioristic-materialism is reflected in their evolutionary notion of the origins of the social in its several senses. Inter- and/or multi-personal relations evoke (inter- and/or multi-personal) activity which in turn culminates in society as the most encompassing, persisting, organized group. Relation(-ship) begins as the material-objective likeness of two or more individuals occupying similar or contiguous points in space and time; it involves similarity in the biopsychic nature of the human units in an aggregate existing at a common point in time and so distributed throughout a common or similar habitat that they confront essentially similar conditions of existence. However, the character of the social forces (the imperiousness of human nature needs, especially hunger) in relation to scarcity among the resources required for satisfaction tends to transform the merely multi-individual relationship of coevality (in time) and contiguity (in space) into activity, which is likely to assume the form of competition or even conflict. The likelihood of even more serious threats arising within or on the periphery of the habitat prompts individuals to restrain their antagonisms and even eventually to cooperate (albeit antagonistically).[2]

For Sumner and Keller, the group (or society) begins and persists in and through commonly practiced sets of (antagonistically cooperative) behavior which one or a few talented individuals have originated and the masses have adopted because such forms of activity are adaptive or expedient in relation to (survival under the) given conditions of existence. Wittingly or unwittingly, Sumner's choice of the terms 'behavior' and 'collective behavior' (to designate the totality of folkways, mores, laws, institutions, etc.) are appropriate because consciousness and intentionality are not predominantly or characteristically involved in their emergence and dissemination in the aggregate.

A group (or more accurately, a society) comes into existence once antagonistic cooperation and appropriately established modes of behavior become prevalent and recurrent among the members of the aggregate. What began merely as a relationship of (spatio-temporal) likeness and antagonistic activity among individuals was transformed so that what had been a mere aggregate became a cooperative or collaborative entity or group.

Stability remains only so long as the conditions of existence persist unaltered (e.g., the land—man ratio). Once these conditions are altered, the satisfaction of elemental needs disrupted, and pain (more) intensively and extensively experienced (and thus adaptation and survival are made problematic), social change is predestined. Innovation arises with the 'stronger minds' who initiate ideas and acts (1959, p. 19). According to Sumner, 'talent [must have] exerted its leadership at all times' (1959, p. 19). With their greater capacity, the gifted or more talented can respond more effectively to the changed conditions of existence and innovate or adapt (on the basis of past folkways).

By virtue of the operation of suggestion and imitation as men 'notice each other's efforts' in relation to pleasure–pain, the bulk of individuals (the 'masses') come to adopt the ways of doing things which answer 'the purposes better than other ways, or with less toil and pain' (1959, p. 2). Thus, men exhibit a 'concurrence towards that which' proves 'to be most expedient' (1959, p. 2). A mode of behavior becomes a way of the folk or a folkway because the folk or masses have adopted it. It becomes disseminated among the mass of individuals by an automatic, spontaneous, and deterministic process, which is, therefore, congruent with Sumner's and Keller's mechanistic behavioristic-materialism.

(2) The exponents of a second or intermediate position, such as Ward and Giddings, did not adopt a uniform or standardized term to refer to inter- and/or multi-personal activity akin either to Sumner's 'collective behavior' or Cooley's 'interaction.' Rather, they seemed to use such words as 'behavior,' 'conduct,' or 'action' interchangeably. They do, nevertheless, believe that internal, subjective, non-observable consciousness commonly or frequently – though not invariably – possesses a priority or precedence over external, objective, observable behavior such that the former guides or orients the latter. Certainly, the exponents of the orientation did not ignore or deny man's circumscription by and involvement in the domains of biophysical nature and the regularities of physics and biology. Mankind must survive and human species needs require satisfaction by appropriate activity. Social relations, association, and society exist because they are adaptive. However, the nature of the forms of aggregate or collective activity is not immediately specified by the needs of the human organisms or the character of their habitat (though ultimately it is). Accordingly, explanation of the social whole by an exclusively or merely physicalistic or organismic determinism is rejected.

Humanity possesses consciousness which modifies needs and wants into what are more properly desires, interests, and purposes. External activity is no longer necessarily an immediate behavioristic response to stimulus. Feeling and thought, imagery and reflection, sentiment and deliberation, and especially choice and will, can and do occur. The level of the psychic is a new domain within which aggregate analysis must occur and be recognized by attention to intention, volition, motivation. Consciousness, purpose, intention and choice orient relationships and (external) activities. What individuals do can no longer be properly viewed simply as (social) behavior but must be regarded under many circumstances as (social) action or conduct.

Although materialism and idealism are involved to a relatively similar extent, but with some predominance of the latter, in this mixed or intermediate position, the views of the adherents do diverge about the origins of the social. Ward subscribed to the same notion of origins as did Sumner and Keller, but by contrast Giddings contended that human beings as descendants of pack-living anthropoids have always existed in a social condition. Yet the structure of his argument resembles Sumner's. Relations do commence on the basis of interpersonal similarities, though Giddings invokes awareness of likeness between self and others in relation to objective circumstances. Existing as aggregates within a common environment or habitat, individuals are subject to the operation of the process of the struggle for existence, elimination of the unfit, and survival of the fittest. Thus, certain objective likenesses become the basis of subjective likenesses among human beings.

Furthermore, such likenesses and like activity (or behavior) emerge reciprocally in the situation. On the one hand, persons in the aggregate evolve from multi-individual reaction to a common situation or stimulus, to inter-individual stimulation and response, and finally to co-individual behavior. On the other, an inherited sensory or organic sympathy (with which all members of the aggregate are endowed because they are hereditarily alike) becomes reflective sympathy as contacts lead persons to perceive and discuss their likenesses (regarding themselves and their situation (1901, pp. 91–9). They come to like their likenesses (i.e., to like one another). They associate consciously on the basis of likenesses. Like choices are made and like purposes arise. What had been an aggregate of objectively (organically) like organisms becomes a subjective unity of like-minded and consciously like co-acting selves and others (i.e., an organized group).[3] Their activity in concert is more action than it is behavior, though Giddings tends to use the words action and behavior interchangeably.

Although Giddings recurrently alludes to the constraints which the biophysical environment and the nature of the human organism impose, he emphasizes the place of consciousness in human social activity. In particular, human societies are based on the consciousness of kind as it evolves through the several stages of sympathy, especially reflective sympathy. In turn, two forms of

275

like-mindedness may result. On the one hand, reflective or conscious sympathy may elicit a sympathetic, impulsive, or emotional like-mindedness, with crowd or mob behaviors as the consequence. On the other, it may result in rational, deliberative, or formal like-mindedness. Popularly and uncritically accepted beliefs which have been transmitted as part of tradition are subjected to discussion, analysis, argument, and judgment. A public opinion is formed in relation to values. Concerted volition prompts conscious planning involving organization. Rational like-mindedness thus culminates in reasoned, rational cooperation and intended, voluntary preferential association. Undoubtedly, reason in man is a more effective and appropriate form of adaptation than is instinct and, manifestly, rational like-mindedness is a more effective basis for the consciousness of kind than is impulsive or emotional like-mindedness. Giddings seems to believe that reason operating through the uniquely endowed intellects of gifted individuals will increasingly be the basis for concerted volition through which adaptation to changing conditions will occur in modern society.

Ward is also disposed to accord reason an expanding role in evolving human societies in the future. His reason manifestly encompasses both a theoretical or scientific reason and a practical or a moral reason. In Ward's view, the gradual emergence of an equilibrium and then a structuring of the social forces are also accompanied by the development of reason or intellect as an adjunct to aid man in adapting and satisfying his desires effectively in the environment. Reason evolves instrumentally as a grasp of broad generalizations with a capacity to foretell results. (It becomes institutionally incorporated as science.) Reason evolves morally as man's sympathies expand and each person (rationally) admits and accepts the need for rules to protect himself and thereby abjures the resort to personal violence. (Reason in this sense is incorporated in normative codes and becomes group reason (1970, p. 419).) Ward characterizes human society as 'essentially rational and artificial' (1968, I, p. 92) and, accordingly, stresses the role of reason and intellect in its further evolutionary development (e.g., the prospect of a sociocracy). Presumably the uniquely endowed intellect will continue to have a major role in articulating collective desires and telesis.

Ross and Small require separate consideration, for they seem to be less materialistic than Ward and Giddings but less idealistic than Cooley. They do adopt a terminology which would seemingly align them with Cooley's idealism. Ross, for instance, remarks that whatever is social is so because 'it arises out of the interplay of minds,' i.e., psychic interaction (1912, p. 3). Social relationships are 'essentially psychic . . . [the] mind' (1919, p. 152). Small's insistence that the activity of the whole is the result of the 'play of mind upon mind,' of the interchange of psychical influences, of a 'giveness-and-takeness' in contact, ascribes a similar significance to consciousness in the social process, with its waxing and waning of the boundaries of inter- and/or multi-personal association and dissociation. For him (and for Ross), relationships must be envisaged teleologically, i.e., from the perspective of the ends of conscious individuals who are involved (Small, 1905, pp. 636–7). Each person is a unique center of consciousness and desire, who is also aware of others as centers of consciousness and desire. Thus, the character of the relationship and activity pivot substantially around the sensed convergence or divergence, conjunction or disjunction, consensus or dissensus of like or unlike, compatible or incompatible purposes on the part of individuals in the aggregate. Both sociologists agree that both intellect and affect, reason and emotion, are more or less involved. But Small is perhaps more inclined to emphasize reason and Ross less inclined.

They did disagree over their conceptions of the origins of the social. Ross accepted an original egoistic and atomistic condition for earliest humankind. Small argued that homo sapiens had always been more or less social in inclination and in conditions of life.

Both sociologists acknowledged the importance of the contribution of individuals with unusual capacities or talents in innovation. For Ross and Small, the process by which innovation was socially appropriated and disseminated involved social or collective decision. Some modicum of consciousness was clearly required. But Ross also made considerable use of Tarde's (more mechanical) rational-imitation and conventionality-imitation to account for adoption and dissemination of the new. In contrast, Small insisted that generally when men act, they are conscious and attentive, judge or evaluate, and select means to ends.

Both of them were exponents of the prevailing notion of social forces with which all individuals are endowed and which direct attention toward a common habitat or environment for satisfaction. As more or less committed to organic evolution, these early theorists thus conceived of the human units in the aggregate as subject to the constraints of common conditions of (material) existence and as thus relatively materially and objectively similar. Inter- and/or multi-personal relationships and activities are thus

277

basically defined and prompted by a set of common biopsychic appetites and desires, which are initially innate and organic, subsequently undergo differentiation and elaboration, and eventually permit an increasingly learned or acquired dimension.

Yet there remains a residuum of innate and organic force that retains a significant element of (materialistic) determinism for both Ross and Small. Despite their substantial idealism, it cannot be ignored. It accounts for their positional ambiguity: they seem to be more idealistic than Ward and Giddings and yet less idealistic than Cooley.

(3) Among early American theorists, Cooley is perhaps the ideal exemplar of the preponderantly idealist notion of the social in its three senses. Inter- and/or multi-personal activity is conceived of as 'social interaction' and reflects a more insistent and pronounced commitment to the idealist-subjectivist tradition than is found among the adherents of the intermediate viewpoint. Internal, subjective, non-observable consciousness has such a precedence or predominance over the external, objective, observable that the former may be said to control and direct the latter in the activity of the whole. Thus entailing consciousness, interaction can be identified both in terms of what it denies and what it affirms. It denies both deterministic materialism and behaviorism and the egoistic hedonism linked with behaviorism. In its fully developed sense, it affirms that reciprocal action between individuals is preceded, or at least accompanied by, the use of symbolic communication and by a structuring of the response to the other such that ego dialectically takes both his own position and the perspective of the other.

For Cooley, a social relationship thus involves two or more individuals who have been or are in contact with one another and are reciprocally (and subjectively) aware of one another and oriented (consciously) toward one another. Each individual is aware of himself and others as selves and others, with a more or less 'vivid sense of personal traits and modes of thought and feeling' derived through communication, discussion, and more or less mutual understanding (1962, p. 11). Such reciprocal awareness does involve personal ideas of self and others in each mind or imagination in contact with others. As a holist, Cooley insisted (1962, p. 10) that each person's ideas are 'closely connected with those that other people have, and act and react upon them to form a whole.' Most distinctively, Cooley's notion of the social basically incorporates affect or emotion and he is thus a romantic or affective idealist (Hinkle, 1967, pp. 13–14).[4] A relationship will, accordingly, entail a feeling or affective component which has been directly derived from (or is a correlate of) universal socialization experiences in primary groups. Fundamental is some modicum of interpersonal sympathy such that each person lives in the imaginations of others and exercises some claim on the others (and reciprocally, they on him or her) as ego comes to contemplate activity. Although Cooley tends to avoid resort to the doctrine of (human nature) social forces, he does hold that inter- and/or multi-personal activity is prompted and oriented by commitment to primary ideals or sentiments (or their derivatives). This activity typically tends to be characterizable basically as interaction: it not only involves reciprocal consciousness of selves and others but an interpersonal responsiveness in conduct that is relatively symmetrical, dialectical, and indeed antiphonal. Assuming humanity to have been in a state of association *ab initio* (as did Small and Giddings), Cooley is thus not compelled to account for the appearance of permanent association. (Nor does he imply that relationship, activity, and group necessarily emerge in sequence.)

A group is thus not only a unity of personal ideas but also of personal feelings of concrete personalities in direct contact, each of whom has ideas and feelings of self and others. Furthermore, it is an interrelated, interdependent, and interconnected unity or whole – as are all nature, life, and human life (1962, p. 255fn; 1966, pp. 49, 44, 26). What each member of the group thinks, feels, says, and does is influenced by the thoughts, feelings, comments, and actions of others and in turn influences them (1962, p. 4). Innovation necessarily arises in and through interaction in the situation and achieves acceptance through (interpersonal) valuation, public opinion, and public will.

Thus, theorists from two of the three basic social ontological positions were more or less inclined to emphasize consciousness to some degree (excluding only the behavioristic-materialism of Sumner and Keller). Admittedly, Giddings and Ward occupy a more intermediate position as compared with Ross and Small and with Cooley. Although Giddings regards social phenomena as based on aggregation and dispersion, which are more remotely caused by physical forces, he notes that the 'secondary [and derived] causes of social phenomena are conscious motives' (1896, p. 363). Ross's declaration that social phenomena are 'essentially psychic' has already been noted. Small holds that the human group is what it is primarily because men are ordinarily conscious, self-conscious if not always socially conscious (1905, p. 636). Although Cooley cautions that consciousness and behavior 'cannot be disjoined without denaturing both,' he insists nevertheless that 'the social and moral reality is that which lives in our imaginations and affects our motives' (1927, p. 151; 1964, p. 120).

Further evidence of the idealism of the social ontology of early American sociology can be found in the terms employed to communicate the character of the model of the social. Such terms as 'social mass,' 'social molecule,' or 'social atom' with their materialistic implications are rarely encountered. Neither Sumner nor Keller even invokes 'social molecule' or 'social mechanism.' Small and Cooley do use 'social organism' but it is devoid of actual organismic or biological taint. In *An Introduction to the Study of Society* (1971, p. 88) Small and Vincent insist that such use of organism implies only that 'interrelation and interdependence of parts' are entailed. No special order of life, either botanical or zoological, is intended (1971, p. 88). A holistic conception through consciousness is to be conveyed. Other more unambiguously idealistic notions occur in the literature. 'Social ego,' 'social intellect,' and 'social conscience' are infrequent, but 'social' or 'public will' are more common. And 'social mind' and especially 'social consciousness' are relatively frequent. Thus the prevalently idealist outlook seems to be expressed in the character of the terms used to symbolize or to be a model of group or society generically.

A dualistic but prevailingly idealist notion of social reality

Although social reality or the reality of the social is certainly distinctive generally in its dualistic conception and more especially in the varying emphasis on consciousness (and thus on idealism) in early American sociology, it cannot be accurately characterized merely in terms of the social extension of an older philosophic designation and view. It requires further specification in relation to the problem of the nature of the parts or parts to the whole (i.e., of individuals or individual members to the social ensemble) which has been the source of considerable controversy in the earlier and more recent history of European sociology. This dispute manifests certain aspects of the argument over materialism and idealism but it is also somewhat independent or autonomous. Yet it has been cast in the terms of the medieval dispute over the reality of parts in wholes and wholes as wholes. Nominalism had argued that the concept, category or logical universal (*universalia*) had no reality apart from the (composite summary of the) characteristics or properties of the particulars (or *singuli*) to which it refers. Reality resides in the particulars (or *singuli*). But realism had argued that the concept, category, or logical universal represents something different from and organizes the properties or characteristics of the particulars to which it refers. Reality resides in the universal, the idea, ideal, the logical whole.

Early American sociologists became overwhelmingly exponents of the sociological adaptation of nominalism. The position is often designated as social nominalism (or social atomism, or individualism or analytical individualism). It signifies that either the group as a whole has no reality in itself or that whatever reality it does possess is acquired secondarily or derivatively on the basis of the features of the particulars (or individuals) who are conceived to form the aggregate. More fully, social nominalism holds that the group is only a concept or category whose characteristics are derived summatively from the characteristics of the component parts which are assumed to be individuals or persons. It may involve a materialistic view of social reality. But in American sociology it has been pervasively advanced from an idealist stance, especially a subjectivist idealist perspective, in which whatever character the social aggregate possesses is alleged to stem from the features of conscious persons and especially the choices they make. Thus, in American sociology social nominalism is usually linked to a voluntarism. The group is the outcome of choice by individuals (i.e., a voluntaristic nominalism).[5] American sociologists were ordinarily political individualists (i.e., democratic) in the sense that the body politic is assumed to acquire its features through those of individual members (and their choices). But generally they were not economic individualists in the classical *laissez-faire* sense.

Social nominalism

Because Sumner and Keller do represent a somewhat unique position, their views may usefully be examined first. They are committed to a nominalistic notion of the origins of the relatively permanently structured group, though it is cast generally within the perspective of a behavioristic-materialistic-objectivist-deterministic rather than within a prevailingly interactionist-idealist-subjectivistic-voluntaristic standpoint. Their nominalism is evident not only in the origins of the group, but in the structure which arises and in the genesis of change. However, the distinctively Sumnerian analysis of cohesion-solidarity-integration, on the one hand, and of social identity, on the other, seems virtually to imply social realism.

Sumner presupposed that originally human individuals were aggregated within common environments in which they engaged in their struggles for existence and in sufficient proximity so that one another's presences could not be ignored (1959, p. 16). In at least some habitats, the scarcity of needed objects was sufficiently severe that harsh and violent collisions occurred, considerable pain was occasioned, and persons were induced to reflect and conclude that 'all shall fail' (1959, p. 16). (Presumably the hazards of surrounding biophysical nature and adjacent human aggregates might constitute common external threats.) Egoistic reflection and choice (however limited they may be) are implied by Sumner's use of the word 'an alternative' – such that men 'may so interfere with each other that all shall fail' or that 'they may combine' and thus by organized 'cooperation raise their efforts against nature to a higher power' (1959, p. 16). Accordingly the association culminating in the emergence of permanent human society had its beginnings in the separate but widely (if not universally) shared atomistic experiences (of pain, reflection and presumably choice) of individuals in the aggregate. In effect, Sumner has explained the origins of the social, the collective, and the societal multi-individually and nominalistically (as well as atomistically and reductivistically).

Continued social existence is accompanied by and characterized by antagonistic cooperation. Interpersonal competition and strife evoke individual differences in capacity and the action and reaction resulting will become crystallized into a series of different positions as parts in a division of labor which will effectively incorporate and use these different capacities, etc. (1959, pp. 34–5). The division of labor is thus the consequence of the mobilization of individual differences in relation to a natural, automatic, spontaneous process under the given conditions of existence. (Yet it is true that the consequent organization prompts Keller to declare – suggestive of realism – that society 'has a life different from that of the individual and is not simply aggregated or multiplied from the life of individuals' (1927, p. 2220).

Clearly, Sumner's explanation of the phenomena of social cohesion-solidarity-integration, on the one hand, and of social identity, on the other, is not predominantly nominalistic. These phenomena do not have their rise in separate, aggregated individual experiences but rather in a collective experience of an in-group more or less threatened by conflict with an out-group or out-groups. Consequently, the characteristics by which the society identifies itself also arise in relation to threatening other societies, as are evident in the phenomena of ethnocentrism and the ethos. Thus a Hegelian dialectical explanation is proffered with the implications of a social realism which seems to become more prominent as society persists or is maintained across the generations.

And yet the process by which adaptive innovation occurs is predominantly nominalistic or individualistic. Some minor 'give and take' in suggestion and imitation may occur between man and man, but it is minor or secondary in comparison with the primary invention of the man of genius or talent.

Sumner and Keller consistently deny any peculiar power of emergentism from association so that the aggregate can be said to have 'a mystic power in it greater than the sum of the powers of its members' (1959, p. 19). Sumner rejected the emergent inter-actionism of *Völkerpsychologie*. He argues that cooperation and constant suggestion together are so highly productive in a crowd only because 'it draws out latent power, concentrates what would otherwise be scattered, verifies and corrects what has been taken up, eliminates error, and constructs by combination' (1959, p. 20).

Viewed in relation to other prominent sociologists, Sumner does have a distinctive social ontology. It combines nominalism and realism.

In contrast, Giddings, Ward, Ross, Small, and Cooley do evidence a pervasive social nominalism which is predicated on their subjective idealist stance. They do assume the necessity of action on the part of the aggregate, but it is action stemming from the consciousnesses of the relations of selves and others in the aggregate. Each individual is uniquely a center of consciousness from which social consciousness derives. Early American socio-logists believed that each individual is uniquely different from every other one in the aggregate, possesses a conception of self as relatively different and unique, and is endowed with some modicum of independence, freedom, or will. These essentially nominalistic assumptions underpin the notion of the structured group and intrude into each of its features.[6] They appear in each of the major features of the persisting group or society: the notion of social desires, ends, or purposes; in the process of social decision, volition, or will; in social organization or structure; in the development of normative obligation as incidental to a judgment of the good of the whole or common welfare; in cohesion and solidarity; and most emphatically in social consciousness as the basis of social identity.

Undoubtedly the similarity of the needs or wants in humankind's common biopsychic human nature (i.e., the social forces) in relation to the persistent availability of certain objects in the environment for their satisfaction, along with common experiences over time, is the basis for the development of common, general (i.e., aggregational) ends, purposes or goals and provides the foundation for the genesis of a particular social situation (or environment). Nevertheless, each individual is unique and that singularity cannot be ignored in the formation of a social purpose. As Small holds (1905, pp. 483, 596), each person is a unique combination of 'primal motives and a mixture of their qualities.' This view seems to enter into Ward's collective desires, Giddings's concerted volition, Small's and Ross's social or collective decisions, and Cooley's social ends and public will. American sociologists of the early period seemed to assume that instances of sheer absolute (external) coercion or entirely (and internally induced) emotional action on the part of an aggregate are comparatively rare. Thus, the necessity for the aggregate to act, i.e., act in concert, ordinarily presupposes the formation of a concerted volition, social decision, or public will.

The basic nominalism lying behind the conception of the emergence of a social or public will is evident in numerous attestations of early American sociologists. Cooley proclaims (1962, p. 121) that the 'group "makes up its mind" in very much the same manner that the individual makes up his.' Giddings insists (1896, p. 151) that the social mind 'is astonishingly like the individual mind [in its operations].' (In the same way that a social mind is actually the likeness of many individual minds, so a social will is the likeness of many individual wills.[7]) And as has been noted in many instances above, Ross holds (1919, p. 80) that a social phenomenon has as many causes 'as there are human wills involved.' Ward declares that the social will 'is nothing more than what takes place in the acts of will on the part of individuals' (1901, p. 301). Small (and Vincent, 1971, p. 311) finds that the 'volitions of individuals combine to produce social . . . will.' Public will, concerted volition, or social decision is thus a process of aggregating and combining individual wills, volitions, and decisions.

However, the process of decision was inextricably linked with the process of organization. And it is in this context that early American sociologists' commitment to a belief in the efficaciousness of differential talent or genius in individual differences becomes unmistakably evident. They simply did not believe that all men possessed the same capacity or aptitude for developing a plan of action which is part of the social volition and which contains the bases of organization for executing that decision. Ward suggested, for instance, that those individuals with favored endowments and opportune circumstances also possess a surplus of energy which can be expended in innovation (1970, pp. 243–6). Ross refers to the 'natural inequality of men' in general and to the unique capacities, talents, and gifts of the exceptional man or genius in particular (1969, pp. 275–8, 350). Small also notes the 'exceptional individuals whose marked differences from other men' and 'particular talents distinguish their possessors from others' (1905, p. 711). Idealistically-oriented like Cooley, he also emphasized the indispensability of an interpersonal and social context for stimulating and developing such differences. Cooley is perhaps the unique embodiment of romantic idealism in early American sociology, with his commitment to the belief in the beneficence of variety, diversity, dissimilarity, or heterogeneity of things in general and of individuals in particular. Individual differences are indispensable in the formation of any social whole, for a whole implies an organization of different parts. *E pluribus unum* had a comprehensive social significance for Cooley. Human nature inclines all of us to be somewhat individualistic, idiosyncratic, or different from everyone else. Each of us does 'everything a little different from anyone else' (1966, p. 300). Each person 'as a whole is always more or less novel or innovating' (1964, p. 355). Each differs in physical appearance, temperament, emotion, socialization, experience, tastes, values, norms, and ideas (1962, p. 9). But it is the individuality of each person in energy potential, capacity, and talent that especially 'gives each member his peculiar importance' for the whole (1964, pp. 36, 318–19). That individuality is the basis of his 'special function' and 'peculiar value' for the whole which is a unity only as the unique potentialities of all individuals as parts are released and mutually interrelated.

Manifestly, a technologically efficacious mode of action may not necessarily be a morally justifiable one in terms of a criterion of the good of the whole or welfare of the group or society. Most early sociologists did subscribe to a democratic notion of the majority as a sanction of or legitimation of decision. Yet even the subjective idealists also assumed the necessity of survival and might be inclined to argue that the common good or welfare of the whole is (technically or technologically) what is conducive to the survival of the whole (or a majority of the whole?). It is not too difficult to understand why Cooley was so eager to assert that the 'many have the sense to adopt' the finer judgments of the few (1962, p. 125). (However, the democratic assumption of the moral legitimating function of common participation in a social decision is evidence of the pervasive individualism or nominalism of early American sociology. The perplexities encountered do require more consideration below in connection with the analysis of voluntarism.)

The features of social cohesion and solidarity also entail nominalistic or individualistic assumptions. Cohesion and solidarity tend to be construed motivationally by early sociologists of the idealistic-subjectivistic outlook. Ward's approach through sympathy and altruism is consistent with the prevailing nominalism. Giddings's references to 'spontaneous sympathy,' 'agreement in opinion,' and 'loyalty' are indicative of individual members' attitudes, though he does seem to suggest that these attitudes focus on a relatively transpersonal unity (1896, p. 148; 1898, p. 166). Cooley's personal discipline and emulation, which are contributory to solidarity, do involve certain distinctive attitudes of persons towards standards, shared ideals, and their contributions to the whole. These attitudes are, in turn, associated with the sympathy and we-feeling engendered by the social participation and experiences in what Cooley terms the primary group (and Ross the community).

Admittedly, some congruencies with realism do exist in the notion of solidarity and integration. Cooley, for instance, specifies that cultural variations in the emphasis and interpretation of personal differences, individuality, variation, freedom, aggressiveness, and power versus likeness, conformity, the unity of the whole, its authoritativeness, and its success in past conflicts may affect the nature and vigor of solidarity of different societies. And like Sumner, Ross reveals an inclination to construe integration as a property or feature of (the consistency, harmoniousness, and interconnectedness of) the parts of the social structure as opposed to the subjective characteristics of members.

But perhaps the most conspicuous confirmation of the prevailingly nominalistic view of the nature of the group in early American sociology is to be found in the character of 'social consciousness' as the basis of the last feature of social identity as conceived by the idealist-subjectivists among the early theorists. Ward's position seems to be typical of early sociologists. Social consciousness is the multiple awarenesses of each individual in an aggregate of the desires, feelings, beliefs, and intentions of the persons in that aggregate. This view is clearly consistent with the claim that 'Society, in its literal or primary sense, is simply an association of individuals' (1968, I, p. 460). For Ward, 'society is [thus] only an idea – a Platonic idea, like genus, species, order etc., in natural history. The only real thing is the individual' (1901, p. 99).

Giddings's social consciousness and social self-consciousness derive from multi-individual consciousnesses of similarities or like-consciousnesses and, accordingly, are nominalistic in character. Thoughts 'that appear simultaneously in many individual minds which are acting upon one another' constitute social consciousness (1896, p. 137). In turn, social self-consciousness arises when each individual in the aggregate makes both his and others' feelings, thoughts, and judgments objects of reflection, judges his and others' mental contents to be identical, and then 'acts with a full consciousness that his fellows have come to like conclusions, and will act in like ways' (1896, p. 137). Social reality for Giddings ultimately 'exists only in individual minds, and we have no knowledge of any consciousness but that of individuals' (1896, p. 134).

Undeniably, Giddings's remarks do contain certain features which might be construed as other than entirely nominalistic. For instance, he does refer to 'many individual minds in interaction,' their communication and continual 'influence [upon] one another,' and the mental combinations culminating in mental products 'which could not result from the thinking of an individual who had no communication with fellow-beings' (1896, pp. 120, 121). Yet he does not conceive of interaction dialectically: it does not evoke emergent, creative qualities, i.e., it does not engender something new which is not already within the parts or individuals of the aggregate.[8] (Instead, the source of the socially creative response lies within some one or more gifted or talented individuals.)

Though the concepts of social mind and social consciousness do not have the prominence in Ross's writings that they display in Giddings's or Cooley's analyses, they are basically presupposed. (And they also display, it must be conceded, some realistic implications.) Society is envisaged in terms of a social or collective mind, which originated in the 'community of many consciousnesses,' 'the play of mind on mind,' the awareness of human beings of others and their judgments, and in the 'interactions of individuals and generations' (1919, pp. 293, 4, 7). Just how creatively emergent interaction or the interplay of minds is is difficult to establish, but Ross does assert that 'from the interactions of individuals and generations there *emerges* a kind of collective mind' (author's italics) (1969, p. 293). Apparently, collective normative ideas begin as the ideas of specific individuals which precipitate as a typical or average opinion (1969, p. 341).

287

Such norms may become more or less impersonal – they become 'detached from persons' – as a result of general 'social reflection' or 'the social mind' (1969, p. 340). Presumably this impersonalization or depersonalization is further accentuated because transmission of the ideas to others occurs only as the notions are believed to conform to the approval of others or to what others should want (1969, pp. 343–5). The normative structure undergoes a constant selection, becoming more generalized, more comprehensive, more elevated as it is communicated in the succession of generations (1969, pp. 342–5).

However, Ross is manifestly loath to ascribe an impersonal, deterministic quality to the social consciousness of society. He objects to any conceptualization of society as a complete perceivable 'social organism' or 'as a mass rather than consensus, as an aggregate of bodies rather than an accord of minds' (1919, pp. 3, 47). Arising 'in the community of many consciousnesses,' society 'does not place itself over against the individual in order to bully, browbeat, and exploit him if it can' (1969, p. 293). Self and other consciousnesses, the separate personalized locus of awareness, does not apparently disappear. Accordingly, he remarks that society is 'a kind of fiction . . . [is only] people affecting one another in various ways' (1969, p. 293). It 'is not a being, but just people in their collective capacity' (1969, p. 418).

Even in the cases of Small and Cooley, who are interactionists and holists, the notion of social consciousness remains particularized and personalized and thus nominalistic. For Small, the declaration that social consciousness in its earliest form is merely the individual members' perception that the group exists is still essentially only an aggregate of personal awarenesses of selves and others. Cooley's notion of social consciousness is precisely an aggregate of individual consciousnesses of egos and alters. Derivatively, his public consciousness (like Giddings's societal self-consciousness) requires communication and especially discussion. Not only is it thus awareness of one another, but reciprocal awareness of ideas about selves and others in the aggregate.

Nevertheless, Cooley's analysis resists simple and facile characterization. He does recognize that the association of two persons brings a 'new whole whose life cannot altogether be understood by regarding it merely as the sum of the two' (1966, p. 8). Presumably, it is the common experiences arising from interaction that prompts individuals to feel and think of one another reciprocally as associated selves and others in imagination – as a group. He does regard organization as necessary to the very nature of the group

288

and such organization, he notes, is a coordinated system of activities 'that is not apparent in the parts [i.e., the individuals]' (1964, p. 38). He also acknowledged impersonal as well as personal and intermediate forms of social life. An impersonal form is 'one whose life history is not identified with particular persons' and whose development 'is organized along lines other than those of personal consciousness' (1966, pp. 4, 6). His most explicit illustrations of unqualified impersonal forms are actually prevailingly cultural in nature (e.g., fashion, myths, language, traditions, and customs). His allusions to more social varieties, such as voluntary associations, cities, or modern nations, involve an insistence that both personal and impersonal characteristics are present. Though voluntary associations 'are of a character chiefly impersonal' they do tend to include one or more individuals 'who do identify themselves with the life of the association and put personality into it' (1966, p. 7). Larger communities and even nations do have 'a life history that must be seen as a whole and can never be embraced in any study of persons as such' but they are still 'thought of as aggregates of persons' (1966, p. 7).

Furthermore, the individual can become 'aware of great social wholes, like a nation, or epoch, . . . [or] ideas or sentiments which are attributed to his countrymen or contemporaries in the collective aspect' only as they are embodied, represented, and personalized in the particular aspect of society of which he is aware (1964, p. 119). Although a country – for example – will be linked with 'many sensuous symbols – such as flags, music, and the rhythms of patriotic poetry – that are not directly personal . . . it is chiefly an idea of personal traits that we share and like as set over against others that are different and repugnant' (1964, p. 113).

It would be manifestly false to deny that Cooley's interactionary emergentism, his holistic notion of organization, his allusion to impersonal (in addition to personal and intermediate) forms of social life, and his commitment to a view of reality as a teleological, religio-moral whole are congruent with social realism.[9] But they remain only congruencies. Cooley did not make an actual transition to social realism, to the position that the phenomena of the group are decisively emergentistic, existing *sui generis*, as shared, common, general, public, and objective, as transpersonal and impersonal, as different from – if not greater than – the mere summative characteristics of particular individual members. To have accepted social realism would have meant abandonment of many of the aspects of his romanticism. It would have undermined the valuation of individual differences, the basis for the significance of opposition and conflict, the perduring impact of the primary group-induced human nature sentiments, and his optimism about the future role of voluntarism in social conduct.

However, it is inappropriate and inaccurate to categorize Cooley as a conventional social nominalist. Admittedly he does assert that society is not 'a thing by itself,' that it is artificial to consider society apart from individuals, that the group is simply a general or collective view of persons, and even in one context that society is 'a large number of individuals' (1964, pp. 135, 37, 38, 42; 1966, p. 158). But he also rejects the usual, more traditional forms of social nominalism in which the group is regarded as a mere aggregate, summary, or average of what individuals are apart from contact, association, and interaction. 'The average theory,' he insists, 'is wholly out of place' (1962, pp. 124, 123).

Cooley appears to be what might be termed a social neo-nominalist. He pervasively recognizes social (or interpersonal) interaction and its emergent qualities. He alludes to the possibility of larger, more impersonal social wholes, though he is disposed (as above) to depreciate their efficacy vis-à-vis more personalized relations and traits.[10] He is analytically inclined to conceive of the group as essentially an aggregate of personal consciousnesses (feelings) and ideas of specific individuals who imagine themselves as particular selves in association with particular others by virtue apparently of the changing extent, intensity, and modes of interaction. His neo-nominalism is thus distinctively linked with his subjective romantic idealism.

Voluntarism

However correct any nominalistic characterization of the (subjective idealism of the) social ontology of early American sociology may be, it is nevertheless incomplete. The nature of the social is also commonly, typically, and certainly ideally voluntaristic. Indeed, nominalism and voluntarism seem to be inextricably joined. Although other evidences of nominalism have been cited, its ideal manifestation exists in the process of decision by which American sociologists tended to believe that the whole was mobilized for action by the emergence of more or less consensus on the part of the wills of the individuals involved. The frequency of such terms as social decision-concerted volition, or public will in early theory, has been invoked to indicate a pervasive nominalism, for social will is a process of aggregating and combining individual wills. But it is equally important to acknowledge the relevancy and significance of will itself.[11] For early American theorists, social structure and change are both peculiarly exhibited in social decision or choice. What the structure of the group is was believed to be manifested finally in group action, which for early theorists means more or less (inter-individual) choice, will, decision, or volition. In addition, the explanation of (the introduction and dissemination of) social change also becomes crucially a matter of multi- and inter-individual choice, will, decision, or volition.

An initial caution must be issued. Early subjective idealist sociologists did accept a modicum of evolution but they often failed to distinguish earliest primitive man and society from later primitive man and society. Certainly, Ward, Giddings, Ross, and Small seemed to believe that an evolutionary (and progressive) trend from instinct, impulse, and affect to choice, deliberation, and reason was evident biopsychically and socially. Giddings, for example, specifies that social evolution is associated with a transition from instinct to habit, to reason and choice.[12] Nevertheless, some minimum or modicum of reason, choice, and deliberation is evident from the very outset of biopsychic and social development.

At some point in biopsychic and social evolution, the requirements of technical (or instrumental) rationality and moral rationality may come into conflict. The problem of achieving a technically efficient decision is not necessarily the same as or consistent with the process by which a morally justifiable or binding decision is arrived at. What works, is expedient, or adaptive and conducive to objective survival may not be congruent with a notion of moral good, good will or common will, or the interpersonally defined welfare of the whole. The differential evaluation of the distribution of individual differences, i.e., talent or genius, might not necessarily be harmonious with the moral demand that a decision is legitimate only if everyone participates and 'counts equally' in the aggregate. However, early American theorists did endeavor to resolve, if not to preclude even the appearance of, the contradiction between popular Darwinism and the moral assumptions of the Judaic-Christian tradition.

For early American sociologists, the doctrine of individual differences does imply individual inequality: not all men are equally possessed of the rationality, training, or expertise required to formulate effective options for a social decision. The elitist implications are clear. According to Ross (1912, p. 351), it is a 'falsehood that one man is as good as another' in determining the content of public opinion and social will. If sufficient time elapses to permit the formation of a free and mature discussion, some persons will have many 'times the influence' of others (e.g., the philosopher versus the field hand) in the outcome (1912, p. 351). Collective rumination and social decision will then reveal (retrospectively) 'an intelligence and foresight far above that of the average man' (1912, p. 351). Nor is Ross implying that emergence in interaction elevates technical efficiency. Rather he seems to be suggesting what Cooley asserted explicitly: the 'many have the sense to adopt' the finer judgments of the few, have a 'general capacity for recognition and deference' to the superior, and have a natural tendency 'to defer to . . . [the] most competent members [of the group]' (1962, pp. 125, 146).

Giddings's views are substantially similar, though perhaps less optimistic. On the one hand he notes that nearly every individual of ordinary intelligence may to some extent share in the formation of the critical judgments constituting public opinion and the emergence of rational social will. On the other hand he advises that as the number of individuals participating in a collective decision decreases the intellectual quality of the decision rises.

However, it is Cooley's confident assertion that actually conceals but points to a basic predicament: the alternatives (from which selection can be made) can be instrumentally effective only if they have been devised by the few who have the talent, whereas the choice of a social decision is morally binding only if the many have participated. (Thus, it becomes possible to account for his eagerness to claim that the 'many have the sense to adopt' the finer judgments of the few, etc.) Understandably, Ross, Small, and Cooley deny that the opinions and will of the social whole are simply 'an aggregate of separate individual judgments,' or 'a mere accumulation,' 'a mere addition' or 'arithmetical sum,' or an average of the convictions, decisions, or wills of individuals.

Nevertheless, early American sociologists do not question the view that the common good, good of the whole, or welfare of society can only be established through freely given individual decisions or consent. Most of the early sociologists assumed that the will or action of a majority is morally binding on and to be interpreted as the will or action of the society as a whole, though they are silent on the rationale of assimilating the latter to the former. Ward's willingness to identify the will of the majority with the will of society seems to suggest that the good as defined by the majority is the good of the whole or the 'good of society' (1901, pp. 325, 202). Even though his ideal sociocracy will presumably use scientific sociological knowledge as a basis for majority action, the nature of the good of the whole is still essentially nominalistic. But he also alludes to a common good as that upon which 'all . . . are agreed' (1901, p. 325).

Small is among those early sociologists who seem to imply a distinction between a social will (determined by the majority) and a common will (involving unanimity), with the former eventuating in the 'good of the whole' and the latter in the 'common good.' For Small, a notion of the good of the whole develops from a common interest, a social end, or general purpose which emerges out of the interaction of individual interests, purposes, or ends of members of an aggregate in a given situation (and Vincent, 1971, pp. 349, 352, 356–7; 1905, p. 583). The notion of common interest is transformed into a conception of the good of the whole by the contributions of influential persons, a sense of community (feelings of participation in a common, shared lot), and feelings of vicariousness (with awareness of the contributions of others to the welfare of self and of self to others) (1905, p. 246). Usually, this notion of the 'good of the whole' (as 'paramount to the good of the parts') is reflected in the acceptance of some 'minimum established limits of struggle' which special or particular interests will not or cannot violate (1905, pp. 242, 328, 340). Basically a notion of the good of the whole is a judgment of utility for all (everyone) (1905, pp. 668–9). However, a majority vote 'does not succeed in forming a genuine common will,' for the wish of the minority is not included (1971, pp. 352, 353). A common good is thus like a common volition: it must be unanimous and involve (complete) consensus (1971, p. 351). Presumably for Small, the common will is morally more compelling and preferable to the mere majority of social will.

In Ross's and Cooley's views, some departures from strict nominalism are suggested. Interestingly, Ross asserts that individual views of the good are necessarily particularistic, egoistic and aggressive (1969, p. 343). The notions of a(n interpersonally) desirable good which are communicated to others (i.e., alters) in direct and recurrent contact tend, the Wisconsin sociologist argues, to be interpersonally appealing, sharable, and generalizable because they sustain and preserve association. A 'man recommends to others, not what he likes, but what he likes others to like' (1969, p. 345). Presumably, each one in the aggregate is concerned with the interests and approval of the others so that he treats each other as another in a certain way. As generations come and go, the particularism of egoism is slowly and gradually sloughed off. What is selected and what survives is what can appeal to others.

Only those suggestions and ideas are retained that are 'felt to comport with' social welfare (1969, p. 327). There results a judgment of group will which 'measures things from the standpoint of society and not from the standpoint of the individual' (1969, p. 327).

Nevertheless, he insists that these collective appraisals 'are ever in contact with private valuations, and are perpetually modified by them' (1969, p. 327). Persistent egoism makes 'it impossible for social valuations to rise clear of private judgments,' though the former tend to have a constantly elevating effect on individuals (1969, p. 328). If the will of the whole and the good of the whole are emergents, they are manifestly restricted by the character of individual and private judgments.

Furthermore, Ross does contend that the 'only welfare there is is the welfare of persons present or to come . . . "Social welfare" is merely a synonym for the gain that comes [to the individual] through joint action [as opposed to the welfare secured by his own free individual action]' (1969, p. 418).

Cooley explicitly rejects the distributive formula of 'the greatest good of the greatest number' as 'dispersive, numerical, un-inspiring' (1966, p. 417). He declares that 'those nations were not wholly wrong who, rejecting the extreme doctrines of utilitarian individualism, have maintained the idea and feeling of a transcendent collective reality' (1966, p. 418). He seems to be repelled by any narrowly nominalist formula of the common or general good. Still, his assertion that Hegel's social realism is no more mystical 'than our exultation of the individual' is not an outright endorsement of any realist notion of common good or of realism in general (1966, p. 418).

What seems to be evident is that even those early American sociologists who were most conspiciously committed to idealistic interaction were reticent to conceive of the social will and its common good as so emergent that something new could result substantially different from the consciousnesses and experiences of individuals in the aggregate. Ross, Small, and even Cooley seem to fall within the scope of this characterization. Ross does advance a notion of group will involving the 'interactions of individuals and generations' (1969, p. 293). He does indicate that this 'intercourse' of associates 'begets reciprocal suggestion and transfusion of feelings,' which apparently develop 'a mass of beliefs and desires' constituting the social mind and will (1969, p. 327). Nevertheless, the collective appraisals developed cannot rise 'clear of [or transcend the] private judgments' and the persistent egoisms of individuals (1969, p. 328). Social welfare remains only the 'welfare of persons present or to come' (1969, p. 418).

Small's social volition arises from the interaction or influence of mind upon mind and the mutual reaction of individual wills. Interaction occurs through discussion, criticism, disapproval, repudiation, and approval and confirmation of individual opinion and will. A social or collective will becomes an organized, coordinated, unified product (Small and Vincent, 1971, pp. 309, 310). It does entail emergence and creative synthesis, but they are limited and restricted, for social volition differs only 'in some degree' or 'in greater or lesser degree' from individual volitions (1971, pp. 305–8).

Constituted an organized synthetic whole by communication and reciprocal influence in the course of discussion, dispute, and compromise from prior individual views, opinions, and valuations, Cooley's public will is an emergent from public opinion. The will to which public opinion gives rise is organic and differentiated; it involves neither unanimity or uniformity. Disagreement and divergency of views often persist. Cooley's notion of a social or public will thus reflects his romantic commitment to the beneficence of difference (as linked to his acceptance of a theory of plenitude). This interaction of individual opinions, valuations, and wills does elicit a dialectical, emergent, and synthetic or holistic quality such that social volition does exist on a plane differing from 'that of the individual thinking [or willing] in separation' (1962, p. 124).[13] Interpersonal valuation by which social or public will is constituted does rest on a constant test of (pragmatic) workability, fit, or adaptation of an object or objects in the situation. As indicated above, the common good is thus not to be incorporated in any simple distributive formula. And yet, in Cooley's case also, the emergent quality of the social will is limited by the nature of individual wills. As surely as social consciousness is a consciousness of specific and particular selves and others, so social will tends to retain a distinctively personal quality of individual (selves and other) wills. Cooley seems to recoil from a realistic and impersonal will, despite his references to impersonal social entities.

Thus, no early American sociologist genuinely espouses the position of Durkheim for whom the common good of a moral act is necessarily disinterested and impersonal. For him, egoism must be eliminated and the goal or end cannot be the advantage of any one particular individual. Each person as an individual must be eliminated in the moral act. Morality must entail an impersonal or disinterested object of devotion (as develops out of the effervescence of interaction and collective experience). For Durkheim, the common good of morality cannot be predicated on individual goods, no matter whether they be those of a majority or, presumably, even a summary aggregate. Concerted volition and common good or social welfare do retain a peculiarly personalistic, individualistic, or nominalistic quality in early American sociological theory.

What must not be ignored or forgotten in this broad summary characterization of early American social ontological theory as substantially idealistic, nominalistic, and voluntaristic is that the typifying features are not only accurate for structural theory but also for change theory. The features are apparent in the components of the modus operandi or explanatory formulation of change irrespective of the divergence between evolutionary and processual theories of social change.

Nevertheless, the differences between the two dynamic theories and their protagonists must be recognized. As social evolutionists, Ward, Keller, and Giddings did invoke the organismic growth analogy and the comparative method, assumed that the social units undergoing change were comprehensive or macrocosmic in nature, regarded rate and magnitude as relatively slow and small-scale and adhered to a linear or rectilinear notion of directionality of change (as exhibited in a temporal succession of stages). As processualists, Ross, Small, and Cooley rejected the monistic and, indeed, monolithic view of the unity of all human societies as one, controverted the conventional organismic growth analogy, repudiated the use of the comparative method, allowed for considerable variation in the rate and magnitude of change (even though slow, gradual, small-scale change might be most common), and might deny directionality altogether, reject the notion of a straight and uniform line of development, or might accept some general directionality in conjunction with progress (as opposed to the necessity of adaptive social differentiation).

Undeniably, too, social evolutionists and social processualists disagreed over certain aspects of the modus operandi of change. Ward, Keller, and Giddings adopted Darwinian (or Darwinian-Lamarckian) principles in their explanations (which also presupposed that naturalness, necessity, internality, and uniformity in the causal components were involved). Ross, Small, and Cooley (and also Sumner) denied the tenability of both (social) Darwinian and Lamarckian notions of the mechanisms of change. (Small was more inclined to accept the predominance of conflict in earliest human existence than was Cooley but both opposed the view that conflict invariably deteriorated into struggle, extermination, and annihilation of the vanquished.) As the term processualist suggests, change involves a sequence of phase-processes more or less in accordance with the dialectic of the Hegelian tradition. Tension, conflict, contradiction, or divergence comprise the initial phase (thus representing thesis and antithesis), but some degree of compromise, accommodation, adaptation, or adjustment ensue among opposing parties or contestants, with innovation emerging eventually as a concomitant (i.e., synthesis).

Notwithstanding the importance of the differences between their positions, evolutionists and processualists did ascribe a central and pivotal significance to the function of individual differences in the emergence of the socially new which tended to make the innovative process increasingly conscious, nominalistic, and voluntaristic. (Undeniably, Sumner's and Keller's behavioristic-materialisms are an exception.) Evolutionists did tend to conceive of a relatively small segment of the aggregate as contributing the biophysical-psychic variations as the basis of an appropriate adaptive response to the changing conditions of existence. And certainly in the initial stages of human social experience the (external) conditions of existence seemed to be more potent in dictating the adaptive response than individuals' consciousnesses and their choices were. However, it is manifestly evident that Giddings and Ward did envisage the process of innovation as increasingly conscious and intentional (through concerted volition and collective desire respectively). For the processualists, the socially new tended to be engendered out of interaction which included the less favorably as well as the more favorably endowed members of the group. Although evolutionists were inclined to include the role of emotion or emotionally-related factors in the development of an adaptive response and in its consentient dissemination among members of the group, they were more disposed to emphasize reason and rationality. Processualists were perhaps more prone to accord equal stress on or importance to rational and emotional components (e.g., temperament, courage, resolution, initiative, assertiveness, imagination, sensitivity, etc.). For the bulk of early theorists, i.e., for Ross, Small, and Cooley and also for Ward and Giddings, innovation was more or less a process of interpersonal decision, volition, or valuation in which each individual's uniqueness as a biopsychic entity and self was a crucial aspect in the emergence of an adaptive or adjustive response and in the dissemination and adoption by the group.

Manifestly, therefore, early sociological theory was prevailingly an ontological theory rather than an epistemological-methodological theory (even though its epistemology was discernibly dualistic and its methodology divergently positivistic and humanistic). Predicated on the three tenets of evolutionary naturalism, its social ontological theory was primarily concerned with the problems of social origins and social change and only secondarily with the problems of social structure. This theory was predominantly idealistic, nominalistic, and voluntaristic – as has just been indicated.

Only one more major problem thus remains. It is necessary to determine just how long these features predominated in theory, i.e., how long early theory continued. Use of the analytic scheme is required to establish or fix the temporal boundaries of the early or founding period of American sociological theory.

12 Toward discontinuity and continuity in the history of American sociological theory

Undeniably, that which may appear as a discontinuity at one level of intellectual analysis may, however, reappear as part of a continuity at another level. Periodicization of the history of theory does indeed anticipate that features different from and thus to some extent discontinuous with the traits in the summary, synoptic characterization of early theory provided in the last chapter will be discoverable in the literature. If the analytic (i.e., the classificatory-periodicizing) scheme has the utility intimated in the first chapter, it should be able to facilitate the final temporal demarcating of the first era of theory.

By the same token, confidence in the utility of the scheme will presumably be further enhanced if it can aid in detecting continuities in the character of the assumptions of general theory across several different periods. Accordingly, what may appear as part of something discontinuous at one more concrete or specific level of analysis (as characteristic of one period) may be restatable and reappear again as part of a more generalized, comparative formulation of (inter- or multi-period) continuities. Detection and identification of such continuities will be tantamount to the discovery of a 'deep structure' of basic assumptions of theory persisting across several periods. (Admittedly, the considerable detail of analysis required to study one era of theory makes it evident that only a tentative, preliminary verdict can be rendered.)

However, it is necessary first to ascertain discontinuity before contemplating the possibility of continuity. The analytic scheme must be used in an effort to determine the datable closing or ending boundary of the period of founding theory.

Discontinuity: delineating the terminal boundary of the founding period

In some respects, the difficulties which are encountered in delineating the closing or ending temporal boundary of the 'founding era' would seem to be more typical of the problem of periodicization than the comparative ease with which the beginning or onset of the period was established. The dating of the 'initial' boundary was accomplished rather simply by reference to the earliest of the published works in the continuous output of books and/or journal articles in the field. Published in 1883, Ward's *Dynamic Sociology* appears to have been the first major work in general theory. (However, one of Sumner's essays on the field of sociology which was subsequently published as part of a collection seems to date from 1881.) Consequently, the early 1880s appear to constitute the 'beginning boundary' of the founding period.

Undeniably, an element or elements of arbitrariness (or of personal judgment) enter into the determination of temporal boundaries in a periodicizing endeavor. Change in the dominant or majority characteristics of a period rarely occurs instantaneously. Instead, a somewhat varying number of years seem to be involved and it becomes a problem of ascertaining, through the use of the scheme, which realms of theory undergo change, in what respects, and how much, and what in retrospect seem to be the major indicator(s), symptoms, barometers, precedents or harbingers of the emerging change.

In the case of the founding era, substantial evidence exists that the years of World War I (*c*. 1915–18) constitute the time interval in terms of which the closing or ending boundary of the founding period occurs. (Indeed, the significance of the changing notions of science, epistemology, and methodology, and the necessity of first-hand empirical inquiry in the changing conception of theory might well suggest that Thomas's and Znaniecki's *The Polish Peasant in Europe and America* is the most apt indicator of the oncoming change.) Nor should the theoretical importance of designating or characterizing the temporal ending of the founding era in terms of a system of events outside of theory or sociology itself (i.e., World War I) be ignored. This circumstance may suggest that periodicization itself is especially a function of the intrusion of a system outside of theory itself, of something which dislocates the more or less stable relationships of theory with sociology, the other social sciences and the various domains of knowledge, the universities or institutions of higher learning and their relation with American society and culture in the most comprehensive sense. (At the very least, it appears that explanatory accounts of change which are endogenous or internal to the structure of theory itself are likely to be incomplete and unsatisfactory.)

It is initially of paramount significance that both the theory of American sociology and the knowledge which the discipline itself offers as a whole are alleged to have their justification in the practical benefits which will accrue to American society itself. Basically, sociological theory was associated with sociology's own development and its promise to contribute to the advancement of progress in American society. Now this faith in the possibility of continuous advancement of science and the furtherance of progress was predicated on the belief that man was essentially rational. As man's reason or intellect makes possible technical and material progress, so social scientific knowledge was held to advance society in harmony with humanitarian ideas and, accordingly, assure constant progress. However, the occurrence of World War I undermined many intellectuals' belief in man's rationality and their faith in progress. In the evolutionism so often associated with progress, violence was regarded as part of an earlier primitive social condition and a prevailingly irrational human nature. Thus, mankind's advance was suspect and the possibility of continuous progress in doubt. (Often, this apprehension was expressed as a lag between science-technology and man's nature, as in the writings of Groves and Weatherly.)

Differences often existed between those sociologists who had substantially developed their careers before World War I and those who entered the profession afterwards. Many of the older sociologists did continue to adhere to progress with little modification or qualification. But frequently the oncoming post-World War I generation of sociologists manifested considerable pessimism and others actually came to subscribe to a more secular, instrumentalist view that sociology as a form of scientific knowledge had its justification in (sheer) utility.

As the justification of the discipline altered, so the character of its inquiries and methods changed. Concrete, inductive, empirical research acquired an unprecedented prestige. The nature of science was debated vigorously and problems and issues of methodology came to occupy a central position in the field. Sociologists' participation in the Social Science Research Council, in various symposia on the state of the social sciences, and in such interdisciplinary ventures as *The Encylopedia of the Social Sciences* and *Social Trends* enhanced their awareness of and sensitivity to the status of their own discipline vis-à-vis others and in relation to the requirements of natural science, methods, and research. During the 1920s the general nature of the papers in the journals (*American Journal of Sociology, Social Forces,* and *Sociology and Social Research*), the attitudes of figures at the major graduate institutions, and the character of the doctoral dissertations attest the ·increasing respect for the prestige of concrete, empirical, inductive research, which is based on primary (rather than secondary) data. Major controversies developed over the nature of science and the appropriate methodology, with two somewhat divergent stances emerging. One was objective, positivistic, statistical, descriptive, and (more or less) atomistic. The other was subjective, idealist, case-study, explanatory and (more or less) holistic. (Giddings, Chapin, Ogburn, Rice, Gillin, and Lundberg came to be associated with the former position, whereas Thomas, Park, and Faris came to be champions ᴑf the latter view.)

The ċonsiderable interest generated in the debate over the nature of science and appropriate methodology had fundamentally negative consequences for general, comprehensive, or macro-theory as it had been envisaged in the years before 1915. Generally, such theory was attacked and (often) abandoned because it was held to be abstract, conjectural-speculative, abstruse, deductive, subjective, unreliable, and was based on indirectly acquired (or secondary) data. These objections, which reflected a new notion of acceptable knowledge, new disciplinary models (e.g., psychology and physics), and coincided often with sociologists' disillusionment with the idea of progress, tended to undermine the older type of interest in general, comprehensive, or macro-theory.

Significantly, the thrust of both (empiricist) positivistic and (idealist) humanistic methodologies was such as to indict the assumptions of the content of much of older theory in general and the social forces doctrine in particular:

(1) Both methodological positions found the concept of social forces objectionable because no explicit methodology or definite set of data had been employed in its formulation.

(2) Both positions objected to the assumption that social forces are the normal and natural ends of individuals and collectivities, and with a fixed, universal normative measuring rod entailed. An ethnocentric or personal bias was involved.

(3) Presumably both positions would object to the instinctivism at the base of the social forces notion. The newborn infant is equipped only with a number of relatively inchoate and vague

impulses which are defined and given meaning only as the individual acts and interacts with his social environment.

(4) Methodological positivists would presumably object to the notion because – despite its implications – it is not readily measurable or quantifiable.

(5) Methodological idealists would object because the notion fallaciously imitates the atomistic conceptions of physical phenomena, with the characteristics of irreducibility, permanence (indestructibility), basicness, and universality. A force in physical nature is not a particular agency by virtue of which activity occurs independently of the situation. The phenomena to which the social forces refer involve activity because things exist in relationships, as parts of wholes, not atomistically. Social and cultural diversity defeats any attempt to conceive of all human behavior as variations from and combinations of categories of social forces, which are elemental, fundamental, permanent, and universal units.

But the most significant modification of general theory occurred in consequence of the attacks launched against social evolutionism which seemed to stem especially from the data and inferences provided by the allied disciplines of psychology (especially behaviorism) and anthropology (particularly from the findings of concrete enthnographic research). Symposia, specialized conferences, round tables and sessions at professional meetings, journal articles, and frequent academic contact within the same departmental organization (in the case often of sociology and anthropology) provided sociologists with access to information and arguments from these allied disciplines. Alexander Goldenweiser, Wilson Wallis, Melville J. Herskovits and Malcolm Willey, William Fielding Ogburn, and Ellsworth Faris were major figures in the development of the indictment of (classical) social evolutionism. They offered six major arguments:

(1) The considerable cultural variation among modern primitives seemed to refute the assumption of the existence of a common set of primordial social institutions which have derived adaptively from a primordial human nature (Herskovits and Willey, 1923, p. 191).

(2) The study of extensive cultural diffusion appeared to controvert a conception of culture as a self-contained expression of a people's biopsychic traits (Herskovits and Willey, 1923, p. 196; Ogburn, 1950, pp. 80 ff).

(3) Biological, archaeological, ethnographic data suggest that the notion of a parallel bio-psychic-socio-cultural evolution is unsupportable. Apparently, human nature and the human organism

have remained constant over the last several thousand years while culture itself has changed rapidly (Ogburn, 1950, p. 286).

(4) Ethnographic and geographic data indicate that culture and culture change are relatively independent of physico-geographical environment (Goldenweiser, 1916, p. 630; Wallis, 1926, pp. 703–7).

(5) Invention cannot be construed simply as a rational process resembling the discovery of the solution to a problem by unusual, talented, or gifted individuals (Goldenweiser, 1925a, p. 20; Goldenweiser, 1925b, p. 220).

(6) Ethnographic analysis requires the rejection of the notion of a universally valid fixed sequence of institutional stages (Lowie, 1914, pp. 68–97; Goldenweiser, 1925a, pp. 28–9).

Unfortunately, the analysis so far presented may convey the erroneous impression that only the particular content and structure of general theory as envisaged before World War I was seriously disputed. In actuality, the very notion of any general theory was fundamentally questioned. The overwhelming significance of the persistent methodological disputes centering around the problem of what constitutes science and the rapid ascent of a positivistic methodology had consequences which were generally inimical to general theory. On the one hand, the concern with methodology developed to such proportions that it became a field of its own seemingly detached from interests in substantive theory. The developments of the 1920s brought a peculiar hiatus between the epistemological-methodological division of theory and the social ontological realm so that theory without any qualifying designation tends now to mean substantive theory. On the other hand, the prestige which positivistic methodology acquired tended to demand such a rigorously defined problem, a delimited range of accessible data, and requisite specifiable techniques such that the pursuit of general theory became well-nigh an intellectual impossibility. Use of secondary data became suspect and the practical limitations in acquiring primary data tended almost to preclude cross-societal inquiries and to transform American sociology into a sociology of (restricted aspects of then contemporary) American society. Indeed, if theory were to be legitimate at all, it had to become identified with small-scale inductive, empirical generalizations.

Although older sociologists with established reputations did continue their interests in general theory, younger sociologists entering the discipline after World War I were generally apprehensive about identifying themselves with the field. True, Giddings and Cooley continued their general interests during the

304

1920s. Keller's (and Sumner's) *The Science of Society* appeared in 1927. Furthermore, such students of Small's as E. C. Hayes (at University of Illinois), Charles A. Ellwood (first at University of Missouri and later at Duke University) and Floyd N. House (at University of Virginia) reflected an espousal of the older notion of general theory.

Such prominent figures as William Fielding Ogburn and F. Stuart Chapin, who had been students of Giddings at Columbia and were conspicuously associated with Sociology Departments at the Universities of Chicago and Minnesota, were really transitional personalities. Both of their publications exhibit some marked continuities with the older macro-theory interest (e.g., their *Social Change* (1950) and *Cultural Change* (1928) books) and yet their positivistic methodological commitments and specific research inclinations were decisively hostile to much of the content, if not also the structure, of founding (general) theory. Only Chapin's student Lundberg seems to have maintained an interest in general theory.

Robert E. Park was also a transitional figure. He had received a German doctorate in the early 1900s and entered sociology around the time of World War I. His macro-theory interests are reflected in (his and Burgess's) *Introduction to the Science of Sociology* and in his journal or periodical publications. He did develop a conception of general sociological theory such that his graduate students were able to locate and pursue specific researchable problems. Yet only two of his students in the 1920s (Louis Wirth at Chicago and Howard P. Becker at Wisconsin) became persistently associated with macro-theory throughout their careers.

In some respects it would appear that the emergence of marked field differentiation within sociology during the 1920s was also somewhat inimical to the vigorousness of interest in general theory. Specialization, which seems to be a necessary accompaniment of professionalization, probably represented an obstacle to the ready persistence of a general theory interest, given the ascendance of a strongly positivistic methodological orientation.[1] Most particularly, the problem-foci which had been relatively unified and coherent within general theory became fragmented and disparate under the impact of specialization. Curiously, a field of 'general sociology' sometimes made its appearance as part of the curriculum in larger departments and thus afforded a vehicle for maintaining some interest in 'general theory.' But many, if not most, of the older general concerns were redistributed among and submerged within more specialized fields. Although the problem of 'social origins' was assimilated within social change, it seems to have become increasingly suspect as a legitimate problem of investigation in the decade or decade and a half after World War I. ('Origins' came to be defined as unscientific because they required a maximum of conjecture and a minimum of data. 'First-hand' information had not been and would not become available.) Problems of social alteration and transformation, especially in their older conceptualization as social evolution, also tended to loose their legitimacy because the requisite kind of data and research techniques could not be secured and/or employed, though vestiges of the older concern persisted in courses in social change, historical sociology, cultural sociology, and social disorganization. The older interest in the theory of human nature (centering especially in the doctrine of social forces) became a part of the subject-matter and the debates (especially on instincts) in (sociological) social psychology and biological sociology.

Although the intellectual consensus on which founding general theory had rested was undermined substantially after 1915, the bases of its eventual reconstruction and recovery were being developed. The frequent publications on the state or condition of the social sciences or merely on sociology itself (which would tend to be organized in terms of the major developments within each of the sub-fields of the discipline) did articulate both the controversies and the possible foundations for their resolution. Paradoxically, too, the very necessity to write textbooks for undergraduates compelled sociologists to produce syntheses of sociological knowledge and to construct more or less generalized, if not actually general, theories about man, nature, personality, society, and culture.

Continuity: detecting and characterizing persisting assumptions of later periods

Although some substance for the claim of the utility of the analytic scheme has presumably been won by the successful delineation of the beginning and ending temporal boundaries and major characteristics of the first, founding period of theory, the claim would be further enhanced by a demonstration of the applicability of the scheme of the analysis of the demarcations and characteristics of theory across several successive periods in the history of American sociological theory. However, such an undertaking would seem to be almost impossible of fulfillment in less than a chapter in view of the more than ten chapters required to analyze only one period. Yet the attempt becomes almost mandatory if the possible charge of the restricted or selective use of the scheme is to be met.

Manifestly, some simplification and circumscription of objectives and relaxation in the rigor of analysis are compelled to achieve even the most preliminary and tentative results. Thus, the objective is to be limited simply to an effort to detect, delineate, and basically characterize major continuities and/or discontinuities in the basic assumptions of general social ontological theory throughout the several periods. In addition, it will be impossible to provide complete details about the dating of periods and about the full range of acceptance of major characteristic theories or theoretical orientations during given periods. (Optimally, it would be desirable to know just how widely dominant orientations were disseminated among general theorists and even how extensively they were accepted in fields other than general theory itself.) It will thus be necessary to center attention only on the principal figures and major features of their views of general theory in given periods.

But before any analysis of the actual content of theory and theorists can begin, the demarcation and characterization of the successive periods must be preliminarily indicated. Four periods can be delineated in succession after the initial period of 'founding theory' which extends from the early 1880s to c. 1915–18. A second period involving the 'Declining Interest in General Theory' (with a heterogeneous content) prevails from about 1918 to 1930. A third period characterized by a 'Revival of Interest in General Theory and (by the Prominence of) Social Action Theory' can be dated from the years c. 1930 to c. 1945. A period from about 1945 to 1965 is aptly characterizable as one of 'Structural-Functional Orthodoxy.' Most recently, 'Theoretical Dissensus and Heterodoxy' have been evident (i.e., after 1965).

Park as a general theorist

The effort to offer details about the closing or ending of the founding period in the previous section almost expanded into a full exposition of the changing position and characteristics of theory during the next decade and a half as just typified as the 'Declining Interest in General Theory.' These years correspond to the early period of what has often been designated as the dominance of the Chicago School in the broader or more general history of American sociology. Much of what transpired – as was observed above –

entailed a substantial repudiation of much of the earlier social evolutionism. Patently, not all that occurred was merely a negative response to or a destruction of that past. Some reconstructive syntheses were attempted. Interestingly, Park perhaps most nearly succeeded in developing a general or comprehensive sociological theory, even though his name has been conspicuously associated with intellectual developments in a variety of fields. Although now largely ignored, if not unknown, W. I. Thomas's significant collaboration in the genesis of the Park and Burgess *Introduction to the Science of Sociology* provides an important datum for interpreting just what Park's dominant theoretical stance was. Faris's own efforts to work within and elaborate the intellectual perspective of George Herbert Mead (which culminated in his book on *The Nature of Human Nature*, 1976) also contained many of the basic ingredients of a general theory. And in many respects Ogburn's volume on *Social Change* (which presents his culture lag thesis) may also be said to possess many of the features of a general theory. Yet Park seems to have exercised the greatest influence in his volume of publications and in the number of doctoral dissertations for which he had major responsibility.

Like the predecessors of the founding era, Park espoused a general sociological theory which was predicated on both social epistemological-methodological and social ontological premises. For his epistemological-methodological views, he drew on Windelband's and Rickert's differentiation of the science-nomothetic disciplines from the history-idiographic disciplines. He regarded sociology as part of the science-nomothetic disciplines. Interestingly, his social ontological theory embodies a peculiar 'double' dualism in which human societies are conceived to operate as they do because humankind is partially in nature (as living matter) and partially outside (as conscious beings) and because the social is sometimes explicitly declared to be realistic and at other times implied to be nominalistic. In addition, Park also reflected the growing effort to develop a division of labor between anthropology and sociology by allocating the study of primitive, aboriginal, or nonliterate societies to the former and the inquiry into modern, civilized, or literate societies to the latter. Furthermore, the city or urban community occupied a central position in the emergence and persistence of civilized societies.

Park's insistence that the study of social phenomena must proceed by analysis of and equal attention to the two levels of the more or less unconscious ecological and the more or less conscious moral does indeed seem to reflect his inclination to construe humankind as both inside and outside of biophysical nature. The two levels do incorporate distinctive sets of sociological traditions: (1) the ecological is derived from Spencer's emphasis on the role of the struggle for existence and competition among humans as organisms in a biotic habitat, and (2) the moral is ascribed to Comte's stress on consensus and communication in the emergence of social order. Enmeshed in the web of nature and implicated in struggle or conflict and competition, human individuals are part of a natural order and economy in which they find their proper niche in accordance with a (competitive) territorial or spatial distribution along with other animals and plants of the habitat or geographical locale.

However, Park is also convinced that persistent relationships among an aggregate of homo sapiens will also reveal another facet of human nature (sympathy or altruism as opposed to an egocentric survival preoccupation) so that a conscious level of orderliness emerges, is definable in Comte's terms, and is organized around consensus and communication (rather than conflict and competition). Park insists (1952, p. 182) that humans cannot long continue to treat one another as mere utilities, as part of the flora and fauna of the habitat. Humans can and do communicate. Consequently, conflict or struggle does not generally tend to culminate in extermination, but is rather transformed into and succeeded by the processes of accommodation and assimilation. At some point, humans will endeavor to act collectively (in relation to problems of the biophysical habitat?). Out of accommodation will emerge social organization with stable relationships which are customary, conventional, institutional, moral, and cultural. Consciousness and understanding with intent, design, purpose, and consensus issue. Accommodation leads to assimilation which produces a characteristic personality type and cultural heritage.

But it is the city as the functionally strategic community in civilized societies rather than any type of community or any type of society which is of primary and crucial interest to Park. Centered in market or exchange relations, the city naturally tends to develop differentiated and specialized 'natural areas' as a consequence of the (ecological) processes of competition, segregation, and dominance. These natural areas have their distinctive ecological characteristics. However, the natural areas tend (1952, p. 201) to become 'cultural areas,' with their own peculiar traditions, customs, conventions, standards of decency and propriety, and a typical universe of discourse and meaning.

Park's dichotomy of the natural and the cultural, the ecological and the moral, and community and society – all of which really express a distinction between the physical (or matter) and consciousness (or mind) – is really the basis of a fundamental problem in his conception of the part–whole or whole–part relationship in the nature of the social. He never directly and systematically accounts for the genesis of society, culture, and morality out of the natural, ecological, or community. Nevertheless, he apparently explicitly commits himself to social realism both in his (and Burgess's) *Introduction to the Science of Sociology* (1924, p. 508) and in later articles (1955, pp. 16, 17, 18). But many of his statements raise serious questions about how consistent, rigorous, fundamental, and comprehensive his profession of social realism was. To hold (1952, p. 181) that 'Societies are *formed for* and in action' and 'grow up *in the efforts of individuals* to act collectively' (author's emphasis) is to presuppose the priority of individual experience and to suggest the importance of individual consciousnesses and choices in the emergence of society or societies. Park significantly interprets (Park and Burgess, 1924, p. 37) Dewey's process of communication as commencing with experiences which are 'individual and private' and as culminating in an experience which is 'common and public.' But he does not himself explain or emphasize (in contrast to Durkheim) how a situation involving individual private experiences and different individual purposes can elicit or engender (emergentistically?) through communication a common public experience and a common purpose. Although Park does argue that the social and the (inter-?) individual, culture and personality, society and the person 'somehow are different aspects of the same thing,' he also insists (1952, pp. 203–4, 81) that 'social relations are finally and fundamentally personal relations. . . .' Indeed, the ultimate key to (cultural) meaning is afforded by the personal experiences of individuals as revealed through life histories (1952, pp. 201–9). Furthermore, the changes in society can become comprehensible only by reckoning 'with the changes' taking 'place in the individual units' (1952, p. 174). Park agrees (1952, p. 175; Park and Burgess, 1924, p. 438) that attitudes – 'the individual's tendency to act' – are the social elements producing change (or maintaining social organization). But even more fundamental psychologically are the basic wishes (envisaged originally within the social forces tradition) that give 'the attitude its kick' or dynamic, activating quality (1955, p. 280; 1924, pp. 438–43). Understandably, the 'elementary units' in social relations – 'that is to say, the individual men and women who enter into these different combinations [of relations] – are notoriously subject to change' (1952, p. 173). Society is thus the more or less integrated and coordinated actions of motivated individuals who are more or less conscious and act intentionally and voluntarily. Certainly, Park's social realism was not sufficiently pervasive or intense so as to issue in an explicit repudiation of the arguments of earlier American sociologists or to preclude collaboration with and endorsement of Thomas who opposed Durkheimian realism and espoused in effect a social nominalism.

Social action theory (MacIver, Znaniecki, Parsons, and Becker)

Between the years 1930 and 1945 – the period of the depression and World War II – interest in general theory revived and was especially expressed in the social action orientation. This renewal of concern with theory involved both epistemological-methodological and ontological preoccupations. Within the former domain, both empiricist-positivist and idealist-humanistic stances were assumed. Again, the social ontological developments were dualistic, though some were especially behavioristic-materialistic and many were actionist-idealistic.

The crises of the period were important in the changing attitude toward theory. Some sociologists apparently concluded that the particularistic, descriptive studies actually provided no aid in coming to terms with the crises. Such inquiries were generally devoid of a specific theoretical stance and were not readily generalizable. Even empiricists and positivists became aware that their two model sciences of physics and biology ascribed their success not only to methodological precision but also to theoretical elaboration. Indeed, facts were often claimed not to speak for themselves but to require interpretation in terms of a theoretical system.

Two movements in the discipline attest the more favorable attitude toward theory. One was represented by the continuing Committee on Conceptual Integration in the American Sociological Society. The other was evident in the attempt to develop theoretical systems, often modelled on the lines of the physical sciences or a combination of the physical and biological sciences.

Developments both inside and outside of American sociology facilitated the revitalization of general theory. Presumably the increasing availability of translations of such European theorists as Durkheim, Weber, Freud, and Pareto was of consequence. Relocation of many refugee intellectuals and professors who were themselves theoretically trained and concerned (e.g., Gerth, Speier, von Hentig, Heberle, etc.) had a major favorable impact. In addition, the increased importance of prestigious Columbia and Harvard Universities as centers of graduate training in sociology was significant. Each institution had theorists of major stature on its staff (Abel, MacIver, and later Merton at Columbia and Sorokin and Parsons at Harvard). As their graduate students entered the profession, the interest in and status of general theory as a recognized and legitimate specialization was enhanced appropriately.

Although advocates of general theory can be found among the empiricist-positivists and behavioristic-materialists (e.g., Lundberg), the major elaboration of theory came from the idealist-humanists and actionist-idealists. Robert MacIver's articles on social causation in the late 1920s were probably the first contribution of the orientation. But Talcott Parsons, Howard P. Becker (University of Wisconsin), and Florian Znaniecki (later at the University of Illinois) also joined in the advocacy of the position. (Interestingly, MacIver and Znaniecki had been born and educated abroad, whereas Parsons and Becker had been born in the US but had graduate training and/or major experience abroad. But only Becker had had training in American sociological theory at Chicago which suggests the compatibility of earlier American traditions with social action.) Undeniably, some differences in commitment and in terminology exist among the four, but they do tend to concur in the major basic assumptions of the social action orientation.[2]

(1) In contrast to (mere or sheer) objectively conditioned or determined 'behavior,' 'action' designates that human activity is typically and/or prevailingly oriented in and by consciousness. Znaniecki's 'humanistic coefficient' and MacIver's 'realm of conscious being' reflect this view as does Parsons's analysis of the subjective, the perspective of the actor, and the nature of the ego. Becker is distinctive in emphasizing Mead's role-playing and symbols as indispensable to consciousness. The very use of the term 'actor' or 'agent' is significant precisely because the conscious initiation of activity is assumed (i.e., a subject and subjectivity).

(2) 'Action' is social to the extent that the plurality of persons involved are each aware of (them-) 'selves and others' as acting subjects and objects of action. (Indeed, the very conception of others as objects of action must entail the attribution of some modicum of subjectivity and agency to them.) This second feature is embodied in Znaniecki's 'attitude-value' and 'social agent– social object' conceptualizations; MacIver's 'inner and outer

orders' (and the 'attitude–interest' distinction); Parsons's earlier 'actor–situation' dichotomy; and Becker's 'selves–others' notion.

(3) If activity is action, it characteristically is teleological or purposive in that it is oriented toward or by intention, purpose, end, or goal. Although Znaniecki does not formally and explicitly define an end or purpose, he implies its existence as the outcome of the successful influencing of the actions of others. Parsons proposes the concept of end as a future state of affairs which the actor seeks to attain by his purposive intervention or non-intervention in the situation. MacIver prefers the notions of objective and motive to separate out different aspects of intention. Becker adopts W. I. Thomas's notion of the four wishes (for security, response, recognition, and new experience) as categories of ends.

(4) Action is more or less rational in the sense that purpose can be realized only with some modification in the external situation by a resort to (Parsons's) 'means,' or (MacIver's) 'technique, procedure, and instrument,' or (Znaniecki's) 'social instrument' and 'social method' (which Becker also adopts). Becker invokes Weber's distinctive types of means–ends relations as 'expedient rationality,' 'sanctioned rationality,' 'traditional nonrationality,' and 'affective nonrationality.'

(5) Certain aspects or components of the situation which are designated 'conditions' are unchangeable or unmodifiable. For Parsons, these aspects are whatever the actor regards as given or unmodifiable. Less relativistic, MacIver restricts (1964, p. 331) 'conditions' to the biophysical realm 'as relevant to and prerequisite for the particular action.' Znaniecki apparently envisages conditions as referring more simply and broadly to the variety of objective features in the external situation in which action occurs.

(6) In genuinely social action, actors are always more or less regulated in their selection of means to ends and of ends in relation to ends by moral rules, norms, standards, or principles. Parsons is most emphatic and precise about the normative component in his scheme. The means cannot be regarded as either random or as dependent wholly on the conditions of action. They must in some sense be subject to the influence of an independent and determinate selective factor. Interpersonal relations can be orderly only if they are oriented to and governed by rules.

But MacIver, Znaniecki, and Becker do not introduce a concept of a norm as a major social action component. Still all of them do insist that action within structured social relations requires on the part of the persons involved a mutual acceptance and performance of prescribed, sanctioned duties which imply the existence of moral rules.

(7) Important as these constituents of action are, they achieve their crucial significance only as aspects of action if they presuppose and involve a fundamental voluntarism. A coherent line of activity relating means to ends, rules, and the conditions of the situation demands of any actor the exercise of a modicum of will, evaluation, assessment. As Parsons argues, action is action only if it is generically 'voluntaristic.' In MacIver's case, choice operates through his notion of 'dynamic assessment' which subjectively interrelates objective, technique, social relations, and biophysical conditions. Znaniecki's conceptualization of the elements of action also presupposes that the (social) agent or subject can choose (especially methods and instruments) and that the (social) object is necessarily ascribed some degree of spontaneity or voluntarism in making his social reaction. Becker's formulation assumes the operation of choice but it does not offer a distinctive conceptual designation.

(8) Finally, the social action orientation entails a specific epistemological-methodological stance. It demands that the researcher employ an appropriate investigative technique, method, or approach which Parsons earlier designated as 'verstehen,' Becker as 'interpretation,' MacIver as imaginative or 'sympathetic reconstruction,' and Znaniecki as 'vicarious experience.' The approach insists that the subjective experience of each actor in the social situation is relevant to and must be understood and taken into account in the total outcome. Social action requires a humanistic methodology which is congruent with its prevailingly subjective idealist social ontology.

However, a caution – if not a caveat – must be entered. Not one of the four sociologists regarded social action as a complete system of theory. Social action was the infrastructure for each of them. In MacIver's case, social action was explicitly a part of his major work on *Social Causation* (1942), his *Society: Its Structure and Changes* (1931), *Society: A Textbook of Sociology* (1937), and (with Charles Page) *Society: An Introductory Analysis* (1949). Unfortunately, Znaniecki never lived to complete his magnum opus on systematic sociology in which social action in some version would presumably have entered as a foundation for his four social systems: social relations, social roles, social groups, and societies (1965, p. xvii). For Becker, action theory was a prerequisite for and basis of his theory of sacred–secular societies as substantially developed

314

during the last ten years of his life (1950, chapter V; 1957, pp. 133–85). Yet it was Parsons's distinctive fusion of the action orientation and structural functionalism which dominated sociological theory in the US in an unprecedented fashion from the mid-1940s to the mid-1960s.

Parsons and structural functionalism

In retrospect it may seem curious – but it is significant none the less – that structural-functionalism has appeared to be inextricably bound with social action throughout its years of pre-eminence in American sociology, which coincided roughly with the end of World War II, the advent of the 'cold war,' the effort to return to normalcy, the years of Civil Rights protest, the rise of student activism on college campuses, and the country's gradual involvement in the Vietnamese conflict (1945–65). Certainly the absence of any association of action theory with structural-functionalism in anthropology and the examples of social action theorists in sociology who never espoused functionalism should have been a warning against any assumption of an intrinsic connection between the two. Why the realism of Durkheimian and Radcliffe-Brownian functionalism was ignored is itself an interesting problem. True, occasionally some analyst claimed that Parsonsian voluntarism seemed to be weakening or that Parsons's *verstehende* commitment was less evident and the signs of positivism more dominant. However, the various elaborations of structural functionalism continued to contain persistent claims of loyalty to the action orientation, even though definitions might seem to vary considerably.

Initially Parsons pursued his effort to develop a structural-functional theory both at the level of the social (or society, i.e., a (total) social system) and at the level of the interconnections among society, culture, and personality as sub-systems (of action). His point of departure (both in *The Social System* and *Toward a General Theory of Action*) is Hobbes's formulation of the problem of social order as it might be represented in the relations of a hypothetical pair or dyad (ego and alter) who are assumed to confront the prototypical and primordial problem of social existence (or interpersonal coexistence). Ego and alter must meet and resolve the problem of adjusting a potential incompatibility of claims in the face of the scarcity of desired objects (both social and non-social) in the situation. Conflict can be precluded (i.e.,

315

interaction can be stable or stabilized) only if ego's and alter's expectations are complementary. In turn, such a condition rests more broadly on the (organization of) personality and (the patterning of) culture. Expectations can be complementary only if the personalities of the (two) actors have been socialized generally to want approval from one another and only when they share appropriate (cultural) value orientations, norms, or rules. (On the basis of this argument, Parsons possesses the basic components to derive the notions of role, collectivity (and social system), norm, and value.)

Put somewhat more abstractly, a social order (or orderliness) can exist (and be maintained) only if relations are part of a persisting social system, but it in turn requires a minimum of support from the other two sub-systems of action, personality and culture. Similarly, organized personalities are possible only if a certain minimum of support from society and culture are forthcoming. In turn, culture can presumably persist as a patterned entity only if it receives appropriate support from society and personality.

Simultaneously, Parsons identified certain functional imperatives (i.e., adaptation, goal-attainment, integration, and pattern-maintenance) which at first seemed to have primary relevancy only for the social and personality systems, each with its own peculiar manifestation of these demands. But once Parsons introduced the conception of a cybernetic control hierarchy (in *Theories of Society*), each system was construed to have a unique functional problem and distinctive contribution to make to each of the others. Parsons also extended his analysis to include the behavioral organism and the physical environment (at one end and ultimate reality at the other). Thus, pattern maintenance is the distinctive problem (and contribution) of culture (which provides a system of control relative to social systems); integration is the central problem of the social system (which comprises a system of control over personality); goal-attainment is the major problem of personality (which exercises control over the behavioral organism); and adaptation is the distinctive problem of the behavioral organism (which is the point of articulation of the sub-systems of action with the anatomical physiological features of the physical organism and its point of contact with and basis of control over the physical environment).

Manifestly, functional analysis for Parsons entails an examination of the interrelations among society and its five environments of ultimate reality, cultural system(s), personality (systems), behavioral organisms, and the physical organic environment.

Parsons defines (or redefines) society as a type of social system which attains the highest level of self-sufficiency as a system relative to its environments. In effect, then, the self-sufficiency of a society is a function of the balanced combination of its controls over its relations with these five environments and of its own state of internal organization. Stability is the maintenance of an appropriate balance of inputs and outputs of society (or the societal community) and each of its environing systems (i.e., each system is involved in a set of input/output relationships with every other system). Instability involves some disruption of the appropriate balance between inputs and outputs between or among one or more of the several systems (and/or of the components of the social system itself). (By the mid-1960s Parsons was convinced that such instability and change might eventuate in social evolution.)

In spite of the modifications constantly introduced into his theoretic system, Parsons's explanation of structure and change continues to center on the relative balance of tendencies to conformity or deviance in the motivations of the individual actors in the social system. Any social unit or social system is a whole only as individuals are motivated to certain lines of activity (as defined by relevant values). Such activity is action by virtue of the formation of meaningful intentions and their more or less successful implementation by human beings in concrete situations (1966, p. 5; cf. 1951, p. 4). Accordingly, 'There is a sense in which all action is the action of individuals' (1966, p. 5). Ultimately, change means disturbances in individuals' motivations at the role level (Parsons *et al.*, 1961, p. 74). Alterations in motivations occasion modifications in intentions, i.e., 'decisions' (1966, p. 20). Admittedly, Parsons's endorsement of voluntarism has apparently become more oblique, if not more muted, than it was in *Toward a General Theory of Action* in which references to choice, selection, evaluation, appraisal, and assessment were conspicuous (e.g., pp. 63–4, 70–2). Nevertheless, the assumption that a collectivity is the motivated, intentional action in concert of a plurality of individuals (i.e., involves a voluntaristic nominalism) is still necessary and remains.[3]

Early action antecedents and symbolic interactionism (Mead, Blumer)

Before examining the variety of theoretical movements which have arisen since the mid-1960s to contest the (earlier) dominance of social action-based structural-functionalism, it is necessary to

317

consider two other intellectual developments in sociology, one of which existed prior to the emergence of the social action orientation and the other of which has co-existed with that orientation at least since the 1930s. The implications of both of these 'developments' are such as to augment the intellectual significance of the assumptions which are represented in the social action orientation both for theory in particular and for American sociology in general.

The first development is, paradoxically, identifiable only retrospectively after the ascendance of social action itself. It involves the discovery that early American sociological theory (of the founding era) anticipated the action orientation. Ward, Giddings, Ross, Small, and Cooley do refer to the terms of an action vocabulary, including 'consciousness,' 'teleology,' 'end,' 'desire,' 'means,' 'devices,' 'strategy,' 'implement,' 'instrument,' 'principle,' 'standard,' 'rules,' 'judgment,' and 'choice' (and also in Cooley's case, 'sympathetic introspection'). Admittedly, the terms do not appear conspicuously and do not constitute basic concepts in any sense because these early idealistic subjectivist sociologists (except for Cooley) construed early man as frequently (if not substantially) instinctive, impulsive, and irrational. But they did assume that early human circumstances were such as to permit occasional instances of 'consciousness,' 'reason,' the envisagement of more or less explicit ends or objectives, plans using objects, instruments, and techniques as means, the exercise of foresight, judgment, choice in relation of means to ends and conditions and rules.[4]

Unlike his colleagues, Cooley was unwilling to draw a sharp distinction between reason and emotion or between so-called primitive and modern mankind. Cooley's notion of valuation, which is a precursor of Thomas's (and Znaniecki's) 'definition of the situation,' and MacIver's 'dynamic assessment,' does seem to embody essentially all of the components of the action orientation and does seem to be applicable both to early man and modern man. Cooley's concept identifies a subject oriented to an object or objects in a situation (1966, pp. 283–5). Using a scale of values or judgments of worth, the subject compares, weights, organizes, integrates, and chooses among the objects of the situation in order to solve a problem (1966, pp. 283, 289–91, 331, 338, 311, 312, 332). What works or seems to fit or integrate the situation is the criterion of choice (1966, pp. 284; 1962, p. 121). Valuation seems to imply consciousness, reflection, choice, and purposive or ends-oriented conduct. Admittedly, valuation must be conceived within the context of his analysis of suggestion, choice and moral judgment (1964, pp. 51–80, 358–60). He certainly recognized the nature and function of principles, rules, or standars in social conduct (1964, pp. 287–8, 295, 382). Though he explicitly invoked the notion of ends, he only infrequently used means–ends as such (1962, p. 261).

The second development involves Herbert Blumer's elaboration of symbolic interactionism which displays important congruence with the assumptions of social action (of the third period, c. 1930 – c. 1945), has claimed the work of George Herbert Mead as its major point of departure, and has continued to remain at the micro-theoretical, interpersonal, or social psychological level rather than successfully becoming a foundation for a more comprehensive or general theory. If Blumer's orientation is to be understood, its putative relation to Mead's views must be confronted and examined.[5] In Mead's analysis of the nature and development of human conduct the act is crucially central, though it is explicitly analyzed only in his *The Philosophy of the Act.* Signifying self-caused movement as opposed to motion caused by external impact, the act tends to set human beings apart from the rest of the animal world. According to Mead, the act emerges in the four stages of impulse, perception, manipulation, and consummation. Each stage is meaningful only in relation to its place in the total act in the situation.

The symbol is indispensable in Mead's account of the act. Once in possession of symbols, the human individual can be self-conscious and reflective. Impulse can be symbolically defined as desire and as a conscious end in view to be gratified. Perception is not merely dependent on an immediate sensuous stimulation in relation to objects in the situation. Symbols allow the individual to delay his response, to pick out particular characteristics of the objects in the situation so that they can be regarded as means to ends, to engage in internalized conversation through which the situation can be imaginatively reconstructed. Symbols permit the identification of alternatives, their organization, testing, and selection (or choice) to constitute a plan of action in advance of an overt response. Symbolic thought is thus the foundation of human reason, reflection, rational (or deliberative) choice, and the delayed response. The symbol occupies a strategic position in the human capacity to act rather than merely to behave. Mead's pragmatism does involve a reconstituted idealism. Humans can be unique: they can be subjects (of action), be conscious of means and ends, choose rationally or deliberatively in relation to one another and the situation.

It is on the intellectual foundation provided by Mead that Blumer developed his view of symbolic interaction as a reciprocal, interconnected process of (inner) symbolization, construction, or interpretation and (outer) activity or conduct involving inter-changes between aspects of the self (the 'I' and the 'me') and between self and others. Symbolic interaction is a conscious taking account of self and another or others. In taking account of self, various things and objects are indicated, defined and assessed for self; wishes, wants, and objectives, along with available means for their achievement are specified; likely actions of others are considered; different possibilities and outcomes of act for self are projected; selections are made and then pieced together; and finally the individual is organized for action (Blumer, 1969, pp. 96, 95, 15, 55).

Taking account of another means that each step in the eventual construction of a plan of action is made contingent on the assessment of the intentions and probable actions of the other. To take account of the other is to regard the other as a subject in relation to one's self as subject. 'Each has to experience the other as the initiator and director of his acts so that one can identify what the person means, what his intentions are and how he may act. Each takes the other into account as one who, in turn, is taking him into account' (Blumer, 1969, p. 109). Such awareness is the basis for a given actor's orientation of himself and direction of his own conduct.

As the exchange of symbols and overt actions occurs, each is presumably ready to reconstruct his definitions of the other and his action contingent upon what the other says and does. Each is dialectically involved with the other. Thus, a person may start his line of action, suspend, postpone, check it at one point or other, confine it to mere planning or reverie, revise it or transform it, or devise a substitute (Blumer, 1969, pp. 55, 16).

For Blumer, collective action is joint action and is thus peculiarly conscious, subjective, intentional, volitional and voluntary, inter-pretive, or constructive. Such action is an 'articulation or linkage' of individual actions which must be consciously initiated and reinitiated (Blumer, 1969, p. 17). Thus, an element of precarious-ness in sustaining the set of meanings is always present. The contingent relationship between personal–interpersonal inter-pretations (and the set of relevant meanings) and the emerging interactive conduct always makes stability problematic (Blumer, 1969, p. 18).

Schutz and phenomenological sociology

No period in the history of American sociological theory has exhibited more diversity than the years from the mid-1960s to the present. Structural-functionalism has persisted but has lost its pre-eminence. Symbolic interactionism also continues. But conflict theory (sometimes with a strongly Marxist accent and at other times without), social exchange theory (ordinarily based on some variant of behavioristic hedonism), neo-Marxist theory, critical theory (sometimes with a substantial indebtedness to Hegel as well as Marx), a (reconstituted) phenomenology and ethnomethodology, and structuralism are all part of the current theoretical scene. All are distinctively theoretical, though in many cases much more elaboration and development are possible. With the possible sole exception of the behaviorism of social exchange theory, all of them have been substantially inspired by or influenced by European antecedents.

Manifestly, not all are equally compatible with the substantial idealism, nominalism, and voluntarism of social action (whether associated or unassociated with structural functionalism) and symbolic interaction theories. Many analysts have acknowledged the evident individualism or nominalism of social exchange theory (although its behaviorism is more congruent with ontological materialism than idealism and its methodology more clearly positivistic than humanistic). Critical theory is insistent on freedom or emancipation and on moral or practical reason but it also demands a distinctive aloofness from the present social order. At the other extreme are neo-Marxism and structuralism both of which deny any compelling and distinctive status to empirical social reality and tend to espouse a social realism.

Of all of these newer intellectual developments of the last two decades, socially (or sociologically) oriented phenomenology (and ethnomethodology) is (are) the chief expositor(s) of a subjective idealism, nominalism, and voluntarism. Alfred Schutz has been the main figure in the emergence of a socially or interpersonally oriented phenomenology (and ethnomethodology). Significantly, Schutz's own views are substantially indebted to Edmund Husserl's reformulation of idealism. The 'phenomena' or phenomenology refer to that which is given indubitably in the consciousnesses of individuals and which must, therefore, not be subjected to the categories of external (physical) nature. For phenomenology, both consciousness and activity are intentional. Mind or consciousness is construed as a relation between a subject and an object, i.e., consciousness is always consciousness of something. Furthermore, human activity is always oriented by and in terms of the 'goals, projects, motives, and so on,' that human beings entertain (Winter, 1966, p. 124).

Following Husserl, Schutz also holds (1966, p. 116) that consciousness is directed toward the life-world, to which we all belong in the pre-scientific natural attitude and in which 'we, as human beings among fellow-beings, experience culture and society, take a stand with regard to their objects, are influenced by . . . and act upon them.' Characteristically, this life-world is interpersonal or intersubjective and cultural, for it involves the reciprocity of perspectives between selves and others (including the inter-changeability of standpoints). But the world of each self is not fully accessible to others even in the most intimate relationships. No one can ever inwardly experience in his or her consciousness 'the richness and particularity of the other's consciousness – if only because his [her] 'here and now' as well as . . . total biography, furnishes a unique perspective on the world' (Winter, 1966, p. 119). The meaning of the situation to the other can only be approximated roughly through common cultural understandings and the recipro-city of perspectives (based on the interchangeability of standpoints and the congruence of the system of relevances). Each then tends to take for granted that his interests are similar enough to others so that things appear similarly to all in the situation.

The common culture includes the typical course of events, meanings, and symbols of the workaday world. It provides the 'understood typifications of modes of acting and 'reasons' for acting which are available or 'at hand' in the everyday experience of the society' (Winter, 1966, p. 129). Pre-given, these typifications involve the taken-for granted understandings of how things should go and thus facilitate routine-problem-solving efforts and the management of affairs of everyday life (1966, pp. 125, 126). Such typifications tend to become interrelated as 'schemes of inter-pretation,' which 'order phases of the cultural and social world – for example, a linguistic system, a scientific system, a legal system, etc.' (1966, p. 129).

Most (individual) activity entails more than 'lived' experience or the enactment of the pre-given of the culture. It involves reflective self-consciousness in which meaning is apparent. Such meaning arises as the reflective consciousness elicits what was intended or is being intended. That is, meaning can be retrospective or prospective. The decisive criterion of meaning 'is the project of the actor,' either an anticipated or prospective state of affairs in his or her 'own pre-remembrance' or the retrospective recovery or recollection of that project as completed or elapsed. (Winter, 1966, p. 131).

But whether prospective or retrospective, the formulation of the project arises within individual consciousness and is intrinsically voluntaristic. True, the choice process appears different in the prospective as opposed to the retrospective. In the prospective, an earlier 'here and now' of the actor is assumed. 'The prospective meaning of choosing is the spontaneous creation of alternatives' using the 'pregiven materials of previous syntheses of experience' (Winter, 1966, pp. 128, 129). The process has not yet been completed. But in the retrospective, a later 'here and now' is taken as perspective and choice becomes selection among completed alternatives. Retrospective meaning 'is an allocation among fixed alternatives' (1966, p. 128). An 'illusion of determinism' is created so that the 'shaping process by which alternatives come into existence' is transmuted 'into a predetermined choice among preset alternatives' (1966, pp. 128–9).

Manifestly, the distinction between the prospective and retrospective perspectives, meanings, and choice process departs from Schutz's distinction between in-order-to and because motives. Basically, the in-order-to motive 'starts from the project and explicates the constituting of the action,' whereas 'the because motive starts from prior experiences and explicates the constitution of the project' (Winter, 1966, pp. 146–7). A prospective state of affairs in terms of what it will be when it will have happened constitutes the in-order-to motive. The project of action is the motive for acting – the why (1966, p. 146). A retrospective view 'on the meaning of experience or action treats the project as completed . . . and attempts to give an account of the conditions leading to the project' (1966, p. 146). For example, a 'retrospective view of going shopping for a hat attempts to account for' the action 'recollectively in terms of prior experiences – he had lost his hat' (1966, p. 146).

Elemental and elementary, this account of the Schutzean phenomenological stance in sociology does indicate that the position involves a basic continuity with the earlier predominant idealism, nominalism, and voluntarism of earlier American sociological theory. It must be conceded that this analysis of the founding figure of American phenomenologically-oriented sociological theory is itself only partial and preliminary. Nor is it possible to represent here the complexity and variety of the current versions of this stance.[6] Only the character of the early basic assumptions has been suggested.

Although the need for brevity has precluded consideration of the evidence of the actual dates of the several periods (*c*. 1915–30, *c*. 1930–45, *c*. 1945–65, *c*. 1965 to the present) and the bases for inferring the dominance of the theoretical orientations in the periods, the basic assumptions of the social ontology do seem to be essentially the same and thus appear to be continuous through the several periods in the history of American (macro-) sociological theory. A prevailing idealism and a voluntaristic nominalism are inferrable for the near-century duration of American sociological theory. (But all theoretical variation and divergence are not thus precluded. Evidence of exchangist, neo-Marxist, even structuralist orientations (along with the possibility of social realist assumptions) is not being denied or ignored.) All that is being argued is that the assumptions of voluntaristic nominalism appear to be continuous through different theoretical stances from the earliest to the most recent period(s) in the history of American sociological theory. Manifestly, this conclusion is tentative and preliminary and must be subject to more extensive study (akin to the inquiry of the first period and to possible additional specification, refinement, qualification, and revision). But assuming that this preliminary, tentative verdict is supported by subsequent investigation, the question must still be posed as to how the character of the inter-period prevalent assumptions can be interpreted or explained.

A 'structure' of persisting assumptions

In spite of the evident differences in the dominant theoretical orientations throughout the several periods of the history of American sociological theory, a more or less sub-surface structure of persisting basic ontological assumptions can be identified. Whether this 'structure' is a genuinely 'deep' structure akin to the 'deep structure' of (Lévi-Strauss's) transformational structuralism would be difficult to claim at this stage of theoretical inquiry.

Obviously, theorists have been aware of the ontological distinctions between a (social) materialism and a (social) idealism, between a (social) nominalism and a (social) realism, such as have been incorporated in the analytic (classificatory-periodicizing) scheme. But apart from portions of the present analysis, investigators of the broad sweep of theoretical developments have not generally identified a persisting core of basic assumptions in American (general) sociological theory. Accordingly, it appears appropriate to construe this 'structure' of persisting assumptions as sub-surface, if not also deep!

(Admittedly, it is necessary to recognize now that although this set of assumptions is attached to more broadly, generally, or comprehensively defined notions which together constitute various versions of general theory, the assumptions under consideration are more micro- than macro- in character. Except for a very few theorists, such as Parsons, little systematic effort has been directed toward the elaboration of their implications for culture, personality, group and society, for structure (e.g., of primitive and modern societies), or for change. Specifically, the assumptions concern the nature of human nature and the related bases for direct interpersonal relations and activities which can become the foundations for a persisting order or structure or group.)

To claim – in advance of the full inquiry into the nature of the dominant theoretical orientations after 1915 – that this 'structure' of assumptions should be studied in terms of a particular model of structuralism may be to risk denial by subsequent experience. For instance, the acceptance of the view that linguistic structuralism is appropriate may be confounded by contradictory results. All versions of 'theory' (of sociological theory in the future) may not necessarily possess the structure of a language and thus be analyzable in terms of syntagmatic and paradigmatic relationships. It may be to assert too much to view social nominalism and social realism as intrinsically a part of a bivalent logic. On the other hand, the genetic structuralism of Lucien Goldmann and Maurice Godelier are less dogmatically universalistic and offer an initially attractive plausibility.

What this 'structure' of social ontological assumptions insists is merely that the dominant view within and about American sociological theory holds that social reality is prevailingly idealist, nominalist, and voluntarist in nature. Specifically, these assumptions declare that:

(1) The nature of the social depends substantially and characteristically on human beings' possession of consciousness. (Presumably, this consciousness is developed naturalistically. It may be regarded as innate but more likely it will be conceived to be acquired through interaction.) Association-dissociation, interpersonal relations and activities, structure and change derive primarily, substantially, or significantly from consciousness – directly or indirectly.

(2) Although humans are considered to possess consciousness generically, each and every human organism is different from every other in terms of its genetic legacy, its constitutional attributes, and its socialization experiences. These primordial nature-nurture individual differences are the bases for differences in (individual) consciousnesses. In particular, these differences are manifested in variations in needs, wants, desires, goals, aims, ends, objectives, and wishes – all of which must be taken into account, must be made the analytic point of departure and return, in the analysis of association. This irrepressibly different sense of 'I-ness' means that the social is always inter- and multi-personally construed. The social is always a more or less personalized (but multiple) 'you' – 'I' relationship. It will tend to be a more or less genuine 'we' but it will tend to remain personal. The social cannot 'naturally' and 'normally' be impersonal or transpersonal.

(3) Constituted of selves and others, the social is believed to exist and persist, to remain the same (structurally) or to become different (change) naturally and ordinarily through will, choice, or consent. Power and coercion are ultimately immoral, reprehensible, and unnatural for American theorists. As a persisting structure of interpersonal relations and activities, the group has its existence and legitimate *raison d'être* in consensus. The failure of consensus is ordinarily taken to mean the advent of dissensus. Social change is assumed to mean (at least ultimately) a breakdown in consent and structural change becomes complete with the emergence of a new consent or consensus.

Simply and briefly put, these three assumptions signify the structure of the prevailing idealism, nominalism, and voluntarism of American sociological theory. Number one identifies idealism. Number two identifies nominalism (which is also sometimes designated as analytic individualism). Number three identifies voluntarism.

At this point, no effort has been made to identify different sub-positions within voluntaristic nominalism. (It is true that rationalistic and romantic, transcendentalist, etc., versions of idealism *might* be designated.) Eventually, it may become possible to separate out different notions or sub-positions of nominalism and voluntarism and thus arrive at a statement of different combinations and permutations of the two which could become the basis for a dynamic or transformational formulation (à la Lévi-Strauss).

Undeniably, this 'structure' of social ontological assumptions is couched or characterized relatively, i.e., in context and by comparison (coexistentially and/or sequentially). Of course, no assumption is made that the present formulation of idealism is the only one possible or that it is a full achievement or expression of idealism. (Indeed, this American version of idealism is part of a dualism.) Certainly, the present statement or characterization does not assume that this version is the only one possible. It does not assert that it is impossible for any other theory or doctrine to be more nominalistic or voluntaristic than American sociological theory has been. The present formulation must be envisaged and understood in context and by comparison.

Insistence on the contextual and comparative nature of the prevailing idealism and voluntaristic nominalism has several implications which must be made explicit now. For instance, early theory in American sociology may indeed have been less nominalistic and voluntaristic than were the views of the figures in the earlier American Social Science Association (who were not necessarily consistently committed to naturalism).[7] However, characterization can be made more fairly and appropriately by comparison with the theoretical stances of other early American social sciences or (then contemporary) versions of European sociologies. Certainly, American sociological theory appears to be indisputably more nominalistic and voluntaristic if it is juxtaposed, for instance, with the views propounded by Durkheim and his disciples. (Tarde is nominalistic but the adjective voluntaristic would appear to be disputable in his case.)

Toward a structuralist sociology of the history of sociological theory

From the very outset (as indicated in chapter 1), this study of the nature of the assumptions of early American sociological theory was envisaged as part of a broader study of the continuities and discontinuities in the assumptions of theory throughout the several periods of its history which was in turn to be related to continuities and discontinuities in the structure of American society, academia, the social sciences, and sociology. In brief, this study has been conceived as contributing finally to the sociology of the history of sociological theory. The preliminary identification of a (persisting) sub-surface structure of assumptions in the modern structuralist sense also suggests the possibility of the appropriation of the methodology of structuralism, and especially genetic structuralism, as a basic approach to a sociology of sociology. (In spite of his transformationalism, Lévi-Strauss has tended to conceive of his structuralism as synchronic, atemporal, and ahistorical rather than diachronic, temporal, and historical. However, such genetic structuralists as Goldmann and Godelier are by no means in opposition to the study of discontinuity, or change in the passage of time, or to the admission of a historical or diachronic interest. For them, structuralist explanation is to occur by placing any problematic (or partial) structure within the context of a broader or more comprehensive structure or structures. Fundamentally, then, the holism or contextualism of a structural sociology of sociology seems to be highly congruent and compatible with more conventional notions of the sociology of sociology.)

What this procedure of explanation entails, therefore, is the resort to increasingly more comprehensive contexts. It means first the relating of assumptions of dominant orientations from different periods in the history of theory to the broader continuities-discontinuities in the history of sociology as a discipline and profession, then to the continuities-discontinuities in the history of the social sciences (both intellectually and professionally), thirdly to the continuities-discontinuities in the history of academia (both intellectually and professionally), and finally to the continuities-discontinuities in the major periods of the structure of American society and culture. In the broadest context, inquiry would especially involve an effort to relate values and social structure, especially to juxtapose seeming continuities or persistencies in values vis-à-vis shifts or modifications in social structure or, conversely, discontinuities or alterations in values against possible continuities or persistencies in social structure. (Certainly, the waning of supernaturalism, the concern with individual life, self, ego or personality (and the reality of individual experience), equality, freedom, (personalized) morality, activism, and practicality would seem to be among the most relevant of basic American values.) It also appears that explanation of the persisting structure of theoretic assumptions involves a set of peculiarly dialectical relationships between and among theory and sociology as a discipline and profession, the intellectual assumptions and organization of the social sciences, the assumptions-values and structure of higher education (including the nature of knowledge-science), and the very nature of the major values and basic structure of American society itself.

Notes

Chapter 1 Sociological history of theory

1 Except for the figures on New York University, the data are drawn from official figures of the departments or universities in question; e.g., the appendix of Faris's *Chicago Sociology 1920–1932* (1967), pp. 135–7, and from *Theses of the University of Chicago, Doctors of Philosophy, June 1893–December 1921* (Chicago, Ill., Harper Memorial Library, University of Chicago, n.d.), pp. 19–22 (on Sociology and Anthropology); *A Bibliography of the Faculty of Political Science of Columbia University 1880–1930* (Columbia University Press, 1931), pp. 316–28, 345–52, and (Columbia University) *Studies in History, Economics, and Public Law*, ed. by the Faculty of Political Science, (Columbia University Press), vol. V (1896) –vol. LXVII (1915); a mimeographed report of the Department of Sociology, Yale University, entitled 'Doctors of Philosophy (Sociology), Yale University, 1899–1930' (and drawn from *Doctors of Philosophy 1861–1960*, New Haven, Conn., 1961); 'Doctors of Philosophy of the Graduate School, 1889–1927, University of Pennsylvania,' *University of Pennsylvania Bulletin*, vol. 28, no. 7 (November 12, 1927, Philadelphia, 1927), pp. 113–15 (Sociology); Cooley, 1969, p. 11; personal communication from the Chairman (Michael Aiken), Department of Sociology, University of Wisconsin at Madison, October 25, 1978. Figures on New York University are derived from G. Albert Lunday's *Sociology Dissertations in American Universities, 1893–1966*, (East Texas State University, 1969). Unfortunately, Lunday does not indicate the sources of his data which diverge substantially from the above official count. According to him, fifty-six Ph.D.s in sociology had been awarded by American universities by 1915: twenty-seven by the University of Chicago, eight by Columbia, eleven by the University of Pennsylvania, two by Yale, and eight by New York University.

329

2 Information has been drawn from Paul J. Baker, Martha P. Long, and Susan L. Quensel, 'The Pioneers of American Sociology: An Empirical Study' (unpublished paper presented at the 68th annual meeting of the American Sociological Association, New York, August 1973), especially revised calculations of Table 4.

Chapter 2 Contexts of early theory

1 For an earlier presentation of the context(s) of early sociology (the objective of which was somewhat different), see Hinkle and Hinkle (1954, pp. 1–4). Consult also Oberschall's article, 'The Institutionalization of American Sociology,' in A. Oberschall (ed.), *The Establishment of Empirical Sociology* (1972).
2 Consult, among others, F. L. Allen's *The Big Change* (1952), G. D. Nash's *The Great Transition* (1971), C. N. Glaab's *The American City* (1963), A. D. Chandler's article on corporations in S. E. Ambrose (ed.), *Institutions in Modern America* (1967). See also C. A. Ellwood's *Sociology and Modern Social Problems* (1910), J. R. Commons's *Races and Immigrants in America* (1967; originally 1907), H. P. Fairchild's *Immigration* (1920), and E. P. Hutchinson's *Immigrants and Their Children, 1850–1959* (1956).
3 Austria-Hungary was an ethnically heterogeneous entity constituted of Germans, Slavs (Czechs, or Bohemians, Moravians, Slovaks, Poles, and Ruthenians), Magyars, some Italians, and Jews. (The separate segment of 'Greece, Servia, Romania, etc.' presumably also includes Croatians, Dalmatians, and Slovenians who are politically part of Austria-Hungary.) The designation 'Russia' also conceals considerable heterogeneity. Specialists at the time argued that only a very small percentage were actually Russian as such. (H. P. Fairchild (1920, p. 139) insisted that only about one-tenth of those so designated actually were Russians, whereas Commons (1967, p. 87) held that only 2 per cent were ethnically Russian.) The rest were Poles, Lithuanians, Finns, Germans, and Jews.
4 Originally, the section on basic American values was almost as long as the present total chapter on contexts. For relevant analyses, see: T. C. Cochran's chapter in R. E. Spiller and E. Larrabee (eds), *American Perspectives* (1961), H. S. Commager's chapter in J. W. Chase (ed.) *Years of the Modern* (1949), M. Curti, *The Growth of American Thought* (1951), A. A. Ekirsch, *The Idea of Progress in America, 1815–1860* (1944). R. H. Gabriel, *American Values* (1974), P. Miller, *The Life of the Mind in America* (1965), R. Welter's article in the *Journal of the History of Ideas*, 1955, R. M. Williams, Jr, *American Society* (1952), and I. G. Wyllie, *The Self-Made Man in America* (1954).
5 The interpretation in this section is indebted primarily to L. R. Veysey, *The Emergence of the American University* (1965) and to R. Hofstadter and C. DeW. Hardy, *The Development and Scope of Higher Education in the United States* (1952).

6 Data are drawn from the *Statistical Abstracts of the United States*, 1952, Table 142, p. 121. See also Veysey (1965, p. 4).

7 Information in the following three paragraphs derives from an unpublished study of Dorothy Ross, 'The Development of the Social Sciences in America, 1865–1920,' pp. 13–14.

8 The required data have been difficult to secure. But see L. L. Bernard (1909), some amplifications and corrections are included in A. W. Small (1916); F. A. Tolman (1902); H. Becker and H. E. Barnes (1952), vol. II, pp. 953–1001.

9 Cooley's own *Human Nature and the Social Order* (1964) is a warning that infrequency of a citation does not necessarily signify the (relative) insignificance of a figure. Tarde is by no means one of the most frequently cited figures but he is basically an important person in the development of Cooley's own notion of suggestion in chapter II on 'Suggestion and Choice.'

Chapter 3 In the view of a scheme

1 See, for instance, Ward (1908), Giddings (1896, pp. x, xi), Ross (1919, pp. vii, ix), Small (1905 (subtitle)), Cooley (1969 (title), pp. 270, 283).

2 The earliest formulation of a scheme was contained in my paper on 'The Structure of the History of Sociological Theory,' which was presented to the 64th Annual meeting of the American Sociological Association in 1969. A revised version of the scheme was published as part of the author's 'Basic Orientations of the Founding Fathers of American Sociology' (1975, pp. 108–9). Certainly, additional modifications of the scheme are likely.

Certain criteria have been important in the construction of the scheme:

(a) Classifying periodicizing categories should be based on all of the fundamental problems of the discipline (e.g., genesis).

(b) They should be derived from what are basic and generic to the phenomena in question (e.g., association).

(c) They should be constructed in accordance with the requirements of logic and express the *fundamentum divisionis* of the subject (e.g., statics and dynamics).

(d) They should embody what is both historically uniform and continuous and multiform and discontinuous, so that both continuities and discontinuities in time can be identified (e.g., shift from problem of dynamics to statics).

(e) They should permit further differentiation and specification (i.e., subclassification and subperiodicization, e.g., idealism – subjective idealism – objective idealism – rational idealism – romantic idealism).

(f) They should be expressed in a terminology that at least articulates with, and preferably is in fact an extension of, broad and basic distinctions in the social and natural sciences, the humanities and philosophy (e.g., materialism – idealism, atomism – holism, nominalism – realism).

3 Cooley holds (1966, pp. 27–8), 'All are equally real and all are aspects

of a common whole.' Each one has its distinctive unity of parts and each has its distinctive tendency to change within a total life-history (1966, p. 14). Each organic unity or system is also interconnected with and understandable only in relation to the other two. If all persons were removed, for instance, 'there would be nothing left, the other system would be gone too, because their [concrete] constituents are the same' (1966, p. 6). Conversely, the withdrawal of culture or idea-systems would leave nothing – 'certainly no personality' (1966, p. 6).

4 Evolutionary naturalism is manifestly an orientation which has apparently characterized many of the biological and social sciences at some point in their development. Consult P. F. Boller, Jr, *American Thought in Transition* (1969). For manifestation of the orientation in psychology, H. Cravens and J. C. Burnham's 'Psychology and Evolutionary Naturalism in American Thought, 1890–1940' (1971) is relevant.

Understandably, the explicitness and elaborateness of the commitment of early American sociologists to evolutionary naturalism varied considerably. Ward and Giddings offer the most umambiguous and developed statements of the position (Ward, 1970, pp. 71, 76–9, 80, 85, 90–6, 99–101, 173–6, 178–9; Giddings, 1896, pp. 7–11, 17–20, 21–45, 363–419). By contrast, Small and Cooley provide less explicit and less elaborate accounts (Small, 1905, pp. 408, 420, 426–7, 478; Cooley, 1964, p. 4; 1962, p. 255; 1966, pp. 49, 44, 26; 1969, p. 240). Cooley's holism (or organicism) was vitally related to an evolutionism, which may have been somewhat less obvious in Small. Sumner's evolutionary naturalism is considered by Stow Persons in Sumner's *Social Darwinism: Selected Essays of William Graham Sumner* (1881, reprinted 1963).

5 Ward, Ross, and Small used the designation 'social forces' as an explicit and fundamental concept in their theories. Sumner and Keller employed the terms 'socializing forces' and 'societal forces' as central, though less conspicuous, notions. Giddings used 'socializing forces,' 'social forces,' and 'societal forces,' with the first meaning the forces creating association and society and the last two the forces society itself creates. Presumably he was influenced by Sumner's and Keller's implicit distinction between 'socializing forces' as the stimuli producing original association and 'societal forces' as the associationally-derived influences affecting the nature of society once it has been formed. Cooley rarely employed the social forces notion but his concept of primary ideals or primary sentiments fulfilled a somewhat similar intellectual function in his idealist theoretical orientation. (Consult especially Ward (1970, pp. 256–65), Sumner (1959, pp. 18–19), Giddings (1898, pp. 126–7; 1901, pp. 67–8), Ross (1919, pp. 167–8, 169), Small (1905, pp. 447–68).)

Certainly, Cooley's commitments to an idealist view of social reality and to the related (or humanistic) view of how that reality should be studied were inimical to the adoption of the social forces concept with its materialistic, mechanistic, and positivistic implications. Indeed, he disavowed such implications. Cooley did not regard human social life as explicable as a mere extension of either matter in motion or animal evolution. He certainly did not deny that man had received a hereditary legacy from the evolution of the hominid organism. But he did not accept instinctive hereditary mechanisms as simple explanations of man's social behavior. His own emphasis on plasticity and teachability as the distinctive attributes of man's organic legacy and his comparatively precise and explicit conception of heredity, environment, and learning precludes the vagueness and indefiniteness of the notions of heredity and environment which seem to be associated with the social forces notion as used by other sociologists (Cooley, 1966, pp. 199, 200; and 1927, pp. 160–2). He refused to conceive of social structure and social change, or personality and culture, as organically (or materialistically) dictated by certain fixed organic mechanisms. He recognizes that heredity determines breathing, sucking, crying of infants, and even walking and such physical features as hair, shape of the head, height, pigmentation, and racial differences (1964, pp. 22, 7). He even suggests (1965, p. 202) that hereditary racial and ethnic differences in responsiveness to certain ideas may exist. He accepts (1964, pp. 7, 18) the existence of inherited differences in mental endowment in intellectual abilities, 'capacity, aptitude, disposition,' temperament, emotional gifts, 'lines of teachability, or whatever else we may call the vague psychical tendencies that all of us are born with.' But man does not possess instincts in the sense of a 'system of fixed hereditary responses to fixed stimuli' (1966, pp. 198, 199). Consequently, the word 'instinct' cannot and should not be applied to most human behavior (1964, p. 24). However, human emotions do include 'a hereditary element which seems to remain much the same under the most diverse manifestations' and, accordingly, he refers to 'instinctive emotional dispositions of several kinds' (1964, pp. 24, 25, 30, 170; see also below). Still, all such emotional dispositions are rapidly developed, altered, 'transformed, and interwoven by social experience' so that they become distinctive for different epochs and societies (1964, p. 27). Unlike some of his colleagues who accepted the social forces notion, Cooley does not seem to have been a Lamarckian.

6 All of the major early theorists were cognizant of the contents of the three varieties of social forces, irrespective of the distinctive terms used. Sociologists did vary in the extent to which all three of the above varieties are included within the social forces designation or some cognate term. Giddings and Ellwood are illustrative of sociologists who essentially recognize and accept all types of forces. Sumner and Keller acknowledge both the second and third varieties as forces, though as Darwinists their sensitivities to environmental conditions cannot be questioned.

7 Fundamentally, the human social forces may be divided into two varieties, one original, natural, and physical or organic and the other derived, spiritual, or cultural. The first variety constitutes an organic base of appetites, needs, and wants which humankind shares with the animal kingdom and which involve organic individual (or ontogenetic) and species (or phylogenetic) requirements for survival. Included are hunger, thirst, and demand for bodily protection and physical well-being of the individual, as designated by (Ward's) 'forces of individual

preservation,' (Small's) 'health interest,' (Ross's) 'appetitive desire,' (and Sumner's and Keller's) 'hunger want.' (Both Sumner and Keller and Ward derive economic and technological needs respectively from 'hunger' and the 'forces of individual preservation,' but Small proposed a separate 'wealth interest.') Ward and Sumner and Keller also have second special categories specifying the need for the preservation of the species as represented respectively by 'the forces of race [or species] continuance' and 'sex (-love).' Small's 'health interest' and Ross's 'appetitive desire' also include a sex impulse.

Ward, Sumner and Keller, Small, and Ross also proposed the existence of a second variety of derived, non-organic (or psychic), and cultural (social) forces. Ward elaborated 'moral,' 'aesthetic' and 'intellectual forces' which are paralleled by Small's 'rightness,' 'beauty,' and 'knowledge' interests and by Ross's 'ethical,' 'aesthetic,' and 'intellectual' desires. Sumner and Keller and Ross designated respectively a separate 'ghost-fear' or 'religious' desire. Ross's 'egotic' desire is essentially the equivalent of Sumner's and Keller's 'vanity' or 'self-gratification' impulse which also includes Ross's 'recreative' desire. Small's 'sociability interest,' a demand for contacts with other persons which is based on an 'instinct of personal integrity' (an instinctive assertion of the equal right of personal individuality in relation to others) and a 'craving for reciprocal valuation' or esteem from others, has no parallel in the other taxonomies of social forces. Ross's 'hedonic' desires (fear, aversion to pain, love of warmth, ease and sensuous pleasure) are apparently implied in Ward's 'forces of individual preservation,' Small's 'health interest,' and perhaps even in Sumner's and Keller's 'ghost-fear.' No other social forces theorist seems to have developed a category closely corresponding to Ross's 'affective' desires: the socially or interpersonally oriented sympathy, sociability, love, hate, spite, jealousy, anger, revenge. (Although Cooley never used the social forces as a major concept in his sytem, his instinctive emotional 'dispositions to anger, to fear, to maternal love, to male and female sexual love, and to the emotion of self-assertion or power' certainly do resemble certain of the previous social forces (1964, p. 25).)

8 No more basic dichotomy in the history of Western thought seems to be available for characterizing the nature of social reality than that of materialism and idealism. But in this instance also the impact of evolutionary naturalism is evident. Interestingly, Ward seems to relate consciousness to feeling and feeling in turn to irritability (1970, pp. 101–2, 94–5), which tends to make mind an epiphenomenon (1970, p. 128), to construe it as having an evolutionary origin in the more primitive forms of life. Even Cooley claims 'the rudiments of consciousness and will may be discerned or inferred in the simplest reaction of the lowest living creature' (1964, p. 53). (However, Cooley is the only one among the founders of the discipline who emphasized the peculiarly dialectical relationship between self and others in the genesis

of human consciousness.) Giddings's objections to the notions of J. M. Baldwin – who occupied a somewhat enigmatic position in relation to early American sociology – are illuminating (1922, pp. 162–3, but more especially 1900, pp. 29–40).

Chapter 4 Social epistemological-methodological theories

1 Technically, Cooley seems to have accepted interaction rather than causation as an explanatory formula. As an organicist or holist, he insisted (1966, pp. 44–5) that 'No factor of life can exist for men except as it is merged in the organic system and becomes an effect as much as a cause of the total development. . . What observation shows is a universal interaction, in which no factor appears antecedent to the rest.' Causation seems to entail particularisms for Cooley.

2 Ross conceded (1919, p. 41) that the regularities and constant relations which sociology discovers are likely to be devoid of 'some of the precision and absoluteness of physical and chemical laws.' Sociology can rarely achieve 'anything better than an empirical law. Few, indeed, are the formulas that can be so phrased as to hold for all occasions and circumstances' (1919, p. 41).

3 To those acquainted with the recognized authors of *The Science of Society*, the referential use of Sumner (1927) or Keller (1927) rather than Sumner and Keller (1927) may appear to be a perverse and unwarranted departure from past citational practice. However, the assumption that joint authorship means equal intellectual involvement and responsibility on the part of the two persons is not valid in the case of *The Science of Society*. Keller has acknowledged that he alone determined the contents of the four volumes. He designated Sumner as senior author—seventeen years after the latter's death—in order to provide recognition of basic indebtedness to his mentor (see n. 1 to chapter 9 below). Moreover, any justification of Keller's decision on grounds of known intellectual similarity between himself and Sumner seems to rest more on Keller's own claim (and its widespread acceptance) than on independently confirmed fact. Indeed, a recent investigation of the theories of social change of the two sociologists – using heretofore unexamined (unpublished) manuscripts – reveals substantial divergence in their positions (consult also n. 1 to chapter 9). Accordingly, the present monograph has attempted to identify differences in involvement and responsibility by use of three forms of reference: Sumner (1927) for those few passages of which he was the explicitly recognized author; Keller (1927) for authorship of the overwhelming majority of chapters and sections in *The Science of Society*; and Sumner and Keller (1927) for a limited number of cases of evident intellectual agreement between the two.

4 F. J. Teggart (1977, pp. 5–6, 57, 85, 89–93, 104, 108, 111, 117, 171–2; 219) has provided an account of the Aristotelian view and its trans-

mission to modern social science through Descartes and Comte (cf. K. E. Bock, 1956, pp. 48–53, 5–17, 64–7, 82, 85).

5 See also Teggart (1977) as above.

6 An apt exemplification is to be found in sociologists' (Small, Cooley, Ward) and historians' (G. L. Burr and W. M. West) reactions to Giddings's paper on 'A Theory of Social Causation,' *Publications of the American Economic Association*, 3rd series, vol. 5 (1904), pp. 419–25, 426–31, 431–34, 434–37, 437–43 (pages are listed in accordance with the indicated order of authors).

7 A positivistic methodology must be understood in relation to more general intellectual positivist philosophy and the positivistic movement. Admittedly, the adjective 'positivistic' can and has carried a variety of meanings – perhaps as many as the noun 'positivism' itself. For a contemporary analysis, see Anthony Giddens, 'Introduction' to *Positivism and Sociology* (1974), especially pp. 3–4. Gouldner (1970) offers a study of the original French context of the term (pp. 94–102). Consult also Leszek Kolakowski, *The Alienation of Reason* (1968), especially pp. 1–10; Jürgen Habermas, *Knowledge and Human Interests* (1972), pp. 67–90; F. R. Dallmayr and T. A. McCarthy, 'Introduction' (to the Positivistic Reception), *Understanding and Social Inquiry* (1977), pp. 77–80; and Nicola Abbagnano, 'Positivism,' in *Encyclopedia of Philosophy*, vol. 6, 1967.

8 The comparative method tends to involve an association between temporalism and developmentalism because it is generally employed with the organic growth model of (human) societal change. See chapter 8, p. 194 on The Analogy or Model, below.

9 Sumner adopts (1914, p. 331) a variation of this assumption when he declares that American society at the time he lived displayed 'every intervening stage through which our society has passed in two hundred years.'

At least some sociologists disputed the view that the ethnographic present of modern times actually contains exemplifications of all varieties (and thus stages) in the development of human society. Ward claims that because all branches of mankind have been subjected to some social change, no society can presently be found in the aboriginal, primordial condition of earliest mankind. No race or people is 'very near the base of the [developmental or evolutionary] scale' (1970, p. 449). Small argues (1905, pp. 209–10) that 'we have only the most dubious scientific sanction for assuming that we know the "original" social condition.' Keller warns (1915, p. 50) that in both organic and societal evolution 'there can be no comprehensive view of variation over long epochs' because 'transitional, non-advantageous variants' tend to be eliminated. In both lines of evolution, 'many a mean between extremes has been preserved, if at all, only under the protection of isolation or in the form of a fossil or survival' (1915, p. 50).

10 Although evidence of a prevailing epistemological idealism is found in all of his volumes, it is most obvious in the article on 'The Roots of

Social Knowledge' in *Sociological Theory and Social Research*, in chapters on 'Intelligence and Social Function,' 'Social Science,' and 'Art and Social Idealism' in *Social Process*, and in sections on 'Art, Science and Sociology,' 'Thinking,' and the 'Larger Life' in *Life and the Student*. (For an earlier version of this analysis of his prevailing epistemological idealism, consult R. Hinkle, 1967, pp. 7–8, including footnotes on these pages.)

11 Cooley's divisions into personal, social knowledge and spatial, material knowledge are reminiscent of Dilthey's 'Naturwissenschaften' and 'Geisteswissenschaften,' although he makes no explicit reference to Dilthey. (See especially *Sociological Theory and Social Research*, pp. 289–309, and *Social Process*, pp. 395–404.) Cooley actually used the term 'humanistic studies' (one of the English translations of 'Geisteswissenschaften') in *Life and the Student*, p. 145. As one of the humanistic studies, sociology would apparently use typologies. Note his endorsement of the development of various kinds of types in *Social Organization*, p. 22, and *Social Process*, pp. 198, 201.

Chapter 5 Social origins

1 Indeed, the stance of early social science, including sociology, cannot be understood without a recognition of the basic opposition of conservative-fundamentalist Protestantism and its vigorous espousal of supernaturalism as against the naturalism of evolutionary science. Certain aspects of this conflict are revealed in the article of J. D. Heyl and B. S. Heyl, 'The Sumner–Porter Controversy at Yale: Pre-Paradigmatic Sociology and Institutional Crisis' (1976).

2 To note, as Ward did (1970, pp. 548, 511, 378), that man 'acquired the social habit' and that he 'early saw the advantages of association' is certainly to argue for the existence of a 'presocial man.' According to Ward (1898, p. 90), apes and monkeys 'can scarcely be regarded as gregarious.' Certainly, the simian-like (Ward does not use the term 'primate') animal from which man has been descended 'was not even gregarious by instinct' (1898, p. 90). In addition, modern exploration and research have discovered contemporary primitive peoples who 'scarcely possess anything that can be called society, and seem to live solitary lives or in pairs, the children separating as soon as able to subsist alone' (1968, I, p. 454). Accordingly, Ward postulates an earliest solitary or autarchic stage of human existence. It was a presocial condition in which 'man must have been as far removed from a social state as is possible for a species to be and continue propagation of its kind' (1968, I, p. 464).

Although Sumner is not as direct and explicit about the earliest condition of humankind as might be desired, his intellectual expositor and academic successor, Keller, is unmistakably definite. 'As we retrace the course of civilization toward its beginnings, we note a progressive shrinkage in both the extent and complexity of association' (1927, p.

15). Less 'and less perfect types of association' are encountered until, by inference, association substantially ceases (1927, p. 15). Cases drawn from the life of primitive societies show 'that the capacity to live in society is not there at the outset, but has to be won' (1927, p. 13). Certainly, early man was not 'outfitted with any innate quality of sociability' or gregariousness (1927, pp. 11, 12).

Ross concedes that we 'do not know whether our simian ancestor was most akin to the solitary ape, or to the sociable chimpanzee, but it is safe to say that man was never so thoroughly sociable as the horse, the prairie dog, or the grass-eating animals generally' (1969, p. 14). Even in the best strains of early man, 'the gregarious instincts do not seem to have very long roots' (1969, p. 14). Humankind's 'social union comes late and is not easy to maintain' (1969, p. 14). The import of Ross's argument about the increasing emphasis on altruistic, social, and amiable dispositions in biopsychic evolution (1969, pp. 7–8) does suggest earlier human nature characteristics which are associated with the position of earliest human isolation, solitude, and atomism adopted by Ward and by Sumner and Keller.

3 Giddings contended that all 'existing varieties of human beings are social,' including the lowest savage hordes who possess 'sympathetic instincts and habits of cooperation' in some degree (1898, p. 232). Apes and monkeys – the animals most nearly approaching man in anatomical and psychological characteristics – are predominantly social in instinct, habit, and affections (1898, p. 233). To assume that man as a social creature had derived from a non-social and isolated form intermediate to the 'social species from which man is known to be descended' would be strange and unwarranted (1898, p. 233).

Small's concurrence with Giddings's position is also indicated by the former's remark that it 'is probably nearer the truth to suppose that originally individuals were differentiations of groups than to suppose that groups were syntheses of individuals' (1905, p. 208).

Cooley's declaration that the assemblies of early man 'are possibly more ancient than human nature itself' is also an assertion that the 'evolution of group life' preceded the origin of humankind as a distinguishable variety of organism (1962, p. 109).

4 Cooley did remark (1962, p. 69) that the word 'usually goes before, leading and kindling the idea' so that 'we should not have the latter if we did not have the word first.'

5 Giddings observes, for instance, that men's variable inheritance of egoism, the persistence of 'instincts of conflict, which are kept alive by the necessity of destroying life to maintain life,' the presence of 'original differences of nature and habitat that have not been blended or neutralized' in the human aggregate, and the inconsistencies of imitations are major sources of conflict among emerging human beings. In addition, the recurrent threat of natural crises or calamities (e.g. starvation) is also a basis for severe conflict (1896, p. 113).

6 Small's actual listing of processes is somewhat more extensive: association (attraction), dissociation (repulsion and conflict), accommodation, differentiation, individualization, moralization, socialization, assimilation, and integration.

7 Giddings separates subjective from more objective processes, with the former only vaguely and the latter more clearly demarked. For the former, see *The Elements of Sociology*, pp. 58–65; and for the latter, consult the analyses of communication, association, assimilation, and cooperation in the same work, pp. 67, 49, 70, 77.

8 Early, if not earliest, man is moved by the 'daily flow and ebb of energy, the unsteady pull of instinct, the rhythm of appetite, the irregular pulse of desire, the explosions of passions' (Ross, 1969, p. 180).

Chapter 6 Primordial social structure

1 In some of Ward's earlier works, the concept of social consciousness occupies a central position. His *The Psychic Factors of Civilization* includes chapters on 'Social Consciousness,' 'Social Will,' and 'Social Intellect.' These ideas are not, however, rigorously developed. Social consciousness seems to mean the composite consciousness of individuals (in an aggregate) about the feelings of one another (possibly towards others). Government is the organ by which such consciousness is ascertained and appropriate action taken. In his later *Pure Sociology*, social consciousness loses its conceptual prominence. It is also conceived as the 'product of the spontaneous creative synthesis of all individual [consciousnesses or] minds' (1970, p. 91). It exists as an average, somewhere between the lowest and highest psychic phenomena of individual members of the aggregate (1970, p. 91).

2 American sociologists today generally credit Sumner with coining the term 'ethnocentrism' – apparently unaware that Sumner was thoroughly acquainted with Gumplowicz's early *Der Rassenkampf*, a last section of which is entitled 'Ethnocentrismus'!

3 They essentially view an institution as 'the most general and appropriate name for social structure' (Ward, 1970, p. 185; cf. Small and Vincent, 1971, p. 270). But structure or organization is invariably regarded as adaptive, instrumental, or utility-oriented. Small and Vincent thus construe institutions as 'attempted solutions to the problem of social adjustment' (1971, p. 61).

4 Small regards institutions as stemming especially from human beings, conscious, subjectively-issuing adjustments of their varying convergent and/or divergent interests (1905, pp. 174, 526; cf. pp. 619–20).

5 Basic too in the emergence of the institution is the equilibration of a perpetual and vigorous struggle among antagonistic and more or less conscious desires (as based on social forces) in accordance with the basic principle of synergy.

6 Thus, Ward invoked the notions of 'mos' and 'mores,' but later sociologists ignored his use and associated the terms with Sumner.

7 Sumner's notion of institution does presuppose and build upon his ideas about the folkways and mores, but the notion of institution is a more complex structure than a single mos, folkway, or even law. It entails a series of folkways and laws in a complex society. By interlinking several mores (and folkways) to form a system of prescribed positions for persons who are in persisting, enduring relations, the institution is a mechanism of organization affording prescribed routines of cooperation. The activities become publicly approved and enforced (or sanctioned) (1959, pp. 54). They have been 'instituted' or established (1959, p. 55). The persons who engage in the activities have rights and duties associated with their 'prescribed positions' or statuses (1959, p. 55).

Basically, his notion of institution as constituted of a concept and structure is consistent with his behavioristic materialism. Apparently, the concept develops around a need and functions more or less as an end or its equivalent, whereas the structure functions as a means to satisfy the need. In primitive societies, the concept is represented rudimentarily as an interest, which – Keller cautions – 'is sensed rather than consciously realized' (1927, p. 523). The concept is found in civilized societies as an idea, notion, or abstract doctrine 'upon which the institution in question is formed' (1927, p. 522; cf. Sumner, 1959, p. 53). Whether in primitive or in modern societies, the concept really stands for a need so fundamental and, apparently, multi-dimensional, as to evoke the development of a cluster of mores (cf. 1959, p. 395). As a means, the structure 'is a framework, or apparatus, or perhaps only a number of functionaries set to cooperate in prescribed ways at a certain conjuncture' (1959, p. 53). Prerequisite, of course, to the development of structure is the emergence of persisting or enduring relationships as engendered by a basic or fundamental interest (1959, p. 395). Structure is evident in a definite and specific 'system of acts,' which are defined by rules,' consist of 'prescribed positions,' and involve the use of 'apparatus,' materials or instrumentalities by the functionaries in a cooperative endeavor (1959, pp. 395, 4).

8 Published some nine years earlier than Ross's *Foundations of Sociology* and perhaps a precedent for Ross's position, Giddings's *The Principles of Sociology* (1896, p. 314), defines social institutions in terms of coercive sanctions. According to Giddings, the coercive sovereign power of the state establishes institutions by consciously, purposively, and systematically authorizing and sanctioning social relations. This reference to consciousness and purposiveness accords, of course, with the broader idealistic component of Giddings's consciousness of kind.

9 His analyses tend to be scattered and fragmentary. For his notion of rules, see especially *Social Process*, p. 384, *Social Organization*, pp.

42–3, and *Human Nature and the Social Order*, pp. 371–5. Values are accorded relatively extensive treatment in *Social Process*, pp. 283–5, 293. Also treated in a number of different contexts in his several works, his notion of institution suggests the possibility of a more systematic and coherent formulation. When the varied instances are integrated and synthesized, they reveal a view of institutions that is pervaded by idealism with a strong emphasis on affectivity, holism, and – to some extent – spontaneity. Cooley regards institutions as having evolved essentially as instrumental elaborations of a rule or rules which serve to adjust and satisfy the basic sentiments or permanent 'needs of human nature' in relation to a recurrent situation (1962, pp. 55, 57, 71). Basically, institutions consist of 'enduring sentiments, beliefs, customs and [permanent] symbols,' such as laws, constitutions, and sacred writings (1962, p. 313; 1964, p. 166). The adaptive quality of institutions is evident in Cooley's claim that they embody 'the sober and tried goodness of the ages, the deposit, little by little, of what has been found practicable in the wayward and transient outreachings of human idealism' (1962, p. 322). Each institution is 'an organic whole of transmitted ideas which has the power to enlist the activities of a group, but does not, for the most part, originate within the group, and cannot be explained as a mere product of their personalities' (1969, p. 318). Institutions of a given society at any one time 'are not separable entities, but [are] rather phases of a common and at least partly homogeneous body of thought' (1962, p. 314). They 'are the "apperceptive systems" or organized attitudes of the public mind' (1962, p. 314).

As phases of social organization, institutions have the aim of expressing human nature by a system of symbols 'which are the embodiment and vehicle of the idea' (1962, p. 343). Initially, spirit and symbol are 'vitally united and the idea is really conveyed' (1962, p. 343). But over time, they may become separated. The institution as symbol becomes an empty shell, largely devoid of freshness and spontaneity demanded by human nature (1962, p. 343). It comes to be more or less mechanical, routinized, and fixed in its operations; powerful, impersonal, and rigid in its procedures; specialized and organized in the purposes, activities, and involvement of its personnel. It develops its own values, which are more transient, special, historically limited, fixed, impersonal and complex. Characteristic especially of civilizations, institutions tend to operate through a network of specialized groups or associations or what Cooley termed the nucleated group.

10 See Percy S. Cohen (1968, pp. 131, 135, 148–9).
11 Sumner's more precise and elaborate exposition was foreshadowed by Ross's rudimentary account of 'group-cohesion' in the latter's *Foundations of Sociology* of 1905. Ross alludes to 'stress and danger' uniting a group 'against a common foe,' the acquisition of 'solidarity' by 'conquest and successes,' and 'war with adjacent peoples' as the basis for welding or compacting a people into a unified whole (1919, pp. 242–3).

Chapter 7 Social and societal structures

1 See nn. 3, 4, 5, 7, 8, and 9 to chapter 6. Many sociologists developed classifications of institutions. (Cooley was an exception: although he might have used the primary ideas or primary sentiments (which were in many respects the intellectual equivalents of the social forces) for this purpose, he did not.) Ward implicitly used his catalog of social forces to present the evolution of social institutions. Keller (1915, p. 133) apparently devised a classification of institutions which stemmed from Sumner's own classification of societal activities 'into societal-self-maintenance [based on hunger], self-perpetuation [founded on sex-love], and self-gratification [arising from vanity], adding to these the mental and social reactions out of which come [via ghost-fear] the religious and regulative systems' (cf. Sumner and Keller, 1927, pp. 89–90).

Other classifications were also proposed or suggested. Sumner himself distinguished between 'crescive' (arising from the gradual and 'instinctive efforts by which the mores are produced') and 'enacted' institutions (as 'products of rational invention and intention,' which occur only in 'high civilization' but on the basis of earlier antecedents (1959, p. 54)). For his part, Ward separated primary from secondary institutions. The former are the 'direct products of fundamental wants and demands of human nature, and are thus intimately connected with psychic and social energy' (Ward, 1970, p. 192). The latter are more or less 'artificial,' intentional (or telic in Ward's sense), derived, and factitious. Ross suggests (1919, pp. 61, 62) a possible classification in the distinction between 'subjective' (lying within man's mind and thus universal) and 'objective' (exterior to the mind). Giddings's differentiation (Giddings, 1922, pp. 14, 10, 11, 15, 16) of the struggle for existence into several different varieties also provides a basis for classifying institutions.

2 Ward obviously regards (1970, pp. 184–5) the social order as the integration, subordination, and coordination of the several social institutions within a society. Sumner's 'strain toward consistency' in the mores has a similar effect on the total structure of society. Sumner remarks (1959, p. 6) that the 'forms of industry, the forms of the family, the notions of property, the construction of rights, and the types of religion show the strain of consistency with each other throughout the whole history of civilization.' Presumably they are all subject to the strain toward consistency 'because they all answer their separate purposes with less friction and antagonism when they co-operate and support each other' (1959, pp. 5–6). Yet it is very evident that the distinction which Keller draws (1927, p. 2239) between primary and secondary institutions signifies that certain kinds of institutions are more important or determinative of the nature of the total structural unity than are others.

3 This list is more elaborate than the one in his *The Principles of Sociology* (1896, p. 73) and his *The Elements of Sociology* (1898, pp.

175–6). In both volumes, the analysis of social composition and social constitution is presented in terms of social evolutionary theory (Giddings, 1896, pp. 155–68; 1898, pp. 186–90). Thus, social composition arises first and is gradually superceded by social constitution. The simplest units of social composition are families (the temporary pair, the polygamous family (both polyandrous and polygynous), and the monogamous family). Families in turn are aggregated into larger units, ethnic and demotic societies. The former are represented first by hordes (or combinations of families), tribes (or aggregations of hordes, which may be either matronymic or patronymic), and confederations (of tribes). The latter (i.e., the demotic societies or civilized states) include the component groups of 'families, neighborhoods, hamlets or villages, parishes, towns, communes, cities, counties, provinces or departments, commonwealths, federal nations' (Giddings, 1898, p. 190; also 1896, pp. 168–9).

4 Presumably, sympathy in the primary group tends to make each member live 'in the imaginative contact with the minds of the others, and each finds in them the dwelling-place of his social self, or his affections, ambitions, resentments, and standards of right and wrong' (Cooley, 1962, p. 34). When a given person acts, he sees himself in terms of the judgments of others. Thus, there are both morality and unity: morality because he acts in terms of the ideals of others and unity because he links himself with them as a whole.

5 Consult Sumner (1959, pp. 12, 496), Sumner and Keller (1927, I, pp. 421, 422, III, pp. 1561, 1562, 1947, 1954–6, 1967–8; I, pp. 429–30, 427, 437, 438, 440); Ward (1970, pp. 276, 213); Giddings (1896, pp. 199–200, 336–41; 1898, pp. 255, 256, 265, 266, 186, 257, 187, 259–60).

6 Note Ward (1970, p. 205–8); Sumner and Keller (1927, pp. 702, 709); Ross (1969, pp. 18, 386); Small (1905, pp. 229, 244).

Chapter 8 Social change and evolution

1 Both Sumner (1959, pp. 45, 84) and Keller (1915, p. 45) emphasize that the mores set limits to variation and it is within the confines of these limits that the bases of (social) innovation must arise and be selected by action of the conditions of existence. Any 'perennial interest' – to which a mos is a response – 'is never more than approximately satisfied' and beyond the relatively uniform actions of the majority of the members of a group are those behaviors being abandoned because they are no longer effective and still other behaviors so far relatively untried in relation to unchanging conditions (Sumner and Keller, 1927, p. 88).

2 The first law asserts that such readiness is based on the directness of the derivation of the invention from a prior invention (in a logical chain of ideas). If an invention can be made directly from available ideas and inventions, it may be said to be in the first degree of probability. But if it depends on the emergence of logically intermediary ideas and inven-

tions, the invention is said to be in the second degree of possibility. A second law concerns the conjuncture of rare or unusual intellectual capacity and necessary ideas. Ross suggests that an invention is easy or difficult to make (and thus likely to appear sooner or later), depending on the availability or accessibility of the ideas in relation to the greater or lesser number of individuals with the requisite intellectual capacity in the population. He actually states (1912, p. 360) that 'the difficulty of making the combination of ideas for any particular invention will depend upon the number of persons who possess these ideas, and on the frequency in this number of individuals with the intellectual capacity necessary to combine the ideas into the invention.' If genius is relatively readily available and the state of inventive ideas is in the first degree of probability, the time is 'ripe' for invention (1912, pp. 359, 285). Ross suggests that this condition is indicated by the 'frequency of nearly simultaneous originations by two or more persons' (1912, p. 285).

3 Plasticity or variability in potential for change is not indefinite. The system may loose its fitness (or – as Cooley would say – 'workability' in relation) to conditions, signifying apparently that the change required from the system is beyond the limits established in the past. Such a system (or more accurately, its particular form or type) will thus fail to survive; it is destined to perish (Cooley, 1966, pp. 13–14, 30).

4 These features have been derived from a systematic study of the main analyses of both British and American investigators of social evolution as a conception of social change. For the former, see Ginsberg (1957), Burrow (1956), and Smith (1973). For the latter, consult Teggart (1977), Hildebrand's 'Introduction' to Teggart (1949), Bock in Cahnman and Boskoff (1964), and Nisbet (1969) and (1970) in McKinney and Tiryakian. See also Roscoe C. Hinkle, 'Durkheim's Evolutionary Conception of Social Change' (1976, p. 337).

5 It must be conceded that Ward does assert (1970, pp. 32–3) that only the (world-) historic races, who are associated with Occidental civilization and its preoccupation with material culture, are of concern to sociology.

6 Some theorists apparently followed Comte's precedent and distinguished between coexistential and sequential coherences of social phenomena. Giddings is illustrative. On the one hand, he defines (1896, p. 64) the comparative method as involving 'an observation of identical coherences of social phenomena [co-existing] in two or more places, or in two or more populations.' On the other hand, the 'historical method is an observation of coherences [in sequence or] through periods of time' (1896, p. 64). Both methods assume that 'phenomena that persist together, or that change together, are cause and effect, or are effects of a common cause' (1896, p. 64). And apparently both methods are to be used in conjunction with the establishment of social classification or types which presuppose that change naturally involves increasing differentiation. If the investigator 'wishes to group societies by types,

he will succeed only if he fixes his attention upon the marks and processes of social differentiation' (1896, pp. 63–4).

7 Note that Keller suggests (1915, pp. 261–2) that a frontier society 'spans the chasm' between the primitive and the civilized in its 'rapid recapitulation of societal evolution.'

8 Common human nature does signify primarily the operation of a relatively common and uniform biopsychic disposition in mankind to respond similarly to similar conditions, though this proclivity might be qualified by the admission of hereditary biogenetic differences (e.g., races). Thus, the recognition of contact, trade, emigration-immigration, war, and conquest, etc., by Ward, Giddings, and Keller in specific instances of change conjoined with the acceptance (more or less) of bipsychic unity and the involvement of particular concrete societies in a common human society tends to reduce the theoretical significance of what came to be construed as the role of contact, diffusion, and external factors in change in the 1920s.

It may be significant that as the least Darwinian of the social evolutionists Ward proposed the 'difference of potential' as a principle of social change. The notion seems to assume a peculiar intermixture of the psychic, social, and cultural in the potential for change on the part of each of two societies in contact with one another. It acknowledges the relevance of the number of accumulated social experiences with past cross-fertilizations and assimilations for future efficient production of change on the part of one society in relation to the other (Ward, 1970, pp. 232–40, 212–15). (The two societies must be different but not too different.) For Ward, a new society is a synthetic emergent of two older societies based on their differences of potential (Ward, 1970, p. 237). Ward's conception is in accord with his Hegelian dialectical notions of synergy and creative synthesis.

9 Note his insistence that 'mind obeys the Lamarckian law of exercise and is strengthened by every fresh effort put forth' (Ward, 1970, pp. 214–15; cf. pp. 34, 272, 498–504, 446). Consult also Stocking (1968, pp. 241–3, 250, 251, 253, 255–6, 258).

Chapter 9 An oppositional stance

1 The two papers were accidentally discovered by Mr Peter Bollier, Yale University archivist, in the course of a complete re-examination and re-classification of the contents of the papers in both the Keller and Sumner Collections in the Yale University Library in 1976. Their existence was reported to Mr Norman Smith who had been researching both collections of papers in the preparation of his M.A. thesis, 'William Graham Sumner, Social Evolutionism and Social Darwinism,' Department of Sociology, the Ohio State University, 1976. Only one of the two papers is complete and can be identified by its original title, 'The Application of the Notions of Evolution and Progress on the Superorganic Domain.' It consists of twenty-seven

typescript pages (plus one introductory page). Keller refers to this paper in his *Societal Evolution* (1915, p. 328) as well as to unpublished essays on 'Evolution and the Mores' and 'Sociology and Evolution,' the latter of which is to some extent summarized in the first paper located. The other unpublished paper is considerably longer than the first, comprising 114 pages. No title is evident, though the paper obviously focuses on the problem of the applicability of the notion of evolution (or more specifically 'progressive evolution') to the domain of the superorganic. It doesn't contain the 'last passages' which Keller claims to have quoted from 'Sociology and Evolution' or from 'Evolution and the Mores' (Keller, 1915, pp. 328, 247). Archivists from the Yale University Library officially identify the paper as 'Untitled Essay on Evolution,' William Graham Sumner Collection. Both papers were apparently written during the last period of Sumner's career, i.e., 1889–1910 (the date of his death), but neither one carries a specific date. Thus, the first (and shorter) paper entitled 'The Applications of the Notions . . .' is listed in the references as 'n.d.*b*' (i.e., as 'no date *b*') and the second (and longer paper) entitled 'Untitled Essay . . .' is listed in the references as 'n.d.*c*' (i.e., as 'no date *c*') to distinguish both from the large mass of writings comprising 'Early Drafts of Societology,' which is also undated and designated as 'n.d.*a*' (i.e., as 'no date *a*'). Originally the materials comprising parts of the 'Early Drafts of Societology' had been arranged in numbered boxes, but the reclassification process destroyed the older numeration. Thus, no explicit citations can be offered for quotations deriving from the writings in the 'Early Drafts of Societology ('n.d.*a*').

Keller was aware of the importance of his own acceptance of an evolutionary interpretation of social change as opposed to Sumner's rejection. On several different occasions, he acknowledged that his own social evolutionary formulation of *The Science of Society* represented a break with Sumner (e.g., Keller, 1915, pp. vii, 329, 330; 1929, p. 315; also 1927, pp. xxv, xxiv). But his apparent refusal to allow the scholarly-scientific community to have access to Sumner's own later papers on social evolution did in effect conceal the significance of the differences between himself and Sumner. In a letter which he wrote to John Chamberlain in 1944, Keller admitted that he had intentionally 'kept out of the library deposit' certain Sumner manuscripts and that he still had them in his possession at that time. Interestingly, the only one Keller specifically mentioned dealt with evolution! See 'Letter to Chamberlain' (1944), Albert G. Keller Collection, Yale University Library.

Apparently, Sumner had envisaged a magnum opus as including a consideration of social change in general and social evolution in particular. He had already developed several papers on the subject when he became preoccupied with the phenomenon of the (folkways and the) mores which he published as *Folkways* in 1907. Under pressure from Keller and others, he deleted all major sections on change (e.g.,

'Evolution and the Mores') from *Folkways*. His plans to have them published later were unrealized because he became ill and died. Keller also expressed an intention to seek their publication but he never did so and apparently retained the papers himself.

What this means is that the social evolutionism expressed in *The Science of Society* is Keller's and not Sumner's. (Sumner died in 1910 and *The Science of Society* was published in 1927.) In effect, Keller was paying homage to Sumner's memory in conferring senior authorship on his old mentor. He acknowledged (1927, p. xxv) that the four volumes of the work contain 'comparatively few passages of any length or consecutiveness which stand exactly as Professor Sumner left them.' Only 'chapter LVIII remains almost as he left it' and sections '458, 459, 460, 461, and 463 [i.e., pages 2209–47] are likewise mainly in his words' (1927, p. xxv). Keller remarks that he was 'perfectly free to omit, to add, and to alter as I saw fit; and I have done so in the spirit which he [Sumner] indicated. I am thus responsible for the book as it stands' (Sumner and Keller, 1927, p. xxiv).

Accordingly, the text of the present volume has frequently departed from the conventional practice of using only the designated authorship (i.e., Sumner and Keller, 1927) to cite *The Science of Society*. In order to represent involvement and responsibility more accurately, it has also employed Sumner (1927) in a few instances and Keller (1927) in the vast majority of instances (along with Sumner and Keller, 1927, in a limited number of cases). See n. 3 to chapter 4.

Basically, the analyses of Keller's and Sumner's positions on social change in this volume are pervasively and substantially indebted to Mr Smith's 1976 thesis cited above. See also N. E. Smith and R. C. Hinkle, 'Sumner versus Keller and the Social Evolutionism of Early American Sociology' (1979).

2 Ross's *Social Psychology* (1912) includes the social psychological processes of suggestion (suggestibility), imitation (custom imitation, conventionality imitation, rational imitation), conflict (silent and vocal), disequilibration, discussion, compromise, union, and accumulation.

3 Cooley is especially conscious of the ways in which the group's structure or organization can facilitate change by recruiting and promoting personalities with appropriate characteristics (1966, pp. 90, 96, 98, 106, 112, 125, 130, 137, 145). Individual differences can be recognized and used as a resource, and change facilitated by competitively distributing persons according to their merit, talent, and training. Subsequently to encourage and reward them for exercising energy and initiative, self-reliance and tenacity, sympathy and adaptability, intelligence and imaginative concern with the social unity as a whole is to foster those personality traits conducive to change. Emulation in terms of appropriate heroes and standards of fame and reputation can afford additional inducements to sustain personality traits favorable to innovation.

Conversely, the structure of the group – Cooley claims – may eventually come to inhibit the expression of the individual's intrinsic tendency to individualize, to vary, to deviate, to express his own uniqueness, to satisfy the primary ideals, sentiments, or human nature values inculcated by experience within primary groups. Each group has its own value system defining its own goals and standards of action. As the social structure adapts, complicates, diffferentiates, and specializes in relation to environmental exigencies, it tends to become rigid and fixed. It develops its own more transient, special, historically limited, and impersonal values (see Cooley, 1962, pp. 342, 343, 320; 1966, pp. 286–9, 300). In turn, they tend to limit, restrict, and impede the full expression of man's primary ideals, sentiments, or human nature values which initially engendered and inspired the structure. As the possibility for spontaneity, flexibility, plasticity, and individuality are narrowed and limited, the tendencies to deviation, non-conformity, and change are augmented.

Broader cultural and organizational features of a society may facilitate or impede innovation. Alluding to Tarde, both Ross (1912, p. 275) and Cooley (1962, pp. 328–9, 335–41) note that at the broadest cultural level are, for example, a society's concern with the present and the new in contrast to the past and the old, its favorable (as opposed to unfavorable) attitude toward change, its inclination to conventionalism (or conventionality-imitation rather than traditionalism and custom-imitation), its expectation of change, its commitment to progress and the future – in contrast to fixity and the past. Ross also refers (1912, p. 276) to such other characteristics as individualism, competition, catholicism, cosmopolitanism, an emphasis on rights rather than duties, and the rejection of the use of family or ancestor as a basis of personal worth. In such a society, social grading is based on 'some present fact – money, efficiency, achievement, education, or character' (1912, p. 276). Enacted law, religious proselytism, and an esteem for philanthropy are other features (1912, p. 276). Sanctioned by public opinion, honor, and self-respect rather than divine command, morality 'summons the individual to sacrifice himself for certain *wide* interests – the public, humanity, posterity, race elevation' (1912, p. 276). Both sociologists also seem to be in agreement that a democratic social organization, a common language, widespread literacy and an extensively developed system of public education, freedom of discussion, access to the varied means and content of communication and transportation, and optional occasions for cooperation are conducive to innovation (Ross, 1912, pp. 231, 234; Cooley, 1969, pp. 121–59).

4 But it is not argued that this dialectical conception is calculatingly oriented to the several meanings of the Hegelian *Aufhebung*: (as) abolish or eliminate; lift up, transcend, realize; (and) preserve. See Alfred G. Meyer, *Marxism: The Unity of Theory and Practice* (Harvard University Press, 1954), p. 37, and Shlomo Avineri, *The Social and Political Thought of Karl Marx* (Cambridge University Press, 1968), p. 37.

5 With social disorganization individual variation is sufficiently common

to disturb and possibly to destroy the articulation and conformation of individuals' activities so that they no longer appear to be parts of a system fitted to circumstances. Persistent and conspicuous departure from a relatively established norm so as to constitute a 'falling away from the standard' is degeneration. When it involves such rapid and radical alteration in a person's life conditions that intimate (primary group) association, which ordinarily functions to maintain social standards, can no longer operate effectively or is destroyed, it is termed displacement. Eventually, compliance or enforcement or both may become so weakened that the coherence of and, indeed, the very existence of, moral standards may become problematic and moral disintegration may be said to have occurred. This circumstance is likely to be accompanied in the individual by demoralization, the deterioration of stable, integrated moral norms to which he feels personally obligated to conform in overt action. These unsettled and transitional processes and conditions may prompt persons to attempt further innovations (Cooley, 1966, pp. 19, 153–4, 180–1; 1962, pp. 330, 347, 351, 352).

6 Small asserts that a judgment of utility or the calculation of consequences or costs ultimately leads to the weakening of (exclusivist) egoistic antagonisms, the emergence of a type of modus vivendi, and an advance toward recognition of the equal value in other individuals (1905, pp. 382, 332, 325). A change occurs in the judgment of the effects of conduct, in the conditions deemed relevant, or in the scope or diameter of the conditions regarded as involved (1905, p. 333).

7 Although the operation of the dialectic seems to be less evident and direct in Ross's analysis of conflict and the derivation of innovation, it is more manifest in other contexts of his inquiry. For instance, he argues that:

1. 'Just as the ego attains self-consciousness . . . through the *non*-ego [so] a nation "finds" herself through her awareness of other nations' (1919, p. 287).

2. To the extent that danger or threat is perceived, the bonds of the group tighten. To the extent that the group feels unthreatened and secure, its bonds relax (1919, p. 287).

3. The more pronounced (extensive and intensive?) is the group-to-group struggle, the less pronounced is the man-to-man struggle. And conversely, 'the more universal the man-to-man struggle, the less pronounced is the group-to-group struggle' (1919, p. 288).

4. Although the individual wishes others to accept the advancement of his own egoistic interests, he will accept from them and they from him only notions and interests which are more altruistic, solidary, and cooperative in nature. Thus, the ideas and interests which tend to be disseminated and transmitted generationally become more general, comprehensive, and elevated (1969, p. 343).

8 Ross doubts that 'ideas ever get into the blood or feelings and [that] dispositions . . . depend on particular ideas . . . Notions and beliefs do not become fixed race-characters, nor do the emotions and conduct

connected with them become congenital' (1919, p. 355 fn). *But* he does affirm that 'differences in motor and emotional response to stimulus' can and do arise among peoples due to winnowings and selections 'by the respective environments, occupations, and histories' (1919, p. 355 fn). He concedes that 'intellectual gains are indefinitely communicable' and thus 'men do not survive according to their predispositions to have or not to have a certain advantageous idea or belief' (1919, pp. 335–6 fn).

9 See his numerous references to 'races' and 'breeds' as conscious, acting groups in the chapter on 'The Causes of Race Superiority' in his *Foundations of Sociology* and also in his *Social Control*, pp. 3, 9, 10, 16, 17, 28, 32, 33, 36, 56, 60, 438–40.

10 In contrast to Ross, Cooley explicitly notes that the hereditary tendencies of human beings which are transmitted through the germ-plasm are vague and plastic and entail essentially 'lines of teachability' (1966, pp. 199, 200).

11 *Social Process*, pp. 283, 284, 285, 291, 311, 312, 331, 332, 338; also *Human Nature and the Social Order*, pp. 53, 54, 68. Choice is itself a comparatively elaborate and selective process of mental organization and synthesis of which individuals are reflectively aware and which is required by the complexity of thought, social organization, and situational demands. But the ideas constituting the hierarchy of preferences or values governing choice derive most often from the influence of suggestion – unconscious, mechanical, and reflexive in character.

12 Ross's position on social evolution seems to involve a paradox, if not an inconsistency. The isolated pieces of evidence indicated above about Ross's views regarding the features of prevailing nineteenth- and early twentieth-century social evolutionism signify that he overwhelmingly rejected social evolution, and yet the early chapters of his *Social Control* suggest that he endorsed at least what he would have regarded as some form of social evolution! He does refer to social evolution in a positive manner (1969, p. 60). Furthermore, the present author's own contribution to the introduction of the new edition of Ross's *Social Control* (p. xxv) ascribes an organic, psychic, and social evolutionism to him. Ross did hold that early man was characterized by a somewhat individually variable human biopsychic nature involving more or less certain (innate) feelings-sentiments which were selected out for survival and persistence in accordance with more or less recurrent conditions of biophysical existence. More or less similar strains of individuals are selected out and aggregates of such individuals (as breeds or races) are characterized by inherited biopsychic dispositions (e.g., sympathy, sociability, resentment). Organic and psychic evolution presumably go hand in hand. Presumably, too, social evolution arises on this biopsychic foundation. However, Ross is disinclined to postulate broad encompassing stages for the development of all mankind. He did reject much of the conventional (unilinear) social stages notion of social

evolution. He was willing to concede evolution in the different institutional spheres of human social existence, but such evolution seemed to be more divergent and multilinear than convergent and rectilinear. Ross's (own endorsed) social evolution in *Social Control* seems to refer broadly to the social changes involved in the shift from (aboriginal) primitivity to (recent civilized) modernity. Social evolution is involved in and accounts for 'the general trend in the transformation of basic human social units from communities into societies' (from communal to associational groups akin to Tönnies's *Gemeinschaft–Gesellschaft* distinction; 1969, p. xxvi). Such social evolution seems to 'entail an expansion of the population in (the) social units, in conjunction with the processes of social differentiation, organizational complexity, economic differentiation, and political organization' (1969, p. xxvi). See also pp. 12, 13, 18, 19, 20, 40, 50–61 in *Social Control*. What Ross seems to have done (as also happened much later in the 1920s) was to continue to use the term 'social evolution' but to exclude – either explicitly or implicitly – those older and more traditional assumptions with which he disagreed.

He disagreed with the Social Darwinists that social selection is the equivalent of natural selection. However, he also believed that societies (or rather their individual members) have been (and presumably still are) subject to natural selection with survival of the fittest in accordance with the biophysical conditions of existence (1969, pp. 8, 29, 60).

13 Conflict must have been present to afford selection over time (cf. 1912, p. 198). Otherwise, adaptation cannot be presumed. Because 'the longer the time elapsed [from the origin of a custom], the greater the amount of change' likely, and thus 'the older an institution, practice, or dogma, the more hopelessly out of adjustment it may be presumed to be' (1912, p. 204). Similarly, the 'fitter it was when adopted, the worse misfit [it is] today' (1912, p. 204).

14 But Cooley was not always consistent, cf. *Social Organization*, p. 112.

Chapter 11 Founding theory synopsized

1 For a preliminary analysis, see Hinkle (1975).

2 On the basis of pains occasioned by the failures or errors of past experience, individuals in the aggregate may reflect and recognize that any of them 'may so interfere with each other that all shall fail, or they may combine, and by cooperation raise their efforts against nature to a higher power' (Sumner, 1959, p. 16).

3 But in the 1920s Giddings's efforts to be objective and behavioristic required a redefinition of consciousness tantamount to a predisposition to act. (Consult Giddings, 1924, p. 14fn.)

4 Cooley rejects any sharp separation of ideas from impulse, feeling, and sentiment. Impulse and reason, feeling and idea, sentiment and concept are interrelated and interconnected. But he does claim (1962, p. 379)

that sentiment is nearer to the core of life than definable thought (cf. Cooley, 1964, p. 370; 1962, p. 177).

5 An early formulation is contained in Hinkle and Hinkle (1954, pp. v, 14–16, 73–4).

6 Pre-World War I American theorists were overwhelmingly nominalistic. E. C. Hayes, one of Small's graduate students, seems to have been the only conspicuous exception (i.e., he was favorably disposed to social realism). See J. David Lewis and Richard L. Smith, *American Sociology and Pragmatism*, chapter 6 (1980).

7 Giddings notes that it is the prevailing nature of the individual wills in the aggregate which substantially determines the character of the social volition 'when men act together in large numbers' (1898, p. 131). That volition may be (predominantly) sympathetic and impulsive, formal and conventional, or deliberative and rational. When individuals who come in contact are predominantly inclined, innately or temperamentally, to be sensitive to impressions, sympathetic and impulsive or quick to imitate, uninhibited or lacking in coolness of judgment, it is likely that their volition will be sympathetic or impulsive in nature. If individuals are prevailingly inclined to respond emotionally and thus uncritically to the confident expectation that what is desired will come true, to what Giddings terms beliefs – either from the present or the past – their judgments will be based on convention or tradition (1898, pp. 145–6). In the circumstances in which two or more individuals are capable of subjecting their 'ideas and inherited beliefs' to argument, dispute, denial, and criticism – accompanied by the presentation of reasons – a public opinion emerges and it becomes the basis for a rational or deliberative concerted volition (1898, pp. 155–6).

8 Neither Giddings's notion of interaction nor of discussion is genuinely emergentist. He construes interaction as interstimulation and response. Among men, interstimulation takes the form 'not only of accidental suggestion and example, but also intended suggestion and example; not only of unconsciously made and unanalyzed impression, but also of premeditated appeal and intended intimidation. Response takes the forms of conscious imitation, of dramatization, of conversation, of discussion and concerted action' (1922, p. 161). The consequence is the selection of some mode of thought and/or action which is construed to be adaptive to the conditions of existence.

In discussion, individuals' beliefs, ideas, and choices are compared, analyzed, and subjected to argument against one another. Eventually, the truth of the more adequately formulated and supported options is revealed until finally only one remains and is confirmed by the verdict of 'an alert and all-searching reason.' Discussion results in the more or less rational selection from the responses formulated basically by gifted or talented individuals – the 'few leading,' 'thoughtful,' or 'clever men' (1898, pp. 104, 108–9, 113–18; 1896, p. 139). It is no more emergentist than Giddings's more encompassing notion of interaction.

9 Admittedly, Cooley contends (1966, p. 418) that those nations who have rejected the extreme doctrines of utilitarian individualism for the 'idea and feeling of a transcendent collective reality' were not wholly wrong. The human mind, he insists (1966, p. 421), needs to merge the 'I' in a 'We' and requires a continuity of social wholes, making an appeal to faith and hope and a demand for devotion and sacrifice, from the visible, such as community, state, and nation, to the invisible, 'also social, of religious faith, to the Great Life in which our life is merged.'

10 Cooley laments (1966, p. 415) that in the contemporary period the 'groups we serve . . . have come to be so vast, and often so remote from the eye, that even the ingenuity of the newspaper and magazine press can hardly make them alive for us' and attract our attention. These 'we's', he continues (1966, p. 415), do 'not live in face-to-face contact, and though photo-engravings and stereopticons and exhibitions and vivid writings are a marvelous substitute, they are often inadequate, so that we do not feel the cogency of the common interest so immediately as did the men of the clans.'

11 Early theorists did recognize circumscriptions on choice. Their writings undeniably acknowledge the constraints imposed by the biophysical conditions under which any group exists. But they seemed to be unaware of or ignored the instances of outright coercion and intimidation of one group by another and certainly they failed to anticipate the significance of the technological-instrumental manipulation or 'engineering' of the bases of consent. Early sociologists were, indeed, middle-class Americans committed to the ethos of their society.

12 See Giddings (1922, pp. 38–42, 156, 181, 222–3, 250).

13 See chapter 9, pp. 244–5.

Chapter 12 Discontinuity and continuity

1 Regrettably, the account offered in these few pages is so brief that distortion and misinterpretation may easily result. For instance, the developing methodological positivism and the emerging field differentiation-specialization apparently *together* tended *to undermine the legitimacy* of abstract general theory aiming at comprehensive (or universal) explanations. It was not one or the other but the two together at that time which seemed to have the negative consequences for general theory.

2 For a preliminary version, see Hinkle (1963, pp. 706–7). Consult MacIver (1931, pp. 6–8, 11, 25–6, 45–50, 249, 292–300, 500–1, 527–44; also 1964, pp. 15–17, 21, 23, 229–37, 240–1, 271, 276–8, 292–7, 301–32, 390–1); Parsons (1949 (originally 1937), pp. 43–51, 762 fn, 765, 768); Znaniecki (1934, pp. 37, 41, 58–9, 60–1, 73, 87, 131–2, 162–3, 167–8; 1936, pp. 1–33, 71–5, 134); and Becker (1950, pp. 14–17 (especially footnotes, pp. 16–17), 192–4, 198–9, 35–42, 201, 22–32, 199–200, 201–3, 18–21, 24 choice is assumed in 'the means he chose'), 189–97). The antecedents of the two most relevant chapters (I and IV) of Becker's work do date from the early to the mid-1940s.

3 Undeniably, the biophysical environment, the behavioral organism, personality system, the social system, the cultural system (and presumably ultimate reality) do function as circumscribing, constraining, or restrictive environments or systems within which choice is exercised. Total determinism is not accepted.

4 Ward (1968, I, pp. 29, 50, 52; II, pp. 319, 329, 378), Giddings (1922, pp. 38, 42, 146, 34), Ross (1919, pp. 158–9, 50, 80, 152, 160–4), Small (1905, pp. 632, 636, 637, 633, 645, 59, 60, 682, 406, 407, 670; 668, 669).

5 It is of the utmost theoretical significance to recognize that a later theorist's own interpretation of his (her) derivation or borrowing from or inspiration by an earlier one may have to become problematic in the course of tracing intellectual continuities and discontinuities. It may become necessary to question the problematic stance, etc., of the later figure in (his-her) interpretation (or re-interpretation) of an earlier one. Blumer seems to insist that his view ('construction') of Mead presents the genuine or authentic Mead. Precisely this question is opened up in the exchange between Lewis and Blumer in the *Sociological Quarterly* articles of (summer) 1976 and (spring) 1977 and in the former's *American Sociology and Pragmatism* (1980). Lewis argues that an accurate and representative conception of Mead's social psychology must depart from Mead's broader philosophical problems and commitments. Accordingly, Mead becomes a social realist and Blumer a social nominalist.

Admittedly, continuities may be partial and selective rather than complete and (totally) representative. Indeed, American sociologists' tendency to be preoccupied with present issues and problems and to take an intellectually utilitarian ('pragmatic') attitude toward theory tends to obstruct their awareness of the problem of distortion which arises from partial and selective appropriation of ideas from more systematic theoretical wholes. The account of Mead offered above is selective and partial (*sic*) to show how *aspects* of Mead can accord with both the action orientation and with Blumer's perspective.

6 In the late 1970s at least Husserlian (rationalist) and Merleau-Pontyan (*emotive-existential*) inclinations can be identified, along with perhaps (social realist) structural proclivities. See K. H. Wolff's chapter on 'Phenomenology and Sociology' in T. Bottomore and R. Nisbet (eds), *A History of Sociological Analysis* (New York, Basic Books, 1978).

7 Accordingly, Haskell's objections (1977, p. 251 fn) to the designation 'voluntaristic nominalism' seem to be ill founded or misplaced.

Bibliography

Primary

COOLEY, CHARLES H. (1904), 'Discussion of Franklin Henry Giddings, A Theory of Social Causation,' *Publications of the American Economic Association*, 3rd series, vol. 5, pp. 426–31.

COOLEY, C. H. (1927), *Life and the Student*, New York, Knopf.

COOLEY, C. H. (1962), *Social Organization*, New York, Schocken (originally published by Scribners, 1909).

COOLEY, C. H. (1964), *Human Nature and the Social Order*, New York, Schocken (originally published by Scribners, 1902).

COOLEY, C. H. (1966), *Social Process*, Southern Illinois University Press (originally published by Scribners, 1918).

COOLEY, C. H. (1969), *Sociological Theory and Social Research*, New York, Augustus M. Kelley (originally published by Holt, 1930).

GIDDINGS, FRANKLIN H. (1896), *The Principles of Sociology*, New York, Macmillan.

GIDDINGS, F. H. (1898), *The Elements of Sociology*, New York, Macmillan.

GIDDINGS, F. H. (1900), *Democracy and Empire*, New York, Macmillan.

GIDDINGS, F. H. (1901), *Inductive Sociology*, New York, Macmillan.

GIDDINGS, F. H. (1904), 'A Theory of Social Causation,' *Publications of the American Economic Association*, 3rd series, vol. 5, pp. 383–418.

GIDDINGS, F. H. (1906), *Readings in Descriptive and Historical Sociology*, New York, Macmillan.

GIDDINGS, F. H. 09(1922), *Studies in the Theory of Human Society*, New York, Macmillan.

GIDDINGS, F. H. (1924), *The Scientific Study of Human Society*, University of North Carolina Press.

GIDDINGS, F. H. (1932), *Civilization and Society*, New York, Holt.

KELLER, ALBERT G. (1915, 1st ed.), *Societal Evolution*, New York, Macmillan.

BIBLIOGRAPHY

KELLER, A. G. (1916), 'Sociology and Science,' *The Nation*, vol. 12 (May 4), pp. 475–8.
KELLER, A. G. (1918), *Through War to Peace*, New York, Macmillan.
KELLER, A. G. (1927) (See Sumner and Keller, *The Science of Society*. Sole reference to Keller means that he alone was the author of the particular passage. Consult also n. 3 to chapter 4.)
KELLER, A. G. (1929), 'Societal Evolution,' in George A. Baitsell (ed.), *The Evolution of Earth and Man*, Yale University Press.
KELLER, A. G. (1931, rev. ed.), *Societal Evolution*, New York, Macmillan.
KELLER, A. G. (1932), *Man's Rough Road*, Yale University Press.
KELLER, A. G. (1938), *Brass Tacks*, New York, Knopf.
KELLER, A. G. (1942), *Net Impressions*, Yale University Press.
KELLER, A. G. (1944), 'Letter to Chamberlain,' Albert G. Keller Collection (New Haven, Conn.), Yale University Library.
KELLER, A. G. (1947), *Starting Points in Social Science*, Yale University Press (originally published by Ginn, 1923).
ROSS, EDWARD A. (1912), *Social Psychology*, New York, Macmillan (originally published 1908).
ROSS, E. A. (1919, 5th ed.), *Foundations of Sociology*, New York, Macmillan (originally published 1905).
ROSS, E. A. (1920), *The Principles of Sociology*, New York, Century.
ROSS, E. A. (1969), *Social Control*, Case Western Reserve University Press (originally published by Macmillan, 1901).
SMALL, ALBION W. (1904), 'Discussion' of Franklin Henry Giddings, 'A Theory of Social Causation,' *Publications of the American Economic Association*, 3rd series, vol. 5, pp. 419–25.
SMALL, A. W. (1905), *General Sociology*, University of Chicago Press.
SMALL, A. W. (1907), *Adam Smith and Modern Sociology*, University of Chicago Press.
SMALL, A. W. (1910), *The Meaning of Social Science*, University of Chicago Press.
SMALL, A. W. (1912), 'General Sociology,' *American Journal of Sociology*, vol. 18, no. 2, pp. 200–14.
SMALL, A. W. (1916), 'Fifty Years of Sociology in the United States, 1865–1915,' *American Journal of Sociology*, vol. 21, no. 6, pp. 721–864 (reprinted in *American Journal of Sociology Index to Volumes 1–52, 1895–1947*, pp. 177–269).
SMALL, A. W. and VINCENT, GEORGE E. (1971), *An Introduction to the Study of Society*, Dubuque, Io., Brown Reprints (originally published by American Book Co., 1894).
SUMNER, WILLIAM G. (1881), 'Sociology,' *Princeton Review*, pp. 303–23 (reprinted in *Social Darwinism: Selected Essays of William Graham Sumner*, with an introduction by Stow Persons, Englewood Cliffs, N.J., Prentice-Hall, 1963).
SUMNER, W. G. (1913), *Earth Hunger and Other Essays* (ed. A. G. Keller), Yale University Press.

BIBLIOGRAPHY

SUMNER, W. G. (1914), *The Challenge of Facts and Other Essays* (ed. A. G. Keller), Yale University Press.

SUMNER, W. G. (1918), *The Forgotten Man and Other Essays* (ed. A. G. Keller), Yale University Press.

SUMNER, W. G. (1923), *Discipline and Other Essays from the Collected Works of William Graham Sumner* (ed. A. G. Keller), Yale University Press.

SUMNER, W. G. (1927) (See Sumner and Keller, *The Science of Society*. Sole reference to Sumner means that he alone was the author of the particular passage. Consult also n. 3 to chapter 4.)

SUMNER, W. G. (1934), *Essays of William Graham Sumner* (ed. A. G. Keller), Yale University Press.

SUMNER, W. G. (1959), *Folkways*, New York, Dover (originally published by Ginn, 1907).

SUMNER, W. G. (1970), *War and Other Essays*, Freeport, N.Y., Books for Libraries Press (originally published by Yale University Press, 1919).

SUMNER, W. G. (n.d.*a*), 'Early Drafts of Societology,' William Graham Sumner Collection, New Haven, Conn., Yale University Library.

SUMNER, W. G. (n.d.*b*), 'The Application of the Notions of Evolution and Progress on the Superorganic Domain,' William Graham Sumner Collection.

SUMNER, W. G. (n.d.*c*), 'Untitled Essay on Evolution,' William Graham Sumner Collection.

SUMNER, W. G. and KELLER, ALBERT G. (1927), *The Science of Society* (4 vols), Yale University Press (and see n. 3 to chapter 4 and n. 1 to chapter 9).

WARD, LESTER F. (1898), *Outline of Sociology*, New York, Macmillan.

WARD, L. F. (1901), *The Psychic Factor of Civilization*, Boston, Ginn (first printed in 1893).

WARD, L. F. (1904), 'Discussion' of Franklin Henry Giddings, 'A Theory of Social Causation,' *Publications of the American Economic Association*, 3rd series, vol. 5, pp. 431–4.

WARD, L. F. (1906), *Applied Sociology*, Boston, Ginn.

WARD, L. F. (1908), 'Social Classes in the Light of Modern Sociological Theory,' *American Journal of Sociology*, vol. 13, no. 5, pp. 617–27.

WARD, L. F. (1968), *Dynamic Sociology* (2 vols), New York, Greenwood Press (originally published by Appleton, 1883).

WARD, L. F. (1970), *Pure Sociology*, New York, Augustus M. Kelley (originally published by Macmillan, 1903).

WARD, L. F. and DEALEY, JAMES Q. (1905), *A Textbook of Sociology*, New York, Macmillan.

Secondary

ABBAGNANO, NICOLA (1967), 'Positivism,' *The Encyclopedia of Philosophy* (vol. 6, pp. 414–19), New York, Macmillan and Free Press.

ALLEN, FREDERICK L. (1952), *The Big Change*, New York, Harper.

BIBLIOGRAPHY

BECKER, HOWARD P. (1950), *Through Values to Social Interpretation*, Duke University Press.
BECKER, H. P. (1957), 'Current Sacred-Secular Theory and its Development,' in Howard Becker and Alvin Boskoff (eds), *Modern Sociological Theory*, New York, Dryden.
BECKER, H. P. and BARNES, HARRY E. (1952, 2nd ed.), *Social Thought from Lore to Science* (2 vols), Washington, D.C., Herren Press.
BERNARD, LUTHER L. (1909), 'The Teaching of Sociology in the United States,' *American Journal of Sociology*, vol. 15, no. 2, pp. 164–213.
BLUMER, HERBERT (1969), *Symbolic Interactionism*, Englewood Cliffs, N.J., Prentice-Hall.
BLUMER, H. (1977), 'Comment on Lewis' "The Classic American Pragmatists as Forerunners to Symbolic Interactionism",' *Sociological Quarterly*, vol. 18 (spring), pp. 285–9.
BOCK, KENNETH E. (1956), *The Acceptance of Histories* (University of California Publications in Sociology and Social Institutions, vol. 3, no. 1, pp. 1–132), University of California Press.
BOCK, K. E. (1964), 'Theories of Progress and Evolution,' in Warner J. Cahnman and Alvin Boskoff (eds), *Sociology and History*, New York, Free Press.
BOLLER, PAUL F., JR. (1969), *American Thought in Transition: The Impact of Evolutionary Naturalism, 1865–1900*, Chicago, Rand-McNally.
BRANDT, GUNTHER (1974), 'The Origins of American Sociology: A Study in the Ideology of Social Science, 1865–1895' (Ph.D. diss. in History, Princeton University), Ann Arbor, Mich., University Microfilms International.
BRYSON, GLADYS (1932a), 'The Emergence of the Social Sciences from Moral Philosophy,' *Ethics*, vol. 42, no. 3, pp. 304–23.
BRYSON, G. (1932b), 'The Comparable Interests of the Old Moral Philosophy and the Modern Social Sciences,' *Social Forces*, vol. 11, no. 1, pp. 19–27.
BUNGE, MARIO (1959), *Causality*, Harvard University Press.
BURR, GEORGE L. (1904), 'Discussion' of Franklin Henry Giddings, 'A Theory of Social Causation,' *Publications of the American Economic Association*, 3rd series, vol 5, pp. 434–7.
BURROW, J. W. (1966), *Evolution and Society*, Cambridge University Press.
CAREY, JAMES T. (1975), *Sociology and Public Affairs: The Chicago School*, Beverly Hills, Calif., Sage.
CHANDLER, ALFRED D. (1967), 'The Large Industrial Corporation and the Making of the Modern American Economy,' in Stephen E. Ambrose (ed.), *Institutions in Modern America*, Johns Hopkins Press.
CHAPIN, F. STUART (1928), *Cultural Change*, New York, Century.
COCHRAN, THOMAS C. (1961), 'The Social Scientists,' in Robert E. Spiller and Eric Larrabee (eds), *American Perspectives*, Harvard University Press.
COHEN, PERCY S. (1968), *Modern Social Theory*, New York, Basic Books.

COMMAGER, HENRY S. (1949), 'Portrait of the American,' in John W. Chase (ed.), *Years of the Modern*, New York, Longmans, Green.

COMMONS, JOHN R. (1967), *Races and Immigrants in America*, New York, Augustus M. Kelley (originally published by Macmillan, 1907).

CRAVENS, HAMILTON and BURNHAM, JOHN (1971), 'Psychology and Evolutionary Naturalism in American Thought, 1890–1940,' *American Quarterly*, vol. 23, no. 5, pp. 635–57.

CURTI, MERLE (1951), *The Growth of American Thought*, New York, Harper.

DALLMAYR, FRED R. and McCARTHY, THOMAS A. (eds), (1977), *Understanding and Social Inquiry*, University of Notre Dame Press.

EFFRAT, ANDREW (1972), 'Power to Paradigms: An Editorial Introduction,' *Sociological Inquiry*, vol. 42, nos 3 and 4, pp. 3–34.

EISENSTADT, S. N. with CURELARU, M. (1976), *The Form of Sociology: Paradigms and Crises*, New York, Wiley.

EKIRSCH, ARTHUR A. (1944), *The Idea of Progress in America, 1815–1860*, Columbia University Press.

ELLWOOD, CHARLES A. (1910), *Sociology and Modern Social Problems*, New York, American Book Co.

FAIRCHILD, HENRY P. (1920), *Immigration*, New York, Macmillan.

FARIS, ELSWORTH (1976), *The Nature of Human Nature*, University of Chicago Press (originally published by McGraw-Hill, 1937).

FARIS, ROBERT E. L. (1970), *Chicago Sociology 1920–1932*, University of Chicago Press.

FRIEDRICHS, ROBERT W. (1970), *A Sociology of Sociology*, New York, Free Press.

GABRIEL, RALPH H. (1974), *American Values*, Westport, Conn., Greenwood Press.

GIDDENS, ANTHONY (ed.) (1974), *Positivism and Sociology*, London, Heinemann.

GINSBERG, MORRIS (1957), *Essays in Sociology and Social Philosophy*, vol. 1, London, Heinemann.

GLAAB, CHARLES N. (1963), *The American City*, Homewood, Ill., Dorsey Press.

GOLDENWEISER, ALEXANDER (1916), 'Culture and Environment,' *American Journal of Sociology*, vol. 21, no. 5, pp. 628–33.

GOLDENWEISER, A. (1925a), 'Diffusionism and the American School of Historical Ethnology,' *American Journal of Sociology*, vol. 31, no. 1, pp. 19–38.

GOLDENWEISER, A. (1925b), 'Cultural Anthropology,' in H. E. Barnes (ed.), *The History and Prospects of the Social Sciences*, New York, Knopf.

GOULDNER, ALVIN W. (1970), *The Coming Crisis of Western Sociology*, New York, Basic Books.

HABERMAS, JÜRGEN (1972), *Knowledge and Human Interests* (trans. Jeremy J. Shapiro), Boston, Beacon Press.

BIBLIOGRAPHY

HASKELL, THOMAS L. (1977), *The Emergence of Professional Social Science*, University of Illinois Press.

HENDERSON, CHARLES R. (1912), 'Applied Sociology (or Social Technology),' *American Journal of Sociology*, vol. 18, no. 2, pp. 215–21.

HERSKOVITS, MELVILLE J. and WILLEY, MALCOLM M. (1923), 'The Cultural Approach to Sociology,' *American Journal of Sociology*, vol. 29, no. 2, pp. 188–99.

HEYL, JOHN and HEYL, BARBARA (1976), 'The Sumner–Porter Controversy at Yale: Pre-Paradigmatic Sociology and Institutional Crisis,' *Sociological Inquiry*, vol. 46, pp. 41–9.

HILDEBRAND, GEORGE H. (1949), 'Introduction,' in Frederick J. Teggart (ed.), *The Idea of Progress*, University of California Press.

HINKLE, ROSCOE C. (1963), 'Antecedents of the Action Orientation in American Sociology Before 1935,' *American Sociological Review*, vol. 28, no. 5, pp. 705–15.

HINKLE, R. C. (1966), 'Introduction' to Charles Horton Cooley, *Social Process*, Southern Illinois University Press.

HINKLE, R. C. (1967), 'Charles Horton Cooley's General Sociological Orientation,' *Sociological Quarterly*, vol. 8, no. 1 (winter), pp. 5–20.

HINKLE, R. C. (1969), 'The Structure of the History of Sociological Theory,' 64th Annual Meeting of the American Sociological Association, San Francisco, Calif., September.

HINKLE, R. C. (1975), 'Basic Orientations of the Founding Fathers of American Sociology,' *Journal of the History of the Behavioral Sciences*, vol. 11, pp. 107–22.

HINKLE, R. C. (1976), 'Durkheim's Evolutionary Conception of Social Change,' *Sociological Quarterly*, vol. 17 (summer), pp. 336–46.

HINKLE, R. C. (1978), 'Toward Periodicization of the History of Sociological Theory in the U.S.,' *Journal of the History of Sociology*, vol. 1, no. 1 (fall), pp. 68–89.

HINKLE, R. C. and HINKLE, GISELA J. (1954), *The Development of Modern Sociology*, New York, Random House.

HINKLE, R. C., HINKLE, G. J. and WEINBERG, JULIUS (1969), 'Introduction' to Edward Alsworth Ross, *Social Control*, Case Western Reserve University Press.

HOFSTADTER, RICHARD (1952), 'The Development of Higher Education in America,' in Richard Hofstadter and C. DeWitt Hardy, *The Development and Scope of Higher Education in the United States*, Columbia University Press.

HUTCHINSON, E. P. (1956), *Immigrants and Their Children, 1850–1950* (a volume in the Census Monograph Series for the Social Science Research Council in cooperation with the US Department of Commerce, Bureau of the Census), New York, Wiley.

KINLOCH, GRAHAM (1977), *Sociological Theory*, New York, McGraw-Hill.

KOLAKOWSKI, LESZAK (1968), *The Alienation of Reason* (trans. Norbert Guterman), Garden City, N.Y., Doubleday.

360

KUHN, THOMAS (1962), *The Structure of Scientific Revolutions*, University of Chicago Press.

LEHMAN, TIMOTHY and YOUNG, T. R. (1974), 'From Conflict Theory to Conflict Methodology: An Emerging Paradigm for Sociology,' *Sociological Inquiry*, vol. 44, pp. 15–28.

LEWIS, J. DAVID (1976), 'The Classic American Pragmatists as Forerunners to Symbolic Interactionism,' *Sociological Quarterly*, vol. 17 (summer), pp. 347–59.

LEWIS, J. D. (1977), 'Reply to Blumer,' *Sociological Quarterly*, vol. 18 (spring), pp. 291–2.

LEWIS, J. D. and SMITH, RICHARD L. (1980), *American Sociology and Pragmatism*, University of Chicago Press.

LOWIE, ROBERT (1914), 'Social Organization,' *American Journal of Sociology*, vol. 20, no. 1, pp. 68–97.

MacIVER, ROBERT M. (1931), *Society: Its Structure and Changes*, New York, Ray Long and Richard R. Smith.

MacIVER, R. M. (1937), *Society: A Textbook of Sociology*, New York, Farrar and Rinehart.

MacIVER, R. M. (1964), *Social Causation*, New York, Harper Torchbooks (originally published by Ginn, 1942).

MacIVER, R. M. and PAGE, CHARLES H. (1949), *Society: An Introductory Analyis*, New York, Farrar & Rinehart.

MARTINDALE, DON (1965), 'Limits of and Alternatives to Functionalism in Sociology,' in Don Martindale (ed.), *Functionalism in the Social Sciences* (Monograph 5 in a series sponsored by the American Academy of Political and Social Science), Philadelphia, Penna., American Academy of Political and Social Science.

MASTERMAN, MARGARET (1972), 'The Nature of a Paradigm,' in Imre Lakatos and Alan Musgrave (eds), *Criticism and the Growth of Knowledge*, Cambridge University Press.

MEAD, GEORGE H. (1972), *The Philosophy of the Act*, University of Chicago Press.

MILLER, PERRY (1965), *The Life of the Mind in America*, New York, Harcourt, Brace & World.

NASH, GERALD (1971), *The Great Transition*, Boston, Mass., Allyn & Bacon.

NISBET, ROBERT (1969), *Social Change and History*, New York, Oxford University Press.

NISBET, R. (1970), 'Developmentalism: A Critical Analysis,' in John C. McKinney and Edward A. Tiryakian (eds), *Theoretical Sociology*, New York, Appleton-Century Crofts.

OBERSCHALL, ANTHONY (1972), 'The Institutionalization of American Sociology,' in Anthony D. Oberschall (ed.), *The Establishment of Empirical Sociology*, New York, Harper.

ODUM, HOWARD (1951), *American Sociology*, New York, Longmans, Green.

OGBURN, WILLIAM F. (1950), *Social Change*, New York, Viking Press (originally published by B. W. Huebsch, 1922).

PARK, ROBERT E. (1952), *Human Communities*, Chicago, Free Press.

PARK, R. E. (1955), *Societies*, Chicago, Free Press.

PARK, R. E. and BURGESS, ERNEST W. (1924), *Introduction to the Science of Sociology*, University of Chicago Press.

PARSONS,·TALCOTT (1949), *The Structure of Social Action*, Chicago, Free Press (originally published by McGraw-Hill, 1937).

PARSONS, T. (1951), *The Social System*, Chicago, Free Press.

PARSONS, T. (1966), *Societies: Evolutionary and Comparative Perspectives*, Englewood Cliffs, N.J., Prentice-Hall.

PARSONS, T. and SHILS, EDWARD A. (eds) (1951), *Toward a General Theory of Action*, Harvard University Press.

PARSONS, T., SHILS, E., NAEGELE, KASPAR D. and PITTS, JESSE R. (eds) (1961), *Theories of Society* (vol. 1), New York, Free Press.

RITZER, GEORGE (1975), *Sociology: A Multiple Paradigm Science*, Boston, Mass., Allyn & Bacon.

ROSS, DOROTHY (n.d.), 'The Development of the Social Sciences in America, 1865–1920,' Paper prepared for the American Academy of Arts and Sciences, Conference on Knowledge in American Society, 1860–1920, New York City.

RUSSETT, CYNTHIA E. (1966), *The Concept of Equilibrium in American Social Thought*, Yale University Press.

SCHUTZ, ALFRED (1966), *Collected Papers* (vol. 3), The Hague, Martinus Nijhoff.

SMITH, ANTHONY (1973), *The Concept of Social Change*, London and Boston, Routledge & Kegan Paul.

SMITH, NORMAN E. (1976), 'William Graham Sumner, Social Evolutionism, and Social Darwinism,' Unpublished M. A. thesis (Sociology), The Ohio State University.

SMITH, N. E. and HINKLE, ROSCOE C. (1979), 'Sumner versus Keller and the Social Evolutionism of Early American Sociology,' *Sociological Inquiry*, vol. 49, no. 1, pp. 41–8.

Statistical Abstracts of the United States, (1952), Washington, D.C., US Government Printing Office.

STOCKING, GEORGE (1969), *Race, Culture and Evolution*, New York, Free Press.

TEGGART, FREDERICK J. (1977), *Theory and Processes of History*, University of California Press.

THOMAS, WILLIAM I. (1909), *Source Book for Social Origins*, University of Chicago Press.

TIMASHEFF, NICHOLAS S. (1955), *Sociological Theory*, New York, Random House.

TOLMAN, FRANK A. (1902), 'The Study of Sociology in Institutions of Learning in the United States,' *American Journal of Sociology*, vol. 7, no. 6, pp. 797–838, and vol. 8, nos 1, 2, 3, pp. 85–121, 251–72, 531–58.

VEYSEY, LAURENCE R. (1965), *The Emergence of the American University*, University of Chicago Press.

WALLIS, WILSON (1926), 'Geographical Environment and Culture,' *Social Forces*, vol. 4 no. 4 (June), pp. 702–8.

WELTER, RUSH (1955), 'The Idea of Progress in America,' *Journal of the History of Ideas*, vol. 16, no. 3, pp. 401–15.

WEST, WILLIS M. (1904), 'Discussion' of Franklin Henry Giddings, 'A Theory of Social Causation,' *Publications of the American Economic Association*, 3rd series, vol. 5, pp. 437–43.

WILLIAMS, ROBIN M., JR. (1952), *American Society*, New York, Knopf.

WINTER, GIBSON (1966), *Elements for a Social Ethic*, New York, Macmillan.

WYLLIE, IRVIN G. (1954), *The Self-Made Man in America*, Rutgers University Press.

ZNANIECKI, FLORIAN (1934), *The Method of Sociology*, New York, Farrar & Rinehart.

ZNANIECKI, F. (1936), *Social Actions*, New York, Farrar & Rinehart.

ZNANIECKI, F. (1965), *Social Relations and Social Roles*, San Francisco, Calif., Chandler.

Index

anti-social, 71; in-group and out-group, 17, 73, 151–3; Lamarckianism, 226, 228; modern societies, 174; mores, 140; notion of theory, 55, 266; panmixia, 227; post-organic theory of social origins, 105, 113–14, 116–17, 118, 119–20, 123–4; and a prevailingly social materialist ontology, 125–6; primitive societies, 164–5, 166, 167, 168–9, 170–1; primordial social structure, 134–5, 137, 140, 144–5; progress: notion, objections, rejection, 184, 253; reasons for inclusion in study, 13–15; science-history antithesis, 91, 268; social change, 74, 184, 185, 186, 187, 188, 194, 199, 207, 216, 217, 218, 219, 220, 222, 223, 224, 226, 227, 228, 229–33; social Darwinism, 223, 226–7; social forces, 69–70, societal forces, 84; social nominalism, 281–3; social origins (near), 71, 104; social processes, 250; social realism, 282–3, 286; social structure, 71; society, 153; sociology as a field of study, 65, in relation to other social sciences, 46, 48; strain toward consistency, 211, 232; summary, 266, 268, 269, 271, 272, 273, 274, 275, 279, 280, 281, 282, 283, 284, 286, 291, 292, 293, 296, 297; syncretism, 227, 231; theoretical works used in study, 56

symbolic interactionism, 319–21
synthesis, 234

Tarbell, I., 35
Tarde, G., 50, 52, 59, 189, 190, 211, 235, 241, 245, 247, 248, 264–5
Thomas, W., 13, 15, 18, 19, 214, 220–1, 224, 300, 302, 308, 313, 318
Timasheff, N., 4, 5, 7
Tönnies, F., 162, 172
Tolman, F., 49
trade unions, 34
Turner, J., 4
Tylor, E., 43, 94, 196, 198
types of social structures: structure as temporary adaptation to conditions of existence, adjustment to situation, equilibrium of forces whose persistence problematic, 149; notions of structure linked to evolutionary naturalism, 149; institutions most

conspicuously and frequently employed notion in early theory, 150; in-group and out-group, 17, 150, 151–3; social composition and social constitution, 17, 153–6; primary group and nucleated group, 17, 150, 156–62; community and society, 17, 150, 162–4
types of society: great variety, 164–5, 173–4; primitive societies, 17, 165–73; modern societies, 17, 173–81

unification, 251, 252, 257
universities: Brown University, 41, 45; University of Chicago, 14, 37, 40, 41, 45, 305; Clark University, 40; Columbia University, 14, 39, 40, 41, 42, 45, 305, 312; Cornell University, 37, 39, 42, 43; Duke University, 305; Harvard University, 37, 40, 43, 312; Johns Hopkins University, 40, 41, 42, 43; University of Illinois, 38, 45, 305, 312; Indiana University, 37, 45; University of Michigan, 14, 39, 41, 42, 45; University of Minnesota, 38, 45; University of Missouri, 305; University of Nebraska, 45; New York University, 14; Northwestern University, 45; Ohio State University, 45; University of Pennsylvania, 14, 42, 43, 45; Stanford University, 38; University of Virginia, 305; University of Wisconsin, 14, 35, 38, 39, 40, 41, 45, 305, 312; Yale College (later University), 14, 39, 41, 42, 43, 45
urbanization, 233

valuation, 234, 244
values in American society, post-Civil War: activism and work, 30; categorical moralism, 30; democracy, 30; education, 30; efficiency and practicality, 30; exploitability of physical nature, 30; external conformity, 30; material comfort, 30, 31; nationalism, 31; occupational achievement and financial success, 30; optimism, 30; science and technology, 30, 31; *see also* humanitarianism; progress; reform
Van Hise, C., 35, 38
Veblen, T., 59

Routledge Social Science Series

Routledge & Kegan Paul   London, Henley and Boston

39 Store Street, London WC1E 7DD
Broadway House, Newtown Road,
Henley-on-Thames, Oxon RG9 1EN
9 Park Street, Boston, Mass. 02108

Strasser, Hermann. The Normative Structure of Sociology. *Conservative and Emancipatory Themes in Social Thought. About 340 pp.*
Strong, P. Ceremonial Order of the Clinic. *About 250 pp.*
Urry, John. Reference Groups and the Theory of Revolution. *244 pp.*
Weinberg, E. Development of Sociology in the Soviet Union. *173 pp.*

FOREIGN CLASSICS OF SOCIOLOGY

● **Gerth, H. H.** and **Mills, C. Wright.** From Max Weber: *Essays in Sociology. 502 pp.*
● **Tönnies, Ferdinand.** Community and Association. *(Gemeinschaft and Gesellschaft.) Translated and Supplemented by Charles P. Loomis. Foreword by Pitirim A. Sorokin. 334 pp.*

SOCIAL STRUCTURE

Andreski, Stanislav. Military Organization and Society. *Foreword by Professor A. R. Radcliffe-Brown. 226 pp. 1 folder.*
Carlton, Eric. Ideology and Social Order. *Foreword by Professor Philip Abrahams. About 320 pp.*
Coontz, Sydney H. Population Theories and the Economic Interpretation. *202 pp.*
Coser, Lewis. The Functions of Social Conflict. *204 pp.*
Dickie-Clark, H. F. Marginal Situation: *A Sociological Study of a Coloured Group. 240 pp. 11 tables.*
Giner, S. and **Archer, M. S.** (Eds.). Contemporary Europe. *Social Structures and Cultural Patterns. 336 pp.*
● **Glaser, Barney** and **Strauss, Anselm L.** Status Passage. *A Formal Theory. 212 pp.*
Glass, D. V. (Ed.) Social Mobility in Britain. *Contributions by J. Berent, T. Bottomore, R. C. Chambers, J. Floud, D. V. Glass, J. R. Hall, H. T. Himmelweit, R. K. Kelsall, F. M. Martin, C. A. Moser, R. Mukherjee, and W. Ziegel. 420 pp.*
Kelsall, R. K. Higher Civil Servants in Britain: *From 1870 to the Present Day. 268 pp. 31 tables.*
● **Lawton, Denis.** Social Class, Language and Education. *192 pp.*
McLeish, John. The Theory of Social Change: *Four Views Considered. 128 pp.*
● **Marsh, David C.** The Changing Social Structure of England and Wales, 1871-1961. *Revised edition. 288 pp.*
Menzies, Ken. Talcott Parsons and the Social Image of Man. *About 208 pp.*
● **Mouzelis, Nicos.** Organization and Bureaucracy. *An Analysis of Modern Theories. 240 pp.*
Ossowski, Stanislaw. Class Structure in the Social Consciousness. *210 pp.*
● **Podgórecki, Adam.** Law and Society. *302 pp.*
Renner, Karl. Institutions of Private Law and Their Social Functions. *Edited, with an Introduction and Notes, by O. Kahn-Freud. Translated by Agnes Schwarzschild. 316 pp.*

Rex, J. and **Tomlinson, S.** Colonial Immigrants in a British City. *A Class Analysis. 368 pp.*
Smooha, S. Israel: Pluralism and Conflict. *472 pp.*
Wesolowski, W. Class, Strata and Power. *Trans. and with Introduction by G. Kolankiewicz. 160 pp.*
Zureik, E. Palestinians in Israel. *A Study in Internal Colonialism. 264 pp.*

SOCIOLOGY AND POLITICS

Acton, T. A. Gypsy Politics and Social Change. *316 pp.*
Burton, F. Politics of Legitimacy. *Struggles in a Belfast Community. 250 pp.*
Etzioni-Halevy, E. Political Manipulation and Administrative Power. *A Comparative Study. About 200 pp.*
● **Hechter, Michael.** Internal Colonialism. *The Celtic Fringe in British National Development, 1536–1966. 380 pp.*
Kornhauser, William. The Politics of Mass Society. *272 pp. 20 tables.*
Korpi, W. The Working Class in Welfare Capitalism. *Work, Unions and Politics in Sweden. 472 pp.*
Kroes, R. Soldiers and Students. *A Study of Right- and Left-wing Students. 174 pp.*
Martin, Roderick. Sociology of Power. *About 272 pp.*
Myrdal, Gunnar. The Political Element in the Development of Economic Theory. *Translated from the German by Paul Streeten. 282 pp.*
Wong, S.-L. Sociology and Socialism in Contemporary China. *160 pp.*
Wootton, Graham. Workers, Unions and the State. *188 pp.*

CRIMINOLOGY

Ancel, Marc. Social Defence: *A Modern Approach to Criminal Problems. Foreword by Leon Radzinowicz. 240 pp.*
Athens, L. Violent Criminal Acts and Actors. *About 150 pp.*
Cain, Maureen E. Society and the Policeman's Role. *326 pp.*
Cloward, Richard A. and **Ohlin, Lloyd E.** Delinquency and Opportunity: *A Theory of Delinquent Gangs. 248 pp.*
Downes, David M. The Delinquent Solution. *A Study in Subcultural Theory. 296 pp.*
Friedlander, Kate. The Psycho-Analytical Approach to Juvenile Delinquency: *Theory, Case Studies, Treatment. 320 pp.*
Gleuck, Sheldon and **Eleanor.** Family Environment and Delinquency. *With the statistical assistance of Rose W. Kneznek. 340 pp.*
Lopez-Rey, Manuel. Crime. *An Analytical Appraisal. 288 pp.*
Mannheim, Hermann. Comparative Criminology: *a Text Book. Two volumes. 442 pp. and 380 pp.*
Morris, Terence. The Criminal Area: *A Study in Social Ecology. Foreword by Hermann Mannheim. 232 pp. 25 tables. 4 maps.*
Podgorecki, A. and **Łos, M.** Multidimensional Sociology. *About 380 pp.*
Rock, Paul. Making People Pay. *338 pp.*

● Taylor, Ian, Walton, Paul, and Young, Jock. The New Criminology. *For a Social Theory of Deviance. 325 pp.*

● Taylor, Ian, Walton, Paul and Young, Jock. (Eds) Critical Criminology. *268 pp.*

SOCIAL PSYCHOLOGY

Bagley, Christopher. The Social Psychology of the Epileptic Child. *320 pp.*

Brittan, Arthur. Meanings and Situations. *224 pp.*

Carroll, J. Break-Out from the Crystal Palace. *200 pp.*

● Fleming, C. M. Adolescence: Its Social Psychology. *With an Introduction to recent findings from the fields of Anthropology, Physiology, Medicine, Psychometrics and Sociometry. 288 pp.*

● The Social Psychology of Education: *An Introduction and Guide to Its Study. 136 pp.*

Linton, Ralph. The Cultural Background of Personality. *132 pp.*

● Mayo, Elton. The Social Problems of an Industrial Civilization. *With an Appendix on the Political Problem. 180 pp.*

Ottaway, A. K. C. Learning Through Group Experience. *176 pp.*

Plummer, Ken. Sexual Stigma. *An Interactionist Account. 254 pp.*

● Rose, Arnold M. (Ed.) Human Behaviour and Social Processes: *an Interactionist Approach. Contributions by Arnold M. Rose, Ralph H. Turner, Anselm Strauss, Everett C. Hughes, E. Franklin Frazier, Howard S. Becker et al. 696 pp.*

Smelser, Neil J. Theory of Collective Behaviour. *448 pp.*

Stephenson, Geoffrey M. The Development of Conscience. *128 pp.*

Young, Kimball. Handbook of Social Psychology. *658 pp. 16 figures. 10 tables.*

SOCIOLOGY OF THE FAMILY

Bell, Colin R. Middle Class Families: *Social and Geographical Mobility. 224 pp.*

Burton, Lindy. Vulnerable Children. *272 pp.*

Gavron, Hannah. The Captive Wife: *Conflicts of Household Mothers. 190 pp.*

George, Victor and Wilding, Paul. Motherless Families. *248 pp.*

Klein, Josephine. Samples from English Cultures.
1. Three Preliminary Studies and Aspects of Adult Life in England. *447 pp.*
2. Child-Rearing Practices and Index. *247 pp.*

Klein, Viola. The Feminine Character. *History of an Ideology. 244 pp.*

McWhinnie, Alexina M. Adopted Children. *How They Grow Up. 304 pp.*

● Morgan, D. H. J. Social Theory and the Family. *About 320 pp.*

● Myrdal, Alva and Klein, Viola. Women's Two Roles: *Home and Work. 238 pp. 27 tables.*

Parsons, Talcott and **Bales, Robert F.** Family: Socialization and Inter-action Process. *In collaboration with James Olds, Morris Zelditch and Philip E. Slater. 456 pp. 50 figures and tables.*

SOCIAL SERVICES

Bastide, Roger. The Sociology of Mental Disorder. *Translated from the French by Jean McNeil. 260 pp.*

Carlebach, Julius. Caring For Children in Trouble. *266 pp.*

George, Victor. Foster Care. *Theory and Practice. 234 pp.*
Social Security: *Beveridge and After. 258 pp.*

George, V. and **Wilding, P.** Motherless Families. *248 pp.*

● **Goetschius, George W.** Working with Community Groups. *256 pp.*

Goetschius, George W. and **Tash, Joan.** Working with Unattached Youth. *416 pp.*

Heywood, Jean S. Children in Care. *The Development of the Service for the Deprived Child. Third revised edition. 284 pp.*

King, Roy D., Ranes, Norma V. and **Tizard, Jack.** Patterns of Residen-tial Care. *356 pp.*

Leigh, John. Young People and Leisure. *256 pp.*

● **Mays, John.** (Ed.) Penelope Hall's Social Services of England and Wales. *About 324 pp.*

Morris, Mary. Voluntary Work and the Welfare State. *300 pp.*

Nokes, P. L. The Professional Task in Welfare Practice. *152 pp.*

Timms, Noel. Psychiatric Social Work in Great Britain (1939-1962). *280 pp.*

● Social Casework: *Principles and Practice. 256 pp.*

SOCIOLOGY OF EDUCATION

Banks, Olive. Parity and Prestige in English Secondary Education: a Study in Educational Sociology. *272 pp.*

● **Blyth, W. A. L.** English Primary Education. *A Sociological Description.* 2. Background. *168 pp.*

Collier, K. G. The Social Purposes of Education: *Personal and Social Values in Education. 268 pp.*

Evans, K. M. Sociometry and Education. *158 pp.*

● **Ford, Julienne.** Social Class and the Comprehensive School. *192 pp.*

Foster, P. J. Education and Social Change in Ghana. *336 pp. 3 maps.*

Fraser, W. R. Education and Society in Modern France. *150 pp.*

Grace, Gerald R. Role Conflict and the Teacher. *150 pp.*

Hans, Nicholas. New Trends in Education in the Eighteenth Century. *278 pp. 19 tables.*

● Comparative Education: *A Study of Educational Factors and Tra-ditions. 360 pp.*

● **Hargreaves, David.** Interpersonal Relations and Education. *432 pp.*

● Social Relations in a Secondary School. *240 pp.*

School Organization and Pupil Involvement. *A Study of Secondary Schools.*

● **Mannheim, Karl** and **Stewart, W.A.C.** An Introduction to the Sociology of Education. *206 pp.*

● **Musgrove, F.** Youth and the Social Order. *176 pp.*

● **Ottaway, A. K. C.** Education and Society: An Introduction to the Sociology of Education. *With an Introduction by W. O. Lester Smith. 212 pp.*

Peers, Robert. Adult Education: *A Comparative Study. Revised edition. 398 pp.*

Stratta, Erica. The Education of Borstal Boys. *A Study of their Educational Experiences prior to, and during, Borstal Training. 256 pp.*

● **Taylor, P. H., Reid, W. A.** and **Holley, B. J.** The English Sixth Form. *A Case Study in Curriculum Research. 198 pp.*

SOCIOLOGY OF CULTURE

Eppel, E. M. and **M.** Adolescents and Morality: *A Study of some Moral Values and Dilemmas of Working Adolescents in the Context of a changing Climate of Opinion. Foreword by W. J. H. Sprott. 268 pp. 39 tables.*

● **Fromm, Erich.** The Fear of Freedom. *286 pp.*

●   The Sane Society. *400 pp.*

Johnson, L. The Cultural Critics. *From Matthew Arnold to Raymond Williams. 233 pp.*

Mannheim, Karl. Essays on the Sociology of Culture. *Edited by Ernst Mannheim in co-operation with Paul Kecskemeti. Editorial Note by Adolph Lowe. 280 pp.*

Zijderfeld, A. C. On Clichés. *The Supersedure of Meaning by Function in Modernity. About 132 pp.*

SOCIOLOGY OF RELIGION

Argyle, Michael and **Beit-Hallahmi, Benjamin.** The Social Psychology of Religion. *About 256 pp.*

Glasner, Peter E. The Sociology of Secularisation. *A Critique of a Concept. About 180 pp.*

Hall, J. R. The Ways Out. *Utopian Communal Groups in an Age of Babylon. 280 pp.*

Ranson, S., Hinings, B. and **Bryman, A.** Clergy, Ministers and Priests. *216 pp.*

Stark, Werner. The Sociology of Religion. *A Study of Christendom.*
Volume II. *Sectarian Religion. 368 pp.*
Volume III. *The Universal Church. 464 pp.*
Volume IV. *Types of Religious Man. 352 pp.*
Volume V. *Types of Religious Culture. 464 pp.*

Turner, B. S. Weber and Islam. *216 pp.*

Watt, W. Montgomery. Islam and the Integration of Society. *320 pp.*

SOCIOLOGY OF ART AND LITERATURE

Jarvie, Ian C. Towards a Sociology of the Cinema. *A Comparative Essay on the Structure and Functioning of a Major Entertainment Industry. 405 pp.*

Rust, Frances S. Dance in Society. *An Analysis of the Relationships between the Social Dance and Society in England from the Middle Ages to the Present Day. 256 pp. 8 pp. of plates.*

Schücking, L. L. The Sociology of Literary Taste. *112 pp.*

Wolff, Janet. Hermeneutic Philosophy and the Sociology of Art. *150 pp.*

SOCIOLOGY OF KNOWLEDGE

Diesing, P. Patterns of Discovery in the Social Sciences. *262 pp.*

● **Douglas, J. D.** (Ed.) Understanding Everyday Life. *370 pp.*

Glasner, B. Essential Interactionism. *About 220 pp.*

● **Hamilton, P.** Knowledge and Social Structure. *174 pp.*

Jarvie, I. C. Concepts and Society. *232 pp.*

Mannheim, Karl. Essays on the Sociology of Knowledge. *Edited by Paul Kecskemeti. Editorial Note by Adolph Lowe. 353 pp.*

Remmling, Gunter W. The Sociology of Karl Mannheim. *With a Bibliographical Guide to the Sociology of Knowledge, Ideological Analysis, and Social Planning. 255 pp.*

Remmling, Gunter W. (Ed.) Towards the Sociology of Knowledge. *Origin and Development of a Sociological Thought Style. 463 pp.*

URBAN SOCIOLOGY

Aldridge, M. The British New Towns. *A Programme Without a Policy. About 250 pp.*

Ashworth, William. The Genesis of Modern British Town Planning: *A Study in Economic and Social History of the Nineteenth and Twentieth Centuries. 288 pp.*

Brittan, A. The Privatised World. *196 pp.*

Cullingworth, J. B. Housing Needs and Planning Policy: *A Restatement of the Problems of Housing Need and 'Overspill' in England and Wales. 232 pp. 44 tables. 8 maps.*

Dickinson, Robert E. City and Region: *A Geographical Interpretation. 608 pp. 125 figures.*

The West European City: *A Geographical Interpretation. 600 pp. 129 maps. 29 plates.*

Humphreys, Alexander J. New Dubliners: *Urbanization and the Irish Family. Foreword by George C. Homans. 304 pp.*

Jackson, Brian. Working Class Community: *Some General Notions raised by a Series of Studies in Northern England. 192 pp.*

● **Mann, P. H.** An Approach to Urban Sociology. *240 pp.*

Mellor, J. R. Urban Sociology in an Urbanized Society. *326 pp.*

Morris, R. N. and **Mogey, J.** The Sociology of Housing. *Studies at Berinsfield. 232 pp. 4 pp. plates.*

Rosser, C. and **Harris, C.** The Family and Social Change. *A Study of Family and Kinship in a South Wales Town. 352 pp. 8 maps.*
● **Stacey, Margaret, Batsone, Eric, Bell, Colin** and **Thurcott, Anne.** Power, Persistence and Change. *A Second Study of Banbury. 196 pp.*

RURAL SOCIOLOGY

Mayer, Adrian C. Peasants in the Pacific. *A Study of Fiji Indian Rural Society. 248 pp. 20 plates.*
Williams, W. M. The Sociology of an English Village: *Gosforth. 272 pp. 12 figures. 13 tables.*

SOCIOLOGY OF INDUSTRY AND DISTRIBUTION

Dunkerley, David. The Foreman. *Aspects of Task and Structure. 192 pp.*
Eldridge, J. E. T. Industrial Disputes. *Essays in the Sociology of Industrial Relations. 288 pp.*
Hollowell, Peter G. The Lorry Driver. *272 pp.*
● **Oxaal, I., Barnett, T.** and **Booth, D.** (Eds) Beyond the Sociology of Development. *Economy and Society in Latin America and Africa. 295 pp.*
Smelser, Neil J. Social Change in the Industrial Revolution: *An Application of Theory to the Lancashire Cotton Industry, 1770–1840. 468 pp. 12 figures. 14 tables.*
Watson, T. J. The Personnel Managers. *A Study in the Sociology of Work and Employment. 262 pp.*

ANTHROPOLOGY

Brandel-Syrier, Mia. Reeftown Elite. *A Study of Social Mobility in a Modern African Community on the Reef. 376 pp.*
Dickie-Clark, H. F. The Marginal Situation. *A Sociological Study of a Coloured Group. 236 pp.*
Dube, S. C. Indian Village. *Foreword by Morris Edward Opler. 276 pp. 4 plates.*
India's Changing Villages: *Human Factors in Community Development. 260 pp. 8 plates. 1 map.*
Firth, Raymond. Malay Fishermen. *Their Peasant Economy. 420 pp. 17 pp. plates.*
Gulliver, P. H. Social Control in an African Society: a Study of the Arusha, Agricultural Masai of Northern Tanganyika. *320 pp. 8 plates. 10 figures.*
Family Herds. *288 pp.*
Jarvie, Ian C. The Revolution in Anthropology. *268 pp.*
Little, Kenneth L. Mende of Sierra Leone. *308 pp. and folder.*
Negroes in Britain. *With a New Introduction and Contemporary Study by Leonard Bloom. 320 pp.*

Madan, G. R. Western Sociologists on Indian Society. *Marx, Spencer, Weber, Durkheim, Pareto. 384 pp.*

Mayer, A. C. Peasants in the Pacific. *A Study of Fiji Indian Rural Society. 248 pp.*

Meer, Fatima. Race and Suicide in South Africa. *325 pp.*

Smith, Raymond T. The Negro Family in British Guiana: *Family Structure and Social Status in the Villages. With a Foreword by Meyer Fortes. 314 pp. 8 plates. 1 figure. 4 maps.*

SOCIOLOGY AND PHILOSOPHY

Barnsley, John H. The Social Reality of Ethics. *A Comparative Analysis of Moral Codes. 448 pp.*

Diesing, Paul. Patterns of Discovery in the Social Sciences. *362 pp.*

● **Douglas, Jack D.** (Ed.) Understanding Everyday Life. *Toward the Reconstruction of Sociological Knowledge. Contributions by Alan F. Blum, Aaron W. Cicourel, Norman K. Denzin, Jack D. Douglas, John Heeren, Peter McHugh, Peter K. Manning, Melvin Power, Matthew Speier, Roy Turner, D. Lawrence Wieder, Thomas P. Wilson and Don H. Zimmerman. 370 pp.*

Gorman, Robert A. The Dual Vision. *Alfred Schutz and the Myth of Phenomenological Social Science. About 300 pp.*

Jarvie, Ian C. Concepts and Society. *216 pp.*

Kilminster, R. Praxis and Method. *A Sociological Dialogue with Lukács, Gramsci and the early Frankfurt School. About 304 pp.*

● **Pelz, Werner.** The Scope of Understanding in Sociology. *Towards a More Radical Reorientation in the Social Humanistic Sciences. 283 pp.*

Roche, Maurice. Phenomenology, Language and the Social Sciences. *371 pp.*

Sahay, Arun. Sociological Analysis. *212 pp.*

Slater, P. Origin and Significance of the Frankfurt School. *A Marxist Perspective. About 192 pp.*

Spurling, L. Phenomenology and the Social World. *The Philosophy of Merleau-Ponty and its Relation to the Social Sciences. 222 pp.*

Wilson, H. T. The American Ideology. *Science, Technology and Organization as Modes of Rationality. 368 pp.*

International Library of Anthropology

General Editor Adam Kuper

Ahmed, A. S. Millenium and Charisma Among Pathans. *A Critical Essay in Social Anthropology. 192 pp.*
Pukhtun Economy and Society. *About 360 pp.*

Brown, Paula. The Chimbu. *A Study of Change in the New Guinea Highlands. 151 pp.*

Foner, N. Jamaica Farewell. *200 pp.*

Gudeman, Stephen. Relationships, Residence and the Individual. *A Rural Panamanian Community. 288 pp. 11 plates, 5 figures, 2 maps, 10 tables.*

The Demise of a Rural Economy. *From Subsistence to Capitalism in a Latin American Village. 160 pp.*

Hamnett, Ian. Chieftainship and Legitimacy. *An Anthropological Study of Executive Law in Lesotho. 163 pp.*

Hanson, F. Allan. Meaning in Culture. *127 pp.*

Humphreys, S. C. Anthropology and the Greeks. *288 pp.*

Karp, I. Fields of Change Among the Iteso of Kenya. *140 pp.*

Lloyd, P. C. Power and Independence. *Urban Africans' Perception of Social Inequality. 264 pp.*

Parry, J. P. Caste and Kinship in Kangra. *352 pp. Illustrated.*

Pettigrew, Joyce. Robber Noblemen. *A Study of the Political System of the Sikh Jats. 284 pp.*

Street, Brian V. The Savage in Literature. *Representations of 'Primitive' Society in English Fiction, 1858–1920. 207 pp.*

Van Den Berghe, Pierre L. Power and Privilege at an African University. *278 pp.*

International Library of Social Policy

General Editor Kathleen Jones

Bayley, M. Mental Handicap and Community Care. *426 pp.*

Bottoms, A. E. and **McClean, J. D.** Defendants in the Criminal Process. *284 pp.*

Butler, J. R. Family Doctors and Public Policy. *208 pp.*

Davies, Martin. Prisoners of Society. *Attitudes and Aftercare. 204 pp.*

Gittus, Elizabeth. Flats, Families and the Under-Fives. *285 pp.*

Holman, Robert. Trading in Children. *A Study of Private Fostering. 355 pp.*

Jeffs, A. Young People and the Youth Service. *About 180 pp.*

Jones, Howard, and **Cornes, Paul.** Open Prisons. *288 pp.*

Jones, Kathleen. History of the Mental Health Service. *428 pp.*

Jones, Kathleen, with **Brown, John, Cunningham, W. J., Roberts, Julian** and **Williams, Peter.** Opening the Door. *A Study of New Policies for the Mentally Handicapped. 278 pp.*

Karn, Valerie. Retiring to the Seaside. *About 280 pp. 2 maps. Numerous tables.*

King, R. D. and **Elliot, K. W.** Albany: Birth of a Prison—End of an Era. *394 pp.*

Thomas, J. E. The English Prison Officer since 1850: *A Study in Conflict.* *258 pp.*

Walton, R. G. Women in Social Work. *303 pp.*

● **Woodward, J.** To Do the Sick No Harm. *A Study of the British Voluntary Hospital System to 1875. 234 pp.*

International Library of Welfare and Philosophy

General Editors Noel Timms and David Watson

● **McDermott, F. E.** (Ed.) Self-Determination in Social Work. *A Collection of Essays on Self-determination and Related Concepts by Philosophers and Social Work Theorists. Contributors: F. B. Biestek, S. Bernstein, A. Keith-Lucas, D. Sayer, H. H. Perelman, C. Whittington, R. F. Stalley, F. E. McDermott, I. Berlin, H. J. McCloskey, H. L. A. Hart, J. Wilson, A. I. Melden, S. I. Benn. 254 pp.*

● **Plant, Raymond.** Community and Ideology. *104 pp.*

Ragg, Nicholas M. People Not Cases. *A Philosophical Approach to Social Work. About 250 pp.*

● **Timms, Noel** and **Watson, David.** (Eds) Talking About Welfare. *Readings in Philosophy and Social Policy. Contributors: T. H. Marshall, R. B. Brandt, G. H. von Wright, K. Nielsen, M. Cranston, R. M. Titmuss, R. S. Downie, E. Telfer, D. Donnison, J. Benson, P. Leonard, A. Keith-Lucas, D. Walsh, I. T. Ramsey. 320 pp.*

● (Eds). Philosophy in Social Work. *250 pp.*

● **Weale, A.** Equality and Social Policy. *164 pp.*

Primary Socialization, Language and Education

General Editor Basil Bernstein

Adlam, Diana S., *with the assistance of Geoffrey Turner and Lesley Lineker.* Code in Context. *About 272 pp.*

Bernstein, Basil. Class, Codes and Control. *3 volumes.*

● 1. *Theoretical Studies Towards a Sociology of Language. 254 pp.*

2. *Applied Studies Towards a Sociology of Language. 377 pp.*

● 3. *Towards a Theory of Educational Transmission. 167 pp.*

Brandis, W. and **Bernstein, B.** Selection and Control. *176 pp.*

Brandis, Walter and **Henderson, Dorothy.** Social Class, Language and Communication. *288 pp.*

Cook-Gumperz, Jenny. Social Control and Socialization. *A Study of Class Differences in the Language of Maternal Control. 290 pp.*

● **Gahagan, D. M** and **G. A.** Talk Reform. *Exploration in Language for Infant School Children. 160 pp.*

Hawkins, P. R. Social Class, the Nominal Group and Verbal Strategies. *About 220 pp.*

Robinson, W. P. and **Rackstraw, Susan D. A.** A Question of Answers. *2 volumes. 192 pp. and 180 pp.*

Turner, Geoffrey J. and **Mohan, Bernard A.** A Linguistic Description and Computer Programme for Children's Speech. *208 pp.*

Reports of the Institute of Community Studies

Baker, J. The Neighbourhood Advice Centre. A Community Project in Camden. *320 pp.*

● **Cartwright, Ann.** Patients and their Doctors. *A Study of General Practice. 304 pp.*

Dench, Geoff. Maltese in London.*A Case-study in the Erosion of Ethnic Consciousness. 302 pp.*

Jackson, Brian and **Marsden, Dennis.** Education and the Working Class: *Some General Themes raised by a Study of 88 Working-class Children in a Northern Industrial City. 268 pp. 2 folders.*

Marris, Peter. The Experience of Higher Education. *232 pp. 27 tables.*

● Loss and Change. *192 pp.*

Marris, Peter and **Rein, Martin.** Dilemmas of Social Reform. *Poverty and Community Action in the United States. 256 pp.*

Marris, Peter and **Somerset, Anthony.** African Businessmen. *A Study of Entrepreneurship and Development in Keyna. 256 pp.*

Mills, Richard. Young Outsiders: *a Study in Alternative Communities. 216 pp.*

Runciman, W. G. Relative Deprivation and Social Justice. *A Study of Attitudes to Social Inequality in Twentieth-Century England. 352 pp.*

Willmott, Peter. Adolescent Boys in East London. *230 pp.*

Willmott, Peter and **Young, Michael.** Family and Class in a London Suburb. *202 pp. 47 tables.*

Young, Michael and **McGeeney, Patrick.** Learning Begins at Home. *A Study of a Junior School and its Parents. 128 pp.*

Young, Michael and **Willmott, Peter.** Family and Kinship in East London. *Foreword by Richard M. Titmuss. 252 pp. 39 tables.*
The Symmetrical Family. *410 pp.*

Reports of the Institute for Social Studies in Medical Care

Cartwright, Ann, Hockey, Lisbeth and **Anderson, John J.** Life Before Death. *310 pp.*

Dunnell, Karen and **Cartwright, Ann.** Medicine Takers, Prescribers and Hoarders. *190 pp.*

Farrell, C. My Mother Said. . . . *A Study of the Way Young People Learned About Sex and Birth Control. 200 pp.*

Medicine, Illness and Society

General Editor W. M. Williams

Hall, David J. Social Relations & Innovation. *Changing the State of Play in Hospitals. 232 pp.*

Hall, David J., and **Stacey, M.** (Eds) Beyond Separation. *234 pp.*

Robinson, David. The Process of Becoming Ill. *142 pp.*

Stacey, Margaret *et al.* Hospitals, Children and Their Families. *The Report of a Pilot Study. 202 pp.*

Stimson G. V. and **Webb, B.** Going to See the Doctor. *The Consultation Process in General Practice. 155 pp.*

Monographs in Social Theory

General Editor Arthur Brittan

● **Barnes, B.** Scientific Knowledge and Sociological Theory. *192 pp.*

Bauman, Zygmunt. Culture as Praxis. *204 pp.*

● **Dixon, Keith.** Sociological Theory. *Pretence and Possibility. 142 pp.*

Meltzer, B. N., Petras, J. W. and **Reynolds, L. T.** Symbolic Interactionism. *Genesis, Varieties and Criticisms. 144 pp.*

● **Smith, Anthony D.** The Concept of Social Change. *A Critique of the Functionalist Theory of Social Change. 208 pp.*

Routledge Social Science Journals

The British Journal of Sociology. *Editor – Angus Stewart; Associate Editor – Leslie Sklair. Vol. 1, No. 1 – March 1950 and Quarterly. Roy. 8vo. All back issues available. An international journal publishing original papers in the field of sociology and related areas.*

Community Work. *Edited by David Jones and Marjorie Mayo. 1973. Published annually.*
Economy and Society. *Vol. 1, No. 1. February 1972 and Quarterly. Metric Roy. 8vo. A journal for all social scientists covering sociology, philosophy, anthropology, economics and history. All back numbers available.*
Ethnic and Racial Studies. *Editor – John Stone. Vol. 1 – 1978. Published quarterly.*
Religion. Journal of Religion and Religions. *Chairman of Editorial Board, Ninian Smart. Vol. 1, No. 1, Spring 1971. A journal with an inter-disciplinary approach to the study of the phenomena of religion. All back numbers available.*
Sociology of Health and Illness. *A Journal of Medical Sociology. Editor – Alan Davies; Associate Editor – Ray Jobling. Vol. 1, Spring 1979. Published 3 times per annum.*
Year Book of Social Policy in Britain, The. *Edited by Kathleen Jones. 1971. Published annually.*

Social and Psychological Aspects of Medical Practice

Editor   Trevor Silverstone

Lader, Malcolm. Psychophysiology of Mental Illness. *280 pp.*
● **Silverstone, Trevor** and **Turner, Paul.** Drug Treatment in Psychiatry. *Revised edition. 256 pp.*
Whiteley, J. S. and **Gordon, J.** Group Approaches in Psychiatry. *256 pp.*